Creating Cool VBScript Web Pages

Bill Hatfield

Creating Cool VBScript Web Pages

Bill Hatfield

IDG Books Worldwide, Inc.
An International Data Group Company

Foster City, CA ♦ Chicago, IL ♦ Indianapolis, IN ♦ Southlake, TX

Creating Cool VBScript Web Pages

Published by
IDG Books Worldwide, Inc.
An International Data Group Company
919 E. Hillsdale Blvd.
Suite 400 Foster City, CA 94404
www.idgbooks.com (IDG Books Worldwide Web Site)

Library of Congress Catalog Card No.:   96-79593
ISBN 17645-3031-3
Printed in the United States of America
10 9 8 7 6 5 4 3 2 1
IB/RX/RS/ZW/FC
Distributed in the United States by IDG Books Worldwide, Inc.
Distributed by Macmillan Canada for Canada; by Contemporanea de Ediciones for Venezuela; by Distribuidora Cuspide for Argentina; by CITEC for Brazil; by Ediciones ZETA S.C.R. Ltda. for Peru; by Editorial Limusa SA for Mexico; by Transworld Publishers Limited in the United Kingdom and Europe; by Academic Bookshop for Egypt; by Levant Distributors S.A.R.L. for Lebanon; by Al Jassim for Saudi Arabia; by Simron Pty. Ltd. for South Africa; by Pustak Mahal for India; by The Computer Bookshop for India; by Toppan Company Ltd. for Japan; by Addison Wesley Publishing Company for Korea; by Longman Singapore Publishers Ltd. for Singapore, Malaysia, Thailand, and Indonesia; by Unalis Corporation for Taiwan; by WS Computer Publishing Company, Inc. for the Philippines; by WoodsLane Pty. Ltd. for Australia; by WoodsLane Enterprises Ltd. for New Zealand. Authorized Sales Agent: Anthony Rudkin Associates for the Middle East and North Africa.

For general information on IDG Books Worldwide's books in the U.S., please call our Consumer Customer Service department at 800-762-2974. For reseller information, including discounts and premium sales, please call our Reseller Customer Service department at 800-434-3422.

For information on where to purchase IDG Books Worldwide's books outside the U.S., please contact our International Sales department at 415-655-3172 or fax 415-655-3295.

For information on foreign language translations, please contact our Foreign & Subsidiary Rights department at 415-655-3021 or fax 415-655-3281.

For sales inquiries and special prices for bulk quantities, please contact our Sales department at 415-655-3200 or write to the address above.

For information on using IDG Books Worldwide's books in the classroom or for ordering examination copies, please contact our Educational Sales department at 800-434-2086 or fax 817-251-8174.

For authorization to photocopy items for corporate, personal, or educational use, please contact Copyright Clearance Center, 222 Rosewood Drive, Danvers, MA 01923, or fax 508-750-4470.

About the Author

Bill Hatfield

Bill Hatfield is the author of the bestselling book *Developing PowerBuilder Applications (Sams)*, the first book published on PowerBuilder. He is also the co-author of the bestselling *Visual Basic 4 Unleashed*.

In addition to his writing, Bill Hatfield is also the Editor of Pinnacle Publishing's Delphi Developer, a technical journal for professional Borland Delphi programmers. He is a Certified Visual Basic Instructor and a Certified PowerBuilder Instructor and frequently does training and consulting for medium- and large-scale Internet and client/server development projects.

You can visit his web site at **www.edgequest.com**.

Bill Hatfield works from his home in Indianapolis, Ind., where he lives with his wife, Melanie, and their "kids" Coco, Tiger, and Frisky.

ABOUT IDG BOOKS WORLDWIDE

Welcome to the world of IDG Books Worldwide.

IDG Books Worldwide, Inc., is a subsidiary of International Data Group, the world's largest publisher of computer-related information and the leading global provider of information services on information technology. IDG was founded more than 25 years ago and now employs more than 8,500 people worldwide. IDG publishes more than 275 computer publications in over 75 countries (see listing below). More than 60 million people read one or more IDG publications each month.

Launched in 1990, IDG Books Worldwide is today the #1 publisher of best-selling computer books in the United States. We are proud to have received eight awards from the Computer Press Association in recognition of editorial excellence and three from *Computer Currents'* First Annual Readers' Choice Awards. Our best-selling *...For Dummies®* series has more than 30 million copies in print with translations in 30 languages. IDG Books Worldwide, through a joint venture with IDG's Hi-Tech Beijing, became the first U.S. publisher to publish a computer book in the People's Republic of China. In record time, IDG Books Worldwide has become the first choice for millions of readers around the world who want to learn how to better manage their businesses.

Our mission is simple: Every one of our books is designed to bring extra value and skill-building instructions to the reader. Our books are written by experts who understand and care about our readers. The knowledge base of our editorial staff comes from years of experience in publishing, education, and journalism — experience we use to produce books for the '90s. In short, we care about books, so we attract the best people. We devote special attention to details such as audience, interior design, use of icons, and illustrations. And because we use an efficient process of authoring, editing, and desktop publishing our books electronically, we can spend more time ensuring superior content and spend less time on the technicalities of making books.

You can count on our commitment to deliver high-quality books at competitive prices on topics you want to read about. At IDG Books Worldwide, we continue in the IDG tradition of delivering quality for more than 25 years. You'll find no better book on a subject than one from IDG Books Worldwide.

John J. Kilcullen

John Kilcullen
President and CEO
IDG Books Worldwide, Inc.

Eighth Annual Computer Press Awards ➤1992

Ninth Annual Computer Press Awards ➤1993

Tenth Annual Computer Press Awards ➤1994

Eleventh Annual Computer Press Awards ➤1995

IDG Books Worldwide, Inc., is a subsidiary of International Data Group, the world's largest publisher of computer-related information and the leading global provider of information services on information technology. International Data Group publishes over 275 computer publications in over 75 countries. Sixty million people read one or more International Data Group publications each month. International Data Group's publications include: **ARGENTINA:** Buyer's Guide, Computerworld Argentina, PC World Argentina; **AUSTRALIA:** Australian Macworld, Australian PC World, Australian Reseller News, Computerworld, IT Casebook, Network World, Publish, Webmaster; **AUSTRIA:** Computerwelt Österreich, Networks Austria, PC Tip Austria; **BANGLADESH:** PC World Bangladesh; **BELARUS:** PC World Belarus; **BELGIUM:** Data News; **BRAZIL:** Annuário de Informática, Computerworld, Connections, Macworld, PC Player, PC World, Publish, Reseller News, Supergamepower; **BULGARIA:** Computerworld Bulgaria, Network World Bulgaria, PC & MacWorld Bulgaria; **CANADA:** CIO Canada, Client/Server World, ComputerWorld Canada, InfoWorld Canada, NetworkWorld Canada, WebWorld; **CHILE:** Computerworld Chile, PC World Chile; **COLOMBIA:** Computerworld Colombia, PC World Colombia; **COSTA RICA:** PC World Centro America; **THE CZECH AND SLOVAK REPUBLICS:** Computerworld Czechoslovakia, Macworld Czech Republic, PC World Czechoslovakia; **DENMARK:** Communications World Danmark, Computerworld Danmark, Macworld Danmark, PC World Danmark, Techworld Denmark; **DOMINICAN REPUBLIC:** PC World Republica Dominicana; **ECUADOR:** PC World Ecuador; **EGYPT:** Computerworld Middle East, PC World Middle East; **EL SALVADOR:** PC World Centro America; **FINLAND:** MikroPC, Tietoverkko, Tietoviikko; **FRANCE:** Distributique, Hebdo, Info PC, Le Monde Informatique, Macworld, Reseaux & Telecoms, WebMaster France; **GERMANY:** Computer Partner, Computerwoche, Computerwoche Extra, Computerwoche FOCUS, Global Online, Macwelt, PC Welt; **GREECE:** Amiga Computing, GamePro Greece, Multimedia World; **GUATEMALA:** PC World Centro America; **HONDURAS:** PC World Centro America; **HONG KONG:** Computerworld Hong Kong, PC World Hong Kong, Publish in Asia; **HUNGARY:** ABCD CD-ROM, Computerworld Szamitastechnika, Internetto online Magazine, PC World Hungary, PC-X Magazin Hungary; **ICELAND:** Tolvuheimur PC World Island; **INDIA:** Information Communications World, Information Systems Computerworld, PC World India, Publish in Asia; **INDONESIA:** InfoKomputer PC World, Komputek Computerworld, Publish in Asia; **IRELAND:** ComputerScope, PC Live!; **ISRAEL:** Macworld Israel, People & Computers/Computerworld; **ITALY:** Computerworld Italia, Macworld Italia, Networking Italia, PC World Italia; **JAPAN:** DTP World, Macworld Japan, Nikkei Personal Computing, OS/2 World Japan, SunWorld Japan, Windows NT World, Windows World Japan; **KENYA:** PC World East African; **KOREA:** Hi-Tech Information, Macworld Korea, PC World Korea; **MACEDONIA:** PC World Macedonia; **MALAYSIA:** Computerworld Malaysia, PC World Malaysia, Publish in Asia; **MALTA:** PC World Malta; **MEXICO:** Computerworld Mexico, PC World Mexico; **MYANMAR:** PC World Myanmar; **NETHERLANDS:** Computer! Totaal, LAN Internetworking Magazine, LAN World Buyers Guide, Macworld Netherlands, Net, WebWereld; **NEW ZEALAND:** Absolute Beginners Guide and Plain & Simple Series, Computer Buyer, Computer Industry Directory, Computerworld New Zealand, MTB, Network World, PC World New Zealand; **NICARAGUA:** PC World Centro America; **NORWAY:** Computerworld Norge, CW Rapport, Datamagasinet, Financial Rapport, Kursguide Norge, Macworld Norge, Multimediaworld Norge, PC World Ekspress Norge, PC World Nettverk, PC World Norge, PC World ProduktGuide Norge; **PAKISTAN:** Computerworld Pakistan; **PANAMA:** PC World Panama; **PEOPLE'S REPUBLIC OF CHINA:** China Computer Users, China Computerworld, China InfoWorld, China Telecom World Weekly, Computer & Communication, Electronic Design China, Electronics Today, Electronics Weekly, Game Software, PC World China, Popular Computer Week, Software Weekly, Software World, Telecom World; **PERU:** Computerworld Peru, PC World Profesional Peru, PC World SoHo Peru; **PHILIPPINES:** Click!, Computerworld Philippines, PC World Philippines, Publish in Asia; **POLAND:** Computerworld Poland, Computerworld Special Report Poland, Cyber, Macworld Poland, Networld Poland, PC World Komputer; **PORTUGAL:** Cerebro/PC World, Computerworld/Correio Informático, Dealer World Portugal, Mac*In/PC*In Portugal, Multimedia World; **PUERTO RICO:** PC World Puerto Rico; **ROMANIA:** Computerworld Romania, PC World Romania, Telecom Romania; **RUSSIA:** Computerworld Russia, Mir PK, Publish, Seti; **SINGAPORE:** Computerworld Singapore, PC World Singapore, Publish in Asia; **SLOVENIA:** Monitor; **SOUTH AFRICA:** Computing SA, Network World SA, Software World SA; **SPAIN:** Communicaciones World España, Computerworld España, Dealer World España, Macworld España, PC World España; **SRI LANKA:** Infolink PC World; **SWEDEN:** CAP&Design, Computer Sweden, Corporate Computing Sweden, Internetworld Sweden, it.branschen, Macworld Sweden, MaxiData Sweden, MikroDatorn, Nätverk & Kommunikation, PC World Sweden, PCAktiv, Windows World Sweden; **SWITZERLAND:** Computerworld Schweiz, Macworld Schweiz, PCtip; **TAIWAN:** Computerworld Taiwan, Macworld Taiwan, NEW ViSiON/Publish, PC World Taiwan, Windows World Taiwan; **THAILAND:** Publish in Asia, Thai Computerworld; **TURKEY:** Computerworld Turkiye, Macworld Turkiye, Network World Turkiye, PC World Turkiye; **UKRAINE:** Computerworld Kiev, Multimedia World Ukraine, PC World Ukraine; **UNITED KINGDOM:** Acorn User UK, Amiga Action UK, Amiga Computing UK, Apple Talk UK, Computing, Macworld, Parents and Computers UK, PC Advisor, PC Home, PSX Pro, The WEB; **UNITED STATES:** Cable in the Classroom, CIO Magazine, Computerworld, DOS World, Federal Computer Week, GamePro Magazine, InfoWorld, I-Way, Macworld, Network World, PC Games, PC World, Publish, Video Event, THE WEB Magazine, and WebMaster; online webzines: JavaWorld, NetscapeWorld, and SunWorld Online; **URUGUAY:** InfoWorld Uruguay; **VENEZUELA:** Computerworld Venezuela, PC World Venezuela; and **VIETNAM:** PC World Vietnam.   10/1/96

Dedication

This book is dedicated to a woman I love and respect deeply. She worked very hard under seemingly unbearable circumstances to raise two children with little money but a lot of love. Her sacrifices have paid off in the lives of her children and grandchildren many times over. Through it all, she still knows how to laugh, love, and enjoy life. To Francis Hatfield, my grandma. Your life and kindness are an inspiration to me.

Credits

Senior Vice President and Group Publisher
Brenda McLaughlin

Managing Editor
Andy Cummings

Acquisitions Editor
Greg Croy

Software Acquisitions Editor
Tracy Lehman Cramer

Marketing Manager
Melisa M. Duffy

Executive Managing Editor
Terry Somerson

Editorial Assistant
Sharon Eames

Production Director
Andrew Walker

Supervisor of Page Layout
Craig A. Harrison

Developmental Editor
Erik Dafforn
Pat O'Brien

Copy Edit Coordinator
Barry Childs-Helton

Editor
Hugh Vandivier

Editorial Assistant
Timothy Borek

Project Coordinator
Katy German

Layout & Graphics
Mario Amador
Andreas Schueller

Technical Reviewer
Greg Guntle

Quality Control Specialist
Mick Arellano

Proofreader
Christine Sabooni

Indexer
Ty Koontz

Production Administration
Tony Augsburger
Todd Klemme
Jason Marcuson
Leslie Popplewell
Theresa Sanchez-Baker
Melissa Stauffer

Book Design
Theresa Sanchez-Baker

Acknowledgments

First, I want to think all the folks at IDG who made this book possible: To Greg Croy, Acquisitions Editor, for inviting me into the IDG fold with open arms. To Hugh Vandivier for all his great Copy and Development Editing work — I really appreciate it. To Erik Dafforn and Pat O'Brien, Developmental Editors. And to all the rest of the folks at IDG who worked on this project:

Thanks to Greg Guntle for great tips and suggestions he provided as Technical Editor.

Thanks also to Adam Hecktman from Microsoft who was there for answers to key questions when I needed him.

Thanks to my wonderful wife, Melanie, for being so supportive. You're the best!

Thanks to my parents, Melvin and Barb, for always being there to talk and share my ups and downs.

And finally, thanks to the Magic cards crew Brad, Mike, and Paul for providing necessary distractions. They're good at that.

Contents at a Glance

Introduction

In this Introduction, you'll learn what this book is about, who it is for, how it is organized, and what the heck VBScript is anyway. A few moments here can help you plan how you want to approach this book, what chapters you want to read, and what you want to skip to get the most value for your time.

What This Book is About

Through Dave Taylor's *Creating Cool Web Pages with HTML* and other primers on HTML, thousands of people have begun expressing their thoughts and ideas through the World Wide Web by creating their own home pages and even electronic newsletters and magazines. For the first time in history, the average guy, for a relatively small amount of money, can publish anything he wants in an international forum.

As interest in the Web grows and more and more people get online, the investment in technologies to make the Web a more engaging and interactive place increases. A problem arises, however: HTML has its limits. It isn't a programming language, so it can only do so much.

This book is for those who are ready to take their web pages to the next level. To do it, you need the intelligence and power of a real computer language. Although the idea of learning a computer language might seem dull or scary at first, I'm certain that you'll find that it is, in fact, a very exciting journey — and it's not nearly as difficult as it sounds at first.

The language that you'll learn is Visual Basic, Scripting Edition, often simply referred to as *VBScript*. It is probably the easiest computer language to learn, yet it is incredibly powerful, and it is optimized to help you create the best pages on the Web.

Who This Book is For

This book is for you if you are interested in creating really cool web pages. Whether you are developing pages for your company, for a client, for a friend, or for yourself, this book can help you do it better.

You don't have to be a professional programmer. You don't need to have any exposure to computer languages or even HTML, but I will assume that...

⮕ You are comfortable and familiar using Windows 95 or Windows NT.

⮕ You know how to connect to the Internet (either through a permanent connection or dial-up).

⮕ You have at least a basic knowledge of how to surf the Web.

It also helps if you have seen a variety of different web sites and thought about some of the things you'd do if you were designing them.

If you don't know HTML, Chapter 2 will give you a crash course in everything you'll need to begin creating sharp-looking, cutting edge pages. Then, in the pages that follow, I'll show you how to go beyond HTML to create effects that would be impossible without the power of a programming language like VBScript behind you.

In short, if you want to gain a lot more control over your web pages and need a tool to magnify your creativity, but you don't want to wade through difficult syntax or go back for a Computer Science degree, VBScript and this book are for you.

About VBScript

Although Java and JavaScript have been available for some time and have attracted developers to their many impressive capabilities, they require developers to learn the arcane syntax of C++ before they can begin using the capabilities of these languages. Because of this, programming web pages has remained the elite realm of the professional developer.

Now, with VBScript, Microsoft is doing for web development what it did with Windows programming when Visual Basic was first released: opening it up to the rest of us. You no longer have to spend hours in front of the computer learning arcane computer languages to give your web pages that added punch. Visual Basic is already famous for letting hobbyist programmers develop impressive standalone Windows applications and for making professional developers much more productive. VBScript promises to do the same for the Web.

What, exactly, will VBScript do for the Web? VBScript makes it possible to do many things in a web page that you previously had to program the web server to do. Before scripting languages, you often had to write CGI applications to run on the server to accomplish even the simplest tasks, and when you were using someone else's server, you didn't always have that option. Now, with VBScript, you can program the intelligence right into your web page.

What kind of things can you do with it? Your imagination is the limit! You can look at the CD-ROM that comes with this book for a few ideas, and you can check out the Cool Sites sidebars throughout the book to begin to get an idea. You can use VBScript to:

- Liven up your web page with spinning logos, animated graphics, and bouncing text
- Create a recipes page that will automatically adjust the ingredient amounts based on the number of servings
- Include a mortgage calculator on your realestate page
- Make a quick lookup database for zip codes, time zones, and area codes
- Develop educational programs to teach spelling, math, and science
- Dream up cool games like an illustrated text adventure, tic tac toe, hangman, and lots of card games

As I mentioned, many of these ideas or variations of them are on the CD-ROM in the back of this book. You can take these ideas and adapt them to your own use or simply use them as a starting point for creating something totally new!

 Looking for more fun examples of what's possible with VBScript? Check out Microsoft's VBScript Samples page:

```
http://www.microsoft.com/vbscript/us/vbssamp/vbssamp.htm
```

For a list of links to other sites that are using VBScript, check out Microsoft's HotLinks:

```
http://www.microsoft.com/vbscript/us/vbsmain/vbslinks.htm
```

See the section titled "This Book's Web Site" later this chapter for more places to look for fun VBScript examples and ideas.

What Software Do You Need to Use VBScript?

Not much at all, actually! There is no VBScript development environment that requires you to go out and spend $100. You write VBScript right alongside your HTML. So, if you are already creating web pages with HTML, chances are you can use whatever you are using now. I'll show you how in Chapter 3.

If you are not yet creating your own pages, you can use any editor — including Windows Notepad — so long as it saves your work as a simple text document with the extension .HTM.

The only other thing you'll need is Microsoft Internet Explorer 3.0 or higher to see what your pages look like after you create them. If you don't have it already, you're in luck! It is included on the CD-ROM in the back of this book.

In Chapter 5, I'll introduce you to a cool little application called Control Pad. It makes using ActiveX controls a breeze and even helps you code your VBScript applications. It is free from Microsoft's web site, and it also comes on the CD-ROM that accompanies this book.

How This Book is Organized

I've always been a firm believer in the idea that the best way to learn anything about the computer is with your hands on the keyboard and mouse. This book is written with that assumption in mind. Throughout the text I will provide small examples for you to type in (or steal off the CD-ROM that came with the book) and try out right away. These will demonstrate the concepts and ideas in a way that will make them easy to understand and remember.

And don't worry. This isn't going to be a boring Computer Programming 101 class or a dull thesis on correct software engineering principles. Instead, it will be a fun romp through the capabilities VBScript offers so you can make your web pages cooler than ever.

Here's how the chapters fall together.

Chapter 1: Internet Development: Past, Present, and Future

This chapter walks you through a little history before discussing all the current trends and technologies available to us today. It ends by peeking into the plans beyond the plans to see what tomorrow may hold for the Internet world.

Chapter 2: A Crash Course in HTML

This chapter provides a quick review of HTML for those who don't know it or those who need to brush up a bit. You may safely skip it if you feel comfortable with your HTML skills.

Chapter 3: Creating Your First VBScript Page

This chapter describes how to set up your development environment so that you can easily try out new things and quickly see the results. Then, you learn about the `<SCRIPT>` tag and how to use it to create VBScript pages. Finally, you create your very first VBScript web page.

Chapter 4: The VBScript Language

This is your first lesson in programming! I'll introduce the language in a painless, easy-to-understand way and illustrate new concepts with fun examples that you can try out right at your computer.

Chapter 5: Control Pad and ActiveX Objects

Here, I'll introduce you to a Microsoft's Control Pad, a cool utility included on the CD-ROM that accompanies this book. With Control Pad, you can easily add ActiveX Controls to your web page. Then, I'll introduce you to the concept of an object and describe their makeup. Finally, you will use ActiveX control objects to create a really cool page with spinning, jumping, and flashing text and graphics.

Chapter 6: Internet Explorer Objects

This chapter explores all the cool stuff you can do with the objects that are built into the Internet Explorer browser itself. These include the Document, Window, and History objects.

Chapter 7: Advanced Data Handling

This chapter delves deeper into the more intermediate or advanced commands and capabilities of VBScript. It is divided into more or less standalone sections with associated examples.

Chapter 8: Arrays

An entire chapter is dedicated to this very important way of storing data in VBScript, and you'll learn ways to create some cool attention-getting headlines for your web pages in the process.

Chapter 9: Debugging and Error Handling in VBScript

These closely related topics are essential to developing any application, but facilities for them in VBScript are very limited. I'll show you how to work around these limitations and create clean, bulletproof scripts.

Chapter 10: Cool VBScript Web Page Examples

This is the fun chapter. Here, you'll take a break from learning new concepts and put everything you've been learning to use in creating several real-world VBScript-enhanced web pages. You'll create a cool and addictive puzzle game, a dynamic cookbook, and an educational page for teaching math skills.

Chapter 11: Serverless Databases

This is another fun chapter. You'll learn a really flexible strategy for implementing purely client-side databases where smaller amounts of data that don't change very much are needed for lookup or reference. The applications for this strategy are virtually unlimited!

Chapter 12: Data Entry Forms, Validation, and Formatting

This chapter shows you how to accept data and send it off to the server, but before you do, you can perform validation and formatting in VBScript that will help assure that once the data gets there, it will be right.

This Book's Web Site

If you're interested in seeing more VBScript examples, interesting tips, and ideas or errata from this book, check out the *Creating Cool VBScript Web Pages* Web site at this address:

```
http://www.edgequest.com/coolvbs
```

You'll also find links to lots of other cool sites using VBScript.

Text Conventions Used In This Book

Text that you type in or appears on the screen will appear in a monospace font that looks like this: text you type in. Listings of HTML and VBScript will appear in listings like this one.

```
<HTML>
<HEAD>
<SCRIPT LANGUAGE="VBScript">
<!--
MsgBox "Hello World!"
-->
</SCRIPT>
<TITLE>New Page</TITLE>
</HEAD>
<BODY>
This is my first VBScript page.
</BODY>
</HTML>
```

I also use *text in italics* for two different reasons. First, when I introduce a new term that you haven't seen before, I will put it in italics. I will almost always immediately define the word so that you'll know it when I mention it in the future. These terms are usually also defined in the Glossary, Appendix A.

The second reason I might put a word or phrase in italics is to emphasize something. Because a sentence can be read in many different ways, it is easy to misunderstand if you don't know what word is the focus of a sentence. If I were speaking, I could emphasize the words so you'd understand. Because I can't, I use italics instead.

You will also notice sidebars with these icons scattered throughout the text.

 A Note is a brief sidelight that runs parallel with the topic being discussed but isn't necessary to understand it. Sometimes I'll let you in on confusing terminology that programmers use with a note.

 A Tip is a short tidbit that offers advice, a trick, or a technique that you can use.

 A Warning alerts you to bugs, confusing features, or situations where you could potentially cause yourself pain and grief if you aren't careful.

A Cool Site is a place you can go on the Internet to find examples of VBScript used for strange and interesting things. This is intended to give you an idea of the tremendous capabilities of VBScript and offer a launching pad to spark your own creative ideas.

Internet Development: Past, Present, and Future

I'll start off this chapter with a brief history of the Internet and then dive into the ways it has been used in the past. If you are familiar with the Internet, FTP, Telnet, and all the rest, you might want to skip ahead to the section titled "Technology Trends of Today." If not, I think you'll find this section brief and valuable.

After that, I'll talk to you about how the market sits right now. Each section is devoted to a different technology. I spend a lot longer discussing ActiveX and VBScript because those topics are closest to the heart of this book.

Finally, I'll finish the chapter by peering through my crystal ball into a future that moves even faster every day.

The Spirit of the Information Age

Perhaps Alexandria, Egypt should be called the birthplace of the spirit of the Information Age. While they didn't have computers or even printing presses in the third century B.C., they did have the one essential ingredient: a desire for knowledge, and this desire gave birth to one of the greatest efforts ever undertaken: the collection of all the world's knowledge into one place, the great Library of Alexandria. Located at the meeting point of three continents, this center for trade was an ideal place to collect, copy, and house a collection of over 400,000 papyrus scrolls, but these buildings were more than a home for books. They were a museum and a university that had among its instructors the likes of Archimedes and Heron. They were a nexus of worldly knowledge in the greatest Greek tradition.

But it didn't last. Once again, as throughout history, the desire for knowledge was overcome by the lust for blood, and the Library was burned to the ground.

But even the burning of this great library couldn't destroy the spirit of the Information Age. Many people throughout history carried it forward. Eventually, papyrus scrolls gave way to books with bound pages, and the handwritten, hand-copied script gave way to the printing press. These changes in technology helped accelerate the dissemination of knowledge, and this was only the beginning of the new technologies to come.

No technology on Earth has ever held so much promise for the Information Age as the Internet does today. Like the great Library of Alexandria, the Internet has become a common storehouse of the world's knowledge. Beginning in the universities scattered throughout the world, this technology has spread to our corporations, our schools, and now, our homes. Unlike the Library of Alexandria, the Internet is not bound by geography. It is accessible from every major land mass in the world, and anyone can access its pages at the speed of light.

The Beginnings of the Internet

The Department of Defense — specifically the Advanced Research Projects Agency (ARPA) — first created the predecessor to the Internet, ARPANET, in 1969. It connected the Department of Defense with people performing military research for the government.

ARPANET and Dynamic Routing

One of the interesting things about the design of ARPANET, and of the Internet today, is that it is very resilient. With many computer networks, if the line is broken at one point, your computer can't communicate with any of the computers beyond that point, just like breaking a bulb in a string of Christmas tree lights causes all the lights beyond it to go out. But ARPANET was different. All the computers on the network were connected to all the other computers in many different ways so that if a break occurred in the line, the network would realize it and just route information around the break. This was called *dynamic routing*. The government wanted to make sure that a bomb or even a nuclear weapon couldn't destroy the network and stop communication. Because of this, our new storehouse of the world's knowledge, the Internet, is not likely to suffer the same fate as Alexandria's library.

In fact, that resilience of this dynamic routing was recently used against the same Department of Defense that created ARPANET. During the Gulf War with Iraq, even our vastly superior fighters had a very difficult time disabling the Iraqi communications network that used dynamic routing. Technology does not respect political alliances!

ARPANET: Too Successful

The popularity of ARPANET grew, and the network grew in response. Finally, it was divided into two networks: MILNET, to continue to provide communication among military researchers, and ARPANET, for other kinds of university research and education communication. ARPANET continued to expand rapidly and was quickly overcome by too much network traffic. The information exchange became as slow as an L.A. freeway at rush hour.

NSFNET

That's when the National Science Foundation (NSF) entered the picture. They were working on a project to give universities access to super-computers. Although most universities couldn't afford to buy one of these multimillion dollar beasts, the NSF believed they could afford to *rent* them (buy some computing time) to perform particularly difficult or time-consuming calculations. So, this became NSF's mission, but to do it, NSF needed a network to provide access to the Supercomputers. ARPANET, it was decided, was not the way to go, for both political and technical reasons.

So NSF set out to create a better network, and that's how NSFNET was born. NSFNET was similar to ARPANET, but it was much faster and could carry a lot more information. It grew very quickly. More and more universities wanted to connect to it, not because of the supercomputers, but because of the opportunities to communicate and share research with other universities. In fact, the supercomputer idea failed, but by the time it did, NSFNET had gained a life of its own.

The Internet Emerges

As the NSFNET grew in popularity, other independent and commercial networks sprang up and connected to each other and to NSFNET. Today, what we know as the Internet is a very complex interconnection of all of these networks.

In recent years, Internet providers have begun offering access to anyone with a computer and a modem by allowing you to dial up and use the provider's connection to the Internet. This effectively extends the reach of the Internet to anywhere you can make a phone call.

Cool Site

If you are interested in reading more of the fascinating history of the Internet, here are a couple of great places to start:

```
http://www.pbs.org/internet/history/
```

The online version of the PBS series *Life on the Internet*. A time line implemented as a Java applet allows you to scroll forward or backwards as you learn all the key historical landmarks of the Internet's evolution.

```
http://www.forthnet.gr/forthnet/isoc/short.history.of.internet
```

The great science fiction writer Bruce Sterling writes this very readable history reprinted from *The Magazine of Science Fiction and Fantasy*.

Using the Internet: History, Present, and Future

The Internet is really nothing more than a bunch of computers around the world connected by wires. In itself, this isn't a very exciting idea, but when you add the brilliant minds of the faculty and students in universities throughout the world to the equation, you end up with some very creative and exciting technologies.

Then, when you add all the nonprofit institutions, corporations, and individuals to the mix, you end up with a melting pot of ideas as big as the world. This is what makes the Internet so compelling.

In this section, I'll explore how the Internet has been used in the past, what technologies are molding it today, and how those technologies will work together to bring a very exciting future for an interconnected humanity.

Those Thrilling Days of Yesteryear

From a user interface perspective, the early years of the Internet were a very primitive time. In the days when GUI described peanut butter and WYSIWYG was just gibberish, simple text was the paradigm of the day. Using the Internet in those days was a far cry from point and click.

The Dark Days Before the Web

In fact, what we call the World Wide Web didn't even exist. There were, however, several ways of communicating, which are often referred to by Web folks as *protocols*. A protocol is nothing more than an agreed upon way for two or more computers to talk to each other. I'll discuss some of these other protocols here because many of them are still very much in use today.

File Transfer Protocol (FTP) is used to transfer text, binary files, and graphics from one machine to another. FTP programs allow you to navigate the host machine's directories, find what you need, and then receive (download) it from the other machine. It was one of the first protocols used on the Internet.

Telnet is a way of logging onto another system just as you might if you were using a terminal connected directly to the machine. It offers a free-form interaction between the user and the server machine. Often, the user can run programs and even interact with other users who are also logged into the same server.

e-Mail is, of course, a way of sending a text document from one individual to another. It is probably the single most popular form of Internet communication — even more popular than the World Wide Web.

Gopher attempts to make the Internet easier to navigate. It created a standard way of organizing a site's information using simple menus. This protocol came out at about the same time as the World Wide Web and has been widely accepted, but it hasn't seen the same incredible growth that the Web has.

A New Paradigm: the Web Brings Multimedia to the Internet

Around the same time the Windows revolution was hitting the average computer user's desktop, a new protocol called *HTTP* was developed. HTTP stands for the Hypertext Transfer Protocol. It uses a concept called a *markup language* that allows web sites to create pages that can be viewed through special client software called a *browser*. The browser presents the information to the user using both text and graphics, but more importantly, it defines a way to connect one document to another through *hyperlinks*. These specially highlighted words can be selected or clicked on by a mouse to whisk the user off to another document associated with the present one. This linking to links which link to still more links can continue indefinitely. This simple foundation was a profound step forward in organizing information on the Internet.

Browser wars

Although the Web was a cool idea, the first browsers didn't really leverage the Web's capabilities very well. This didn't happen until 1993 when the

National Center for Supercomputing Applications (NCSA) used federal grant money to create Mosaic. Mosaic was the fulfillment of the web vision. It is easy to use and powerful. Anybody, even those that have never used a computer, could pick it up quickly, and it was addictive, too.

Mark Andreesen was the lead developer at NCSA and the man responsible for creating Mosaic. When he saw the incredible business potential that the Web represented, he left NCSA and founded Netscape Communications. Netscape came out with its own browser not long after called Navigator. Navigator had all the capabilities of Mosaic and more. It was quickly followed by Navigator 2.0, which had far-and-away the most complete functionality of any browser available. It quickly displaced Mosaic as the standard web browser and was used by nearly everyone.

Suddenly, there came a stirring in a small suburb near Seattle. Microsoft realized that a tremendous movement was afoot in this strange new world called the Internet. Terrified that this new opportunity would leave him behind, Bill Gates turned Microsoft on a dime and refocused the entire corporation's efforts on the Internet. Not surprisingly, only a few months passed before Internet Explorer appeared.

Although Explorer was an impressive product, and even did a few tricks not even Netscape offered, it did not make a major dent in Netscape's hold on the market. Microsoft quickly followed up with a version 2.0. The new version, along with Microsoft's policy to give Explorer away free to anyone who wanted it, began to have an impact, and Microsoft, following Netscape's lead, began offering prerelease beta versions of its browser available for download on its web site. Explorer 3.0 quickly closed any remaining gaps between Netscape's functionality and Microsoft's, and it also offered some major new advances of its own.

Web Content Development

While Microsoft and Netscape slugged it out on the browser frontier, the Web continued to grow. Most people think the critical mass occurred in 1995 when it seemed that every major corporation had created a web presence and every single advertisement, whether television or newspaper, included a web address.

Cool Site

If you want to keep up with the ongoing battle of the Titans, the best place to go is to the horse's mouth. Microsoft's web site is

```
http://www.microsoft.com
```

and Netscape's site is

http://www.netscape.com

Both sites are full of information about the latest and greatest products on their way, in beta or available today and why those products are so much better than those offered by the other company.

But the state of web development, even through all this, had not changed that much. It was still text and graphics pages with links to other text and graphics pages. Of course, the browser wars had generated a variety of new HTML commands that made some things easier and many things possible that weren't before, but overall, the Web was still the Web.

So what's wrong with this? Well, it seemed a little dead. Although the user could thrash from one page to the next, that was pretty much the limit of the interactivity offered. There was a technology called the Common Gateway Interface, which allowed web pages to fire off applications on the web server, pass them information, and get new information sent back. This created some basic interactivity, like allowing the reader to sign a guest book, send an e-mail message to the web administrator, or fill out a survey, but whenever the user interacted, the browser had to send the information back to the server, the server had to run a special program that sent back information that the browser displayed. Network traffic and overtaxed servers ensured that the interactivity never became very sophisticated.

Technology Trends of Today

That leads us to today. This desire for more interactivity as well as more sound, graphics, animation, and video has been identified as a key business opportunity for many organizations who want to cash in on the Worldwide Web bonanza, and everybody is looking for ways to make it happen.

The key players in the market today are still Netscape and Microsoft, however. Each company has laid out very different visions describing how it will happen, each with its own company right in the middle of it all, of course. In the following sections, I will describe several new technologies and how they are being put to use. All of these technologies are supported by Microsoft Internet Explorer 3.0 and most of them are supported by Netscape Navigator 3.0, too. My emphasis will be on ActiveX and VBScript, though.

New HTML Tags

Netscape has been a pioneer in extending the capabilities of HTML in bold, new directions, and the entire industry has applauded its efforts. Since Microsoft has entered the picture, however, both companies have created and adopted new HTML tags at a rapid pace. Key areas enhanced by the new tags include:

➥ Tables to organize data into neat rows and columns

➥ Frames to divide the browser window into different sections that can each scroll independently of the others

➥ More complete multimedia support including enhanced graphics, sound, animation, video, and real-time audio

➥ The display of different font sizes, colors, and typefaces

➥ New image alignment options that let text and graphics look natural together

 In Chapter 2, I will not only introduce you to the basic HTML tags you need for creating a web page, I'll also show you how to take advantage of these new capabilities. So, even if you are familiar with the basics of HTML, you might want to skim over the chapter looking for tags you haven't worked with before.

Plug-Ins

Netscape plug-ins let you extend the capabilities of Netscape to present animation or real-time audio or a host of other features. They do this by associating a separate program that you have downloaded and installed with a particular file type (usually indicated by the file's extension).

For instance, you might download a real-time audio control that lets you listen to live radio broadcasts and replay prerecorded programs. You install this program and then indicate to Netscape that any time it sees a file with the extension .RA (or whatever the installed program uses) it should download the file, launch this new application, and let the new application handle the file.

Netscape has supported plug-ins since Navigator version 2.0. Microsoft Internet Explorer 3.0 also supports plug-ins.

Java

Java is definitely one of the hottest new technologies on the Internet today. It is a language created by Sun Microsystems originally to control home automation systems. When that industry didn't take off like Sun expected it to, the company began looking for a new home for Java and found it on the Internet.

Java is based on C++, but is simplified so that it doesn't have some of the problems and the extended learning curve that C++ has. Most languages compile into the machine code for a particular computer. Java compiles into what are called *byte-codes* that run on a software platform called the Virtual Machine (VM). That means that any computer, be it Windows, Mac, Unix, or anything else that can run a Virtual Machine program can run Java applications. This makes it truly multiplatform and ideal for the Internet.

Netscape was a very early licenser of Java and built into Navigator the capability to download and run small Java applications called *applets*. These applets are simply small programs that run on the client machine that allow true interactivity with the person browsing the page.

Both Netscape Navigator 3.0 and Microsoft Internet Explorer 3.0 support Java applets

Cool Site

For more information on Java, go to Sun's Java home page at

```
http://java.sun.com/
```

There you'll find discussions, news, products, and even a Java store with Java mugs and baseball caps.

Java Beans

Java Beans is an initiative led by Sun Microsystems to standardize a way to create useful tools or user interface elements that integrate with your web pages. Think of a button, a text box, a slider bar, or an animation viewer. All of these things can be created as Java Beans controls and dropped onto your web page when you create it to make the page more entertaining and interactive.

But HTML already offers the capability to create simple controls like a button, a text box, a check box, or a radio button. How are Java Beans controls different from these controls?

The main difference is that the browser has to support the built-in HTML controls in order for them to work. Every browser supports a basic set of controls, but if you want to do anything different or unusual, you're stuck.

You can write Java Beans controls in Java to look and act any way you like. Then, you can add them to a page, and they will be displayed and work correctly on any browser that supports Java. The control itself is downloaded by the browser and installed automatically when you first go to a page. From then on, whenever you return to that page or go to another page that uses that control, your browser doesn't have to download it again. It just uses the one it already has, and, as you might have guessed, Java Beans controls are written in Java, so they will run on any machine that supports Java.

Cool Site

For a general description of Java Beans, check out the Java Beans home page at

http://splash.javasoft.com/beans/

For a technical white paper detailing how Java Beans works, see

http://splash.javasoft.com/beans/WhitePaper.html

Microsoft's ActiveX Strategy

The theme of Microsoft's Internet strategy from its (somewhat belated) beginning has been "embrace and extend." This means that Microsoft isn't interested in doing something completely different from everyone else and then forcing the industry to follow its lead (as it has sometimes been accused of in the standalone software market). Instead, Microsoft wants to embrace the technologies that are currently out there (including those developed by other companies) and extend its capabilities even further. While some in the industry may question the sincerity of this conviction, Internet Explorer, beginning with version 3.0, *does* support plug-ins, Java applets, and both JavaScript and VBScript (discussed later) as well as almost all of the HTML extensions that Netscape Navigator supports. Microsoft, however, has not simply turned into another "me, too" company. It has a variety of technologies that both extend and compete directly with Netscape solutions.

Cool Site

Microsoft's ActiveX Resource Area is the place to find all the information you need about this exciting new technology. If it isn't here, there's a link to it from here! Check it out at:

http://www.microsoft.com/activex

ActiveX Technology

ActiveX is a generic name that refers to the technologies Microsoft is using to *activate* the Internet. Instead of just viewing web pages that present text and graphics, ActiveX technologies seek to liven up the experience by adding elements like animation, sound, and video to pages to make them more engaging and more interactive.

ActiveX Controls

ActiveX controls are a direct competitor to Java Beans controls. They have all the same benefits as Java Beans controls, and they have the added benefit that they are based on well-established technology: OLE.

You might have heard of OLE or OLE Controls (sometimes called OCXs) in the past. Microsoft has been working hard for years to create standards for dividing large applications down into smaller pieces and then allowing those pieces to communicate and be put together in different ways to solve problems. This initiative has been called *OLE* (which originally stood for *object linking and embedding*). OLE Controls or *OCXs* are a part of all that. They are generic controls that software developers can use in any Windows programming environment.

You can think of ActiveX controls as leaner, meaner cousins of OCXs. They are trimmed down to reduce download time and optimized for use on the Internet. You can write ActiveX controls in any language you like, but if you write them in Java, you will also gain the same multi-platform support that Java Beans controls have.

Microsoft Internet Explorer 3.0 fully supports ActiveX controls. Netscape has decided (so far, at least) not to support ActiveX controls. At least not directly. There is a company called NCompass which has created a Netscape Plug-In which allows users of Netscape Navigator to see and use ActiveX controls just like Internet Explorer does.

For more information on the specifics of how OLE Controls and ActiveX controls relate, see Appendix B.

Internet Scripting

Once you have all these cool ActiveX controls on your web page, you will want to be able to tie them together and use them to solve problems.

ActiveX controls are written as independent pieces of code to solve particular problems. They do what they do very well. But an animation control can only show an animation. Combine it with a control that plays music and another that provides narration, though, and get them all working together and you have a multimedia experience!

But to make several controls work together to solve a problem, you have to have some way to coordinate them all and get them working together. Although HTML continues to be modified and extended with every new browser release, it will never be a complete programming language — and that's what you really need.

Internet scripting languages are simple programming languages that are written alongside your HTML to manipulate and control the browser, the elements of your web page, and ActiveX controls.

Since a scripting language is written right alongside your HTML, it is interpreted by the browser in much the same way as the HTML is. The browser runs the script, so it happens right on the computer of the person accessing your page. With a scripting language, you can now do many of the things that you would have had to use a CGI script for in the past. And it executes faster because it doesn't have to send a request to the server asking it to run an application and then wait for it to send the results back. It all happens right there in the browser.

The Contenders: VBScript and JavaScript

There are two major scripting languages available today: JavaScript and VBScript. Both have very similar capabilities. JavaScript is rather loosely based on the incredibly popular Java language, which, in turn, is loosely based on C++, a very popular PC programming language.

VBScript is based on Visual Basic, another popular programming language. The difference is that Visual Basic is a high-level language. This means that it is more English-like and easier to understand and program, especially for those who have never programmed before. C++, Java, and JavaScript are lower-level languages and are a lot tougher to learn. They are designed more for professional programmers.

Microsoft Internet Explorer 3.0 supports both JavaScript and VBScript. Netscape Navigator 3.0 supports JavaScript but does not support VBScript (not *yet*, anyway).

Cool Site

The Netscape JavaScript home page is at

```
http://home.netscape.com/eng/mozilla/Gold/
        handbook/javascript/index.html
```

The Microsoft JavaScript home page is at

```
http://www.microsoft.com/jscript
```

The Microsoft VBScript home page is at

```
http://www.microsoft.com/vbscript
```

VBScript Versus Java

If you've been involved with the Internet at all, I'm sure you've heard all the hype about Java. What is Java? Java is not the same as JavaScript. Java is a low-level language that computer programmers use to write standalone applications and applets that run efficiently on any computer. Since the

Internet is a place where you can find lots of different kinds of computers, Java is very popular.

Is VBScript a competitor to Java? No, not at all. Java is used to create complete, standalone applications and applets. It can also be used to create ActiveX controls.

VBScript, on the other hand, is a language that is interpreted by your browser and it runs as part of your web page. Instead of creating complete applications, it works together with the browser, your web page, and the Java applets or ActiveX controls to make them all work together smoothly.

So VBScript works alongside Java very well. It is the high-level command and control center that brings the best controls together to make them work the way you want.

VBScript Versus Visual Basic and VBA

Visual Basic is designed to help software developers quickly and easily create intricate Windows applications that solve problems. When it was introduced, it was revolutionary. It did for computer programming what What-You-See-Is-What-You-Get (WYSIWYG) word processors did for the task of typing in documents. It made the whole process more visual and much easier to understand. Because of this, Visual Basic is easier to learn and allows programmers to write applications much faster than traditional programming languages like C or C++.

Visual Basic for Applications (VBA) is a subset of Visual Basic. This means that it is very similar, but doesn't have all the capabilities of Visual Basic. VBA is integrated with desktop applications like Microsoft Excel. This allowed advanced users of Excel to extend and customize its capabilities. With Office 97, VBA is integrated with Microsoft Word and all the other members of the Office family of products. Many other non-Microsoft applications are using VBA now, too.

VBScript is a subset of VBA. It is a very simple, but complete, programming language. It doesn't have all the bells and whistles that Visual Basic and VBA have, but it doesn't need them. It is optimized for Internet scripting and makes it easy to tie together ActiveX controls and make them work as part of a whole web application.

 Microsoft sees VBScript filling a bigger role than just Internet client-side scripting. It will be made available for web server scripting, taking the place of languages like Perl that were often used in the past to create CGI scripts.

Microsoft is also offering VBScript to standalone software developers to use in their own applications as a scripting language, much as VBA does in Microsoft Excel. Although Microsoft also licenses VBA for a fee, VBScript is free to anyone who wants to use it. They are even offering the source code to those who are interested in porting it to new hardware platforms. All this is in an attempt to make VBScript the most prevalent, widely used scripting language available, both for the Internet and for standalone applications.

This is good news for you. Once you learn VBScript for web page development, which is the focus of this book, you will be ready to use it in all the other places it's bound to pop up, from your web server to your favorite software applications.

Is VBScript Secure?

You can't pick up an Internet magazine or news article without hearing all the hype about security. Although security is an important issue on the Internet, confusion about how the technology works and a general sense of anxiety about technology compromising our everyday lives has led to a disproportionate emphasis on this topic.

But, again, this is an important issue. Is VBScript secure? The answer is yes. Perhaps too secure.

VBScript uses the *sandbox* approach to security. The idea is that VBScript gets a portion of the machine's resources and memory set aside solely for its use. It can play in that sandbox all it wants, but it can't get out of the sandbox and muck up stuff on the rest of your machine. That means that VBScript cannot access memory directly and it cannot create or manipulate files on a hard drive. In fact all commands that were in any way "dangerous" (meaning they could potentially be used to create a virus) have been removed.

Although this leaves us with a highly secure environment, it also leaves us with a little less power than we might have otherwise had. But, as always, there is a loophole. ActiveX controls can be created to do anything they like on a system. So, theoretically, an ActiveX control could be created that does file manipulation and then is used with VBScript to give it back some of those features. In fact, it wouldn't surprise me at all to see a third party come out with an ActiveX control that gives you back *all* the features that were removed for security reasons. While this would effectively destroy the sandbox security, it would give you as the developer the greatest flexibility and power. The days ahead will definitely be interesting.

The Future: the Internet in Everyday Life

Today we are witnessing the transformation of the web from simple text documents into interactive, exciting, multimedia applications. This trend will continue until the applications you access on the web are indistinguishable from those you might run today on your standalone PC from a CD-ROM.

In fact, Microsoft has very imminent plans of blurring the line between standalone PC applications and Internet web pages almost completely. Microsoft Internet Explorer 4.0 will be completely integrated with the Windows 95 and Windows NT desktop operating system environments. When you view your desktop, you will be looking at an HTML web page. When you click on the My Computer link, another web page will be displayed that presents its own links to your floppy and hard drives. Clicking one of these links will display yet another page with links to all the files and folders on your drive. Navigating your computer will be no different than navigating the web. If you have a permanent connection to the Internet, you won't be able to tell the difference between data stored locally on your hard drive or data stored on a computer across town. And you won't be able to tell the difference between running an application from your hard disk or accessing a web application on a server across the country or around the world. Terms like *Internet-enabled* and even *client/server* will fall out of common usage. The technology will become so pervasive, there won't be any other kind of application.

You can also expect that computing will become much more a part of your everyday life. A few years from now, you won't have a single computer in your den that you go to only when you want to look at your finances or write a letter. In fact, you will begin to see fewer separate appliances like computers, TVs, and telephones. Instead you will see more general screens and control pads scattered throughout the home. These will work as a television, a video phone, or a place to view images from security cameras. They will also control everything electrical in your house, like your heating and cooling, lighting, and the hot tub.

Bill Gates speculates in his book *The Road Ahead* that you will carry with you a wallet sized device that will not only serve up electronic money and credit card reserves, but also display a photograph album's worth of family pictures as well. This device would be all you'd need to start the car before you go out on a cold winter's morning or put on dinner a half an hour before you get home so it is ready to pull out of the oven when you get there.

In fact, it is likely that you won't even leave home to go to work if you don't want to. The trend is toward faster and cheaper Internet connections. If that continues, you will have a super-fast connection to the world from home. So why do you need to work anywhere else? The increasing number of people working at home today indicates a definite trend in that direction already.

If you are interested in reading more on this topic, I recommend Bill Gates' book mentioned earlier, *The Road Ahead*. He describes, in very easy to understand language, how all this will change the way we work and live in the future. And if you decide you need a monthly dose of futuristic exploration, no magazine out there beats *Wired*.

Summary

I began with ARPANET and continued through the early Internet technologies including FTP, e-mail, Gopher and finally the development of the Worldwide Web. Then I described today's technologies impacting the web including Java, ActiveX, and Internet scripting. Finally I finished this chapter by imagining a future where the Internet became integrated with everything we do. You now have a foundation that should place the rest of the book in context and help you understand how your web development strategy fits into the bigger picture.

In the next chapter, you get to dig in and begin developing a very cool home page while learning or sharpening your HTML skills.

A Crash
Course in
HTML

HTML is the language that makes the World Wide Web possible. All web pages use it as their foundation and use its rapidly expanding capabilities to enhance the presentation of information.

After you see the tremendous flexibility of what you can do with HTML and the number of consulting companies springing up around the world to create web pages for clients, you might assume that HTML is difficult to learn, but you'd be wrong. HTML is a very simple language. In fact, it is so simple that most programmers don't even consider it a full-fledged computer language. It is a *markup language*, which means that, instead of giving the computer commands about what it is supposed to do, it focuses on presenting information in the quickest and easiest way possible.

In this unit, I am going to give you a crash course in HTML. If you are already familiar with HTML, you might want to skim over the chapter and make sure you are comfortable with all the examples. If you are not familiar with HTML, you will be by the time you finish reading this chapter.

Of course, I won't cover every tag and every technique you might use in creating a web page, but I will show you all the basics, and I'll go beyond the basics to show you the standard tags that have been added by the newest revision of the HTML standard and by Microsoft in its Internet Explorer 3.0. I think you'll find the experience a lot of fun and rewarding.

Everyone Needs a Home...

Over the last couple of years, the Internet and the World Wide Web have really been pushed into the limelight. Now, you can barely find a commercial on television, in magazines, or in the newspaper that doesn't include a web address beginning with the now familiar.

```
http://www...
```

This is, of course, the address or URL (Universal Resource Locator, pronounced like *Earl*) of that company's home page, and today it seems like you aren't anybody unless you have a home page.

Feel left out? Well don't. In this chapter, you are going to create your own home page. Starting with a simple outline of a basic web page and a text file, it will go from ugly to masterpiece in one chapter. I guarantee it. You'll also learn many of the secrets web masters use to create their works of art.

Tag, You're It!

Before you begin, though, I want to lay a little groundwork.

HTML is based on the idea of typing simple text into a document. That's easy enough, but as soon as you begin typing in text, you are going to want to format it in different ways. You'll want to add a line break here, emphasize this text there, and set that other text apart in one way or another. So, to meet these demands, HTML offers something called a *tag*.

A tag is simply a bit of text enclosed within less-than and greater-than symbols (<, >). Therefore, a tag called TagName would look like this:

```
<TagName>
```

This tag is not directly a part of the document. In other words, the reader of the document will not see the tag's text. Instead, the reader will see the results of the tag: formatted text.

Sometimes tags are used alone, and sometimes they come in pairs. When they come in pairs, the are called *start* and *end* tags. A start tag called TagName would look like this:

```
<TagName>
```

The end tag would look like this:

```
</TagName>
```

The slash always indicates that this is an end tag. You use start and end tags to enclose parts of your document. This is how you indicate which parts should be formatted.

HTML is not case-sensitive. In other words, it doesn't care whether you use `<TagName>`, `<TAGNAME>`, or `<tagname>`. It's all the same. In this book, I will usually put tag and attribute names in all capital letters just so they stand out from the rest of the page.

The Tags Every HTML Document Has

Certain tags are so common that you will see them in almost every HTML document you see. Listing 2-1 shows you a bare-bones HTML document that only includes these common tags.

Listing 2-1: A bare-bones HTML document.

```
<HTML>
<HEAD>
<TITLE>New Page</TITLE>
</HEAD>
<BODY>

</BODY>
</HTML>
```

The first tag you see is `<HTML>`. It surrounds the entire document and, as you might expect, indicates that this is, in fact, an HTML document (as opposed to a document using some other markup language). No big deal.

The second tag is `<HEAD>`. This creates a header for your document. The `<TITLE>` tag is included within the header and surrounds text that will appear in Internet Explorer's title bar. It is also the name that is given if you save a reference to this page as a shortcut.

`<BODY>` surrounds the real work you'll do in creating your document. The vast majority of your document will appear inside the body.

Your First Home Page

Now is the time for this book to get interactive. If you are new to HTML, I don't want you to read this chapter. I want you to do this chapter. I am going to walk you through the process of creating a home page and then enhancing it with new tags as you learn.

Choose an Authoring Tool

Start off by choosing a tool for creating your web page. Creating web pages is not usually referred to as programming, but rather as *authoring*. Therefore, these tools are often called *authoring tools*, and no, you don't have to go out and by some $100 HTML development environment. You can download shareware and freeware HTML development tools from the Web and other online sources for free.

If you decide not to use HTML Assistant Pro or one of the others suggested here, be sure you don't pick up a What-You-See-Is-What-You-Get (WYSIWYG, pronounced *whizzy-wig*) HTML editor. These editors try to hide the HTML tags from you so that you can use them as you would a word processor. You usually then apply styles which change the way text looks.

The reason you don't want to use these right now is because you want to learn HTML. These tools try to shield you from the HTML and then they do the work behind the scenes. While this may sound appealing, you will be much better off seeing a how HTML is done from scratch. Then, if you want to move on to one of these tools in the future, you will have a much better idea of how to use it because you will know something about what it is doing behind the scenes.

Examples of WYSIWYG HTML editors you should avoid for now are Microsoft FrontPage and Internet Assistant for Word.

Probably the most commonly used HTML authoring tool in Windows is Notepad. That's right. The silly little editor that came with Windows is elegant in its simplicity. Just fire it up and start typing!

Because I don't know what editor you'll be using for this chapter, I won't tell you step by step every move to make. Instead, I'll depend on you to know how to use the specific tool and remember to save your work after making your changes.

Setting Up Your Environment

When you type in your HTML, you will most likely want to see what it looks like in a browser immediately. That way, you can find problems and make corrections right away and then test your document again.

To do this the easy way, start up your editing environment, create a new page, and then save that page. For now, just create a page like the one in Listing 2-2.

Listing 2-2: A simple page to begin.

```
<HTML>
<HEAD>
<TITLE>New Page</TITLE>
</HEAD>
<BODY>

</BODY>
</HTML>
```

You'll notice right away that this looks strikingly similar to the bare-bones HTML page I showed you earlier. You'll remember I said that nearly every web page out there includes most or all of these tags. They are the foundation on which you'll want to build. Save this page under the name HOME.HTM or something equally descriptive.

Once you have the document in your editor and saved to a folder on your hard disk, you can boot up your browser. Launch Microsoft Internet Explorer. Once you are looking at a page, you can choose File⇨Open and click Browse on the Open dialog box that appears. Now, you can search your system for that folder where you saved the HOME.HTM document you just created. Once you find it, select it and open it in Explorer.

 Throughout most of this book, I'll assume that you are using Microsoft Internet Explorer. Because it's free and it is on the CD-ROM, it should be an easy one for you to pick up if you don't use it already. It is probably the best platform for ActiveX controls and VBScript because it comes directly from Microsoft.

If you do use another browser and prefer it for developing active Internet pages, you'll need to know how it works. If you do, you'll probably be able to translate my instructions for using Explorer to whatever you prefer.

You should now see a completely blank web page. Believe it or not, that's a good sign. Just to make sure it is displaying the correct blank page, look up in the title bar of Explorer. You should see New Page - Microsoft Internet Explorer. Look back at the listing, and you'll see that New Page is the title we gave this document in the header portion of our HTML code.

Now, every time you make a change to your document in the HTML editor, be sure and save it. Then, switch over to the Internet Explorer, and click the Refresh button. That will retrieve the newly saved copy and show you your latest work. Always be sure to save and then always press the Refresh button; otherwise you'll be looking at an older version of your page.

A First Cut

Now, I want you just to type your web page. First, type a new title in between the <TITLE> tag pair. Then, go to the <BODY> tag and enter everything else between that tag pair.

What should you type? Tell the reader about yourself. Who are you? What do you do for a living? Where do you work? What do you like to do for fun? What hobbies do you have? Do you like movies? What sort of music do you like? What bands are your favorites? What are your all-time favorite songs? Do some brainstorming.

Listing 2-3 shows you my page. Take mine and model your formatting after it. If you want to add additional sections, feel free, but I'd like the formatting to at least include all the elements I've included there. For instance, you should have a line at the top identifying this as your home page (it doesn't have to be the same as the TITLE, but it often is). You will also want some introductory paragraphs, a separating line (I just used a bunch of dashes here), a list of something (not necessarily hobbies), and a top five or top ten list of something else. You will, however, probably want to do your Surfing section similar to how I've done mine. You can insert your own favorite pages, though, of course. Finally, you'll want a line at the bottom identifying the creator of the page.

I'm not trying to cramp your style, but I do want you to be able to follow along and enhance your page as I'm enhancing mine. As you learn the tags, feel free to add new sections and new formatting as you see fit. It's your page, after all!

Listing 2-3: A first cut at a simple home page.

```
<HTML>
<HEAD>
<TITLE>Bill Hatfield's Home Page</TITLE>
</HEAD>
<BODY>
Bill Hatfield's Home Page

Welcome to my home on the World Wide Web. This page will
tell you about me, my hobbies and my interests.

First, a little about me. I am a computer programmer and
consultant who works in Indianapolis, IN. I do training
for TASC, Inc., and I write.

I really enjoy spending time with friends and playing
games of all types. In fact, I am going to finish my
basement as a game room so I'll always have a place to
```

```
play.

-----------------------------

My Hobbies
I have a wide variety of interests and often enjoy just
chatting about what interests other people. Here are a few
specifics:
Reading
Writing
Computer, Board, and Card Games
British Comedies
Philosophy/Psychology/Religion


-----------------------------


Best Movies Ever
This is a list of the best movies ever, in my humble
opinion. Actually, there are probably a dozen more that I
enjoy just as much. It is so hard to narrow it down...
1. Airplane
2. Star Wars
3. Toy Story
4. Batman
5. Dead Poet's Society



-----------------------------


Surfing
I also love surfing the web. Here are a few of my favorite
places to visit:
Site                    Address
Yahoo                   http://www.yahoo.com
Microsoft Corp.         http://www.microsoft.com
CNet Central            http://www.cnet.com
Windows 95              http://www.win95.com

Designed by Bill Hatfield Consulting.
</BODY>
</HTML>
```

Just use spaces to space out the little list of sites and their addresses. You
probably won't be able to line up all the addresses with each other, but just
get as close as you can and you can work on it later.

Now that you've entered your nifty new page, it's time to see how it looks in Internet Explorer. Save your document, switch over to Explorer, and click Refresh (see Figure 2-1).

Wow. Not exactly what you expected, eh? Don't worry. You'll have it looking a lot better in no time. I promise.

 After you install the CD-ROM that came with this book, you'll find a folder named Chap02. This folder contains the HTML pages created in this chapter. Home.htm and Books.htm are the final product, but also included are the pages as they look as they are being created, one step at a time. That way, if you are having trouble with a specific part of this chapter, you can go out to the Chap02 folder and see what yours should look like. The numbers used correspond to the figures in this chapter, so Home06.htm is the HTML file that was used to produce Figure 2.6, and Home19.htm is the figure that was used to produce Figure 2.19. If you get lost, just look for the nearest figure and check the solution!

Making It Look Reasonable

We first need to address the fact that HTML doesn't pay one bit of attention to where you break your lines. When you typed it in, you carefully created paragraphs and used Return to break up the information, but all of this was lost when you displayed it in Explorer.

The Paragraph and Line Break Tags

If you want HTML to break up lines and paragraphs, you have to tell it specifically to do so. To tell it about paragraphs, you use the <P> tag. You add the <P> tag at the end of every paragraph where you want a paragraph break.

A paragraph break is different from a line break, however. If you just want to break up a line into multiple lines, you will want to use the line break tab instead: <BR>.

What's the difference between <BR> and <P>? Because you use <P> for the end of a paragraph, Explorer will not only break the line but also add a bit of space before the next line so that the reader can tell that a new paragraph has begun. If you had several short lines and you used <P> at the end of each, you would end up with the lines spaced out more than you probably would want.
 doesn't add any space at all, it simply breaks the line.

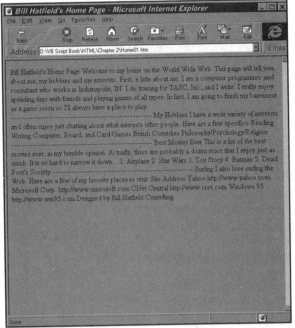

Figure 2-1: A (very) rough first cut at your home page.

Remember when I told you about tags I mentioned that some tags are used alone and some come in pairs. You've seen four different tags that come in pairs already: `<HTML>`, `<HEAD>`, `<TITLE>`, and `<BODY>`. Both `<BR>` and `<P>` are usually used alone, wherever you want to put the break.

My new web page, adding `<BR>` and `<P>` tags in all the right places, is in Listing 2-4. Look at it and then add these tags to your web page where appropriate.

Listing 2-4: The home page with line break and paragraph tags.

```
<HTML>
<HEAD>
<TITLE>Bill Hatfield's Home Page</TITLE>
</HEAD>
<BODY>
Bill Hatfield's Home Page<P>

Welcome to my home on the World Wide Web. This page will
tell you about me, my hobbies and my interests.
<P>
```

(continued)

(continued)

First, a little about me. I am a computer programmer and consultant who works in Indianapolis, IN. I do training for TASC, Inc., and I write.<P>

I really enjoy spending time with friends and playing games of all types. In fact, I am going to finish my basement as a game room so I'll always have a place to play.<P>

--------------------------<P>

My Hobbies<P>
I have a wide variety of interests and often enjoy just chatting about what interests other people. Here are a few specifics:<P>
Reading
Writing
Computer, Board, and Card Games
British Comedies
Philosophy/Psychology/Religion

--------------------------<P>

Best Movies Ever<P>
This is a list of the best movies ever, in my humble opinion. Actually, there are probably a dozen more that I enjoy just as much. It is so hard to narrow it down... <P>
1. Airplane
2. Star Wars
3. Toy Story
4. Batman
5. Dead Poet's Society

--------------------------<P>

Surfing<P>
I also love surfing the web. Here are a few of my favorite places to visit:<P>
Site   Address
Yahoo   http://www.yahoo.com
Microsoft Corp.   http://www.microsoft.com
CNet Central   http://www.cnet.com
Windows 95   http://www.win95.com

Designed by Bill Hatfield Consulting.
</BODY>
</HTML>

Save it, switch over to Internet Explorer, and do a Refresh (see Figure 2-2).

 You may be wondering, if you wanted to use the characters < or > in a web page, how would you do it? If you used them, the browser might think you were trying to specify another tag. Well, there are special ways of displaying symbols that HTML normally uses for other things.

Character	HTML
<	&lt;
>	&gt;

That's easy enough, but now what if you want to use the ampersand (&) for something? How will the browser know you aren't trying to display some special character?

&	&amp;

You can use this same technique to create a foreign language page or maybe just use some foreign words in your page.

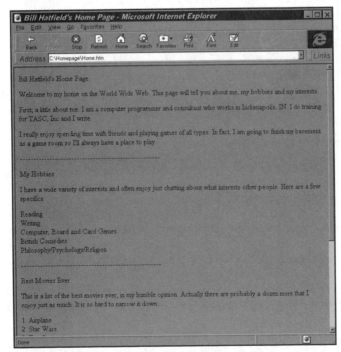

Figure 2-2: A little formatting goes a long way!

This is *much* better! At least now you can tell what it is supposed to look like. Also, notice the difference between ⟨P⟩ and the ⟨BR⟩.

á	&aacute;
à	&agrave;
â	&acirc;
Æ	&aelig;
ä	&auml;
å	&aring;
ç	&ccedil;
ñ	&ntilde;
∅	&oslash;
§	&szlig;

If you want the uppercase equivalent of any of these characters, simply capitalize the first letter of the symbol, like this: &Aacute. In addition, if you want to use an accent with another vowel, simply substitute the vowel in the symbol, like this: &egrav;.

Some problems still exist, of course. The Site and Address table is all collapsed together, as if Explorer decided you didn't really need all those spaces in there. Beyond that, it just looks really bland. Nothing stands out or grabs your attention.

Preformatted Text

Sometimes you want to set up the text to look exactly like you want it, and you don't want the browser to mess with it. That's the purpose of the ⟨PRE⟩ tag. *PRE* stands for *PREformatted text*. You use it as a pair of tags to indicate what portion of the document should be left alone. This is the tag you'll use for the Site/Address table to tell Explorer not to take out your spaces.

Browsers usually use a monospace font to display the text surrounded by the ⟨PRE⟩ tag. A monospace font uses the same amount of room for a *W* as it does for an *I*. While that makes the font less attractive, it allows you to use spaces to line up the text like you want to do for the Sites/Addresses table.

Add the ⟨PRE⟩ tag around your Site/Address table. Listing 2-5 shows the last part of my page after the ⟨PRE⟩ tag pair has been added.

Listing 2-5: The Surfing section of the page using the <PRE> tag to help create a simple table.

```
...
---------------------------<P>

Surfing<P>
I also love surfing the web. Here are a few of my favorite
places to visit:<P>
<PRE>
Site                     Address<BR>
Yahoo                    http://www.yahoo.com<BR>
Microsoft Corp.          http://www.microsoft.com<BR>
CNet Central             http://www.cnet.com<BR>
Windows 95               http://www.win95.com<BR>
</PRE>
<BR>
Designed by Bill Hatfield Consulting.
</BODY>
</HTML>
```

Save your document and Refresh Explorer to see what it looks like. The spacing might still be a bit off, but just note which addresses need to move forward and backward and guess how much. Then, go back to your editor and add or delete spaces as needed. It might take a couple of tries, but you should get them to line up exactly as you want them to in Explorer (see Figure 2-3). (They may or may not end up lining up in the editor.)

Comments

I want to tell you about one more element before you go on: *comments*. Comments don't improve the way your page looks. In fact, they have no impact on the final page at all. So why use them? They place reminders and remarks about the page for others to see who might work on your page later. Or, if no one but you will be working on it, they function as a note to yourself to remind you why you did certain things.

For instance, you might want to remind yourself why you used the <PRE> tag in the Surfing section. This is easy to do with the comment characters. A comment always begins with <!— and ends with —>. So, your Surfing section might look like Listing 2-6 with comments.

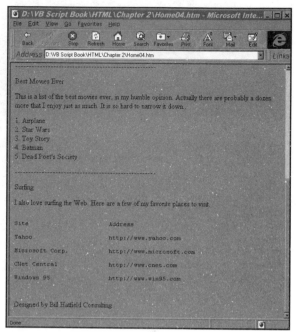

Figure 2-3: The table finally lines up correctly.

For instance, you might want to remind yourself why you used the <PRE> tag in the Surfing section. This is easy to do with the comment characters. A comment always begins with <!– and ends with –>. So, your Surfing section might look like Listing 2-6 with comments.

Listing 2-6: Comments added to explain the <PRE> tag.

```
...
-----------------------------<P>

Surfing<P>
I also love surfing the web. Here are a few of my favorite
places to visit:<P>
<!– I used <PRE> here so that I could get all the



Addresses to line up in a row –>
<PRE>
Site                       Address
Yahoo                      http://www.yahoo.com<BR>
Microsoft Corp.            http://www.microsoft.com<BR>
CNet Central               http://www.cnet.com<BR>
```

```
Windows 95                 http://www.win95.com<BR>
</PRE>

Designed by Bill Hatfield Consulting.
</BODY>
</HTML>
```

As you can see, a comment can continue over as many lines as you like. As long as you end it with the —>. Now anyone who looks at the HTML can read the text, but it won't appear when the page is displayed in Internet Explorer.

Formatting Text and Making It Look Nice

In this section, you'll go beyond looking OK and delve into the features that start to dress up your web documents. You'll add headers and format lists and make use of font styles like bold and italic to add emphasis.

Headers

Whenever you write anything even moderately long, you should always divide it up into sections. If you start off writing from an outline, you can make the major and minor points on your outline break out into major and minor section headers. As an example, each chapter in this book is divided up into sections. The major section heading for this text is "Formatting Text and Making It Look Nice." It is also under the subheading "Headers." You can tell the difference in the headings by their font size and style.

HTML makes headers easy with the <H1> tag pair. Actually, there is an <H2> tag pair, an <H3> tag pair, all the way to <H7>. These allow you to specify primary headers (<H1>), secondary headers (<H2>), and so forth.

In your HTML page, you will want to make the first line a primary header so it will stand out. You will probably want to make the rest of the headers secondary headers. Unless you are creating a complex document, you won't often go beyond <H3> or so.

Listing 2-7 shows what my home page looks like with headers added.

Listing 2-7: The home page with headers in all the right places.

```
<HTML>
<HEAD>
<TITLE>Bill Hatfield's Home Page</TITLE>
</HEAD>
<BODY>
<H1>Bill Hatfield's Home Page</H1>

Welcome to my home on the World Wide Web. This page will
tell you about me, my hobbies and my interests.
<P>

First, a little about me. I am a computer programmer and
consultant who works in Indianapolis, IN. I do training
for TASC, Inc., and I write.<P>

I really enjoy spending time with friends and playing
games of all types. In fact, I am going to finish my
basement as a game room so I'll always have a place to
play.<P>

--------------------------<P>

<H2>My Hobbies</H2>
I have a wide variety of interests and often enjoy just
chatting about what interests other people. Here are a few
specifics:<P>
Reading<BR>
Writing<BR>
Computer, Board, and Card Games<BR>
British Comedies<BR>
Philosophy/Psychology/Religion<BR>
<BR>
--------------------------<P>



<H2>Best Movies Ever</H2>
This is a list of the best movies ever, in my humble
opinion. Actually, there are probably a dozen more that I
enjoy just as much. It is so hard to narrow it down... <P>
1. Airplane<BR>
2. Star Wars<BR>
3. Toy Story<BR>
4. Batman<BR>
5. Dead Poet's Society<BR>
<BR>
--------------------------<P>
```

```
<H2>Surfing</H2>
I also love surfing the web. Here are a few of my favorite
places to visit:<P>
<!- I used <PRE> here so that I could get all the
Addresses to line up in a row ->
<PRE>
Site                        Address<BR>
Yahoo                       http://www.yahoo.com<BR>
Microsoft Corp.             http://www.microsoft.com<BR>
CNet Central                http://www.cnet.com<BR>
Windows 95                  http://www.win95.com<BR>
</PRE>
<BR>
Designed by Bill Hatfield Consulting.
</BODY>
</HTML>
```

The first line (Bill Hatfield's Home Page) is a primary header (H1). All the rest are secondary headers (H2). I don't need to go any deeper than that for this document. I didn't put header tags around the title because, as you remember, this only appears in the title bar of the browser window anyway. Notice that I removed the <P> tags for the lines that I made headers. If I'd left them in, they wouldn't hurt anything, but they aren't needed for headers. A line feed and spacing are already built in.

Figure 2-4 shows what it looks like in Explorer.

Headers definitely make your document stand out and look more interesting.

Lists

I have a couple of lists on my home page. They look OK, but my Hobbies list would look a lot nicer if I could add bullets. Of course, HTML makes that easy.

Unordered Lists

The <UL> tag pair surrounds an unordered list. *Unordered* simply means that they aren't steps and don't require numbers beside them. Within the <UL> tag section, you can use the <LI> tag to indicate the beginning of a list item. You don't use an end tag with <LI>. Explorer knows when the list item is done when it runs into another <LI>. The hobbies section of my page looks like Listing 2-8.

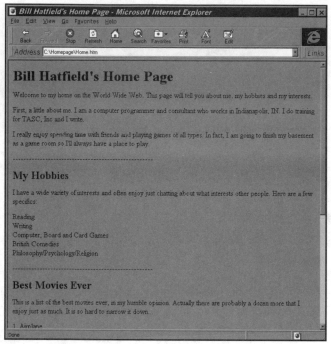

Figure 2-4: The new page, with headers.

Listing 2-8: The Hobbies section as an unnumbered list.

```
...
---------------------------<P>

<H2>My Hobbies</H2>
I have a wide variety of interests and often enjoy just
chatting about what interests other people. Here are a few
specifics:<P>
<UL>
<LI>Reading
<LI>Writing
<LI>Computer, Board, and Card Games
<LI>British Comedies
<LI>Philosophy/Psychology/Religion
</UL>
<BR>
---------------------------<P>
...
```

Because Explorer already knows that each list item should be on a separate line, I can eliminate of all those ⟨BR⟩ tags. It ends up looking pretty spiffy in Explorer (see Figure 2-5).

You can even create a list within a list. For instance, that third line is a little cumbersome. What if I reworked it so it looked like Listing 2-9?

Listing 2-9: A list within a list.

```
...
--------------------------⟨P⟩


⟨H2⟩My Hobbies⟨/H2⟩
I have a wide variety of interests and often enjoy just
chatting about what interests other people. Here are a few
specifics:⟨P⟩
⟨UL⟩
⟨LI⟩Reading
⟨LI⟩Writing
⟨LI⟩Games
```

(continued)

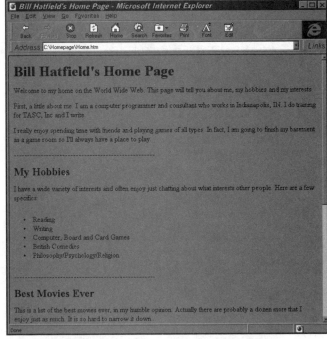

Figure 2-5: Bullets for the unordered list of hobbies.

```
(continued)
<UL>
<LI>Computer
<LI>Board
<LI>Card
</UL>

<LI>British Comedies
<LI>Philosophy/Psychology/Religion
</UL>
<BR>
------------------------<P>
. . .
```

This is an unordered list within another unordered list. This is referred to as a *nested* unordered list. I put an extra line on either side of the nested list just to set it off a bit and make the HTML clearer. These extra lines don't have any effect on how the document is displayed. Speaking of how it's displayed, take a look at Figure 2-6.

Explorer even knows to indent the nested list to show that it is subordinate to Games.

Ordered Lists

If there are unordered lists, you can bet that there are *ordered* lists. Ordered lists always have numbers. The nice thing is that, once you tell Explorer that a particular list is an ordered list, it will automatically handle the numbers for you. The tag for ordered lists isn't tricky at all: <OL>. You also use the same list item tag (<LI>) within the <OL> tag pair. So, if I redo my Best Movies section, it might look like Listing 2-10.

Listing 2-10: An ordered list.

```
. . .
------------------------<P>



<H2>Best Movies Ever</H2>
This is a list of the best movies ever, in my humble
opinion. Actually, there are probably a dozen more that I
enjoy just as much. It is so hard to narrow it down... <P>
<OL>
<LI>Airplane
```

```
<LI>Star Wars
<LI>Toy Story
<LI>Batman
<LI>Dead Poet's Society
</OL>
<BR>
-------------------------<P>
...
```

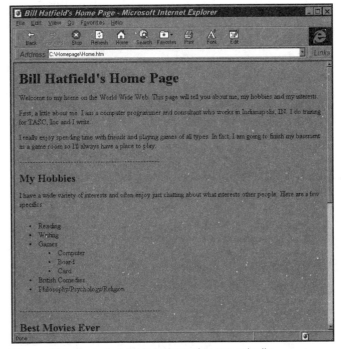

Figure 2-6: A nested list is indented automatically.

Again, I can remove the `<BR>` tags because Explorer knows that it is a list. I also got rid of the numbers because the `<OL>` tag does that for me. Figure 2-7 shows the result.

If you need to add a new item later, you don't have to renumber. Just stick the new one in the middle, and Explorer will figure it out and renumber the items correctly. This is especially nice for really long lists.

By default, your items will be numbered with standard numerals 1, 2, 3, and so on. You can change this, though. Just use the TYPE attribute of the `<OL>` tag to specify any of the following.

Tag	Result
`<OL TYPE="A">`	A, B, C, and so on
`<OL TYPE="a">`	a, b, c, and so on
`<OL TYPE="I">`	I, II, III, IV, and so on
`<OL TYPE="i">`	i, ii, iii, iv, and so on

Definition Lists

Definition lists (sometimes called *glossary lists*) are a little different from ordered and unordered lists. As the name implies, they were originally created for defining terms in a glossary or other situations where you have a word or phrase and then a definition, but you can use them for a broad variety of things.

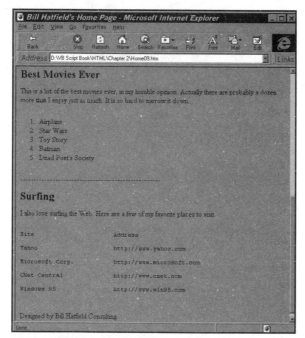

Figure 2-7: The numbered list in Explorer.

Although I don't have a use for definition lists on my home page, I'll create a new page that uses them and then I'll associate the new page with my home page later.

Listing 2-11 shows my new page.

Listing 2-11: A new page demonstrating definition lists.

```
<HTML>
<HEAD>
<TITLE>Bill Hatfield's Favorite Fiction</TITLE>
</HEAD>
<BODY>
<H1>Bill Hatfield's Favorite Fiction</H1>
This is a list of my favorite books of fiction. For each
book, I'll tell you the title, the author, and a brief
summary of the plot. If you want to have a good time, go
out, buy them all, and start reading!<P>
<DL>
<DT>Interview With The Vampire, Anne Rice
<DD>Although the movie was a good adaptation, it still
pales in comparison to this excellent book. A reporter has
an extended discussion with a person who claims to be a
real vampire and has the stories to prove it. Anne Rice is
an absolute master of the language and creates a very
believable, dark mythic world that draws you in from the
first page.
<DT>Terminal, Robin Cook
<DD>A breakthrough cure for a rare form of brain cancer is
discovered. A medical student, fascinated by the
discovery, begins work at the lab but is barred from
participating. As he digs deeper, he finds that a
frightening conspiracy is afoot. This is a high-tech,
biomedical thriller with lots of twists and turns.
<DT>Sphere, Michael Crichton
<DD>A lesser known work from this excellent writer, Sphere
tells the story of a strange object discovered at the
bottom of the sea that isn't a sunken ship or submarine.
It is clearly a spaceship, and it is 300 years old! In an
attempt to find answers, four scientists arrive and
descend to the depths, but what they discover raises even
more questions.
<DT>The Chamber, John Grisham
<DD>This one is very different from The Firm and The
Pelican Brief, and many say it harkens back to Grisham's
first book, A Time To Kill. A young lawyer fights to keep
a convicted murderer from the electric chair. This
impressive work of legal suspense will keep you on the
edge of your seat until the very end.
<DT>Degree of Guilt, Richard North Patterson
<DD>If you like Grisham, you must read Richard North
Patterson. In this mystery/thriller, a world-famous
novelist is murdered, and a famous TV journalist is the
suspect. She pleads guilty to murder in self-defense, but
```

(continued)

```
(continued)
as the trail unfolds, her alibi begins to fall apart.
</DL>

</BODY>
</HTML>
```

You can create your own page on a different topic if you like. Anything will do: a list of your favorite music groups, select pieces from your coin or stamp collection, or a list of cars you've owned in the past.

Notice how the definition list works. The whole thing is contained with the <DL> tag pair. Then, inside the tag pair, you use <DT> to identify the *term* and <DD> to identify the *definition*. Both <DT> and <DD> are used alone, without an end tag.

My page ends up looking like Figure 2-8.

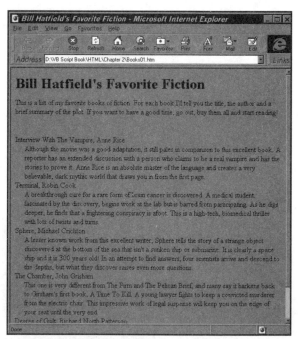

Figure 2-8: The definition list.

Text Style Formatting

Before you finish up that definition list, look at it again. Those book titles and authors (or whatever it is that you ended up using for your definition list terms) sort of just blend in with everything else. Is there a way that you can make the terms stand out more? Could you maybe set the author name apart from the book name?

Bold, Italic, and Underline

Simple type styles are easy with HTML. You can use the <I> tag pair to surround any text you want to appear italic, you use the <B> tag pair for bold text, and you use (you guessed it) a <U> tag pair for underlined text. Listing 2-12 puts this information to work on my book list. (The three periods indicate that I've left out part of the listing. I did the exact same thing to all the book titles and authors.)

Listing 2-12: Making the titles and authors stand out with bold, italic, and underline tags.

```
<HTML>
<HEAD>
<TITLE>Bill Hatfield's Favorite Fiction</TITLE>
</HEAD>
<BODY>
<H1>Bill Hatfield's Favorite Fiction</H1>
This is a list of my favorite books of fiction. For each
book, I'll tell you the title, the author, and a brief
summary of the plot. If you want to have a good time, go
out, buy them all, and start reading!<P>
<DL>
<DT><B><U>Interview With The Vampire</U>, <I>Anne
Rice</I></B>
<DD>Although the movie was a good adaptation, it still
pales in comparison to this excellent book. A reporter has
an extended discussion with a person who claims to be a
real vampire and has the stories to prove it. Anne Rice is
an absolute master of the language and creates a very
believable, dark mythic world that draws you in from the
first page.
<DT><B><U>Terminal</U>, <I>Robin Cook</I></B>
<DD>A breakthrough cure for a rare form of brain cancer is
discovered. A medical student, fascinated by the
discovery, begins work at the lab but is barred from
participating. As he digs deeper, he finds that a
frightening conspiracy is afoot. This is a high-tech,
```

(continued)

```
(continued)

biomedical thriller with lots of twists and turns.

...

</DL>

</BODY>
</HTML>
```

I made the entire term line bold, underlined the title, and italicized the author. Perhaps it's a bit much, but it certainly looks a lot better than it did (see Figure 2-9).

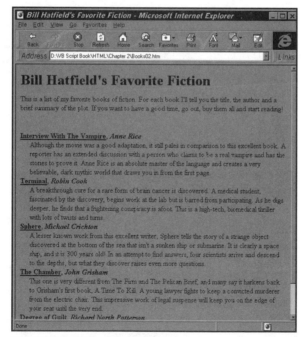

Figure 2-9: The new list of fiction.

Center

Save your definition list document and go back to your home page. I want to show you another text formatting feature: the <CENTER> tag pair. Go up to the top of the HTML document and place the <CENTER> tag pair around your first header (see Listing 2-13).

Listing 2-13: The `<CENTER>` **tag pair is added around the first header.**

```
<HTML>
<HEAD>
<TITLE>Bill Hatfield's Home Page</TITLE>
</HEAD>
<BODY>
<CENTER><H1>Bill Hatfield's Home Page</H1></CENTER>
...
```

The header is now centered (see Figure 2-10).

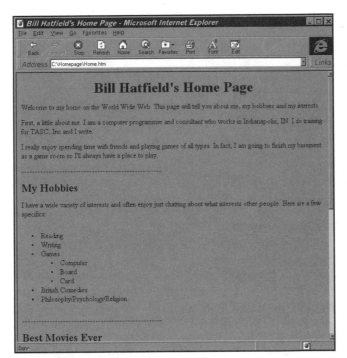

Figure 2-10: The header is centered.

Logical styles: Emphasis, Strong, and Address

HTML supports several tags that do not have specific text styles associated with them. These logical styles simply inform the browser that you want to emphasize a particular bit of text, for instance. The browser decides what that means and displays it appropriately. One browser might choose to italicize the text whereas another browser might choose to underline the text. Or, a browser might provide customization options that let a user choose how emphasized text should appear.

Table 2-1 lists the three logical styles you'll probably run into most. The table shows the tag, how Explorer presents text tagged this way, and a description. These tags are always used in pairs to surround the text they identify.

Table 2-1	The Logical Styles	
Tag	**Explorer Style**	**Description**
`<EM>`	Italics	Emphasis
`<STRONG>`	Bold	Strong Emphasis
`<ADDRESS>`	Italics	Info on page's subject or creator

For my page, I'll go down to the bottom, where I identified the creator of the page, and place an `<ADDRESS>` tag pair around it (see Listing 2-14).

Listing 2-14: The `<ADDRESS>` tag pair is added around the last line.

```
...
<BR>
<ADDRESS>Designed by Bill Hatfield Consulting.</ADDRESS>
</BODY>
</HTML>
```

Figure 2-11 shows what it looks like in Explorer.

Horizontal Lines

One easy way to dress up your home page is with Explorer's built-in capability to create horizontal rules or lines for you. You just identify where you want the line with the `<HR>` (horizontal rule) tag. Go through and replace all those silly dashes with `<HR>` tags. The entire page should look like Listing 2-15.

Listing 2-15: The entire home page listing with horizontal rules.

```
<HTML>
<HEAD>
<TITLE>Bill Hatfield's Home Page</TITLE>
</HEAD>
<BODY>
<CENTER><H1>Bill Hatfield's Home Page</H1></CENTER>
```

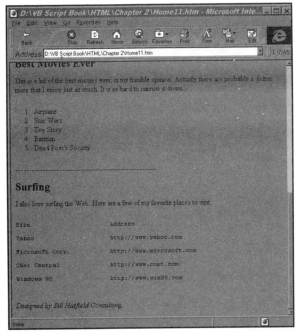

Figure 2-11: The "Designed by" line is in italics.

```
Welcome to my home on the World Wide Web. This page will
tell you about me, my hobbies and my interests.
<P>


First, a little about me. I am a computer programmer and
consultant who works in Indianapolis, IN. I do training
for TASC, Inc., and I write.<P>

I really enjoy spending time with friends and playing
games of all types. In fact, I am going to finish my
basement as a game room so I'll always have a place to
play.<P>

<HR>

<H2>My Hobbies</H2>
I have a wide variety of interests and often enjoy just
chatting about what interests other people. Here are a few
specifics:<P>
<UL>
```

(continued)

```
(continued)
<LI>Reading
<LI>Writing
<LI>Games

<UL>
<LI>Computer
<LI>Board
<LI>Card
</UL>

<LI>British Comedies
<LI>Philosophy/Psychology/Religion
</UL>
<BR>

<HR>

<H2>Best Movies Ever</H2>
This is a list of the best movies ever, in my humble
opinion. Actually, there are probably a dozen more that I
enjoy just as much. It is so hard to narrow it down... <P>
<OL>
<LI>Airplane
<LI>Star Wars
<LI>Toy Story
<LI>Batman
<LI>Dead Poet's Society
</OL>
<BR>
<HR>

<H2>Surfing</H2>
I also love surfing the web. Here are a few of my favorite
places to visit:<P>
<!- I used <PRE> here so that I could get all the
Addresses to line up in a row ->
<PRE>
Site                    Address<BR>
Yahoo                   http://www.yahoo.com<BR>
Microsoft Corp.         http://www.microsoft.com<BR>
CNet Central            http://www.cnet.com<BR>
Windows 95              http://www.win95.com<BR>
</PRE>
<BR>
<ADDRESS>Designed by Bill Hatfield Consulting.</ADDRESS>
</BODY>
</HTML>
```

Figure 2-12 shows what it looks like in Explorer.

Colors and Background Pictures

One aspect of your page probably has more of an affect on your reader's perceptions than any other: colors. You can control the background color, text color, and even the color of the links. Or, instead of setting a background color, you can choose a bitmap to serve as a background picture or design.

You don't even need to learn a new tag to do it, but you do need to learn a few more attributes. You remember when I showed you the bare-bones web page at the beginning of this chapter? I discussed each of the general tags there, including the <BODY> tag. Well, it turns out the <BODY> tag has several interesting attributes.

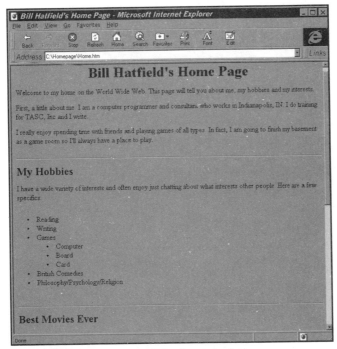

Figure 2-12: The page with horizontal rules.

Colors

BGCOLOR is the attribute that allows you to set the background color. TEXT allows you to set the color of the standard text. LINK and VLINK make it possible to change the color of the links and visited links. All of these are attributes of the `<BODY>` tag and as many or as few of them can be specified after the opening tag as you like.

How do you specify what color you want? Here is a list of standard colors that Internet Explorer supports.

Table 2-2 The Standard Colors That Internet Explorer Supports			
Aqua	Black	Blue	Fuchsia
Gray	Green	Lime	Maroon
Navy	Olive	Purple	Red
Silver	Teal	White	Yellow

If you want to use these colors, just assign them directly to the attribute, like this:

```
<BODY BGCOLOR=Olive LINK=Green VLINK=Lime>
```

I'll change the background color in my page to Aqua, my link color to Blue, and my visited link color to Navy. I'll leave my text black. Listing 2-16 shows you the line that does it.

Listing 2-16: Changing the background, link, and visited link colors.

```
<HTML>
<HEAD>
<TITLE>Bill Hatfield's Home Page</TITLE>
</HEAD>
<BODY BGCOLOR=Aqua LINK=Blue VLINK=Navy>
<CENTER><H1>Bill Hatfield's Home Page</H1></CENTER>
...
```

Of course, there aren't any links in this document yet, but if you check out the page in Internet Explorer, you'll at least see the background color.

 With HTML, you can identify nearly any color you like and assign these color attributes to your page. If you want to use one that is not in the predefined list, however, you have to learn a bit more about how HTML understands colors. HTML identifies colors as a mixture of Red, Green, and Blue, just like your TV set. In order to tell it what color you want to assign to these attributes, you have to give it some mixture of these three colors. Each color can have a value from 0 to 255. If you gave it 0 for Red, Green, and Blue, you would see the color black. If you gave it 0 for Red, 255 for Green, and 0 for Blue, you'd end up with a bright green. If you gave it 150 for Red, 0 for Green and 150 for Blue, you'd end up with a darker purple. See how it works? It's just like mixing paints in elementary school.

The problem is that the value you assign to these attributes must be in hexadecimal. Hexadecimal is a numbering system that the computer uses, but it isn't very intuitive for humans. This means that you will need a tool for translating values. It just so happens that you'll find such a tool on the Web. You can find it at:

```
http://www.microsoft.com/vbscript/vs/vbssamp/colortime/
colortime.htm.
```

You just slide the scrollbars for red, green, and blue until you see the color you want. As you do, the associated decimal and hexadecimal numbers for each part of the color and for the whole color appear below.

In case you'd rather work from a table, Table 2-3 provides some colors you might want to use; the three decimal values for Red, Green, and Blue; and the hexadecimal number you need to assign to the attribute in your web page.

Here's an example, setting the background to Antique and the text to Magenta:

```
<BODY BGCOLOR=#f9e8d2 TEXT=#ff00ff>
```

Table 2-3	Some Common Colors			
Color	Red	Geen	Blue	Hexadecimal
Cyan	0	255	255	#00ffff
Magenta	255	0	255	#ff00ff
Gray*	128	128	128	#808080
Antique (Off White)	249	232	210	#f9e8d2
Sky Blue	130	202	250	#82cafa
Gold	212	160	23	#d4a017
Orange	248	122	23	#f87a17
Pink	250	175	190	#faafbe
Sienna (Brown)	138	65	23	#8a4117
Turquoise	67	198	219	#43c6db
Violet	141	46	201	#8d38c9

* You can produce different shades of gray by increasing or decreasing these numbers. As long as all three numbers stay the same, it will be some shade of gray.

Be careful which colors you use for the background. If your video card doesn't support the specific color you've chosen, the video card may simulate the color by dithering. Dithering is a process where two different colored dots, say red and blue, are used in a checkerboard pattern to try to fool your eyes into believing it is seeing a different color. Red and blue dots in this pattern would create something that looked purple. Sort of. Actually it ends up being very grainy, and if there is text on it, the text is often hard to read.

Remember that even if your graphic card supports 16 million colors, your users might be working with one that only displays 16.

Background Pictures

BACKGROUND is one other interesting attribute for the <BODY> tag. BACKGROUND allows you to specify a background picture that is tiled underneath your text in the browser. Often, small bitmaps that provide a texture like sand or marble are used to make the page more interesting.

You should be concerned about two things when choosing a background picture for your web page. First, do not pick a picture that is too busy or near the same color as your text. Nothing is more frustrating than trying to read a page where the background gets in the way of the text.

Second, choose a reasonably small bitmap. Just like other graphics on the page, backgrounds can slow the page loading down on dial-up lines.

If you had a bitmap named sand.gif that was in the same folder as your web page, you could tile it as your background using this syntax:

```
<BODY BACKGROUND="sand.gif">
```

Fonts

Varying font sizes or styles in your HTML document used to be difficult. Any time you wanted a bigger font, you'd have to use one of the header tags. Both Netscape and Microsoft have addressed this problem and vastly expanded the options. In the next three sections, I'll show you how you can change the size, typeface, and color of your text anywhere in your document. I won't be putting any of these to immediate use in my home page, but feel free to add them to yours anywhere you like.

Size

<BASEFONT> and <FONT> are two tags that will help you with font size. <BASEFONT> allows you to choose the standard size for all the text in your document. The size is measured on a scale from 1 to 7, 7 being the largest. The numbers don't represent point size; they are just arbitrary numbers designed to indicate relative font size. The default <BASEFONT> is 3. If you were creating a page for folks who are likely to have difficulty reading small fonts, you might want to use a line like this:

```
<BASEFONT SIZE=5>
```

The <BASEFONT> tag does not have an end tag and affects the entire document, from the tag downward.

<FONT> is used for more temporary font size adjustments. You might use it to emphasize a word in text by increasing the font size:

```
I couldn't believe he ate the <FONT SIZE=4>whole
thing</FONT>!
```

<FONT> is used with an end tag and encloses the section containing the text where the font is to be changed. The font returns to the base font after the end tag. You can also use <FONT> simply to increase or decrease the font size without regard to what the base font is. You do this by prefixing the number with a plus or minus:

```
When it happened I felt <FONT SIZE=-2>very, very
small</FONT>.
```

This line reduces the font size for the words *very, very small* two levels. If the base font is already 1, this <FONT> would have no affect.

Typeface

One innovation that Microsoft pioneered is the capability to let you specify exactly what font is used to display your text. This is powerful. It gives you much more control over the way your web page looks:

```
They call him <FONT SIZE=5 FACE=Brush Script MT>Mr. Fancy-
Pants</FONT>.
```

The attribute FACE allows you to choose the specific font you want to display. You can see the results in Figure 2-13.

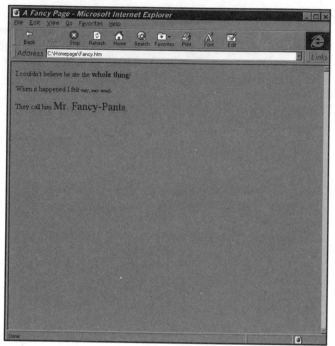

Figure 2-13: Using a specific font.

The downside of setting a specific font is that your user may not have the font on his system. To allow for this, you can specify several fonts, and the browser will try to use each one in order until it finds one or runs out of options.

```
<FONT FACE="Britannic Bold", "Bookman Old Style", "Times
New Roman">His gate was unusual.</FONT>
```

In this case, the browser would first look for Britannic Bold on the system. Failing that, it would try Bookman Old Style and then Times New Roman. If the browser did not find any of these fonts, it would go to the default font normally used in the browser.

Color

In a previous section, you learned that you could change the color of your web page as well as the text and the links on your page. Although you could change the color of all of the text, you could not change the color of just one phrase or paragraph. Again, the <FONT> tag has an attribute for that.

```
As the boat rocked back and forth, I began <FONT
```

```
COLOR=Green>feeling a little sick</FONT>.
```

All the standard colors available for the `<BODY>` tags `BGCOLOR` discussed previously are also available with the `COLOR` attribute for `<FONT>` (see Table 2-2 earlier this chapter).

You can use all of these `<FONT>` attributes together to get your point across exactly the way you want.

Adding Anchors

All of this formatting goes a long way toward making your documents easier and more enjoyable to read, but the whole point of the web is that content is more than fancy pages in a book. Information is connected to other information through *hyperlinks*. Hyperlinks are created with *anchors* in HTML. You use the `<A>` tag pair to create an anchor.

Links to Other Sites

Creating an anchor that links to another page somewhere else is easy. I'm talking specifically about the kind of links you want to create for the Surfing section of your home page. Instead of just telling your readers what sites you enjoy, make links to them so that they are only a mouse-click away.

The anchor tag pair always surrounds the text you want to become the hyperlink, but the anchor tag is never used by itself. It always has the `HREF` attribute defined. The `HREF` attribute identifies where the link should take the reader if she clicks on the text.

Listing 2-17 shows the surfing section reworked to provide links to the sites mentioned.

Listing 2-17: The Surfing section with links.

```
...
<H2>Surfing</H2>
I also love surfing the Web. Here are a few of my favorite
places to visit:<P>
<!— I used <PRE> here so that I could get all the
Addresses to line up in a row —>
<PRE>
Site                    Address<BR>
<A HREF="http://www.yahoo.com">
```

(continued)

```
(continued)

Yahoo</A>                    http://www.yahoo.com
<A HREF="http://www.microsoft.com">
Microsoft Corp.</A>          http://www.microsoft.com
<A HREF="http://www.cnet.com">
CNet Central </A>            http://www.cnet.com
<A HREF="http://www.win95.com">
Windows 95 </A>              http://www.win95.com</PRE>
<BR>
<ADDRESS>Designed by Bill Hatfield Consulting.</ADDRESS>
</BODY>
</HTML>
```

The site name and the address were left in the table format just as they were. I just added anchor tags around each of the site names so that they would jump to their associated sites when the user clicks on them. Figure 2-14 shows the result.

Links to Other Documents on Your Site

In addition to linking to other cool sites, you are likely going to want to link to other pages to your own site, such as that definition list page that you created a few pages back. Because mine was on fiction I enjoy reading, I'll link it to the place where I mention Reading in the Hobbies section (see Listing 2-18).

Listing 2-18: Linking to the book.htm page on this site.

```
. . .
<H2>My Hobbies</H2>
I have a wide variety of interests and often enjoy just
chatting about what interests other people. Here are a few
specifics:<P>
<UL>
<LI><A HREF="books.htm">Reading</A>
<LI>Writing
<LI>Games


<UL>
<LI>Computer
<LI>Board
<LI>Card
```

```
</UL>

<LI>British Comedies
<LI>Philosophy/Psychology/Religion
</UL>
<BR>
...
```

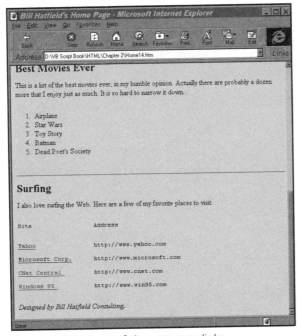

Figure 2-14: The surf sites are now links.

If the page is in the same subdirectory where the current page is, you can simply type the page name in the value for HREF.

Links to a Particular Part of a Page

If you have a very long page, it is courteous to give your readers a table of contents at the top of the page with links so that when the user clicks on a link, the page automatically scrolls to that location. It is also good in this situation to provide links throughout the page and at the bottom that scroll the reader immediately back up to the top.

My fiction page isn't all that long, but I'll use it to show you how this is done with the anchor tag. See Listing 2-19.

Listing 2-19: Making the titles and authors stand out with bold, italic, and underline tags.

```html
<HTML>
<HEAD>
<TITLE>Bill Hatfield's Home Page</TITLE>
</HEAD>
<BODY>

<A Name="Top"></A>
<H1>Bill Hatfield's Favorite Fiction</H1>
This is a list of my favorite books of fiction. For each
book I'll tell you the title, the author, and a brief
summary of the plot. If you want to have a good time, go
out, buy them all, and start reading!<P>
Click on any book to see its description. <P>




<A HREF="#Interview">
Interview With A Vampire<BR>
By Anne Rice<BR></A>
<BR>

<A HREF="#Terminal">
Terminal<BR>
By Robin Cook<BR></A>
<BR>

<A HREF="#Sphere">
Sphere<BR>
By  Michael Crichton<BR></A>
<BR>

<A HREF="#Chamber">
The Chamber<BR>
By John Grisham<BR></A>
<BR>

<A HREF="#Degree">
Degree of Guilt<BR>
By Richard North Patterson<BR></A>
<BR>

<DL>

<A Name="Interview"></A>
<DT><B><U>Interview With A Vampire</U>, <I>Anne
```

```
Rice</I></B>
<DD>Although the movie was a good adaptation, it still
pales in comparison to this excellent book. A reporter has
an extended discussion with a person who claims to be a
real vampire and has the stories to prove it. Anne Rice is
an absolute master of the language and creates a very
believable, dark mythic world that draws you in from the
first page.

<A Name="Terminal"></A>
<DT><B><U>Terminal</U>, <I>Robin Cook</I></B>
<DD>A breakthrough cure for a rare form of brain cancer is
discovered. A medical student, fascinated by the
discovery, begins work at the lab but is barred from
participating. As he digs deeper, he finds a frightening
conspiracy is afoot. This is a high-tech, biomedical
thriller with lots of twists and turns.

<A Name="Sphere"></A>
<DT><B><U>Sphere</U>, <I>Michael Crichton</I></B>
<DD>A lesser known work from this excellent writer, Sphere
tells the story of a strange object discovered at the
bottom of the sea that isn't a sunken ship or submarine.
It is clearly a spaceship, and it is 300 years old! In an
attempt to find answers, four scientists arrive and
descend to the depths, but what they discover raises even
more questions.

<A Name="Chamber"></A>
<DT><B><U>The Chamber</U>, <I>John Grisham</I></B>
<DD>This one is very different from The Firm and The
Pelican Brief, and many say it harkens back to Grisham's
first book, A Time To Kill. A young lawyer fights to keep
a convicted murderer from the electric chair. This
impressive work of legal suspense will keep you on the
edge of your seat until the very end.

<A Name="Degree"></A>
<DT><B><U>Degree of Guilt</U>, <I>Richard North
Patterson</I></B>
<DD>If you like Grisham, you must read Richard North
Patterson. In this mystery/thriller, a world-famous
novelist is murdered, and a famous TV journalist is the
suspect. She pleads guilty to murder in self-defense, but
as the trail unfolds, her alibi begins to fall apart.
</DL>

<A HREF="#Top">
```

(continued)

```
(continued)
Go to top<P></A>

</BODY>
</HTML>
```

I introduced a new attribute in this listing: Name. Name simply identifies a point in the document with a name so that another anchor can reference it. Although you must have an end anchor, you won't usually enclose anything when you are just naming a spot in the document.

Next, you'll notice that the links in the first part of the document refer to these names and put a pound sign (#) in front of them. That simply indicates that it is a named anchor in this document. A "Go to top" link was created to go to the named anchor at the top of the page.

Add links like this to your definition list page. It is easy once you get the hang of it, and it is fun to test in Explorer.

 You can use named anchors in other documents on your site with syntax like this:

```
Michael Crichton's book <A
    HREF="books.htm#Sphere">Sphere</A> is a
    fascinating tale.
```

Just use the page name in the HREF as you normally would and add the pound sign and anchor name after it. Likewise, for pages on other sites, use something like this:

```
Michael Crichton's book <A HREF=
    "http://www.iquest.net/~billprsn/books.htm#Sphere">
    Sphere</A> is a fascinating tale.
```

Mail Links

Once you put all this work into your home page, you'll want people to tell you what they think of it and maybe even give you ideas for improving it. You can build an easy feedback mechanism into your pages: a mail link.

A mail link is simply a link that provides your e-mail address. When users click on the link, Explorer brings up a window where they can type in an e-mail message, automatically addressed to you.

I added it to the address line of my home page (see Listing 2-20).

Listing 2-20: A mail link in the address line.

```
. . .
<ADDRESS>Designed by <A
HREF="mailto:72064.3200@compuserve.com">Bill Hatfield
Consulting.</A></ADDRESS></BODY>
</HTML>
```

As you can see, the only difference between a web page link and a mail link is that you put the phrase `mailto:` followed by the e-mail address instead of the web page URL in the `HREF` attribute.

Spit and Polish

In this section, I want to introduce you to three nice HTML capabilities for really adding that extra punch to your pages: images, tables, and frames.

Images

Sometimes there is no quicker way to drive home a point than with a good picture, diagram, or illustration. Whether you are a child or an adult, information is always more engaging when it has pictures.

You always hear that a picture is worth a thousand words, but on the web, it might be more like two or three thousand words worth of download time. There's nothing more annoying than going to a sight you want to use and having to wait for it to download picture after picture. Sure, once they're all downloaded a half hour later, they look nice, but most people aren't that patient.

So, the first rule to remember with graphics is, even if you have a fast connection, remember that not everyone does.

What's the best strategy? Go with small images. You can download a lot of small images in the time it would take to download one big banner for the top of your page.

The <IMG> Tag

HTML, again, makes it easy with `<IMG>` tag. The `<IMG>` tag is another one that you won't ever see without an attribute to give you more information. Probably the most common attribute is SRC, which you set equal to the name of your graphic file (see Listing 2-21).

Listing 2-21: A logo for Bill Hatfield Consulting.

```
...
<ADDRESS>
<IMG SRC="bhc.gif">
Designed by <A HREF="mailto:72064.3200@compuserve.com">Bill
Hatfield Consulting.</A>
</ADDRESS>
</BODY>
</HTML>
```

If you have a picture of yourself, a corporate logo, or other interesting graphics that you want to add to your web page, feel free. You just have to make sure of two things:

➡ The graphics file is in the same folder where your HTML page is

➡ The graphic is in either GIF or JPG format

As long as both of these things are true, you can use syntax just like I have, and you should see the graphic in your web page. If your graphic is in a different folder, you can put that folder's name before the file name to make sure it finds the graphic. You can even put a full-blown URL in the quotes so that it finds a graphic to display on your page on a completely different web site.

Notice that <IMG> is a single tag and does not have an end tag.

When it is displayed in the browser, it looks like Figure 2-15.

You'll notice that the text appears beside it, aligned with the bottom of the figure. This is the default alignment, but you can change that.

Image Alignment

In addition to the SRC attribute, <IMG> also has an ALIGN attribute that can have one of five values assigned to it: TOP, CENTER, BOTTOM, RIGHT, or LEFT. BOTTOM is the default if you don't specify the ALIGN attribute. Listing 2-22 shows the <IMG> tag with the alignment set to CENTER.

Listing 2-22: Aligning the text with the logo.

```
...
<ADDRESS>
<IMG SRC="bhc.gif" ALIGN=CENTER>
Designed by <A HREF="mailto:72064.3200@compuserve.com">Bill
Hatfield Consulting.</A>
</ADDRESS>
</BODY>
</HTML>
```

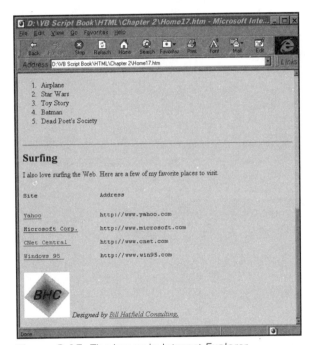

Figure 2-15: The image in Internet Explorer.

Figure 2-16 shows the result in Internet Explorer.

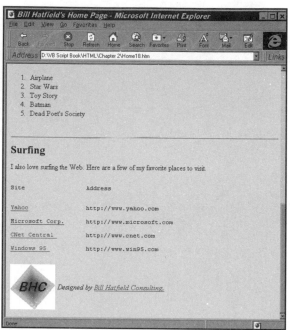

Figure 2-16: The image with CENTER alignment in Internet Explorer.

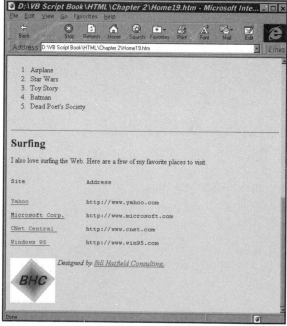

Figure 2-17: The image with TOP alignment in Internet Explorer.

Figure 2-17 shows what would happen if you set the `ALIGN` to `TOP`.

All three of these options, `BOTTOM`, `CENTER`, and `TOP`, allow only one line alongside the image. Often, the preferred way to deal with text and pictures is to allow the text to flow onto several lines along the left or right of a picture in a page. That, of course, is what `ALIGN=LEFT` and `ALIGN=RIGHT` do. Figure 2-18 shows what `ALIGN=LEFT` would look like in the browser if there were a lot of text to wrap around it.

Listing 2-23: No `ALIGN` and a `<BR>` after the image.

```
...
<ADDRESS>
<IMG SRC="bhc.gif"><BR>
Designed by <A HREF="mailto:72064.3200@compuserve.com">Bill
Hatfield Consulting.</A>
</ADDRESS>
</BODY>
</HTML>
```

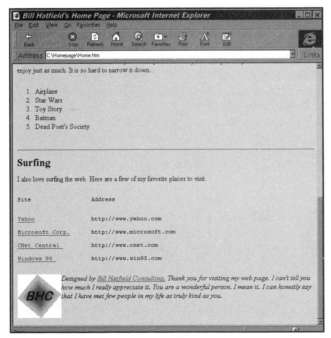

Figure 2-18: The image with `TOP` alignment in Internet Explorer.

There is one more option. If you don't specify an `ALIGN` and place a `<BR>` after the image (Listing 2-23), the text will simply appear below the image (Figure 2-19).

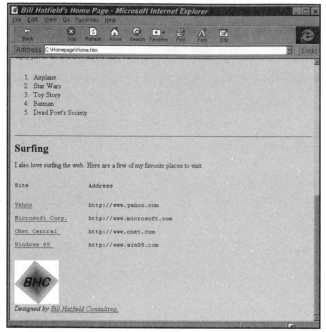

Figure 2-19: The text below the image.

You probably noticed that I put the <IMG> tag inside the <ADDRESS> tag in this example. This is because the <ADDRESS> tag causes an automatic page break when it begins. If I had put the IMG before the <ADDRESS> tag, it would have forced the text to the next line after the image, and I wouldn't have been able to show you the alignment options.

Because I really only have one line of text and I want it to line up nicely with the graphic, I'll use ALIGN=CENTER for my page.

Using the Image as a Link

Just as you can use text to link a user to another page or another site, so can you use graphics. Graphic links use the exact same tag as text links: the anchor (see Listing 2-24).

Listing 2-24: The mailto link also works on the graphic.

```
. . .
<ADDRESS>
<A HREF="mailto:72064.3200@compuserve.com">
<IMG SRC="bhc.gif" ALIGN=CENTER></A>
Designed by <A HREF="mailto:72064.3200@compuserve.com">Bill
Hatfield Consulting.</A>
```

```
</ADDRESS>
</BODY>
</HTML>
```

The additional anchor does the same thing the anchor around Bill Hatfield Consulting does, it simply lets you click on the graphic to do it. Notice that an outline of the link color appears around the graphic (see Figure 2-20).

 One strategy for displaying images and diagrams is to place a small version of the image on the page where it is first displayed but then make that image a link to display a larger image. This is an intuitive way to offer a more detailed graphic without forcing the user to sit through a long download when the page initially loads.

Transparent GIFs and Other GIF89a Tricks

If you enjoy integrating graphics into your web pages, you will want to check out the GIF89a format. This special GIF graphics format lets you do a variety of very nice things on your web pages. For instance, you can build an entire, simple animation into one GIF file and have it continuously cycle the animation when it displays on your page.

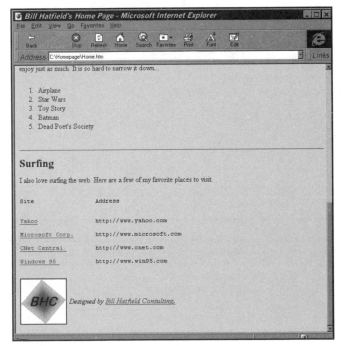

Figure 2-20: The image is a link.

Another cool feature of GIF89a is the capability to identify a transparent color. You probably noticed that my graphic logo appears in a big white box that isn't very attractive. However, if I translated my GIF into a GIF89a format and identified white as my transparent color, my web page would look like Figure 2-21.

To make use of all these neat features, you will need a paint package that supports these features. Table 2-3 provides a list of packages that support GIF89a and their web sites.

One such package is called WebImage, and you can download a demo of it from `http://www.group42.com/webimage.htm`. Another is LView Pro, and you can download a demo of it from `http://www.lview.com/`.

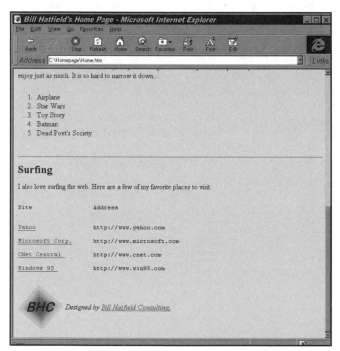

Figure 2-21: The image with white turned transparent.

Table 2-3	Paint Packages That Support GIF89a
Package	Site to Download It
WebImage	`http://www.group42.com/webimage.htm`
LView Pro	`http://www.lview.com/`
GIF Con-struction Set	`http://www.mindworkshop.com/alchemy/gifcon.html`

Multimedia

Want to integrate recorded sound files, music, or video into your web page? It is as easy as creating a link to another web page on your site (see Listing 2-25).

Listing 2-25: Adding multimedia links to my hobbies.

```
. . .
<H2>My Hobbies</H2>
I have a wide variety of interests and often enjoy just
chatting about what interests other people. Here are a few
specifics:<P>
<UL>
<LI><A HREF="books.htm">Reading</A>
<LI>Writing
<LI>Games

<UL>
<LI><A HREF="demo.avi">Computer</A>
<LI>Board
<LI>Card
</UL>

<LI><A HREF="quote.wav">British Comedies</A>
<LI>Philosophy/Psychology/Religion
</UL>
<BR>
. . .
```

Just as I linked Reading to the books.htm web page that is in the same folder as this web page, I can also link to AVI (video) and WAV (recorded sound) files in the same folder. Again, I can also specify a different directory or provide a complete URL, here identifying where the multimedia component is that I want to link to. Internet Explorer knows about all these different file types and will load the appropriate application, if necessary.

You might want to search your hard drive for AVI and WAV files you could use to dress up your web page.

Tables

HTML tables let you organize information into a nice, evenly spaced grid. This gives you more control over the layout and position of elements on your page.

On my home page, for instance, I have a table-like set of information that I had to use with the <PRE> tag and fiddle with quite a bit just to make it line up right. If I replaced the <PRE> tag with a <TABLE> tag and organized it that way, there wouldn't be any guesswork. In fact, Listing 2-26 shows you exactly how that would look.

Listing 2-26: Reformatting the Surfing section as a table.

```
...
<H2>Surfing</H2>
I also love surfing the Web. Here are a few of my favorite
places to visit:<P>
<TABLE BORDER=1>
<TR>
  <TD>Site</TD>
  <TD>Address</TD>
</TR>
<TR>
  <TD><A HREF="http://www.yahoo.com">
  Yahoo</A></TD>
  <TD>http://www.yahoo.com</TD>
</TR>
<TR>
  <TD><A HREF="http://www.microsoft.com">
  Microsoft Corp.</A></TD>
  <TD>http://www.microsoft.com</TD>
</TR>
<TR>
  <TD><A HREF="http://www.cnet.com">
  CNet Central </A></TD>
  <TD>http://www.cnet.com</TD>
</TR>
<TR>
  <TD><A HREF="http://www.win95.com">
  Windows 95 </A></TD>
  <TD>http://www.win95.com</TD>
</TR>
</TABLE>
<BR>
...
```

I've added indentation to make it a bit clearer. This is the most complex HTML you've looked at so far, but it is really just a natural extension of what you've been doing all along. There are three tags: <TABLE>, <TR>, and <TD>. <TABLE> just identifies the entire thing as a table, <TR> surrounds an entire row of the table, and <TD> identifies one bit of data, or *cell*, within the table. So, you can see that each row above has two cells in it, and there is a total of five rows.

All your work is rewarded though, when you see the result (Figure 12-22).

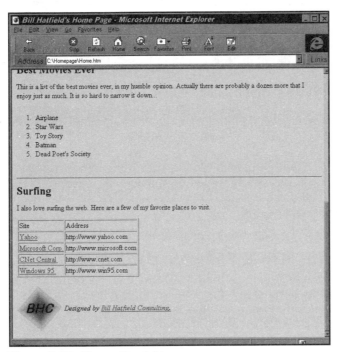

Figure 2-22: The surfing table.

As you can see, you can put both text and links in a cell. You can also put graphics and virtually anything else you can put in a web page into a cell.

There are other options you can specify to customize how your table will look. I assigned the BORDER attribute a 1. That set the width of the lines between the cells in the table. If you set it to 0, the table won't have any lines. This is nice if you want to use the table for placing information on a page at a specific location, but you don't necessarily want the table to be seen.

The WIDTH attribute of a table allows you to specify the width in pixels or as a percentage of the width of the browser's window. The CELLSPACING and CELLPADDING features allow you to specify the spacing between individual cells and the space between the border of a cell and it's actual contents.

Frames

Frames are a very cool extension to HTML that allow web page authors to create several separately scrollable regions on a window. In other words, you could have two web pages displayed in your browser at once (one on the top and one on the bottom) and scroll through each of them independently of the other.

While this is the first thing that comes to mind, frames make it possible to do much more sophisticated layouts. The flexibility makes possible all kinds of interesting strategies. For instance, many sites have designed their web pages with a banner at the top that sits in its own frame and acts as a header for all the other pages on the site. You can scroll up and down in the regular page, but the header at the top stays put because it is in a separate frame.

Another idea is to create a small table of contents and put it in a long narrow frame on the left side. The main window holds whatever document you are currently reading, but just a click on one of the links in the frame on the left takes you to a different document.

I don't have all that complex a document for my home page yet, but it would be nice if the header stayed on the window, even while the reader scrolled up and down through the document. I'll show you how to do this in your own home page.

Create All the HTML Files for the Frames

The first step is to create all the HTML files that will be used in all the frames. For my home page, I'm only going to have two frames: one for the document header and one for the rest of the document. I am going to remove the top header from my main document (Listing 2-27) and create a new document that has the header in it (Listing 2-28).

Listing 2-27: The modified home page, without the header.

```
<HTML>
<HEAD>
<TITLE>Bill Hatfield's Home Page</TITLE>
</HEAD>
<BODY>
Welcome to my home on the World Wide Web. This page will
tell you about me, my hobbies and my interests.
<P>

First, a little about me. I am a computer programmer and
consultant who works in Indianapolis, IN. I do training
for TASC, Inc., and I write.<P>

I really enjoy spending time with friends and playing
games of all types. In fact, I am going to finish my
basement as a game room so I'll always have a place to
play.<P>

<HR>
...
<ADDRESS>Designed by Bill Hatfield Consulting.</ADDRESS>
```

```
</BODY>
</HTML>
```

Listing 2-28: The header page.

```
<HTML>
<HEAD>
<TITLE>Bill Hatfield's Home Page</TITLE>
</HEAD>
<BODY BGCOLOR=Aqua LINK=Blue VLINK=Navy>
<CENTER><H1>Bill Hatfield's Home Page</H1></CENTER>
</BODY>
</HTML>
```

The header page is saved under the name HEADER.HTM. Now it is time to create the layout document.

Create the Layout Documents

Frames are made possible through layout documents. Layout documents are separate HTML files that do nothing but describe how the browser's window will be divided up and what HTML files will fill each. Listing 2-29 shows the layout document that creates the frames for my home page.

Listing 2-29: The layout document.

```
<HTML>
<HEAD>
<TITLE>Bill Hatfield's Home Page</TITLE>
</HEAD>
<BODY>
<FRAMESET ROWS="50,*">
    <FRAME SRC="header.htm">
    <FRAME SRC="home.htm">
</FRAMESET>
</BODY>
</HTML>
```

`<FRAMESET>` surrounds the description of the frame for this document. The attribute ROWS tells Explorer that you want to divide the window horizontally. If you had used the attribute COLS instead, it would have divided the window vertically. Once it knows how you want to divide the window, it needs to know how much room to allot to each frame. In this case, I have said that I want 50 pixels dedicated to the first frame and whatever is left dedicated to the second. That's what the star (*) means in this case: *whatever is left*. You could also specify this in percentages like this:

```
<FRAMESET ROWS="25%,75%">
    <FRAME SRC="header.htm">
    <FRAME SRC="home.htm">
</FRAMESET>
```

This divides the browser window into fourths, giving one-fourth to header.htm and three-fourths to home.htm. The reason I didn't do this is because you never know how big the browser window will be, and you want the header to always have enough room to display its text. A percentage division would be good for other circumstances, though.

My window has only two frames, but you could put as many as you like there simply by adding new <FRAME> tags and providing the SRC attribute with the file name for each. But, however many <FRAME> tags you have, you should have a matching number of entries above set equal to your ROWS or COLS attribute.

Save the layout document as LAYOUT.HTM, and then open it in Internet Explorer. It will create the frames and load in the specified documents (Figure 2-23).

You can scroll up and down in the main document to your heart's content and never scroll the title off the top. That's pretty handy, and it's just the start.

You can also put a <FRAMESET> tag within another <FRAMESET> tag so that you can specify both horizontal and vertical divisions on the same page.

The best way to see all the possibilities is to experiment and look for others on the Web who have done interesting things with frames on their site.

Other Stuff

In a chapter this size, you can't cover everything, but if you've followed along through the entire chapter, you certainly have more than the basics. You are ready to go out and start creating your own web page content, and with the help of the rest of this book, you'll activate your web pages with ActiveX controls and VBScript.

Of course, there are at least a couple of things I didn't have time to cover. I want to mention at least those things here and give you a conceptual feel for what they are.

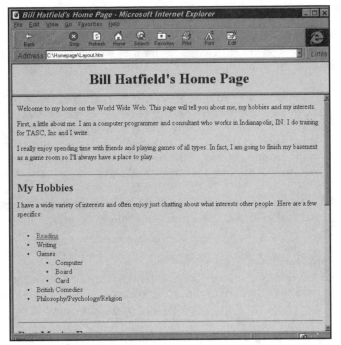

Figure 2-23: The home page with frames.

Forms

HTML provides the capability for users to talk back to you through forms. Forms are places set aside on your page where you can put controls that accept data. Several controls are built in, including a single and multiline text edit, check boxes, radio buttons, dropdown list boxes, and command buttons. You are limited only to using the controls supported by the browser.

Forms are designed to communicate the information entered back to the server for processing, usually with a CGI application. Using attributes, you give the form all the information it needs to send the information back. On the sever, an application runs and can do whatever you like with the data: process it and send back a result, put the information into a database, or send the information through e-mail to someone.

Chapter 12 is dedicated to the topic of creating forms, validating and formatting their data using VBScript, and then sending them off to a server.

Image Maps

Image maps are medium to large images that the user can click to kick off certain functions. For instance, you might see a map of the United States and click on a state to bring up sales information for that state.

Until recently, the only way to create an image map that did anything useful was to write an application on the server and use the CGI interface to interact with the web pages. Today, many client-side solutions don't require your web page to go back and badger the server every time the user clicks on the image. Some of these solutions are accomplished through HTML, and others are accomplished through scripting languages.

I'll show you a technique later in the book for creating image maps easily with VBScript. I'll also show you some alternatives to image maps that are even easier.

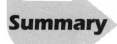

Summary

This has been quite a ride. You began by just typing out a home page in a text editor. Then, after adding a little paragraph formatting, horizontal lines, text formatting, and even an image, you now have a pretty spiffy looking page. Even more importantly, you have all the tools to make it better and to publish anything else you like, just the way you want it, in the international forum of the World Wide Web.

Creating Your
First VBScript
Page

To say that the Internet industry is a rapidly evolving place would be quite an understatement. It is not as mature a part of the computer industry as, say, desktop publishing or word processing is. Because of this, you can't pick one package that will do all the cool stuff you want in one easy-to-use environment. Instead, you have to pick and choose among many tools and use each for what it does best. That's the price you pay for being on the cutting edge!

In this chapter, I'll discuss several common HTML editors and show you how to write VBScript code in them. I'll address HTML Assistant Pro, the Microsoft Word Internet Assistant, Microsoft Front Page 1.1, and Microsoft Front Page 97.

In the next chapter, where I begin teaching you the VBScript language, I'll assume that you are using Notepad or one of the editors discussed in this section to create your HTML and add your VBScript tags.

Using VBScript in Your Web Pages

So how do you actually write VBScript commands that execute when your web page is displayed? You just use the `<SCRIPT>` tag. See Listing 3-1.

Listing 3-1: A very simple web page with a very simple VBScript application.

```
<HTML>
<HEAD>
<SCRIPT LANGUAGE="VBScript">
<!—
MsgBox "Hello World!"
—>
</SCRIPT>
<TITLE>New Page</TITLE>
</HEAD>
<BODY>
This is my first VBScript page.
</BODY>
</HTML>
```

What do the lines above do? Well, you probably recognize most of the tags. HTML simply indicates that this is an HTML document. HEAD determines what happens in the heading. TITLE surrounds the title for the page, and BODY wraps the main body of the page. What is new is the SCRIPT tag inside the HEAD portion of the HTML document.

SCRIPT indicates that the enclosed lines are to be interpreted as a script programming language. The LANGUAGE attribute designates the specific language: "VBScript" in this case. If you were developing JavaScript applications, "JavaScript" would be there instead.

You might recognize the first and last line within SCRIPT as HTML comments (beginning with <!— and ending with —>). This is not required, but is usually done so that browsers that don't support scripting, or don't support VBScript specifically, will not be confused. Those browsers will simply look right over the stuff within the comments. If you didn't do this, those browsers might trigger an error when the page is loaded or simply display these lines thinking they are part of the document.

Finally, there is one line VBScript program inside the comments. This line calls the MsgBox procedure that is built into VBScript (MsgBox stands for *message box*). It displays a separate window showing the text passed to the procedure (inside the parentheses).

Trying it Out

Try creating a new HTML page now. Type in Listing 3-1.

Save the HTML document to any folder you like, naming it VBSTest.HTM.

Now, if Internet Explorer isn't already up, launch it. Then, choose File ⇨ Open from the menu to display the Open dialog box. Click Browse... and then find the folder where you saved VBSTest.HTM. Click it and click OK. Click OK on the Open dialog box, and you are presented with your message box (see Figure 3-1).

Interesting. It first executed the message box line even before it displayed the page. In fact, the page doesn't appear until you press the OK button on the message box.

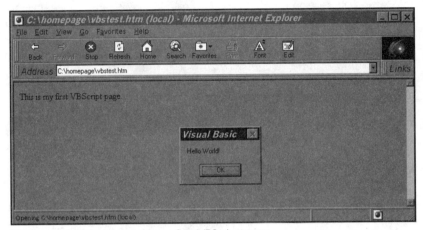

Figure 3-1: The results of your first VBScript page.

What Happened?

I want to go back now and look at what you just did in a little more detail. You'll notice that you put the SCRIPT tag within the HEAD section of your HTML document. You can also put it in the BODY section. It doesn't really make any difference which you choose.

Why did this line of VBScript execute first? If you simply place VBScript commands inside the SCRIPT tag as we did, it will always execute first, even before the page is loaded. I'll show you ways you can better control when your VBScript commands execute in the next couple of chapters.

Finally, notice that you created a page in Notepad and then you viewed the page in Explorer. If you wanted to go back and make changes, all you'd have to do is switch back over to Notepad, make your changes, and save the page again. Then switch to Explorer and click Refresh. This process makes it easy to quickly see the changes you made and know what kind of impact they'll have. You can use this technique with any editor.

VBScript and Other HTML Editors

Can you use your favorite HTML writing tool to write VBScript? Absolutely!

There's just one catch. Many HTML editors out there don't directly support scripting yet. Because of this, you have to find a way to add the SCRIPT tag and your VBScript commands in yourself by hand. I've picked several popular web page development tools and described in the sections below how to add VBScript to them. If you use one of these tools, skip to that section and read it. If you use a tool not listed in the next few sections, skip to the last section titled "VBScript and Other Web Page Development Tools," and read it. It should give you enough information to figure it out for yourself.

Oh, one last note. In the next chapter, I'm going to show you a tool called Control Pad. It has a Script Wizard that makes scripting a breeze. So, you might end up deciding that while doing your HTML in another editor is a good idea, doing VBScript in Control Pad is much better. For now I'll show you how to script in the editors.

VBScript and Notepad

So many people use Notepad to create HTML documents that it has been jokingly referred to as "Visual Notepad or Visual N++." Although there's nothing visual about Notepad, it is a simple, easy-to-use text editor that works fine for simple HTML and scripting chores — as long as you don't mind typing it all in yourself. Other editors can help you out by pasting tags in when you press a button, but in a pinch Notepad is always there.

To add VBScript to your page, you just type in the tag, HTML comments, and code as you did before. No problem!

VBScript and HTML Assistant Pro

HTML Assistant Pro is nothing more than an enhanced text edit tool for writing HTML. It does not try to hide the HTML tags, as Front Page 1.1 does. It simply makes the task of remembering and adding all those HTML tags to your web page easier. So adding VBScript to a document created there works exactly as you've done it above. Simply type in the SCRIPT tag, add the begin and end comment characters, and then type your VBScript commands just as you like.

VBScript and Microsoft FrontPage 1.1

FrontPage is a very handy tool for creating web pages. It doesn't require you to understand all those complex tags or to look at a convoluted representation of what your final page will look like. It is a WYSIWYG HTML editor. This is good, but it can also become a problem especially when you want to add VBScript — a task which FrontPage's designers hadn't anticipated. You can't just type in the SCRIPT tag and write your VBScript commands because FrontPage doesn't work that way.

Fortunately, the designers of FrontPage realized that HTML doesn't sit still for long and is likely to evolve and change very quickly. They added a capability for inserting new tags into the document that FrontPage leaves alone. You can easily add VBScript in this way.

To add a VBScript listing to the current web document in the FrontPage Editor:

1. Click in the document where you want the VBScript tag added. It makes no difference at all. Although you normally put VBScript in the HEAD, you may not be able to when using FrontPage. But again, this isn't a problem. Put it anywhere in the body of your document you like. Where it is placed has no impact on how or when it works.

2. Choose Insert ⇨ Bot... from the menus. The Insert Bot dialog box appears.

3. Choose HTML Markup from the list box. Click OK.

4. The HTML Markup dialog box is displayed.

5. Type the SCRIPT tag, the HTML comments, and your VBScript commands into the big edit box (see Figure 3-2).

6. When you are finished, click OK.

7. The SCRIPT tag will appear as a question mark in a box in your web page (see Figure 3-3). Don't worry, this won't appear in the browser when people see your web page.

VBScript and FrontPage 97

FrontPage 97 is designed for scripting. If you are willing to buy a tool to do web page development and scripting, I would highly recommend buying this one. It has everything you need. Later, when I discuss Control Pad and all its capabilities, you will find that all those capabilities have been incorporated into FrontPage 97. That, combined with the easy WYSYWIG web page development tools, make it ideal.

In addition to adding tools for making scripting easier, FrontPage 97 has also made it much easier to access the HTML than it was with FrontPage 1.1.

1. Load up the page with which you want to work.

2. Choose View ➪ HTML

3. A color-coded editor is displayed with the raw HTML ready for you to edit.

All you have to do now is type in your SCRIPT tag and begin coding. It's as easy as that.

VBScript and the Microsoft Word Internet Assistant

The Microsoft Word Internet Assistant is a free add-on provided by Microsoft that lets you create web pages in Microsoft Word or convert Word documents into web pages.

The Word Internet Assistant works similarly to FrontPage in that it tries to hide the ugly tags and give you a more-or-less WYSIWYG way of working with your pages. Again, this is a stumbling block to you for adding VBScript, but again, there is a way around it.

Your first inclination might be to try the Insert ➪ HTML Markup. This menu option which you can access when you're in Edit mode, allows you to add HTML that Internet Assistant won't interpret. The problem is that you can only enter one line. The better bet is to view the HTML source itself and add your changes right in.

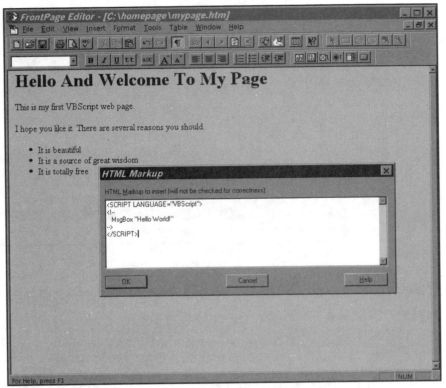

Figure 3-2: Adding VBScript in the HTML Markup dialog box.

To add VBScript commands to a web page being created with Word Internet Assistant:

1. In Edit mode, choose View ⇨ HTML Source.

2. The source is displayed with all the tags, along with a little floating toolbar.

3. Go to the HEAD section and add the SCRIPT tag, the HTML comments, and the VBScript commands (see Figure 3-4).

4. Click the Return To Edit Mode button on the floating button bar.

5. Part or all of the lines you added may appear in the main document (in Edit mode) as blue underlined text (see Figure 3-5).

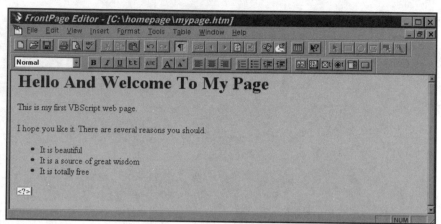

Figure 3-3: The question mark representing where the VBScript was placed.

VBScript and Other Web Page Development Tools

There are really two different kinds of web page development tools. The first type, which I will call enhanced editors, assume that you know HTML and just attempt to make your web page creation process as simple and painless as possible. They are really nothing more than normal text editors with the added capability to paste in common tags easily. They usually either come with their own web browser or allow you to link to your favorite browser to preview your work. HTML Assistant Pro is an example of an enhanced editor.

With an enhanced editor, you just need to add your SCRIPT tag and HTML comment characters and then write the commands that you want in the web page's header as I described earlier this chapter. Although the editor probably won't offer any help to make the process easier (although they probably will in the near future), they also do not get in your way.

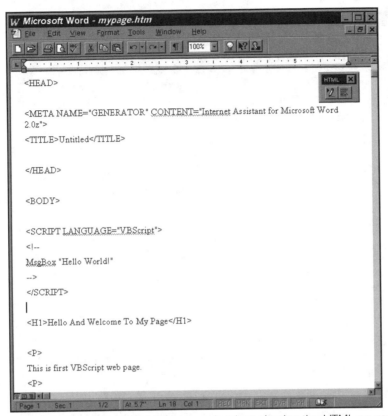

Figure 3-4: Adding VBScript commands when viewing the HTML source in Word Internet Assistant.

The other kind of web page development tool is what I will call a *what-you-see-is-what-you-get* or WYSIWYG editor. WYSIWYG editors look like word processors. They allow you to enter text as you would normally and enhance it with different styles that you choose from a menu or a dropdown list box. These editors try to hide the HTML tags from you and let you work in an environment that is very similar to what the final page will look like in a browser. FrontPage and Word Internet Assistant are two different kinds of WYSIWYG editors.

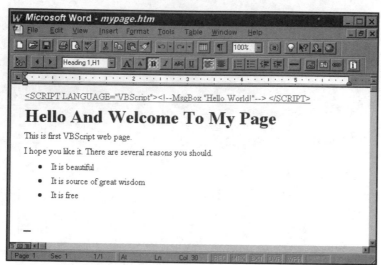

Figure 3-5: *Some or all of the lines you added may appear in the main document as blue underlined text.*

This is a very nice, visual way of creating web pages without learning the sometimes arcane syntax of HTML. The problem is that it is sometimes difficult to add tags to your document that the original developers of the environment hadn't anticipated.

The first step for a WYSIWYG editor is to check to see whether it supports scripting. If it does, you are in business. If it doesn't, you need to find a way of adding an unsupported tag that the editor will not try to interpret. You want the editor to allow you to enter something and trust you that it makes sense. Some WYSIWYG editors allow you to view or even edit the original source for your web document as Front Page 97 does. When you choose this option, you'll see your web page with all the tags. If you can edit this view, you might be able to add your VBScript commands this way. You'll just have to experiment.

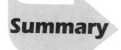

Summary

You have not only created your first VBScript web page in this excursion, you've also learned a lot about the environment in which you'll be working. You saw how to set up Internet Explorer to view web pages as you work on them. Finally, you learned about HTML editors and how they work (or don't work) with VBScript.

The VBScript Language

Programming seems dark and mysterious to many people, but if you've done any programming at all in the past, you know that there's really nothing too mysterious about it.

In fact, if you've ever written a batch file in DOS or you've used a scripting language to customize or enhance an application you use like Microsoft Word or Excel, you've already done some programming. Even if you haven't done any of these things, I'm sure you'll find the whole process much simpler than you expected.

What Is a Program?

A computer program is just a set of directions that tells the computer exactly what to do. You can think of it as a recipe or a to-do list that the computer follows exactly as you tell it to, in exactly the order that you wrote it.

Actually, one of the frustrating things about programming is that the computer follows your instructions *exactly* as you wrote them. Even if that's not exactly what you meant! You can't assume *anything* with the computer.

The programs you write will be a part of a web page. They will use the web page to communicate with the person browsing your page. These programs will be very similar to any other computer program, and if you enjoy what you learn here, it will be easy to move on to writing standalone applications for Windows using Visual Basic.

In the next few sections, I'm going to lay some groundwork you'll need to begin using VBScript in your web pages. Get Control Pad up and running, and save a working document to your hard drive. Then, get your browser looking at that working document as I described in the last chapter. If you'd prefer to use Notepad or one of the HTML tools I talked about in the last chapter, feel free. Control Pad or Notepad would probably be the simplest way.

Once your editor and Internet Explorer are both up and looking at the page on your hard drive that you are working with, you are ready to type in the examples as you go through the chapter and play with them to see how they work. Feel free to experiment as you go along.

Oh, one more thing: be patient. You'll start off with some simple, even trivial examples. The examples you do in this chapter won't look much like web pages yet, but this chapter lays the foundation for the next chapter when you will begin to create some very cool web pages. In the meantime, I think you'll find some exciting and fun ideas here that let you do things you could never have done before with a web browser.

Executing Commands

You use *commands* (sometimes called *statements*) to tell VBScript what to do. They are just key words that VBScript recognizes and responds to.

A series of commands make up a program listing or script. A program listing (or part of it) is often referred to as code. A programmer might say, "That is a pretty tricky piece of code. How does it work?" Or a programmer might say, "I added a couple of lines of code to that program." This is just another one of those words programmer use to confuse the rest of the world.

If you did the sample application in the last chapter, you've already seen one command: `MsgBox`. What did it do? You gave it some text, and it displayed that text in a separate little window that had nothing but an OK button on it. This command allows you to give information to the person using your page.

By the way, that person who reads and interacts with your page is often called the *user*.

When you type the name of a command, VBScript will do what you told it to when the web page appears. Programmers say the command executes or is called or runs. These all mean the same thing. That VBScript went off and did what you told it to.

A couple of sentences ago I said that you *gave the command some text*. What does that mean? First, look at Listing 4-1. It is a repeat of the page you created last chapter.

Listing 4-1: The simple web page/VBScript application you created last chapter.

```
<HTML>
<HEAD>
<SCRIPT LANGUAGE="VBScript">
<!-
MsgBox "Hello World!"
-->
</SCRIPT>
<TITLE>New Page</TITLE>
</HEAD>
<BODY>
This is my first VBScript page.
</BODY>
</HTML>
```

You'll notice that the text Hello World! appears after the command, and it is enclosed in quotes. When you see text inside quotes in a program it is referred to as a *string*. A string is any combination of letters, numbers, or symbols (like the exclamation point) all strung together in a line. It is always set off by double quotation marks.

I capitalized the *M* and *B* in *MsgBox*. That makes it easier to read, but it isn't necessary. You can use any sort of capitalization you want. You can even capitalize things in different places different ways and VBScript won't care. The only time you have to be careful is with text inside a string. The text inside quotation marks is always used exactly as you typed it.

Passing Arguments

By putting the string right after the command, I am telling VBScript that I want to *send* the string to the command. I do this so the command can use it, in this case, so it will know what to display in the little window. When you send information to a command that information is called an *argument* or a *parameter*.

You can send (or *pass*) more than one argument to some commands. In fact, if you want to, you can send MsgBox more than one argument. Look at Listing 4-2. (To conserve space, I am only showing the SCRIPT portion of the HTML page from this listing on. You can assume the rest of the page is the same is it was in Listing 4-1, unless otherwise specified.)

Listing 4-2: Using more than one argument with MsgBox.

```
<SCRIPT LANGUAGE="VBScript">
<!—
MsgBox "Hello World!", 1, "A Greeting..."
—>
</SCRIPT>
```

Try typing this one in and seeing what it does.

Two things are different. First, you'll now find both an OK and a Cancel button on the message box. Second, the title bar reads A Greeting... .

Notice that now you are passing three arguments: a string, a number, and another string. They are all separated by commas. Although you have to have a space after the MsgBox and the first argument, the spaces after the commas are optional.

But how did it know to put Hello World! in the box and A Greeting... in the title bar? Why didn't it do it the other way around? The answer, as you might have guessed, is that the *order* you put the arguments in is important. The first argument of MsgBox is required. It always has to be there, and it determines what appears in the box. The second argument is a number and it is optional. It determines what buttons appear. If you don't use this argument (or if you use it and send a 0), it will just display an OK button. If you send a 1, an OK and a Cancel button are displayed. Table 4-1 shows some of the options for the second argument to MsgBox. Finally, the third argument (an optional string), tells MsgBox what to put in the *title bar* of the message box window.

Table 4-1 Some of the Options for the Second Argument of the MsgBox **Command**

Value	What it does
0	Display OK button only.
1	Display OK and Cancel buttons.
2	Display Abort, Retry, and Ignore buttons.
3	Display Yes, No, and Cancel buttons.
4	Display Yes and No buttons.
5	Display Retry and Cancel buttons.

Remarks

Remarks or *comments* explain to other people who look at your web document what it is doing and how it works. The only time users would see your comments is if they chose to view the source for your HTML document where your VBScript code is. Remarks don't appear on your web page.

 You'll remember that the comments marker in HTML is the <!-- to begin a comment and --> to end a comment. As I mentioned in the last chapter, these surround your entire VBScript program so that non–VBScript-compatible browsers don't get confused when they see your VBScript code.

Within your VBScript code, however, you use a different method to indicate which lines are comments, as you'll see in this section.

To create a remark in VBScript, you use the Rem statement. See Listing 4-3.

Listing 4-3: Using remarks to make your code clearer.

```
<SCRIPT LANGUAGE="VBScript">
<!-
Rem This program greets the user
MsgBox "Hello World!", 1, "A Greeting..."
-->
</SCRIPT>
```

VBScript ignores everything after Rem. These statements don't do anything except help you document and describe what you are doing in your application.

There is also a shortcut. Instead of typing **Rem**, you can use the apostrophe character (') instead. See Listing 4-4.

Listing 4-4: Using the apostrophe for standalone and line-by-line comments.

```
<SCRIPT LANGUAGE="VBScript">
<!-
' An apostrophe character can take the place of Rem
MsgBox "Hello World!", 1, "A Greeting..."      ' A greeting
  is displayed
-->
</SCRIPT>
```

The apostrophe in this listing takes the place of Rem to create a comment line, but with the apostrophe, you can also place remarks on the same line as other VBScript commands. After the `MsgBox` command, I placed an apostrophe and then a short line to describe what that statement did. This is called *line-by-line commenting*. It lets you comment on each line right beside the command. You can only do this with the apostrophe. When you use `Rem`, it must be on a line by itself.

TIP Sometimes when you are testing your VBScript program, you will want to delete some lines to see how the program would work without them. One alternative is just to put an apostrophe before the lines you want to delete. This will cause VBScript to ignore these lines, thinking they are just comments. Then, when you want to add the lines back in, just remove the apostrophes. This technique is referred to as commenting out a line and then uncommenting a line.

Using Variables

Sometimes you need a place to store information temporarily until you can use it somewhere else. You do this with *variables*. Variables are like empty boxes that can hold information.

Using Variables to Hold Numbers

You create variables in VBScript by using the `DIM` statement. See Listing 4-5.

Listing 4-5: Using the `DIM` statement to create variables.

```
<SCRIPT LANGUAGE="VBScript">
<!—
Dim Net, Gross, Tax    ' Create three variables
Gross = 30000          ' Gross income
Tax = 4000             ' Taxes owed
Net = Gross - Tax      ' What's left...?
—>
</SCRIPT>
```

After `Dim`, you see three words separated by commas. These three words are the names I've given to variables I want to use. This statement actually creates three variables for me to use. Programmers would say I *declared* three variables. *Declare* and *create* are basically synonymous here. Once they are created, I can give them values as I do in the next two lines. To put a value in a variable, you just use the equals sign. After the third line executes, `Gross` has the value of 30,000, and `Tax` holds the value 4,000. This is called *assigning* a value to a variable. The very first time you assign a value to a variable it is sometimes called *initializing* the variable. Initializing just means setting the value for the first time.

The fourth line does a little math to figure out what Net should hold. Tax is subtracted from Gross, and the *result* of this math is placed in Net. Type this one in and try it out.

What happened? Nothing!

Not quite. The variables were created, the values were assigned, and the math was calculated, but you didn't ask it to display the results. How do you do that? One way is with the good old MsgBox command. See Listing 4-6.

Listing 4-6: Displaying the results with the MsgBox command.

```
<SCRIPT LANGUAGE="VBScript">
<!-
Option Explicit
Dim Net, Gross, Tax
Gross = 30000
Tax = 4000
Net = Gross - Tax
MsgBox Net                ' Don't forget to display the answer
->
</SCRIPT>
```

Instead of putting an actual string in quotes here, you pass a variable as an argument to MsgBox. MsgBox is smart enough to take the value of this variable and use it as the argument to display. Now try this one.

As soon as you display the page, the message box appears providing the answer: 26,000.

Notice that I added a line at the beginning of Listing 4-6. It is the first line of code:

```
Option Explicit
```

This should be in every VBScript application you create. It ensures that you always declare your variables before you use them. Without it, you could just start using a variable and VBScript would create it for you automatically. While this might sound like a nice feature, it can actually turn out to be a nightmare if you sometimes have fat fingers, like me. For example, look at the following code:

```
Dim AnnualSalary, WeeklySalary
WeeklySalary = 300
AnualSalary = WeeklySalary * 52    ' Calculate annual salary
MsgBox AnnualSalary                ' Show annual salary
```

Without the `Option Explicit` at the top, this little program will work just fine, but it won't display the amount you expect in the message box. That's because when you misspelled `AnnualSalary` in the third line (using only one *n*), VBScript just assumed that you wanted to create a brand new variable. This new variable, then, has the correct salary information in it. This can be a tough bug to find unless you go through and check the spelling of all your variables.

If you had put `Option Explicit` at the top of the listing, though, VBScript would give you an error when you misspelled the variable name in line 3, and you would immediately be able to see it and fix it.

What else can you do with variables? All kinds of things. For instance, any mathematical work you want to do is easy. Here are some examples and descriptions of what they do:

`Total = Current + Reserve`	Adds the values in `Current` and `Reserve`, and places the result in `Total`.
`Check = HourlyRate * HoursWorked`	The * is the multiplication operator (x doesn't work). This multiplies the value in the `HourlyRate` variable by the value in `HoursWorked` and puts the result in the `Check` variable.
`Hours = MilesPerHour / Miles`	The / is the division operator, which divides the value in `MilesPerHour` by the value in `Miles` and puts the result in the `Hours` variable.
`Counter = Counter + 1`	Takes whatever is in `Counter`, adds 1 to it, and then puts the result back into `Counter`. Basically, it just kicks the value in counter up by 1.
`Liters = Liters - 2`	Takes whatever is in `Liters`, and subtracts 2 from it, and then puts the result back into `Liters`. Basically reduces the value in `Liters` by 2.

The +, -, *, and / symbols are referred to as *numeric operators*, which simply means that they operate on numbers or variables with numbers in them.

All the examples listed are *numeric expressions* that are assigned to variables. A numeric expression is just numbers or variables added, subtracted, multiplied, or divided together in different ways. Numeric expressions always boil down to a number, so they can usually be used anywhere you'd use a number. Expressions are often assigned to a variable so the result can be stored and used later.

Using Variables to Hold Strings

Numbers aren't the only thing you can put into variables. Variables can also hold strings. Look at Listing 4-7.

Listing 4-7: Storing strings in variables.

```
<SCRIPT LANGUAGE="VBScript">
<!—
Option Explicit
Dim FirstName, LastName, WholeName    ' Create three
  variables to hold strings
FirstName = "Helen"                   ' Assign first name
LastName = "Everhart"                 ' Assign last name
WholeName = FirstName & LastName      ' Stick them together
MsgBox WholeName                      ' Show the whole thing
—>
</SCRIPT>
```

Two variables are declared: `FirstName` and `LastName`. They are filled with strings. A string, as I mentioned earlier, is any combination of letters, numbers, or symbols all strung together in a line. It is always set off by double quotation marks. In this case, I am using the `FirstName` variable to hold the string `"Helen"` and the `LastName` variable to hold `"Everhart"`.

`WholeName` is another variable, and it is going to hold a larger string that contains both the `FirstName` and the `LastName` strings stuck together using the ampersand (&) symbol. Then, the `MsgBox` command is called.

The ampersand is the string *concatenation* character. Concatenation simply means sticking two things together, so if you want to stick two strings together, you use the ampersand.

 You can also use the plus sign (+) to concatenate two strings, but I don't recommend it. It can become confusing whether you are trying to add two numbers or concatenate two strings. Using the ampersand for concatenation and plus for addition helps keep things straight.

When you execute this, though, you see that it doesn't look quite right. The message box displays `"HelenEverheart"`. The problem is that you need a space between the two names. How do you do it? Just concatenate another string in between `FirstName` and `LastName` (see Listing 4-8).

Listing 4-8: Concatenating the first name, a space, and the last name.

```
<SCRIPT LANGUAGE="VBScript">
<!—
Option Explicit
Dim FirstName, LastName, WholeName
FirstName = "Helen"
LastName = "Everhart"
WholeName = FirstName & " " & LastName   ' Add a space this
  time
MsgBox WholeName
—>
</SCRIPT>
```

Now, you are sticking three things together: the first name, a space, and then the last name. This should look much better when you try it. That next-to-the-last line is an example of a *string expression*. You remember that a numeric expression is a bunch of numbers or numeric variables put together in different ways using the plus, minus, times, and division operators. Well, a string expression is a bunch of strings or string variables put together with the string concatenation character, ampersand (&).

When Lines Get Too Long

Sometimes when you are writing code in VBScript, you'll realize that the line you are typing is getting very long. Fortunately, there is a way you can break your lines in the middle and continue them on the next line. It's done with the line continuation character, which is an underline: _. This is keyed on most keyboards by holding the shift key down and hitting the dash key (usually right after the 0 at the top of the keyboard).

The code below breaks up the line which assigns a value to the whole name. You can break a line anyplace you might normally put a space.

```
<SCRIPT LANGUAGE="VBScript">
<!—
Option Explicit
Dim FirstName, MiddleName, LastName, WholeName
FirstName = "Helen"
MiddleName = "Louise"
LastName = "Everhart"
WholeName = FirstName & " " & _
    MiddleName  & " " & LastName
MsgBox WholeName
—>
</SCRIPT>
```

Calling Subroutines and Functions

Now I'd like to talk a bit more about commands. Commands come in two different flavors: subroutines and functions. MsgBox, as you've been using it in these examples, is a subroutine. You call a subroutine simply typing its name and then any arguments afterward separated by commas.

The other type of command is the function. Functions are similar to subroutines in that you call them by typing their name, and they can receive arguments. The difference is that functions send a value *back* to you.

A Function Example: InputBox

Take a look at Listing 4-9.

Listing 4-9: Functions return values back to you.

```
<SCRIPT LANGUAGE="VBScript">
<!—
Option Explicit
Dim UserName
UserName = InputBox("Enter your name:")
MsgBox "Hello, " & UserName
—>
</SCRIPT>
```

InputBox is a VBScript function that displays a separate window, just like MsgBox. The difference is that with InputBox, the window has an edit where the user can type in information. After they type something and click OK, the text that they typed is *returned* from the function. To have the value returned, you must use the syntax:

```
variablename = function(arg)
```

This one line does two things:

➡ It calls the function and passes whatever arguments are inside the parentheses. You must put parentheses around any parameters you pass when you call a function. With subroutines, you don't use parentheses.

➡ It receives the value sent back from the function into the variable called variablename.

So in Listing 4-9, the second line calls the InputBox function, passing the string as an argument. It also receives the value back from the function which, in this case, is the text the user typed. Finally, the UserName variable is concatenated with "Hello, " to create a greeting.

So, a subroutine and a function have two primary differences:

➡ A function not only receives arguments, as a subroutine does, but it also can pass back a single value. The value is received by setting a variable equal to the function name.

➡ A function, if it has arguments, will always place the arguments inside parentheses after the function name. A subroutine never has parentheses.

 VBScript is an unusual computer language in that it doesn't have a lot of commands for communicating with the user. MsgBox and InputBox are simple commands for telling users something or getting information from them. I'll use it quite a bit in this chapter as you are learning the language, but in the next chapter, you will learn how to write on web pages themselves and how to use information that users type into ActiveX controls. Once you learn how to do this, you probably won't use MsgBox and InputBox as often.

Another Function Example: Rnd

I want to tell you about another function that's built in to VBScript. It is called Rnd, which is short for *random*. A random number is a number you just pick out of the air. That is exactly what this function does. It just picks any old number and returns it to you.

The Rnd function is used a lot for creating games and educational software. Rolling dice, picking a card, and flipping a coin can all be simulated on the computer by using random numbers. Listing 4-10 shows an example.

Listing 4-10: Displaying a random number.

```
<SCRIPT LANGUAGE="VBScript">
<!-
Option Explicit
Dim AnyOldNumber

AnyOldNumber = Rnd        ' Pick a number, any old number
MsgBox AnyOldNumber   ' And show it
->
</SCRIPT>
```

Notice that the Rnd function doesn't take any arguments. Because of that, it doesn't need to have parentheses after it. You could put them there, but they'd just be empty, anyway.

What is the result? Click the Refresh button again. What happened the second time?

You definitely do see a different number each time, but it probably wasn't quite the kind of number you were expecting. Rnd returns a random number between 0 and 1, so it could return .3 or .5 or .9. Usually, though, it returns something like .432843. That doesn't seem very useful, does it?

You might occasionally see a number that looks like this: 4.535276E-02. This number is not four and a half. For some numbers, the computer will revert to scientific notation. Whenever you see the big E at the end of the number, you know that is what it's doing. All it means is that you should move the decimal point either forward or backward the number of digits specified after the E. In this case, because the number is a negative two, you are supposed to move the decimal point back two places. That makes the number .04535276. Why didn't it just write that to begin with? Who knows!

What if you want to simulate rolling dice? You need a number between 1 and 6. How do you coax Rnd into giving it to you? All it takes is a little math. See Listing 4-11.

Listing 4-11: First attempt at a dice roller.

```
<SCRIPT LANGUAGE="VBScript">
<!—
Option Explicit
Dim Dice

Dice = Rnd * 6 + 1     ' Pick a number between 1 and 6
MsgBox Dice
—>
</SCRIPT>
```

This listing points out another interesting thing you can do with functions: use them in an expression. You remember that a numeric expression is a bunch of numbers or variables stuck together with +, -, *, or /. You can also include functions in that mix. That's because, when you call a function and it returns a value, it is as if that value *replaces* the function in the line:

```
Dice = Rnd * 6 + 1
```

Here's how this line works. The first thing that happens is the Rnd function is called and a random number is returned. Then, that returned number is multiplied by 6, 1 is added, and the result is assigned to the variable Dice.

Multiplying the random number (that is between 0 and 1) by 6 gives you a random number between 0 and 5. Adding 1 gives you a value between 1 and 6.

Sort of. Actually, when you run this program, you see values like 3.747829 and 5.43437. They are between 1 and 6, but they aren't exactly what you would see when you roll dice.

Integers to the Rescue

What you need is a way to chop off anything that isn't a whole number, so when Rnd comes up with 4.5, it would just display 4. Believe it or not, a function in VBScript does just that!

A number with no fractional part is called an integer. 5.78 is not an integer, but 5 is. Therefore, the function in VBScript that takes a number and turns it into an integer is called Int. See Listing 4-12.

Listing 4-12: Using Int with Rnd to create a better dice roller.

```
<SCRIPT LANGUAGE="VBScript">
<!—
Option Explicit
Dim Dice

Dice = Int(Rnd * 6) + 1   ' Pick an integer between 1 and 6
MsgBox Dice
—>
</SCRIPT>
```

A new function is added to the numeric expression. Here's how that second to last line works:

1. The Rnd function is called, and it returns a random number between 0 and 1. Let's say it returns .756

2. The number returned from Rnd is then multiplied by 6. If Rnd returned .756, multiplying it by 6 would give you 4.536.

3. The result of the multiplication is sent to the Int function. It chops off anything after the decimal point. If it were sent 4.536, it would return 4.

4. Finally, 1 is added to the result. 4 plus 1 is 5.

This little formula will always generate a number between 1 and 6, or you can replace the 6 with any number you want, and it will give you a random number between 1 and that number.

```
Month = Int(Rnd * 12) + 1
```

This line would pick a random number between one and 12 and put that value in Month.

Asking Questions

In this section, I'll show you how to create programs that can do a little thinking for themselves. In programming, you can do this with *conditionals*. Conditionals are just VBScript statements that allow you to ask questions and then respond in different ways depending on what the answer is.

The Simple If...Then

The most commonly used conditional is the If...Then statement. It works like this:

```
If condition Then statement
```

The *condition* here could be any sort of question. You could replace *condition* with Salary = 30000. Then *statement* refers to any valid VBScript command, so the following line would be valid.

```
If Temperature = 220 Then MsgBox "Boiling!"
```

This line checks to see whether Temperature is equal to the value 220. If it is, the statement executes. If it isn't, nothing happens.

You will want to check for more than just equality, though. Remember the greater-than and less-than signs you learned in school?

> Greater than

< Less than

To these symbols, VBScript adds a few of its own.

>= Greater than or equal to

<= Less than or equal to

<> Does not equal

These are sometimes referred to as *comparison operators* or *boolean operators*. Now to see how these work, here are some examples:

```
If Score > 50000 Then MsgBox "You are a master at this game"
```

If the score is over 50,000, the message box is displayed. If the score was exactly 50,000 or less than 50,000, nothing would happen.

```
If  PercentGrade > 90 Then Response = "Excellent!"
```

If the PercentGrade variable contains a value greater than 90, the Response variable is assigned the string "Excellent!".

```
If Earthquake <= Threshold Then Status = "Tremor"
```

If the variable Earthquake contains a value less than or equal to the value in the variable Threshold, the Status variable is assigned a value of "Tremor".

```
If UserName <> "Fred" Then MsgBox "I don't recognize
  you...", 1
```

If the UserName variable is not equal to "Fred", display a message box that displays the message "I don't recognize you...".

You'll notice in the last example that I used a <> (does not equal sign) to compare a variable to a *string*. As you might guess, you can also use an = (equal sign) with strings, too.

What you might not guess is that you can also use all the other comparison operators (<,>,<=, and >=) with strings, too. When you do, it basically compares the two strings alphabetically so that "apron" < "zygot" and "kiss" > "hug".

You just need to remember a couple of twists if you compare strings like this, though. First, capital letters are always considered less than small letters. Second, punctuation characters (:;+-.,&$ and so on) and numbers are always considered less than capital letters.

Underneath the surface, the computer assigns numbers to every letter and symbol you see. This number (called the *ASCII value*) is actually what is being compared.

The Compound If...Then

Sometimes a simple comparison doesn't cut it. That's when you need *logical operators*. A logical operator is usually something like an And or an

Or that you drop into your If statement so that you can use more than one comparison at the same time.

For instance, if you wanted to assign a letter grade based on a percentage, you might do it like this:

```
If PercentGrade < 60 Then LetterGrade = "F"
If PercentGrade >=60 And < 70 Then LetterGrade = "D"
If PercentGrade >=70 And < 80 Then LetterGrade = "C"
If PercentGrade >=80 And < 90 Then LetterGrade = "B"
If PercentGrade >=90 Then LetterGrade = "A"
```

Using two comparisons joined with an And makes the If statement trigger only if *both* conditions are true. If either one is false, the whole thing ends up being false.

The Or operator, on the other hand, allows you to join two conditions and will trigger the If statement if *either one* of the conditions is true.

```
If Savings < 100 Or Checking < 25 Then MsgBox "Money is
  running low!"
```

If Savings is less than 100 or Checking is less than 25, the message is displayed. If both conditions are true, the message is still displayed. If neither are true, the message is not displayed.

Using Not

There is one other logical operator that you can use in an If...Then statement: Not. Not isn't placed between two conditions like And and Or are. Instead it stands in front of a condition and reverses it, so if it was true before, it becomes false, and if it was false before, it becomes true:

```
If Not PercentGrade >= 60 Then PassFail = "Fail"
```

In this case, if the grade wasn't 60 or better, the student failed. You will never run into a case where you absolutely need to use Not. You could have written the previous condition like this:

```
If PercentGrade < 60 Then PassFail = "Fail"
```

and this would work just as well. Sometimes, though, using Not can make the If...Then condition clearer. Use whatever makes the most sense to you.

If...Then...Else

In all of the examples so far, you were checking for the truth of a condition. If the condition were true, you did whatever came after the Then. If it weren't true, nothing happened. Sometimes, however, you will want to do one thing if the condition is true and another thing if the condition is false. That is what's behind the If...Then...Else statement.

```
If PercentGrade < 60 Then PassFail = "Fail" Else PassFail
= "Pass"
```

If PercentGrade holds a value less than 60, PassFail is assigned the string "Fail"; otherwise, it is assigned the string "Pass".

```
If Temperature > 220 And Condition = "Red" Then MsgBox
"Alert!" Else MsgBox "All is OK"
```

If the Temperature variable holds a value greater than 220, and the Condition variable is equal to the "Red" string, a message box is displayed alerting the user. Otherwise, it tells the user that everything is all right.

Multiline If...Then...Else

Often, when you want to perform a conditional, you want to perform multiple commands if the condition is true and maybe another set of commands if it is false, but the If...Then...Else statements I've shown you so far are all one-line statements. Another way to do it is a lot more flexible: the multiline If...Then...Else statement:

```
If PressureMeter > 320 Then
    MsgBox "Warning — High Pressure"
    Status = "Alert"
Else
    MsgBox "Pressure is acceptable"
    Status = "Normal"
End If
```

If PressureMeter holds a value greater than 320, the warning message box is displayed, and the Status variable is set to "Alert". Otherwise, a "Pressure is acceptable" message box is displayed, and the Status is set to "Normal".

Notice that you should press Enter after the Then and begin your statements on a separate line. This is how VBScript knows you want to do a multiline

If...Then...Else. The Else sits on a line by itself, and the Else
statements begin on the next line. Finally, the whole thing ends with End If
on its own line. This tells VBScript that the If...Then...Else is over.

You can also do a multiline If...Then without the Else.

```
If Height = 6 and Weight > 250 Then
    MsgBox "You are a bit overweight"
    Overweight = True
End If
```

Notice that the lines that are a part of the Then or Else section of an
If...Then...Else statement are indented to make that clear. This makes
it easy to pick out the If, Else, and End If when you look at it. VBScript
doesn't require you to do this indenting, but it does make your code a lot
easier to read.

Using Int with Strings

Earlier, in the section called *Integers to The Rescue*, I told you about a
function called Int. It converted decimal numbers into integers. I want to
take a break now from the If...Then statement for a moment to talk
about another interesting thing you can do with Int.

Suppose you wanted users to enter their age so that you could calculate
how long they have to live. The program might look something like
Listing 4-13.

Listing 4-13: How long do I have?

```
<SCRIPT LANGUAGE="VBScript">
<!—
Option Explicit
Dim Life, Age, Left

Age = InputBox("How old are you?")

Life = 78    ' Average life expectancy
If Age > Life Then
    MsgBox "You should be dead!"
Else
    Left = Life - Age
    MsgBox("You have " & Left & " years left. Enjoy them!")
End If
—>
</SCRIPT>
```

This program looks perfectly reasonable. The Age variable is filled in with whatever the user enters. Life is always filled with 78 (the current average life expectancy). Then, the two are compared to make sure the user isn't already dead, and if not, it figures how many years of earthly pleasures remain.

Try running this one. You'll find that the program thinks you should be dead no matter what age you enter! Why? Because the value that came back from the InputBox function was a string, and therefore Age is holding a string! The If statement is comparing a *string* to a *number* and when that happens, the string is always higher, so it always thinks you should be dead.

The way to fix the problem is with Int:

```
Age = Int(InputBox("How old are you?"))
```

You can use Int not only to turn decimal numbers into integers but also to turn *strings into integers*. Here, you can use Int to take the string that is returned from InputBox and turn it into a number before you assign it to Age. This will make the program work like it should.

While VBScript does sometimes do conversions for you behind the scenes, this example proves that it doesn't always do it. So it is a good idea always to convert a string to a number before you start doing math with it or comparing it to other numbers.

If...Then...ElseIf...Else

Now back to If...Then. I want to tell you about one more variation of If...Then. It throws in another word, ElseIf. Just as it looks, this works as a combination Else and If. It lets you check to see if one thing is true, then another, then another, and finally do something else if none of them is true. Listing 4-14 shows an example.

Listing 4-14: Using If...Then...ElseIf...Else **to figure out the dice.**

```
<SCRIPT LANGUAGE="VBScript">
<!—
Option Explicit
Dim Dice1, Dice2, Total

Dice1 = Int(Rnd * 6) + 1
Dice2 = Int(Rnd * 6) + 1
Total = Dice1 + Dice2

If Dice1 = 1 and Dice2 = 1 Then
    MsgBox "Snake Eyes"
```

```
ElseIf Dice1 = 6 and Dice2 = 6 Then
    MsgBox "Box Cars"
ElseIf Total = 7 Then
    MsgBox "You rolled 7! You're lucky!"
ElseIf Total = 11 Then
    MsgBox "You rolled 11! You're lucky!"
Else
    MsgBox "The total was " & Total
End If

-->
</SCRIPT>
```

You may have to run this one quite a few times to see all the possibilities. Snake eyes and box cars just don't come up all that often.

How does it work? The first and second lines of the If...Then should look familiar to you by now. They simply compare to see if both dice rolled a 1. If they did, you use MsgBox to let the user know.

The ElseIf on the next line only executes if the previous condition failed. It's sort of like "OK, if that didn't work, try this one". A new condition appears here. It checks to see if both dice rolled a 6. If so, it displays a different message box.

The next line contains another ElseIf. Again, this one will only execute if both of the previous conditions failed. So if it isn't snake eyes, and it isn't box cars, you check to see if the total was 7, and if that one fails, you check to see if the total was 11. You can write as many ElseIf lines as you want to cover all the possibilities.

Finally at the end, you have a single Else. This is the catch-all. If all the other conditions failed, the code here executes. You will usually have an Else when you have a statement like this, but you don't have to. If you leave it off, nothing happens when they all fail.

A Coin-Toss Game Example

Here's a challenge for you. Create a game that asks the user to pick heads or tails. The computer simulates a coin toss, displays a message box telling the user how the coin landed, and displays a second message box telling whether the user won or lost. Can you do it? Give it a try....

Want some hints? OK, here they come:

➡ You will need two variables, one for the user's guess and one for the result of the coin toss.

➥ Use `InputBox` to ask the user to type heads or tails.

➥ Use the `Rnd` function in a line like the one used to simulate rolling dice only instead of 6 sides, your dice only has 2 sides.

➥ Make 1 stand for heads and 2 for tails (you could do it the other way around if you wanted to). Use an `If...Then` statement. If the toss is a 1, tell the user it was heads. Otherwise, tell them it was tails.

➥ Use a second `If...Then...ElseIf...Else` statement to check all the possibilities. If they typed **heads** and the toss was 1, they win. If they typed **tails** and the toss was 2, they win. Otherwise, they lose.

➥ Use a message box to inform the user of a win or loss.

Do you have it working yet? Don't give up!

OK, Listing 4-15 shows you my solution.

Listing 4-15: The coin-toss game.

```
<SCRIPT LANGUAGE="VBScript">
<!-
Option Explicit
Dim Guess, Toss

Guess = InputBox("I'm going to flip a coin. Call it heads



 or tails.")
Toss = Int(Rnd * 2) + 1

If Toss = 1 Then
    MsgBox "Heads!"
Else
    MsgBox "Tails!"
End If

If Guess = "heads" and Toss = 1 Then
    MsgBox "You win!"
ElseIf Guess = "tails" and Toss = 2 Then
    MsgBox "You win!"
Else
    MsgBox "You loose!"
End If
->
</SCRIPT>
```

Try running it a few times to test it out. Keep choosing heads until you've both won and lost and then keep trying tails until you've both won and lost.

Nothing is new here. It is just a combination of techniques you've already covered to create a neat little game. First, I create a couple of variables and then ask the user to call it heads or tails. After the user calls it, I flip the coin by calling the Rnd function using a formula that gives me a number between 1 and 2. If the toss is 1, I let the user know it came up heads. Otherwise, it's tails. Then, I check to see if the user guessed heads, and it was heads (Toss = 1). If both of those things are true, the user wins. Another way the user could win is if he or she guessed tails and it was, in fact, tails (Toss = 2). Any other situation counts as a loss.

 I told you at the beginning of this chapter that VBScript was not case sensitive. In other words, it doesn't matter if you type **MsgBox**, **MSGBOX**, or **msgbox**. VBScript will always understand what you mean.

This is true for VBScript commands but not for strings. When VBScript compares two strings, they must be exactly alike before it considers them equal. Because the program in Listing 4-15 compares the user's guess to heads and tails, the user must type them this way for the program to understand. If the user types HEADS or Heads, the program won't understand. The result will be that the user will always lose.

By the way, one of the reasons why programming is so much more fun than mathematics or other subjects you learn in school is that in programming more than one right answer exists. In fact, you can usually write even a simple program dozens of ways, and it will still work. So, if you write a coin-toss game that works but doesn't look like mine, congratulations! If yours didn't quite work, I hope you can figure out how to make it work by looking at the way I did it.

Just don't feel bound to what I show you here. Play with it and experiment. I offer you my solutions to generate new thoughts and ideas, not to show you the "right" way!

Nested If...Thens

You can nest If...Then statements. *Nested* simply means that one is placed inside of another. Listing 4-16 shows another way of implementing the coin-toss game using If...Thens.

Listing 4-16: Another coin-toss game using nested If...Thens.

```
<SCRIPT LANGUAGE="VBScript">
<!-
```

(continued)

```
(continued)
Option Explicit
Dim Guess, Toss

Guess = InputBox("I'm going to flip a coin. Call it heads
  or tails.")
Toss = Int(Rnd * 2) + 1

If Toss = 1 Then
    MsgBox "Heads!"
    If Guess = "heads" Then
        MsgBox "You win!"
    Else
        MsgBox "You loose!"
    End If
Else
    MsgBox "Tails!"
    If Guess = "tails" Then
        MsgBox "You win!"
    Else
        MsgBox "You loose!"
    End If
End If
-->
</SCRIPT>
```

This is where all that indenting of lines within an If...Then pays off. Without it, the code in Listing 4-16 would be very hard to read. After getting the user's guess and tossing the coin, the big If...Then tests to see if Toss equals 1. If it does, the user is informed that it is heads. Then, an If...Then statement executes. Notice that this new If...Then is completely inside the Then part of the first If...Then statement. That means that this If...Then won't even execute unless the Toss equals 1. So in this inner, nested If...Then, you check to see if the user guessed heads. If so, the user won; otherwise, the user lost.

Now there is an End If, but which If does it accompany? An End If always goes with the last If statement executed, which was the nested If. You will always close off your nested If with an End If before you continue on with the outer If statement.

Next comes an Else. This, as you can see by the way it is indented, goes with the outer If statement. Therefore, the code in this section only executes if the very first condition failed: that is, if Toss does not equal 1. In this case, you tell the user it is tails and then check the guess to see if the user won or lost.

Although this might seem a little more complicated at first, when you think about it, it does make a little more sense than the first solution.

So what do you need to know about nested If...Then statements? They are just like normal If...Thens that appear inside of the Then or Else portion of another If...Then. They allow you to ask more questions once you know how the first question was answered.

They also must always be closed off with an End If before continuing.

 So can you have an If...Then nested inside an If...Then nested inside yet another If...Then? Yes. In fact, you can go as deep as you like with it, but use common sense and simplify whenever possible. Otherwise, you are likely to come back and look at the code a couple of months from now and say, "What the heck was I thinking?"

In fact, now that the program is structured this way, you can simplify it even more. You could make it so that it displays only one message box telling the user both what the toss is and whether the user won or lost. Listing 4-17 shows you how this is done.

Listing 4-17: The coin-toss game that displays only one message box.

```
<SCRIPT LANGUAGE="VBScript">
<!-
Option Explicit
Dim Guess, Toss

Guess = InputBox("I'm going to flip a coin. Call it heads
  or tails.")
Toss = Int(Rnd * 2) + 1

If Toss = 1 Then
    If Guess = "heads" Then
        MsgBox "Heads! You win!"
    Else
        MsgBox "Heads! You loose!"
    End If
Else
    If Guess = "tails" Then
        MsgBox "Tails! You win!"
    Else
        MsgBox "Tails! You loose!"
    End If
End If
->
</SCRIPT>
```

I simply removed the first message box in each case and integrated the information into the message box displayed inside the nested Ifs.

Using Variables to Hold True/False Values

Earlier in this chapter, I introduced you to variables and showed you how they could hold both numbers and strings. Variables can hold another type of value: *boolean*. A boolean value is a true/false value. True and False are actual values, just like 58 and "Fred" are real values that you can assign to variables. Boolean variables track on/off-, yes/no-, and available/unavailable-type information. Take a look at Listing 4-18.

Listing 4-18: Boolean variables at work.

```
<SCRIPT LANGUAGE="VBScript">
<!—
Option Explicit
Dim Saturated, WaterLevel

'  Other stuff happens here

If WaterLevel > 5 Then Saturated = True



'  Other stuff happens here

If Saturated Then MsgBox "The ground is saturated"
—>
</SCRIPT>
```

Saturated is set to the value True if the WaterLevel variable is greater than 5. Then, later on in the program, the Saturated variable is checked in an If...Then. You might be surprised to see Saturated by itself in the If...Then. You might have expected something like this instead:

```
If Saturated = True Then MsgBox "The ground is saturated"
```

This works, too, but it is unnecessary. The condition part of an If...Then needs a boolean value. Because Saturated is already a boolean variable (one that holds true/false), it can be used by itself.

Listing 4-19 provides another example.

Listing 4-19: More boolean variables at work.

```
<SCRIPT LANGUAGE="VBScript">
<!—
Option Explicit
Dim TooHot, TooCold, CurrentTemp
TooHot = CurrentTemp > 100
TooCold = CurrentTemp < 32
If TooHot Or TooCold Then MsgBox "The temperature just
  doesn't feel right"
—>
</SCRIPT>
```

After three variables are created, one of them is assigned the value `CurrentTemp > 100`. What kind of value is that? A boolean value, or a *boolean expression* to be exact.

You remember that a numeric expression is a bunch of numbers, variables, and +, -, *, and / symbols that boil down to a number. A string expression is a bunch of strings and variables connected with & that finally boil down to one string. Therefore, boolean expressions are just numbers, strings, or variables compared using the <, >, =, and other comparison operators that finally boil down to a true or false value.

`CurrentTemp > 100` and `CurrentTemp < 32` are the same sort of things you might put in the condition part of an `If...Then` statement. They each work out to be either true or false. `TooHot`, then, ends up holding True or False depending on how the condition `CurrentTemp > 100` works out. The same is true for `TooCold`. Then, the `If...Then` statement uses these variables directly. If either one is true, the message box is displayed.

Select...Case

Often you want to test a single variable and do a variety of different things, depending on the value in the variable. A situation like this is a perfect time for the `Select...Case` statement. Look at Listing 4-20.

Listing 4-20: Using `Select...Case` to evaluate an account's status.

```
<SCRIPT LANGUAGE="VBScript">
<!—
Option Explicit
Dim Status, Description, Penalty
```

(continued)

```
(continued)
'   Other stuff happens here

Select Case Status
Case 1
   Description = "Current"
   Penalty = 0
Case 2
   Description = "30 days past due"
   Penalty = 100
Case 3
   Description = "60 days past due"
   Penalty = 200
Case 4
   Description = "90 days past due"
   Penalty = 300
Case Else
   Description = "Unknown status"
End Select
-->
</SCRIPT>
```

The first line of Select Case, appropriately enough, begins with the words *Select Case*. Then comes the variable on which this whole statement will be based: Status. Next comes a list of possible cases and associated statements. If the value of Status is 1, the two lines after Case 1 execute. You could put as many lines as you want here. If Status wasn't 1, the next Case is checked, and so on, all the way through Case Else. If none of the Case values match what is in Status, Case Else acts as the catch-all and executes. The whole statement ends with End Select.

You can do more than match on a single value, however. Listing 4-21 shows another example.

Listing 4-21: Using Select...Case **with multiple** Case **options.**

```
<SCRIPT LANGUAGE="VBScript">
<!--
Option Explicit
Dim Status, SendNotice, Description

'   Other stuff happens here

Select Case Status
Case 1, 2
   SendNotice = False
Case 3, 4
```

```
    SendNotice = True
Case Else
    Description = "Unknown status"
End Select
->
</SCRIPT>
```

In this `Select Case`, `Status` equals either 1 or 2, and `SendNotice` is set to false. If it is either 3 or 4, `SendNotice` is set to True; otherwise, `Description` is assigned the string `"Unknown status"`. You can put as many values after `Case` as you like, all separated by commas.

Doing It Again, and Again, and...

So far, all the programs you have written start from the top, they run line by line until they reach the last line, and then they are done. This works well, but in the real world, you need more flexibility than that. That's why VBScript has *looping statements*. Looping statements are commands that let you cause certain lines to execute again and again. Some looping statements loop for a set number of times, whereas others continue to loop until a particular condition (like we used in `If...Then`) becomes true.

For...Next

The `For...Next` loop provides a simple way of executing a set of commands a certain number of times.

The Simple For...Next

Listing 4-22 shows an example of a simple `For...Next` loop.

Listing 4-22: A simple For...Next loop.

```
<SCRIPT LANGUAGE="VBScript">
<!-
Option Explicit
Dim Count



For Count = 1 To 3      ' Loop from 1 to 3
    MsgBox Count
```

(continued)

```
(continued)
Next
MsgBox "Done!"
->
</SCRIPT>
```

Everything between the For and the Next statements are *inside the loop*.
The statements inside the loop are the ones that execute again and again.

Look at the For statement. It begins with the word *For* followed by a
variable. In this case, Count, was declared earlier. After Count is an equals
sign which seems to indicate that a value is going to be assigned to Count,
but instead of a single value, the phrase 1 To 3 follows. So what is
assigned: 1, 2 or 3? Actually, all three numbers are assigned to Count, one
at a time.

The first time this For line executes, Count is assigned a value of 1. Then,
the message box is displayed showing the value 1. The Next statement
simply jumps you back up to the For line again. This time, the value 2 is
assigned to Count, and the message box displays 2. The Next statement
again causes you to jump back up to the For line and 3 is assigned to
Count. The message box displays 3.

This time when you reach Next, the Next statement realizes that 3 was the
last number it was supposed to assign to Count (because 3 is the value
that comes after the To on the For line). Therefore, it doesn't send you
back up to the For this time. It just goes to the next line and displays the
Done message box.

So how do you create a For...Next loop? First, you need a variable. The
variable used in a For...Next loop is often called a *counter* or *index*
variable, but it is no different than any other number variable. Then, you
put an equals sign followed by a range of numbers that you want to go
between. The loop will then execute all the lines of code inside the loop
(between the For and the Next) as many times as it takes to go from the
first number to the second number. Look at Listing 4-23.

Listing 4-23: A For...Next loop that starts with 3 and goes up to 5.

```
<SCRIPT LANGUAGE="VBScript">
<!-
Option Explicit
Dim Count

For Count = 3 To 5    ' Loop from 3 to 5
   MsgBox Count
```

```
Next
MsgBox "Done!"
->
</SCRIPT>
```

This listing will work exactly like the last one would, except that the numbers that are displayed in the message boxes will be 3, 4, and 5. That's because the loop started with 3 and ended with 5. You can start with any number you want and end with any number you want, as long as the second number is higher than the first. The For loop will always count by one each time until it reaches the higher number.

 What is the value of the counter variable after the loop is over? For instance, what number would the last MsgBox command display on the screen in Listing 4-24?

Listing 4-24: Displaying the counter value after the loop is done.

```
<SCRIPT LANGUAGE="VBScript">
<!-
Option Explicit
Dim Count

For Count = 1 To 3    ' Loop from 1 to 3
    MsgBox Count
Next
MsgBox Count     ' This will display 4
->
</SCRIPT>
```

You probably expect that the value will be 3 because that is the last value in the loop that it was assigned, but actually, the value is 4. It is a quirk in how the For...Next loop works. The value in the variable after the loop will always be one more than the last value it had in the loop.

A Step Up

A loop that counts for you automatically is a nice thing to have, but suppose you don't want to count by ones. Suppose you want to count by twos or threes? See Listing 4-25.

Listing 4-25: Using Step to count by twos.

```
<SCRIPT LANGUAGE="VBScript">
<!-
```

(continued)

```
(continued)
Option Explicit
Dim Count

For Count = 2 To 10 Step 2   ' Count from 2 to 10 by 2s
    MsgBox Count
Next
MsgBox "Done!"
->
</SCRIPT>
```

Now what you'll see the values 2, 4, 6, 8, and 10 displayed in the message boxes. Step allows you to specify what to count *by*. In this case, the For loop counts by twos. You could just as easily count by threes, fours, or fives.

You can even count backwards! See Listing 4-26.

Listing 4-26: Using Step to count backwards.

```
<SCRIPT LANGUAGE="VBScript">
<!-
Option Explicit
Dim Count

For Count = 5 To 1 Step -1   ' Count backwards from 5 to 1
    MsgBox Count
Next
MsgBox "Done!"
->
</SCRIPT>
```

This code will display five message boxes with the values 5, 4, 3, 2, and 1, in that order. Providing a negative value for Step makes the For loop count backwards.

Remember that anywhere you can use a number, you can also use a variable that holds a number or a numeric expression. Take a look at Listing 4-27.

Listing 4-27: Using a variable in a For...Next loop.

```
<SCRIPT LANGUAGE="VBScript">
<!-
Option Explicit
Dim Count, Times
```

```
Times = Int(InputBox("How many times?")) ' Convert string
returned from InputBox to a number
For Count = 1 To Times
    MsgBox "This is loop number " & Count & " out of " &
 Times
Next
MsgBox "Done!"
-->
</SCRIPT>
```

This time, InputBox asks the user how many times the loop should execute and stores the response in the Times variable. Then, Times is used in the For line to tell the loop how many times to execute. If the user entered 3, he or she would see the following messages in separate message boxes:

```
This is loop number 1 out of 3
This is loop number 2 out of 3
This is loop number 3 out of 3
Done!
```

Do...Loop

If you want a loop that executes a specific number of times, the For...Next loop can't be beat, but if you want to determine how many times the loop happens some other way, you should check out a Do...Loop.

A Do...Loop uses a condition, just like the conditions you used in the If...Then statement, to decide if the loop should continue. Listing 4-28 shows an example.

Listing 4-28: A Do...Loop **uses a condition to determine when the loop should end.**

```
<SCRIPT LANGUAGE="VBScript">
<!--
Option Explicit
Dim Guess, Toss

Guess = InputBox("I'm going to flip a coin. Call it heads
  or tails.")
Do While Guess <> "heads" And Guess <> "tails"        ' If
  they typed it wrong, try again
    Guess = InputBox("Please type the word heads or tails
```
(continued)

```
(continued)
  below.")
Loop

Toss = Int(Rnd * 2) + 1    ' Random number between 1 and 2
  to flip coin

If Toss = 1 Then                        ' If it's heads,
    If Guess = "heads" Then             ' and they guessed
heads,

      MsgBox "Heads! You win!"          ' they win
    Else                                                    ,
otherwise, they loose
      MsgBox "Heads! You loose!"
    End If


Else                                    ' If it's tails,
    If Guess = "tails" Then             ' and they
guessed tails,
      MsgBox "Tails! You win!"          ' they win
    Else                                'otherwise, they loose
      MsgBox "Tails! You loose!"
    End If
End If
->
</SCRIPT>
```

This is yet another upgraded version of the coin-toss game I showed you earlier in this chapter. This version adds a small loop after the InputBox line that compares Guess to the expected values "heads" and "tails". If it is neither one of these, the code inside the loop executes. The code inside the loop asks the user specifically to type the word **heads** or **tails**. After this, the Loop statement causes the execution to jump back up to the top of the loop and compare the response again. If it is still not right, the loop executes again. If it is right, the loop ends, and the execution continues to the line that follows the Loop.

So, instead of looping a predetermined number of times, Do...Loop allows you to loop again and again until a specific condition is met.

You can design this loop to do specifically what you want it to do. For instance, you could have made the loop look like this:

```
Guess = InputBox("I'm going to flip a coin. Call it heads
  or tails.")
```

```
Do Until Guess = "heads" Or Guess = "tails"
   Guess = InputBox("Please type the word heads or tails
 below.")
Loop
```

While tells VBScript to loop as long as the condition is true. As soon as the condition becomes false, it tells VBScript to stop looping.

Until is just the opposite. It says to loop as long as the condition is false. As soon as the condition becomes true, it tells VBScript to stop looping.

You can use either one in any situation, depending on what operators you use. In this case, if I used <> and the And, I could do a While. If I wanted to use Until instead, I had to change <> into an = and the And into an Or. When I do, the statements are identical. Use whichever one makes your code easiest to understand.

You can customize the Do...Loop to your needs in one more way. The loop in Listing 4-28 is a *top-tested loop*. In other words, the condition is checked before the loop ever executes the first time. If the condition fails in Listing 4-28, the loop never executes, not even once.

You could redesign the loop in Listing 4-28 to look like this:

```
Do
   Guess = InputBox("I'm going to flip a coin. Please type
 the word heads or tails below to call it.")
Loop While Guess <> "heads" And Guess <> "tails"
```

This is a *bottom-tested loop*. In other words, the loop always executes at least once, and then the condition is checked. If the condition is true, the loop continues. If not, it stops. This means that you don't need two different InputBox function calls, one before the loop and one inside it. The one inside does it all.

Whether it is a top-tested loop or a bottom-tested loop is determined by where you place the conditional clause: after the Do for top-tested and after the Loop for bottom-tested. Again, the only difference between top-tested loops and bottom-tested loops is that top-tested loops may never execute if the condition isn't met. Bottom-tested loops always execute at least once.

And, in case you're wondering, you can also do a bottom-tested Until loop:

```
Do
   Guess = InputBox("I'm going to flip a coin. Please type
 the word heads or tails below to call it.")
Loop Until Guess = "heads" Or Guess = "tails"
```

Blackjack Example

Here's a whole new example. Listing 4-29 presents the code for a game that simulates Blackjack or 21.

Listing 4-29: A Blackjack game.

```vbscript
<SCRIPT LANGUAGE="VBScript">
<!-
Option Explicit
Dim Decision, Card, Total, Bust, Dealer

Bust = False
Card = Int(Rnd * 12) + 1     ' Draw first card
Total = Card                 ' Add it to total
Decision = InputBox("Your first card is a " & Card & ".
Do you want to hit or stay?")
Do While Decision = "hit" And Bust = False  ' Go till the
   user stays or busts
    Card = Int(Rnd * 12) + 1       ' Draw another card
    Total = Total + Card           ' Add card to total
    If Total > 21 Then             ' Check for bust
        MsgBox "Your next card is a " & Card & ", for a
        total of " & Total & ". You busted!"
        Bust = True
    Else
        Decision = InputBox("Your next card is a " & Card &
        ", for a total of " & Total & ". Do you want to
        hit or stay
    End If
Loop

Dealer = Int(Rnd * 21) + 1  ' Figure wimpy dealer total

If Bust = False Then          ' If they didn't bust
    If Total > Dealer Then    ' Check to see who won
        MsgBox "Dealer had " & Dealer & ", you had " &
Total & ". You win!"
    Else
        MsgBox "Dealer had " & Dealer & ", you had " &
        Total & ". You loose."
    End If
End If
->
</SCRIPT>
```

Whew! That's a big program, but again, there is nothing new here. This code pulls together a lot of the things we've discussed so far.

After you create all the variables you need, you set Bust to False. Bust will keep track of whether the user has gone over 21. Then, Card is assigned a random value between 1 and 12 to simulate a card draw (Ace, 2, 3, up through 9, Jack, Queen, and King), and the Total so far is just the one card that was drawn.

The user is told about the card and asked if he or she wants to hit (to get another card) or to stay with the total he or she has.

Now, the big loop starts. The loop is a top-tested While loop that will go as long as Decision = "hit" and the user hasn't busted.

Inside the loop, a card is drawn and added to the total. If the total is over 21, the user has busted. The user is informed, and the Busted boolean variable is set to true. If the total is 21 or less, the user is told what the new total is and is given the chance to hit or stay.

Loop causes execution to go back to the top and check the While conditions again. If they are met, the code inside the loop executes again. If not, the code after Loop executes.

After the loop, the dealer must have a score to compare to the player's score. Just to make it simple, I generated a random number between 1 and 21 for the dealer. This makes the dealer usually have a pretty low value, so he's easy to beat.

Finally, if no bust occurs, the user's total is compared to the dealer and the best score wins.

While...WEnd

While...WEnd is a looping structure that works very much like a Do While...Loop, without the Do and the Loop. Here's an example:

```
Card = Int(Rnd * 12) + 1     ' Draw first card
Total = Card
While Total < 18 And Bust = False  ' If I'm under 18 and
  I haven't busted, hit me
    Card = Int(Rnd * 12) + 1    ' Draw next card
    Total = Total + Card
    If Total > 21 Then Bust = True   ' Did I bust?
WEnd
```

While indicates the start of the loop, and WEnd indicates the end. As long as the condition after While is met, the loop keeps on going.

You probably won't ever use `While...WEnd` because `Do...Loop` lets you do the same thing plus a whole lot more. `While...WEnd` is really a holdover from an earlier version of Visual Basic before the `Do...Loop` was available. I mention it here because you may see other people use it from time to time.

Loops Inside of Loops

Remember nested `If...Then` statements? A nested `If...Then` occurs when you used an `If...Then` statement inside the `Then` or `Else` portion of another `If...Then`. We indented the code in the nested `If...Then` an additional level.

Just like `If...Then` statements, loops can also be nested. A nested loop is a loop that exists completely inside of another loop. Here is an example (see Listing 4-30).

Listing 4-30: A nested `For...Next` loop.

```
<SCRIPT LANGUAGE="VBScript">
<!--
Option Explicit
Dim Garland, JCount, OCount
Garland = ""
For JCount = 1 To 5
    Garland = Garland & "J"
    For OCount = 1 To 3
        Garland = Garland & "o"
    Next
Next
MsgBox Garland
-->
</SCRIPT>
```

Did you ever string garland for a Christmas tree? The idea is that you take popcorn or candy canes or whatever and string them together on a long thread that is then wrapped around a Christmas tree. In Listing 4-30, I've used string concatenation (sticking strings together to make longer strings with the & operator) to do the equivalent of a Christmas garland. The little *o*'s represent popcorn while the *J*'s represent candy canes (that are upside down).

The purpose of this is to show you how a nested loop works. When you run this code, you see this in a message box: JoooJoooJoooJoooJooo. Can you figure out how the loops work from that?

The `Garland` variable is set equal to `""` to start. Two quotes together like this represent an empty string. Setting a variable equal to an empty string clears out anything else that was in there.

Then, a `For` loop increments `JCount` from 1 up to 5. The first line inside the loop puts a *J* onto the end of the string. Then, another loop starts incrementing `OCount` from 1 to 3. Inside that loop, an *o* is placed on the end of the string. From the string you saw in the message box, you can tell that this inside, nested loop executes all three times before the outer loop gets to loop again. Then, another *J* and another 3 *o*'s are added. This continues until 5 *J*'s and 15 *o*'s have been put on the string.

You can also nest a `Do...Loop` inside of a `For...Next`, a `For...Next` inside of a `Do...Loop`, and a `Do...Loop` inside of another `Do...Loop`. Yes, you can even nest a loop inside of a nested loop. Also, just like `If...Then` nesting, you can go as deep as you like.

The key thing to remember about loops inside of loops, though, is that the inner loop goes all the way through all of its looping before the second loop of the outer loop begins.

Writing Your Own Subroutines and Functions

When I refer to commands and statements I'm talking about those things that are built into Visual Basic, but those aren't the only subroutines and functions that exist. In fact, you can make your own subroutines and functions and call them. This actually allows you to extend the VBScript language and make it work the way you want it to work.

A New Way to Greet the User

Listing 4-31 is a different way of writing something you did earlier this chapter.

Listing 4-31: Greeting the user using a function and a subroutine.

```
<SCRIPT LANGUAGE="VBScript">
<!—
Option Explicit
Dim UserName

Function GetName
```

(continued)

```
(continued)
    GetName = InputBox("Please Enter Your Name:")
End Function

Sub Greet(Name)
    MsgBox "Hello, " & UserName
End Sub

UserName = GetName
Greet UserName
—>
</SCRIPT>
```

After declaring our variable UserName, you create a function called GetName and a subroutine called Greet. These functions and subroutines don't execute right away. All you are doing is telling VBScript that you want to create these functions and subroutines to use later. Then, the actual program begins: the last two lines.

The first line takes the variable declared at the top of the listing and assigns to it the value that comes back from the GetName function, so the GetName function is called.

GetName doesn't take any arguments, and it only has one line. It simply calls the InputBox passing the string "Please Enter Your Name:".

But wait! It is assigning the value that comes back from InputBox to a variable called GetName. We never declared a variable called GetName! So where did it come from? If you notice, GetName is the name of the function itself. By assigning a value to the name of a function, you are telling VBScript that this is the value you want to *send back* to the routine that originally called GetName. In other words, that is the value that will be assigned to UserName in the second to last line of the listing.

Finally, the Greet subroutine is called, and UserName is passed as an argument to it. Look back up to where Greet was declared. There, you find this line:

```
Sub Greet(Name)
```

This declares that you want to create a new subroutine called Greet that accepts one argument. Here, you call that argument Name. When they pass a value in, it may be called something else, but in the body of this subroutine, it is called Name.

Question: Why is Name in parentheses? Didn't I make a big deal about the fact that functions use parentheses and subroutines do not? That is true when you are *calling* a function or subroutine, but when you are creating a *new* subroutine, you always put the arguments inside parentheses on the first line.

All of this makes sense, but why would you want to use this solution which takes a lot more lines to accomplish the same task? Well, perhaps you wouldn't for this situation, but whenever you encounter a problem where you need to do the same thing several times in several different locations, creating a subroutine or function can significantly reduce the amount of program lines you have to write. Not only that, but if you later want to make changes, you only have to make the change in one place.

Yet Another Greeting

Here, in Listing 4-32, is another stab at the same problem.

Listing 4-32: Greeting the user with one subroutine.

```
<SCRIPT LANGUAGE="VBScript">
<!-
Option Explicit
Sub GreetUser
    Dim UserName
    UserName = InputBox("Please Enter Your Name:")
    MsgBox "Hello, " & UserName
End Sub

GreetUser
->
</SCRIPT>
```

This solution is different. It bundles everything up into one routine that you can call with one line. Now any time you want to greet a new user, you can just call the GreetUser subroutine. It doesn't take any arguments.

Local and Global Variables

Notice that the Dim statement has been moved *inside* the subroutine. What significance does that have? Well, it means that UserName is now a *local* variable. A local variable is one that can only be accessed from inside the subroutine or function where it was created.

So what happens if you add a line at the end of the listing like this?

```
MsgBox UserName
```

Give it a try, and see what happens. You receive an error on that line. That's because `UserName` is an unknown variable at that point in the script. Because it is declared inside the subroutine, it is local to that subroutine and can only be accessed there. If you try to access it anywhere else, you receive an error.

If a variable declared inside a subroutine or function is a local variable, what are the variables we've been using up until now that are just declared at the top of the whole script? These are called *script-level* or *global* variables, and they can be accessed from anywhere in the script.

This characteristic of variables that describes where in the script it can be accessed is referred to as a variable's *scope*. In VBScript, a variable's scope can be either global or local.

Scope Strategies

If local variables are more restricted than global variables, why not always use global variables? This is a good question. The answer is that the more global variables you have, the more chances there are for confusion and errors to slip into your code. If you use a variable called `Counter` in one place and then use that same variable in another place for a different purpose, there is a chance you could become confused. You might receive one value when you expect another. If instead you had simply used a local variable in each place, each one would be separate, and you'd always know what you were working with. This becomes more important for bigger programs where it is easy to lose track of what's going on.

So should you always use local variables? Of course not. Just try to figure out which makes the most sense for the situation. Are you really only going to be using the variable in this one place or only in this particular subroutine? Then make it local. Do you need to have access to it in lots of different places throughout the program? Make it global.

Sometimes you can avoid making variables global by passing them as arguments to a subroutine or function. If this works, try to keep the variable local if you can. Otherwise, feel free to make it global. It's your call.

Random Number and Dice-Rolling Functions

As you do more programming with VBScript and look at what other people have done, you'll probably want to begin collecting really cool subroutines and functions that you create or find. Here are a couple to get your collection started (see Listing 4-33).

Listing 4-33: A random number function, a dice rolling function, and code to try it out.

```
<SCRIPT LANGUAGE="VBScript">
<!—
Option Explicit

Dim Total

Function RandNum(ToNum)
RandNum = Int(Rnd * ToNum) + 1
End Function

Function RollDice(NumRolls)
Dim Count, Sum

For Count = 1 To NumRolls
    Sum = Sum + RandNum(6)
Next
RollDice = Sum
End Function

Total = RollDice(2)

If Total = 2 Then
    MsgBox "Snake Eyes"
ElseIf Total = 12 Then
    MsgBox "Box Cars"
ElseIf Total = 7 Then
    MsgBox "You rolled 7! You're lucky!"
ElseIf Total = 11 Then
    MsgBox "You rolled 11! You're lucky!"
Else
    MsgBox "The total was " & Total
End If

—>
</SCRIPT>
```

The first function is one you've needed since you first learned about random numbers. It allows you to call it and send a number. It returns a random integer between 1 and that number. In this case, RollDice sends it 6 allowing it to return a random number between 1 and 6.

The RollDice function accepts an argument that tells it how many dice to roll. It calls the RandNum function to get each dice roll and sums them up using a For...Next loop. Finally, it returns the sum.

In the main portion of the program, the `RollDice` function is called. It is passed a two and the result is placed in the variable `Total` (declared at the top of the listing as a global or script-level variable). Then, a variation on an `If...Then` statement used earlier lets the user know what happened.

Exit Sub and Exit Function

Sometimes you realize that there is no point being in the current subroutine any more and you may as well get out. In fact, this happens so often that VBScript has a special command just for it. It is called `Exit Sub`. It works like this:

```
Sub EvaluateNum(Num)
If Num < 1 Or Num > 100 Then
    Exit Sub
End If
...
End Sub
```

When this subroutine is called, the first thing it does is to look at the value that was passed to see if it falls outside the range 1 to 100. If it does, `Exit Sub` executes. This works exactly like jumping over all the rest of the stuff in the subroutine and going right to the `End Sub`. It is just a quick way to get out if you realize that this isn't going to work out.

If you are writing a function, a corresponding `Exit Function` works exactly the same way.

The Guessing Game

For a final example, I'd like to challenge you to write a game. In this game, the computer will think of a number between 1 and 100. Then, it will ask the user to guess what the number is. The user will make a guess. If the guess is right, he or she wins. If not, the computer gives a hint. It tells the user whether he or she should guess higher or lower than what was last guessed. This continues with the user guessing and the computer advising higher or lower until the user guesses the correct number. The computer then tells the user how many guesses he or she took.

If you've been reading this chapter straight through, you now have all the tools you need to write this game. Give it a try.

Want some hints? Here goes....

➡ Be sure and use the `RandNum` function I showed you to make your code simpler.

- ➡ Use `Int` to convert the user's guess coming back from `InputBox` from a string into an integer.

- ➡ Use a separate variable to keep track of the number of tries.

- ➡ Use a `Do...Loop` to let the user keep guessing until they get it right.

That's all I'm giving you. Now, see what you can create.

Done? OK, Listing 4-34 shows you my solution. Remember, your solution may look very different, but if it works, you got it right!

Listing 4-34: The Guessing Game.

```
<SCRIPT LANGUAGE="VBScript">
<!-
Option Explicit

Dim Number, Guess, Tries

Function RandNum(ToNum)
RandNum = Int(Rnd * ToNum) + 1
End Function

Number = RandNum(100)           ' Get a number in mind
 between 1 and 100
Guess = Int(InputBox("I'm thinking of a number between 1
and 100. " _
   "See if you can guess it."))Tries = 1        ' This is
the first try




Do While Number <> Guess        ' Loop until they get it
right
   If Guess > Number Then
      Guess = Int(InputBox("Lower! Guess Again..."))
   Else
      Guess = Int(InputBox("Higher! Guess Again..."))
   End If
   Tries = Tries + 1            ' Count
another try
Loop

MsgBox "You win! And it only took " & Tries & " tries..."
->
</SCRIPT>
```

First, you see the RandNum function I created earlier. I highly recommend using it anywhere you use random numbers. Then, I generate a number between 1 and 100 to use as the computer's secret number. Then, I ask the user for their first guess. Notice that I convert the answer to an integer from a string. Because this is the user's first try, I set Tries to 1.

Then begins the loop. This is a top-tested loop, so if the user guesses the number the first time (yea, right!), this loop won't even execute. It will just jump down to the end of the loop and tell the user he or she won! In the much more likely event that the user doesn't get it on the first try, the loop begins and an If...Then statement checks and then tells the user to guess higher or lower. The user's response is put into the Guess variable after it is converted to an integer. The last line in the loop counts off another try, and the loop starts over at the top of the loop if the guess wasn't correct.

If the guess was correct, the message box after the loop tells the user the good news.

Whether you were able to create a working Guessing Game without looking at my code, you should take that and think of ways you can expand on this idea. Make it your own, or think of other games and applications you can create using all this new knowledge.

Summary

This chapter has definitely covered a *lot* of ground. You began by learning what a program is and how you'll use VBScript programs in your web pages. Then, you learned about commands that tell the computer what to do and arguments that you can pass when you call a command. You then learned about variables to hold strings and numbers, and then about subroutines, functions, and return values. You learned several common commands including Dim, MsgBox, InputBox, Int, and Rnd.

Then, you moved on to the If...Then, If...Then...Else, and even the If...Then...ElseIf...Else. Nested If...Thens and Choose...Case statements followed. Finally, you began looping with For...Next and all the variations of Do...Loop. Finally, you learned how to create your own subroutines and functions to extend VBScript to work just like you want.

The Guessing Game ended this chapter with an example that drew on all the skills you learned this chapter.

Control Pad and ActiveX Objects

In this chapter, I'll introduce you to a nifty new tool that Microsoft has made freely available on the web site. It's called Control Pad, and it makes it easier to include ActiveX controls in your web page and to write VBScript.

First, I'll show you a little about how it works, and then I'll step back and talk about the idea of objects in VBScript in general. After that, I'll demonstrate how objects work in Control Pad and all the things that they let you do.

A First Look at Control Pad

Control Pad is a simple package. Figure 5-1 shows what you'll see when you first launch Control Pad.

Control Pad works just like other Windows applications you've used. It has a menu bar and a button bar with familiar buttons, and most of its windows will appear inside the main window. It brings up one window by default, titled Page 1, and it even gives you a general structure for starting to create your web page.

Control Pad doesn't give you much help for creating HTML, though. It wasn't designed for that. Because of that, you may want to use a different HTML editor for creating your web pages (like Microsoft FrontPage or HTML Assistant Pro) and then import the document into Control Pad when you are done to jazz it up a bit.

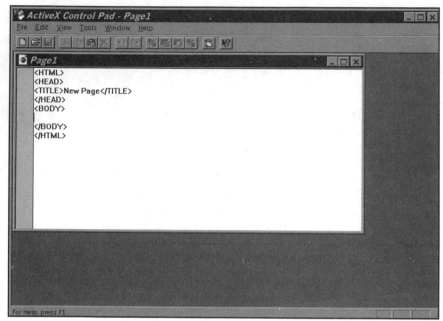

Figure 5-1: Control Pad when it is first launched.

However, if you were just using a very simple editor like Windows Notepad before, you'll find that Control Pad is at least that good, and you might want to start doing your HTML development here.

Creating and Importing HTML Documents

Every time you start Control Pad, it automatically opens an HTML document with which you can work. If you want to create a new one, follow these steps:

1. Choose File ➪ HTML from the menus, or you can click the New button on the button bar to cause the New dialog box to display. Choose Internet Document (HTML) and click OK.

2. A new Page window is displayed with a default, bare-bones HTML document in it.

On the other hand, if you've created an HTML document using some other tool, you'll want to import it. To import an HTML document into Control Pad:

1. Choose File ➪ Open from the menus or click the Open button on the button bar. The Open dialog is displayed.

2. Locate the HTML (or HTM) file you created with another package.

3. Click it to select it and then click OK. The new HTML document opens with its name in the title bar.

Using the HTML Editor

Although it's not as full-featured as other HTML editors, it does provide all the basics:

➡ You can move around using the cursor keys.

➡ You can select text by dragging the mouse over it with the left button pressed, or by holding shift and moving with the cursor keys.

➡ Cut, Copy, Paste, and Delete are available from the Edit menu or by using their standard keystrokes.

➡ Undo and Redo are also on the Edit menu, and you can access them with Ctrl+Z and Ctrl+A, respectively.

➡ The capability to print, open a new document, save this document, and create a new document are all available under the File menu.

 Control Pad offers one other feature that I'm sure you'll find helpful. Under the Help menu, you'll find options for displaying an HTML Reference and a VBScript Reference. These can serve as a great place for quick look-ups of a tag you forgot or the order you are supposed to put the arguments in for a VBScript function.

Adding ActiveX Controls

Perhaps you are wondering what's so impressive about Control Pad. Well, there are several things that make it exciting. The first is the capability to add ActiveX controls to your page quickly and easily.

What's an ActiveX control? ActiveX controls are things like text boxes, buttons, animation viewers, and a variety of other things you can use to spice up your web page. Many ActiveX controls come with Control Pad, but you can find additional ones on the web or through companies that make them. For more information about what they are and how they work, see the section titled "Microsoft's ActiveX Strategy" in Chapter 1.

To add an ActiveX control to your page:

1. Move the cursor to the place in your HTML where you want to place the new ActiveX control.

2. Choose Edit ➪ Insert ActiveX Control. The Insert ActiveX Control dialog is displayed (Figure 5-2).

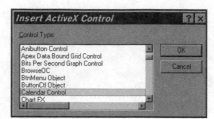

Figure 5-2: The Insert ActiveX Control dialog box lists all the ActiveX controls available.

3.   Choose the name of the ActiveX control you want to add from the Control Type: list box. The ones that came with Control Pad begin with the phrase "Microsoft Forms 2.0" (Microsoft Forms 2.0 Command Button, Microsoft Forms 2.0 Check Box, and so on). You can choose any of these (or any of the other ActiveX controls and click OK.

4.   The control appears in a small window titled Edit ActiveX Control. Another window titled Properties also appears (Figure 5-3).

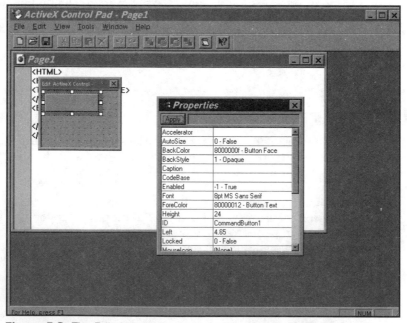

Figure 5-3: The Edit ActiveX Control window and the Properties window.

5.   Set any properties you like in the Properties window. You do this by scrolling up and down to find the property you want to change and clicking on that property to select it. You can then type a value into

the edit at the top of the Properties window located next to the Apply button. That value is assigned to the selected property when you click the Apply button or you click to select a different property.

6. Size the control as you like using the white boxes that appear around it in the Edit ActiveX Control window.

7. Click the close button (the X in the upper right) on the Edit ActiveX Control window. The window disappears. Text is pasted in at the current cursor position in your HTML window. That new text identifies the object and the properties you specified (Figure 5-4).

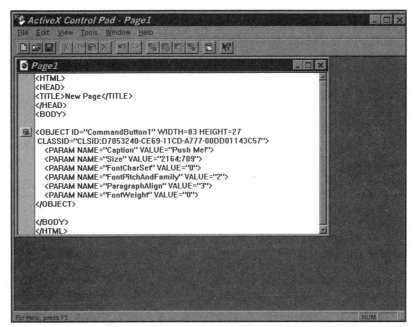

Figure 5-4: New text identifying the object and its properties is pasted in.

Wondering what a property is, why there are so many of them, what they all do, and how you should set them? Relax. I'll talk about all these topics in the sections to come. Right now I just want you to see how the process works.

Look at the lines that Control Pad wrote for you. The OBJECT tag pair that was added to your page is a normal HTML tag. Nothing is special about it. You could have just as easily typed this tag in by hand, but Control Pad lets you tell it everything it needs to know about the object visually and then creates the HTML for you automatically.

So what does the OBJECT tag do? The most important thing it does is specify which ActiveX control you want to place on the page. It does this with CLASSID, which is assigned a very long, ugly number. This number is the unique identifier for the ActiveX control you selected. You can find it in the Windows registry. If you were adding the ActiveX control to your document by hand, you'd have to look up that number yourself. The OBJECT tag also gives it a name (with ID), height, and width. Finally, it also sets all those properties you set in the Property window by using the PARAM tag. Pretty nifty.

Modifying ActiveX Controls Later

What if you realize that you made a mistake and want to change the properties again? Do you have to go in and modify the PARAM tags by hand? Nope.

To modify an ActiveX control after it is created:

1. Locate the ActiveX control in your HTML.
2. Click on the little box icon that appears in the margin beside the HTML OBJECT definition.
3. The Edit ActiveX Control window and Properties window appear again, and you can change the properties as you like.

About Properties...

What is a property and why do you see a window that lists a whole slew of them when you insert a new ActiveX control in your document?

A property is just what you might guess. It is an attribute or characteristic of the ActiveX control. It describes something about that control. You can change that description by changing the value of the property — and thereby change the way the control looks or acts.

Before I go too far in describing properties, I should take a step back and discuss objects in general.

Objects

What is an object? You may have heard the term *object-oriented programming* and decided that it was a very strange and obscure concept. Actually, programming with objects is a lot more intuitive than programming without them.

An object is a thing that holds variables and functions or procedures, so it contains both data (in the variables) and code (in the functions and procedures). It is just a way of bundling things together that seem to go together anyway.

I'll start off with a real-world example to help demonstrate what an object is and what composes it.

Setting Properties in Control Pad

Suppose you are at a car dealership and you are buying a car. You have very specific ideas in mind. You tell the dealer exactly what you want: the color, the type of seat-covers, the engine type, and many other specifics.

The car is an object, and these things you specify about the car are properties. By telling the dealer you want a red car, you are setting the car's Color property. By telling him you want leather, you are setting the Seat-cover property, and so on.

Now let's go back to ActiveX controls and see if we can make any sense of objects in that context. An ActiveX control is an object. The Properties window you saw allows you to set the properties for that object. Follow these steps to see how it works.

1. Insert a "Microsoft Forms 2.0 CommandButton" ActiveX control using the method for inserting controls I described before. You'll see a representation of the button in the Edit ActiveX Control window. You'll also see a separate Properties window with a list of all the things you can change about that command button.

2. Find the property called Caption and click on it. Type some text into the text box at the top of the Properties window. Click Apply.

3. You will see what you typed appear as the text on the button (Figure 5-5).

You have just changed the Caption property of the button so that the text that appears on the button is exactly what you want. Now try this:

1. Click on the BackColor property. You will see something in the edit at the top that reads `8000000f - Button Face`. This tells the button that you want it to be whatever color the user has selected in Windows to be the button face.

2. Click on the dropdown button beside the edit and choose a different color from the list that appears. You will see options like `80000001 - Background` and `80000005 - Window`. These are other colors the user can choose in Windows and are usually set depending on the Windows Theme chosen.

3. Click the dropdown button again to make the dropdown list disappear.

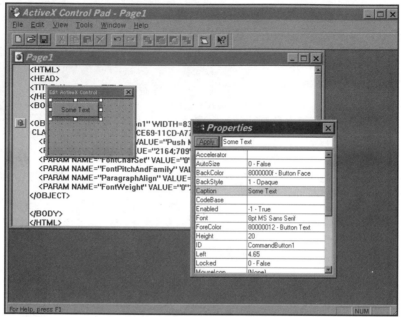

Figure 5-5: The Caption appears on the button after it is changed in the Properties window.

4.   Click the button on the far right beside the edit at the top of the Properties window that has three periods (. . .) in it. This brings up the Color window which allows you to change the background of the button to a specific color.

5.   Click any color, and click OK.

6.   The background color of the button changes to what you select (Figure 5-6). Notice that if you change it to the same color as the button text, you won't be able to read the Caption.

7.   Click the close box in the top right corner of the Edit ActiveX Control window. You are returned to the editor with the object code and parameters set as you specified.

8.   Save the page and view it through Internet Explorer. The button won't do anything when you click it, but it will have the property values that you set (Figure 5-7).

I've gone through these examples just to give you an idea of what properties are and how you can use them to make your ActiveX controls look and work like you want them to. Some of the properties are simple, some have more subtle uses, but all of them help you specify how the control will look and act to your web page users.

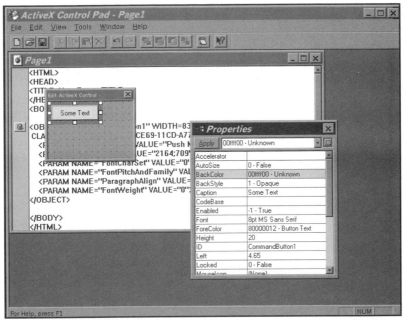

Figure 5-6: The background color of the button changes when the BackColor property is changed in the Properties window.

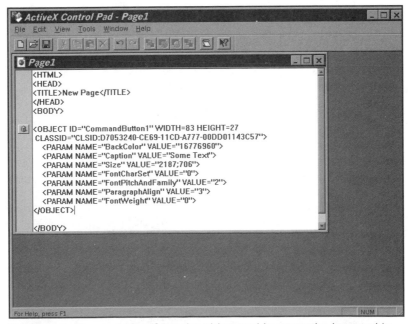

Figure 5-7: New text identifying the object and its properties is pasted in.

Setting Properties in Code

Because a property is nothing more than a variable, you can also set the value of properties in your VBScript code. Add the VBScript code in Listing 5-1 to the page you created in the previous steps. Be sure to place the SCRIPT tag and the VBScript code *after* your command button <OBJECT> tag pair.

Listing 5-1: VBScript code to change the command button's properties.

```
<SCRIPT LANGUAGE="VBScript">
<!—
CommandButton1.Caption = "New Caption!"
—>
</SCRIPT>
```

Now save the page and do a refresh in Internet Explorer to see what it looks like. Instead of the Caption you specified in the Properties dialog, you see New Caption!. Why? The object is initially created with the caption you specified, but almost immediately after that, the VBScript code executes and the caption is replaced with New Caption!. It all happens so fast that you don't ever even see the first caption before it is replaced.

Now look at the line of code used to change the caption. How does it work? Well, if you look at the lines of HTML that Control Pad wrote for you, you'll notice that one of the properties is ID. ID is the name of the control. You didn't change the ID when you were setting the properties for the command button, but you could have. By default, it is given the name CommandButton1. If you put another command button on this page it would be given the name CommandButton2.

So in the VBScript code, you name the control, put a period, the name of the property you want to set, an equals sign, and finally the new value. This is exactly the same syntax you'd use to change the value of a variable, but, in this case, the variable is *inside* the object: it is a property of the object. So to get to it, you have to first say the object name and then the variable name, separated by a dot. This is, likely enough, referred to as *dot-notation*. Just remember that any time you want to get at something inside an object, you have to use the dot-notation and include both the object name and the variable name.

Now wait a minute! Didn't I say in the last chapter that you should always declare a variable before you use it? In the code in Listing 5-1, I didn't declare the variable Caption anywhere. How can I just use it like that without first creating it with a Dim statement?

Well, when you drop an ActiveX control onto your page, all its properties come with it. In other words, adding an ActiveX control to a page causes all its properties to be declared automatically when the object is created, so you don't have to declare them yourself.

Methods

Let's go back to the example of the car. After you specify all the things you want, your car is ordered and finally comes in. All the properties are set just as you like them, but you find that the car is more than just properties. It can also do things. You find if you press the gas peddle it goes forward. You are calling the Go subroutine that is *built into* the car object. If you press the break pedal, it stops. You are calling the Stop subroutine. When a subroutine or function is built into an object, it is often referred to as a *method*. These are capabilities or things the object can do if you ask it to. There is nothing strange about them. They are the same subroutines and functions we talked about in the last chapter; it's just that now they are built into an object.

So what would you use a method to do? Suppose you have a web site that caters to music lovers and you want to find out what the user's favorite musical style is. A first draft of the page might look something like Listing 5-2.

Listing 5-2: Find out what type of music the user enjoys.

```
<HTML>
<HEAD>
<TITLE>Music Lover's Paradise</TITLE>
</HEAD>
<BODY>
<CENTER><H1>Music Lover's Paradise</H1></CENTER>
If you love music, this site is for you. So that we can
customize
this site to your likes and dislikes, please choose the
type of music
you enjoy most.<p>

<OBJECT ID="MusicComboBox" WIDTH=148 HEIGHT=24
  CLASSID="CLSID:8BD21D30-EC42-11CE-9E0D-00AA006002F3">
    <PARAM NAME="VariousPropertyBits" VALUE="746604571">
    <PARAM NAME="DisplayStyle" VALUE="3">
    <PARAM NAME="Size" VALUE="3911;635">
    <PARAM NAME="MatchEntry" VALUE="1">
    <PARAM NAME="ShowDropButtonWhen" VALUE="2">
    <PARAM NAME="FontCharSet" VALUE="0">
```

(continued)

```
(continued)
      <PARAM NAME="FontPitchAndFamily" VALUE="2">
      <PARAM NAME="FontWeight" VALUE="0">
</OBJECT>

<SCRIPT LANGUAGE="VBScript">
<!-
   MusicComboBox.AddItem "Alternative"
   MusicComboBox.AddItem "Rock"
   MusicComboBox.AddItem "Industrial"
   MusicComboBox.AddItem "Metal"
   MusicComboBox.AddItem "Jazz"
   MusicComboBox.AddItem "Reggae"

   MusicComboBox.Value = "Classical"
->
</SCRIPT>

</BODY>
</HTML>
```

The page looks like Figure 5-8 when the combo box is dropped down.

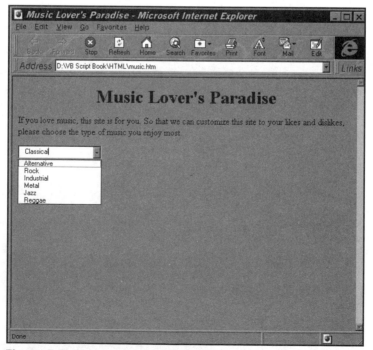

Figure 5-8: The Music Lover's page with the combo box dropped down.

The object here is a combo box ActiveX control (Microsoft Forms 2.0 ComboBox) that is dropped onto the page. The only properties that were changed were the width (it was stretched a bit) and the ID. Instead of `ComboBox1`, I called it `MusicComboBox`.

The combo box allows the user to choose from a dropdown list or type in his or her own value, but in order to fill this list, I used the combo box's `AddItem` method. I call this method in exactly the same way I accessed the command button's Caption property: dot-notation. I just use the name of the combo box (which you can always find in the `<OBJECT>` tag assigned to ID). After the name comes a dot and then the subroutine's name and any arguments I want to pass. In this case, I pass a string that indicates what I want to add to the combo box list.

The subroutines are each called, and the items are added to the list. Finally, the last line assigns a string to the `Value` property of `MusicComboBox`. The `Value` property determines what appears in the editable part of the combo box, so the default will be `Classical` unless the user types something in or picks something different from the list.

In this simple listing, you see both calls to a method and assignments to a property. Both look very similar: they first refer to the object and then use dot-notation to refer to the property or method.

Now that you understand how to use properties and methods inside your VBScript code, you are bound to be wondering what properties and methods are available and what they all do. The best place to look is the Control Pad online help. To the properties or methods for a specific control:

1. Choose Help ➪ Control Pad Help Topics from the menu.
2. Double-click Developer's Reference.
3. Double-click Controls. A list of controls appears.
4. Double-click the name of the control you want more information on.
5. A help window is displayed with general information about the control.
6. If you want to find the properties or methods associated with this control, simply click Properties or Methods at the top of the help window and then choose the property or method you want to know about.

These steps work for the common ActiveX controls that came with Control Pad, but literally hundreds of other controls are available from a variety of sources. If you buy or download a set of ActiveX controls, they should come with documentation that tells you all about what properties and methods are available and what they do.

Events

Objects contain both properties and methods. There is also one other major component of an object: *events*. An event, as the name implies, is something that can *happen to* an object. Allow me to return to my car example one more time to help describe what an event is.

A car has both properties (color, interior, engine type) and methods (Go and Stop). An event is something that can happen to an object. What could happen to a car? Lots of things. Looking on the dark side, it could be in a head-on collision. That would be an event that the car could experience. If that happened, it would be nice if the airbag popped out. This would be a *response* to the event. So when events happen, you can set up things that will happen in response to the event.

Just to clarify, a property *describes* an object. It is implemented as a variable that is built into an object. A method is something the object *can do* if you ask it to. It is implemented as subroutines and functions that are built into the object. An event is something that *happens to* an object, and you can write VBScript code that executes in *response* to the event.

Listing 5-3 extends the Music Lover's page I created in the last section. Now it includes a button and a subroutine.

Listing 5-3: The new Music Lover's page.

```
<HTML>
<HEAD>
<TITLE>New Page</TITLE>
</HEAD>
<BODY>
<CENTER><H1>Music Lover's Paradise</H1></CENTER>
If you love music, this site is for you. So that we can
customize
this site to your likes and dislikes, please choose the
type of music
you enjoy most.<p>

<OBJECT ID="MusicComboBox" WIDTH=148 HEIGHT=24
 CLASSID="CLSID:8BD21D30-EC42-11CE-9E0D-00AA006002F3">
    <PARAM NAME="VariousPropertyBits" VALUE="746604571">
    <PARAM NAME="DisplayStyle" VALUE="3">
    <PARAM NAME="Size" VALUE="3916;635">
    <PARAM NAME="MatchEntry" VALUE="1">
    <PARAM NAME="ShowDropButtonWhen" VALUE="2">
    <PARAM NAME="FontCharSet" VALUE="0">
    <PARAM NAME="FontPitchAndFamily" VALUE="2">
    <PARAM NAME="FontWeight" VALUE="0">
```

```
</OBJECT>
<p>

<OBJECT ID="ContinueButton" WIDTH=96 HEIGHT=32
 CLASSID="CLSID:D7053240-CE69-11CD-A777-00DD01143C57">
    <PARAM NAME="Caption" VALUE="Continue">
    <PARAM NAME="Size" VALUE="2540;847">



    <PARAM NAME="FontCharSet" VALUE="0">
    <PARAM NAME="FontPitchAndFamily" VALUE="2">
    <PARAM NAME="ParagraphAlign" VALUE="3">
    <PARAM NAME="FontWeight" VALUE="0">
</OBJECT>

<SCRIPT LANGUAGE="VBScript">
<!-
    MusicComboBox.AddItem "Alternative"
    MusicComboBox.AddItem "Rock"
    MusicComboBox.AddItem "Industrial"
    MusicComboBox.AddItem "Metal"
    MusicComboBox.AddItem "Jazz"
    MusicComboBox.AddItem "Reggae"

    MusicComboBox.Value = "Classical"

Sub ContinueButton_Click()
Select Case MusicComboBox.Value
Case "Classical"
    MsgBox "Going with the old stand-by, aye?"
Case "Rock"
    MsgBox "Not very imaginative, are you?"
Case "Alternative","Industrial"
    MsgBox "You're a real cutting edge guy..."
Case "Metal"
    MsgBox "Funny, you don't look like a head banger..."
Case "Jazz","Reggae"
    MsgBox "A cool cat, as they say..."
Case Else
    MsgBox "Striking out on your own?"
End Select
End Sub
->
</SCRIPT>

</BODY>
</HTML>
```

The second object I added here was a Microsoft Forms 2.0 ComandButton. The only properties I changed were the Caption (to `Continue`) and the ID (to `ContinueButton`).

Take a look at the subroutine I added. It is a normal subroutine that takes no arguments, but the odd thing is that this subroutine isn't called anywhere. So when is it executed, and why does it have such a funny name?

This subroutine is code that will execute in response to an event. What event? The Click event of the ContinueButton. Now you know why it's named that way. VBScript knows to match up any subroutines with their appropriate objects and events based on the name you give them.

So when you execute this page, choose an item from the dropdown list box, and click the button; the page harasses you with an appropriate message box. If you type in your own text, the `MsgBox` in the `Case Else` portion is called. (See Figure 5-9.)

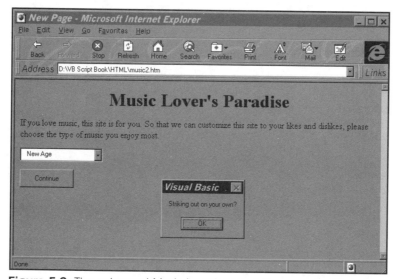

Figure 5-9: The enhanced Music Lover's page harasses you with an appropriate message box.

The next logical question is: What events happen to what objects and when? Again, all that information is in the Control Pad online help. Just follow the steps I outlined in the last section to find help on a particular object and then click Events at the top of the help page. You will see all the events associated with it. Choose one to find out exactly when it happens and why you might want to write code to respond to it.

Again, this works for the ActiveX controls that came with Control Pad, but in the next section I'll show you a way to obtain a complete list of all the properties, methods, and events for any object you'll use. I'll also show you a way to make coding for them much easier.

Control Pad's Script Wizard

If you typed in the previous examples or loaded them in from the CD-ROM, you probably noticed that a little button appeared in the margin beside your <SCRIPT> tag in the HTML page. It looks like the button that appears beside the <OBJECT> tag except that instead of a box, it pictures an open scroll.

If you click on this, you'll open the Control Pad's Script Wizard. Another way to open the Script Wizard is to choose Tools ⇨ Script Wizard from the menus or click the Script Wizard button in the button bar at the top. No matter how you do it, the Script Wizard dialog is displayed (Figure 5-10).

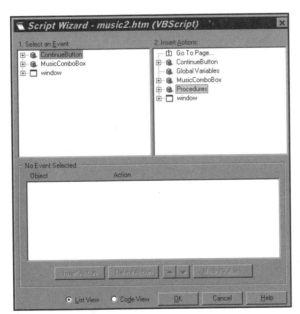

Figure 5-10: The Control Pad's Script Wizard.

This dialog box can be a little confusing at first, but I think once you get the hang of it, you'll like it a lot.

Let the Script Wizard Work its Magic

I think the best way to learn how the Script Wizard works is with an example. In this example, which I call LabelFun, you'll learn how to make text do amazing things with a simple `Label` control. There are lots of good tricks here that you'll be able to use on your web pages right away.

Creating the Page

The first step is to create the page you want to script:

1. If you are in the Script Wizard now, close it and go back to the Control Pad primary window.

2. Close any pages you have open, saving them if you like.

3. Choose File ⇨ New HTML from the menus or click the New button and choose Internet Document (HTML) from the New dialog box.

4. A new page appears. Save it under the name LabelFun.HTM with File ⇨ Save As. After it is saved, the new name will appear in the title bar of the HTML window.

5. Enter the HTML for the page in Listing 5-4. The following description will explain what ActiveX controls were added and what properties were changed.

Listing 5-4: The LabelFun Page.

```
<HTML>
<HEAD>
<TITLE>New Page</TITLE>
</HEAD>
<BODY>
<CENTER><H1>Label Fun</H1></CENTER>
This is the label fun page. It takes a simple ActiveX
control label and
through the magic of VBScript creates something
special.<p>
<p>




<OBJECT ID="MagicLabel" WIDTH=96 HEIGHT=39
 CLASSID="CLSID:978C9E23-D4B0-11CE-BF2D-00AA003F40D0">
    <PARAM NAME="Caption" VALUE="Magic">
    <PARAM NAME="Size" VALUE="2540;1000">
    <PARAM NAME="FontHeight" VALUE="480">
    <PARAM NAME="FontCharSet" VALUE="0">
    <PARAM NAME="FontPitchAndFamily" VALUE="2">
    <PARAM NAME="FontWeight" VALUE="0">
</OBJECT>
<p>
```

```
Now, all you have to do is press the button and see the
magic
begin!<p>

<OBJECT ID="AbracadabraButton" WIDTH=96 HEIGHT=32
 CLASSID="CLSID:D7053240-CE69-11CD-A777-00DD01143C57">
    <PARAM NAME="Caption" VALUE="Abracadabra!">
    <PARAM NAME="Size" VALUE="2540;846">
    <PARAM NAME="FontCharSet" VALUE="0">
    <PARAM NAME="FontPitchAndFamily" VALUE="2">
    <PARAM NAME="ParagraphAlign" VALUE="3">
    <PARAM NAME="FontWeight" VALUE="0">
</OBJECT>


</BODY>
</HTML>
```

The first object is a Microsoft Forms 2.0 Label. I changed the font size to 24 point. To do that, click on the Font property and then on the . . . button at the top right of the Properties window. This will display the font dialog box where you can change the point size.

I also made the label a little taller. To do that, move your mouse to the white box below the label in the middle on the Edit ActiveX Control window. Your mouse pointer will turn into a double arrow pointing up and down. Press and hold the mouse button and move it down a notch or so. This should allow you to see the entire word Magic including the portion of the *g* that goes below the line.

Finally, I changed the ID of the control to `Magic Label`.

The second object is a Microsoft Forms 2.0 CommandButton. I changed its Caption to `Abracadabra!`. I also changed its ID to `AbracadabraButton`.

Of course, when you look at this page in Internet Explorer, it doesn't do anything when you click the button because you haven't written a script for it. Instead of writing your own script, this time you'll use the Script Wizard to do it for you.

Adding the Magic VBScript Code

Now that the page is complete, you are ready to add your VBScript code. Get back into the Script Wizard either by choosing Tools ⇨ Script Wizard... from the menus or by clicking the Script Wizard button on the button bar.

Up until now, most of your code has been written in-line. That means that it was written outside of any subroutine or function and it executed as soon as the page loaded. This kept it simple while you were learning the language, but now I think you'll find that most of your VBScript code will end up being written in a subroutine that is called in response to an event: like the `CommandButton1_Click` subroutine in the example in the last section. This is the assumption that the Script Wizard uses.

The first step is to choose an object and an event you want to write a script for. You do that by double-clicking on the objects in the *left* pane of the window. As you do, the objects are expanded and collapsed to show all the events associated with that object. You can also single-click on the little plus and minus signs that appear beside the object icons. Figure 5-11 shows what you should see if you expand the AbracadabraButton.

You'll notice that the AbracadabraButton has a lot of events: events like `BeforeDragOver`, `BeforeDropOrPaste`, `Click`, `DblClick`, `Error`, `KeyPress`, `MouseUp`, and so on. All of these represent things that can happen to the button. Again, if you want the specifics about when each of these events is triggered, online help is the place to look.

The button event that you are interested in, and the one you will probably write VBScript code most often for, is the `Click` event.

1. Click on the `Click` event listed below `AbracadabraButton`.

2. Look at the right pane on the Script Wizard window. There is another list of the objects here. Double-click the MagicLabel icon.

3. A list of the methods and the properties for `MagicLabel` appear below. Actually, `MagicLabel` has no methods, so all you see are properties.

4. Double-click on the `Caption` property. The MagicLabel Caption dialog box appears asking you to enter a text string.

5. Type this: *** Poof ***

6. Click OK.

7. Notice that on the bottom part of the window a new line was added to the Object/Action list box. The object is `MagicLabel`, and the action is `Change Caption` to "* Poof *".

What you have just done is assigned an action to the `Click` event of the `AbracadabraButton`. Now when you click that button, the label's caption will change, and instead of `Magic Label` you will see * Poof *.

How does it work? The Script Wizard provides this interface to make it easy to add simple actions to your web page without having to write the VBScript code yourself. Of course, all the Script Wizard is doing is writing the code itself behind the scenes. In fact, if you'd rather see the actual code that the Script Wizard is writing, you can perform the following steps:

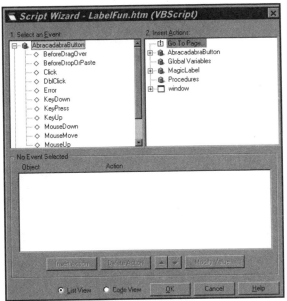

Figure 5-11: The Script Wizard showing the LabelFun page with the AbracadabraButton on the left expanded.

1. At the very bottom of the Script Wizard window, you will see two radio buttons labeled List View and Code View. The List View is the one with the dot inside it.

2. Click the Code View radio button.

3. The bottom part of the window changes from a list box into an editable text area that shows the lines of VBScript that the Script Wizard is writing for you. The name of the subroutine is first, then a line, and then the code in the subroutine. You won't see the End Sub, but it will write that line for you, too.

4. Click OK at the bottom of the Script Wizard window. You are returned to your web page.

Scroll down your web page. You should see the code in Listing 5-5 mixed in there somewhere.

Listing 5-5: The VBScript code written by the Script Wizard.

```
<SCRIPT LANGUAGE="VBScript">
<!—
Sub AbracadabraButton_Click()
MagicLabel.Caption = "* Poof *"
end sub
—>
</SCRIPT>
```

NOTE If you are using Front Page 97, you can access the Script Wizard from there. Just choose Insert ⇨ Script from the menus. This shows the Script dialog box. The VBScript radio button is chosen by default at the top. You can either type a script in there or click the Script Wizard button to associate your script with a particular object and event. The Script Wizard in Front Page 97 works just like the Script Wizard in Control Pad.

Trying it Out

Save the web page and take a look at it in Internet Explorer. Click the button. Hmm... It's not quite right (Figure 5-12).

What happened to that last asterisk? Although the label was wide enough to display Magic, it wasn't quite wide enough to display * Poof *. To make it work right, you'll have to change the width of the label:

1. Click on the box icon that appears in the margin of the HTML page in Control Pad beside the MagicLabel.

2. The Edit ActiveX Control window, and the Properties window appear again.

3. Stretch the label in the Edit ActiveX Control to make it a couple of notches wider.

4. Click the close button in the upper right of the Edit ActiveX Control window.

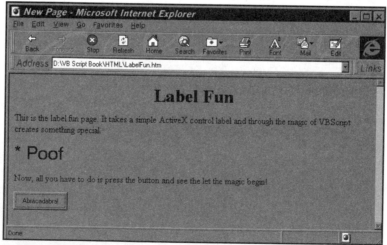

Figure 5-12: The poof didn't poof quite right.

5. The lines of the `<OBJECT>` tag are changed.

6. Save it and look at the results in Internet Explorer (Figure 5-13).

The Script Wizard: a Nice Place to Work

The script wizard can only write VBScript to do simple things like change the property of an ActiveX control or call a method that doesn't require any arguments. Is it really worth using? Absolutely.

The greatest strength of the Script Wizard is not its capability to write code for you. There are really two reasons you should use it for writing your VBScript code:

➡ It provides a way of organizing all your code into the objects and events they accompany. Instead of just looking at a long list of subroutines with strange names, you can click on objects and events and see the code right where it belongs.

➡ It provides a visual interface that makes it immediately obvious what objects, events, methods, and properties are available.

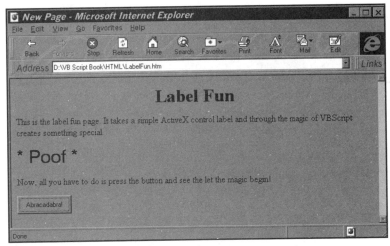

Figure 5-13: A better poof.

In the last section, I walked you through the creation of an example page. I wanted to give you an intuitive feel for using the Script Wizard. Now I'd like to take you back into the Script Wizard to do another example and point out a few things that you might not have noticed.

Writing your VBScript in Code View

Get back into the Script Wizard, and I'll tell you about its key features:

1. Go back to Control Pad.
2. Scroll down the page until you find the <SCRIPT> tag.

3. Click on the scroll icon in the margin beside the `<SCRIPT>` tag.

4. The Script Wizard appears. The Click event of `AbracadabraButton` is highlighted, and the bottom of the window presents the list box of actions.

5. Click the Code View radio button at the bottom of the window.

Even though you changed to Code View before you clicked OK on this window the last time, it still brings up the Script Wizard in List View. This is sometimes annoying because, if you use the Script Wizard all the time, you'll probably end up using the Code View more often than the List View. That's because in code view you can write any VBScript code you like. In List View, you are limited to the kinds of code the Script Wizard knows how to write.

TIP   All events listed in the event pane have a diamond beside them. Some have a white diamond and others have a black diamond. The black diamond indicates that the event has VBScript code assigned to it.

The first thing you should always do before you write code here is to look up to the left pane of the window, called the *event pane*. This tells you what *object* and what *event* you are writing code to respond to. One of the most common mistakes you will make is to put the right code in the wrong place. Then, when you try it out in Explorer, it won't work!

In this case, you are in the Click event of the `Abracadabra` button:

1. Delete the code that is in the event now (the single line assignment of the Caption).

2. Type the code in Listing 5-6.

Listing 5-6: The new `AbracadabraButton` click event.

```vbscript
Dim Red, Green, Blue

Red = Int(Rnd * 255) + 1
Green = Int(Rnd * 255) + 1
Blue = Int(Rnd * 255) + 1

MagicLabel.ForeColor = RGB(Red, Green, Blue)
```

The first line creates three variables. The third, fourth, and fifth lines should be familiar to you. They each generate a random number between 1 and 255 and assign it to each of the variables. Finally, the `ForeColor` property of `MagicLabel` is assigned the return value from the `RGB` function.

What's RGB? You might remember my discussion in Chapter 1 about HTML and how it deals with color. It uses three values (red, green, and blue) and then mixes them in different amounts to produce a color. VBScript color works in exactly the same way, but here, a nifty function makes it easy. The RGB function accepts three numbers, each between 1 and 255 indicating how much red, green, and blue should be mixed into the final color. It returns a long integer (a really big whole number) that identifies that color. So `RGB(0,0,0)` would return a number that indicates black. `RGB(255,0,0)` would return a number that indicates bright red. `RGB(128,0,128)` would return a number that indicates a medium purple (red and blue mixed together). You don't have to worry about what the number it returns looks like. It wouldn't mean anything to you anyway. Just use RGB to tell it what color you want.

So when you click the button, a random color is created (with random amounts of red, green, and blue), and then the label is changed to that color. When you look at this page in Explorer, you'll notice that you can click the button as many times as you like, and you'll see a different color each time.

Simple Property Changes and Cool Effects

In this last section of this chapter, I want to give you the opportunity to put some of the things you've learned so far to use in creating some interesting effects with ActiveX controls for your own pages. I think you'll be surprised at the things you can do by just fiddling with the properties of your ActiveX controls in certain ways.

What You'll Need

In order to create the effects in these sections, you will need a couple of ActiveX controls that didn't come with the ActiveX Control Pad. These are called `Timer Object` and `Label Object`. If you don't have these ActiveX controls already, you can obtain them by visiting the ActiveX page on Microsoft's web site (`http://www.microsoft.com/activex/gallery/`). Locate Microsoft's `Label` and `Timer` ActiveX controls and download them.

About the New ActiveX Controls

You may be wondering why I'm using a different `Label` when a perfectly good label comes with the Microsoft Control Pad. Well, to be honest, the controls that come with Control Pad are nice, but they aren't really as full-featured as others you might find. For instance, the `Label Object` on the

CD-ROM has a property called `Angle`. If you change this property from its default of 0 to, say, 90, the text will stand on end. As you can imagine, you can put this kind of flexibility to use in lots of ways. The Microsoft Forms 2.0 Label simply can't compete.

You may also be wondering what a `Timer Object` is. The `Timer Object` is different from any of the other controls you have seen so far. It is a non-visual control. In other words, the users won't see it when they look at your page. So what good is it? Well, it has a single event that you can write scripts for called the `Timer` event. This event happens again and again at a regular interval, and you can set how long that interval is using the `Interval` property. This allows you to do time-sensitive things. I think you'll begin to have a better feel for exactly what kinds of things it makes possible from these examples.

Zooming In and Out

Here's the effect: the header for the page will begin small. When the user clicks a button, the header becomes bigger and bigger. It will seem as if the letters are coming toward you. Finally, once it reaches to a certain size, it begins shrinking or moving away. This in and out motion continues until the user becomes seasick and clicks the button again to stop it.

Creating the Page

I'm not going to spell out every detail because you should be feeling more comfortable with Control Pad by now:

1. Create a new HTML page.

2. Change the text in the `<TITLE>` tag pair to `Zoomer`.

3. Save it as Zoomer.HTM.

4. Insert a new ActiveX control first thing in the `BODY`.

5. Choose Label Object from the Insert ActiveX Control window. If you don't see Label Object in the list, see the directions in the section titled "What You Need."

6. Move the Properties window to the side and stretch out the Edit ActiveX Control window.

7. Stretch out the label inside the window so it is nice and large. It doesn't have to be exactly the same as mine, but my Height is set to 78 and my Width is set to 276.

The size of the Edit ActiveX Control window doesn't actually have an effect on anything. The reason I had you enlarge it here is just so that you'd have room to make the label bigger. You want the label to be big so that the text inside it will have room to grow as you zoom in and out.

8. Type your name into the `Caption` property.

9. Set `FontBold` to `True`.

10. Leave the `FontSize` at its default of 12. Your name should appear in the middle of the label with plenty of room all the way around. If it isn't in the center, make sure the `Alignment` property is set to 4 - `Centered`. Your window should look like Figure 5-14.

11. Set the control's ID to `ZoomLabel`. Click Apply or press Enter.

I specifically tell you to click Apply here. If you don't click Apply and simply click on another property, that will work, too, but if you change a property and then immediately click the close button for the Edit ActiveX Control window, the change won't happen. So before you close it up, make sure the last change you made has been applied.

12. Click the close button on the Edit ActiveX Control window.

13. Your object is pasted into the web page.

14. Type the lines in Listing 5-7 into the page after the object you just put there.

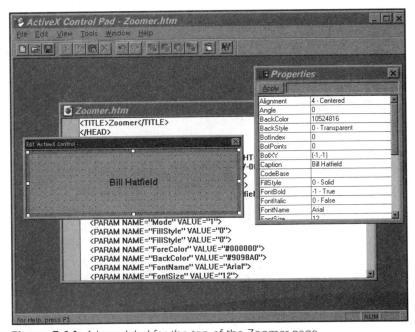

Figure 5-14: A large label for the top of the Zoomer page.

Listing 5-7: The HTML that should appear after the first object is added.

```
<p>
The headline of this text has a tendency to go far away
and then come
back again at a very rapid pace, but it only seems to
happen when you
push this button here:<p>
```

The next thing you need, as you can tell from the text, is a command button. You'll use the normal command button you've used in previous examples.

1. Insert a Microsoft Forms 2.0 CommandButton after the text you added.

2. Change the Caption to Start.

3. Change the ID to ZoomButton.

4. Close the Edit ActiveX Control window to have the HTML <OBJECT> tag pasted in.

Finally, you need a timer control to make this whole thing work. It doesn't really matter where you place this control because the user won't see it when viewing the page. Just to make it easy, put it at the bottom of the page.

1. Insert a Timer Object.

2. Set its Interval to 100.

TIP The Interval is the number of milliseconds to wait between triggering the Timer event. A value of 1000 would trigger the event once a second. The value you put there, 100, will trigger it 10 times every second.

3. Set its Enabled to False.

4. Set the ID to ZoomTimer.

5. Close the Edit ActiveX Control window.

You will notice that an Edit ActiveX Control window still appears and that there is a box with a picture of a clock in it. You can even resize the control if you want to, but it will have no effect. The control does not appear in the final page.

Your page should look like Listing 5-8.

Listing 5-8: The Zoomer page before any scripts are added.

```
<HTML>
<HEAD>
<TITLE>Zoomer</TITLE>
</HEAD>
<BODY>

<OBJECT ID="ZoomLabel" WIDTH=368 HEIGHT=104
 CLASSID="CLSID:99B42120-6EC7-11CF-A6C7-00AA00A47DD2">
     <PARAM NAME="_ExtentX" VALUE="9737">
     <PARAM NAME="_ExtentY" VALUE="2752">
     <PARAM NAME="Caption" VALUE="Bill Hatfield">
     <PARAM NAME="Angle" VALUE="0">
     <PARAM NAME="Alignment" VALUE="4">
     <PARAM NAME="Mode" VALUE="1">
     <PARAM NAME="FillStyle" VALUE="0">
     <PARAM NAME="FillStyle" VALUE="0">
     <PARAM NAME="ForeColor" VALUE="#000000">
     <PARAM NAME="BackColor" VALUE="#9098A0">
     <PARAM NAME="FontName" VALUE="Arial">
     <PARAM NAME="FontSize" VALUE="12">
     <PARAM NAME="FontItalic" VALUE="0">
     <PARAM NAME="FontBold" VALUE="1">
     <PARAM NAME="FontUnderline" VALUE="0">
     <PARAM NAME="FontStrikeout" VALUE="0">
     <PARAM NAME="TopPoints" VALUE="0">
     <PARAM NAME="BotPoints" VALUE="0">
</OBJECT>
<p>
The headline of this text has a tendency to go far  away
and then come
back again at a very rapid pace, but it only seems to
happen when you
push this button here:<p>

<OBJECT ID="ZoomButton" WIDTH=96 HEIGHT=32
 CLASSID="CLSID:D7053240-CE69-11CD-A777-00DD01143C57">
     <PARAM NAME="Caption" VALUE="Start">
     <PARAM NAME="Size" VALUE="2540;846">
     <PARAM NAME="FontCharSet" VALUE="0">
     <PARAM NAME="FontPitchAndFamily" VALUE="2">
     <PARAM NAME="ParagraphAlign" VALUE="3">
     <PARAM NAME="FontWeight" VALUE="0">
</OBJECT>
```

(continued)

```
(continued)
<OBJECT ID="ZoomTimer" WIDTH=60 HEIGHT=49
 CLASSID="CLSID:59CCB4A0-727D-11CF-AC36-00AA00A47DD2">
     <PARAM NAME="_ExtentX" VALUE="1588">
     <PARAM NAME="_ExtentY" VALUE="1296">
     <PARAM NAME="Interval" VALUE="100">
     <PARAM NAME="Enabled" VALUE="False">
</OBJECT>

</BODY>
</HTML>
```

Writing the Scripts

Now that the page looks like you want it to and the controls are in place, it's time to *activate* the page with VBScript!

Creating a Global Variable with the Script Wizard

The first thing you need to do is create a global variable. You remember that *global variables* (also called *script-level variables*) are created with the `Dim` statement outside of any subroutine or function, and they are available in any subroutine or function on the page. How do you create a global variable with the Script Wizard? It's easy:

1. Get into the Script Wizard.

2. Right-click anywhere inside the action pane (the pane on the right). A popup menu appears.

3. Choose New Global Variable from the popup menu. A window will appear asking you to give the variable a name.

4. Type **direction**. Click OK.

5. Double-click on the Global Variables object icon in the action pane. The variable `direction` will now appear under it.

That's all there is to it. Any time you need a global variable, that's all you have to do to create it, but remember to use local variables, declared inside your functions or subroutines instead, if possible. I'll describe why you needed this global in the next section.

 By the way, creating a new function or subroutine is just as easy. Right-click anywhere in the action pane and choose `New Procedure`. Immediately, down on the bottom of the screen you will see (assuming you are in Code View),

```
Sub Procedure1()
```

You can click on the name and change it, and you can add arguments inside parentheses. You can also change the Sub to Function. Then, you can click below in the editor and write the code for your function/subroutine. You should see the name of your function/subroutine on the action pane under the Procedures object icon.

Scripting the Timer

Now you can write the script for the timer:

1. Double-click on the ZoomTimer icon in the event pane (the one on the left). There is only one event: Timer.

2. Click the Timer event.

3. Click the Code View radio button along the bottom. The lower part of the window turns into an editor for the ZoomTimer_Timer event.

4. Type in the code in Listing 5-9.

Listing 5-9: The timer code.

```
If ZoomLabel.FontSize > 30 Then direction = -1
If ZoomLabel.FontSize < 13 Then direction = 1
ZoomLabel.FontSize = ZoomLabel.FontSize + direction
```

What does the timer code do? It increases or decreases the value in the ZoomLabel's FontSize property. FontSize, as you would expect, determines how big the font is for the text in the label. The default is 12, and that's where it starts.

To understand how this code works, the first thing to remember is that this Timer event is triggered again and again, 10 times every second.

So what happens the first time this code executes? The first If fails because the value is not greater than 30. The second If succeeds because 12 is less than 13. The global variable direction is set to 1. Then direction (now with a value of 1) is added to the FontSize, making it 13.

The second time around, the global variable is still 13, so both If statements fail and the direction stays 1. FontSize is increased by 1 again.

The FontSize of the label continues to grow and grow until it reaches 31. Once that happens, the first If statement succeeds and direction is changed to -1. When -1 is added to the FontSize it goes down to 30. It continues to go down until it reaches 12 again. Then, again, the second If statement kicks in and sends the FontSize back up.

Why is `direction` a global variable here? It isn't used in any subroutine other than this one, so why not make it local to this subroutine and put its `Dim` statement here?

If direction were local, it would not remember what direction it was last set to. Each time this subroutine executed, a new direction variable would be created (with an initial value of 0). In order for the code to work, `direction` must maintain the value from one execution to the next, so it had to be global.

Turning it On or Off: Scripting the Button

Finally, the only other script left to write is the command button, which will turn the zooming on and off.

1. Double-click the ZoomButton icon in the event pane (on the left).

2. Click on the `Click` event below `ZoomButton`.

3. The `ZoomButton_Click` subroutine appears in the lower part of the window.

4. Enter the code in Listing 5-10. The timer code.

Listing 5-10: The command button click code.

```
If ZoomTimer.Enabled = True Then
    ZoomTimer.Enabled = False
    ZoomButton.Caption = "Start"
Else
    ZoomTimer.Enabled = True
    ZoomButton.Caption = "Stop"
End If
```

This code only executes when the user clicks the ZoomButton. It first checks to see if the `ZoomTimer` is enabled. When the timer is enabled, it triggers the `Timer` event 10 times a second. When it is disabled, it stops triggering it at all. If the `ZoomTimer` is enabled, this code disables it and changes the `Caption` of this button to read `Start`. Otherwise (if the `ZoomTimer` was disabled), the `ZoomTimer` is enabled, and the `ZoomButton` caption is changed to `Stop`.

This type of button is called a toggle because it alternates between two different states. If the label is on, it turns it off, and if it is off, it turns it on. The caption on the button is changed so that it is clear to the user exactly what will happen when the button is clicked.

Sizing it Up and Trying it Out

Now you are done.

1. Click OK on the Script Wizard window.

2. Your HTML page should look like Listing 5-11.

Listing 5-11: The complete Zoomer page.

```
<HTML>
<HEAD>
<SCRIPT LANGUAGE="VBScript">
<!-
dim direction
->
</SCRIPT>
<TITLE>New Page</TITLE>
</HEAD>
<BODY>
    <OBJECT ID="ZoomLabel" WIDTH=368 HEIGHT=104
    CLASSID="CLSID:99B42120-6EC7-11CF-A6C7-00AA00A47DD2">
        <PARAM NAME="_ExtentX" VALUE="9737">
        <PARAM NAME="_ExtentY" VALUE="2752">
        <PARAM NAME="Caption" VALUE="Bill Hatfield">
        <PARAM NAME="Angle" VALUE="0">
        <PARAM NAME="Alignment" VALUE="4">
        <PARAM NAME="Mode" VALUE="1">
        <PARAM NAME="FillStyle" VALUE="0">
        <PARAM NAME="FillStyle" VALUE="0">
        <PARAM NAME="ForeColor" VALUE="#000000">



        <PARAM NAME="BackColor" VALUE="#9098A0">
        <PARAM NAME="FontName" VALUE="Arial">
        <PARAM NAME="FontSize" VALUE="12">
        <PARAM NAME="FontItalic" VALUE="0">
        <PARAM NAME="FontBold" VALUE="1">
        <PARAM NAME="FontUnderline" VALUE="0">
        <PARAM NAME="FontStrikeout" VALUE="0">
        <PARAM NAME="TopPoints" VALUE="0">
        <PARAM NAME="BotPoints" VALUE="0">
    </OBJECT>
<p>
The headline of this text has a tendency to go far away
and then come
back again at a very rapid pace. But it only seems to
```

(continued)

```
(continued)
happen when you
push this button here:<p>
<SCRIPT LANGUAGE="VBScript">
<!—
Sub ZoomButton_Click()
If ZoomTimer.Enabled = True Then
   ZoomTimer.Enabled = False
   ZoomButton.Caption = "Start"
Else
   ZoomTimer.Enabled = True
   ZoomButton.Caption = "Stop"
End If
end sub
—>
</SCRIPT>
    <OBJECT ID="ZoomButton" WIDTH=96 HEIGHT=32
      CLASSID="CLSID:D7053240-CE69-11CD-A777-00DD01143C57">
        <PARAM NAME="Caption" VALUE="Start">
        <PARAM NAME="Size" VALUE="2540;846">
        <PARAM NAME="FontCharSet" VALUE="0">
        <PARAM NAME="FontPitchAndFamily" VALUE="2">
        <PARAM NAME="ParagraphAlign" VALUE="3">
        <PARAM NAME="FontWeight" VALUE="0">
    </OBJECT>
<SCRIPT LANGUAGE="VBScript">
<!—
Sub ZoomTimer_Timer()
If ZoomLabel.FontSize > 30 Then direction = -1
If ZoomLabel.FontSize < 13 Then direction = 1
ZoomLabel.FontSize = ZoomLabel.FontSize + direction
end sub
—>
</SCRIPT>
    <OBJECT ID="ZoomTimer" WIDTH=60 HEIGHT=49
     CLASSID="CLSID:59CCB4A0-727D-11CF-AC36-00AA00A47DD2">
        <PARAM NAME="_ExtentX" VALUE="1588">
        <PARAM NAME="_ExtentY" VALUE="1296">
        <PARAM NAME="Interval" VALUE="100">
        <PARAM NAME="Enabled" VALUE="False">
    </OBJECT>
</BODY>
</HTML>
```

When you write your code in the Script Wizard as you did for this project, you don't control where it places your VBScript code. If you look at the page now, you'll see that it actually created several <SCRIPT> tags throughout the page.

It put the global variable declaration at the top, and it put the event scripts for the button and the timer right above their associated objects. This keeps all the VBScript code with the objects they belong to. This is not required. If you were writing the code in your web page, you could just as easily have put one `<SCRIPT>` tag at the bottom, just before `</BODY>` and placed all the VBScript code there. It makes no difference, but I think keeping the events with their associated objects is a good idea.

1. Save the page.

2. Switch over to Internet Explorer and load the page (see Figure 5-15).

3. What are you waiting for? Push the button!

4. Feeling seasick yet? Push the button again to stop it.

You may see some flickering the first time the text zooms in and out. This flicker should diminish after the first time. How much flicker you see depends on many factors including how fast your machine and graphics card are, how your monitor works, and how sensitive your eyes are to flicker. To reduce the flicker, you can increase the timer Interval (which will also slow down the zooming movement), and you can decrease the maximum size the text grows to.

Congratulations! You did it, and the good news is that you can take this same framework and create and try out lots of other neat ideas. In fact, let me show you some of my ideas and maybe it will spark some of your own.

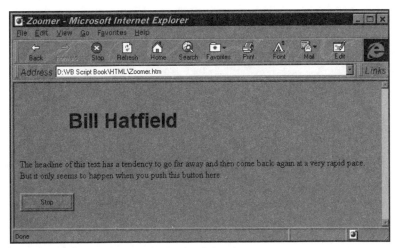

Figure 5-15: The Zoomer page, in all its glory.

A Hanging Sign

Imagine an old sign hanging from the wall with only one nail to hold it up. It's bound to sway back and forth. Now imagine the header for your web page selling western boots doing the same thing.

1. Go back to Control Pad and scroll your page to the <OBJECT> tag for the label.

2. Click the box icon in the margin to edit the label object.

3. Change the FontSize to 25.

4. Change the Angle to 5. You should see the text tilt in the Edit ActiveX Control window.

5. Close the Edit ActiveX Control window.

6. Click the box icon in the margin next to the timer object.

7. Change the Interval to 150.

8. Close the Edit ActiveX Control window.

9. Use Save As to save the page under the name Sign.HTM.

10. Get into the Script Wizard.

11. Edit the script for the Timer event.

12. Change it to look like Listing 5-12.

Listing 5-12: The new Timer event for the hanging sign.

```
If ZoomLabel.Angle > 4 Then direction = -1
If ZoomLabel.Angle < -4 Then direction = 1
ZoomLabel.Angle = ZoomLabel.Angle + direction
```

This is exactly the same type of logic used in the Zoomer example. The Angle starts at 5, so it triggers the first If immediately making direction -1. Angle plus -1 makes angle 4, and it keeps going down until the second If kicks in and reverses it, so the text rocks back and forth between an angle of -5 and 5.

1. Click OK to get out of the Script Wizard.

2. Save the page.

3. Switch over to Internet Explorer, and load up Sign.HTM.

4. Push the button.

Could you make this one better? Here's an idea that I'll leave up to you to try out: Make the sign rock back and forth faster and at a greater angle at first and then make it slow down and rock at lesser and lesser angles until finally it stops, just a little off center. This would take a little more work but would be much more realistic. Adjust the `Interval` from inside the `Timer` event to make it go faster or slower. You might also want to start the rocking as soon as the page loads.

Here's another idea: Combine the concepts used for the last two examples and cause text to spin as it moves from far away to very close. Have it land in place right side up just as the text reaches its largest size.

Attention Grabbers

It's easy to create text that grabs the user's attention by changing its properties dynamically.

Flashy Text

One of the techniques early web pages used to grab attention was flashing text. Whereas this quickly became annoying, a variation on that theme is a little less annoying and just as effective at grabbing attention. It couldn't be simpler:

1. Edit the label control.
2. Change the `Angle` to 0 and the `FontSize` to 30.
3. Edit the `Timer` control.
4. Change the `Interval` to 200.
5. Get into the Script Wizard.
6. Change the code in the `Timer` event to look like Listing 5-13.

Listing 5-13: The Flashy Timer event.

```
If ZoomLabel.FontSize = 35 Then
    ZoomLabel.FontSize = 30
Else
    ZoomLabel.FontSize = 35
End If
```

The font switches back and forth between one size and another size that's slightly bigger. This has the effect of shaking the text in your face, and you can bet it will be noticed!

Flashy Text, Part 2

Another way to do flashing text is to use color:

1.　Get into the Script Wizard.

2.　Change the `Timer` event to look like Listing 5-14.

Listing 5-14: The second Flashy Timer event.

```
If ZoomLabel.ForeColor = RGB(255,0,0) Then
    ZoomLabel.ForeColor = RGB(128,0,0)
Else
    ZoomLabel.ForeColor = RGB(255,0,0)
End If
```

This is exactly the same code used for Flashy, but instead of changing the font size back and forth, I am changing the color between a dull red and a bright red:

1.　Save the page as Flashy2.HTM.

2.　Load it up in Internet Explorer and push the button.

It starts as black, but when you push the button it begins switching back and forth between a dark red and a bright red.

Flashy Text, Part 3

Perhaps a less distracting, more pleasant flash would be more appropriate

1.　Edit the `Timer` and change the `Interval` to 50.

2.　Get into the Script Wizard.

3.　Create another global variable. Call it `labelcolor`. (If you forget how to do this, look back earlier this chapter to the section titled "Creating a Global Variable with the Script Wizard.")

4.　Change the `Timer` event to look like Listing 5-15.

Listing 5-15: The third Flashy Timer event.

```
If labelcolor > 240 Then direction = -10
If labelcolor < 50 Then direction = 10
labelcolor = labelcolor + direction
ZoomLabel.ForeColor = RGB(labelcolor,0,0)
```

This is just another variation on the code used to make the sign rock back and forth and the code used to zoom in and out. The change in direction causes the color variable to sway between 40 and 250. The increment is 10 now instead of 1. That's because it is very difficult to tell the difference between a 200 red and a 201 red. That variable is then assigned to the red portion of the RGB function.

1. Save the page as Flashy3.HTM.
2. Load it up in Internet Explorer and push the button.

It starts as black, when you push the button, it slowly becomes redder and redder until it is glowing bright red. Then it goes back down to almost completely black before it starts up again.

This looks much more pleasant than the other options and is still an effective attention getter.

 If you are not running with 256 colors or more, this example may not look very nice. It looks optimal with high-color (32,000 colors) or more.

Other Ideas

The possibilities for creativity here are endless. Just use your imagination and put the building blocks together to create whatever effects you can dream up. I've shown you quite a few interesting ideas using only the timer and label. Your options only increase the more ActiveX controls you have at your disposal.

Here's one last challenge for you: Try combining the technique used in Flashy, Part 3 with the Zoomer so that when the text is smallest, it is also a dark color. Then, as it gets larger, the color becomes brighter. Then, when the text begins to grow smaller, gradually darken the color again. This will enhance the illusion that the text is coming closer and then moving away.

Summary

I began this unit by introducing you to Microsoft Control Pad, ActiveX controls and the concept of an object, its properties, methods, and events. Then, through a couple of examples, I showed you the wonders of the Script Wizard and how it can help you write VBScript code. Finally, I described and showed you how to write several example pages with concepts you can put to use right away in your own web pages.

In the next unit, I'll introduce you to some more objects you can use: objects that are built into Internet Explorer itself and allow you to manipulate and control the browser from your VBScript code.

Internet Explorer Objects

ActiveX controls aren't the only objects you can access from VBScript. In fact, Internet Explorer itself has several built-in objects that allow you to manipulate and control how the browser behaves from within VBScript just as quickly and easily as you manipulate ActiveX controls. In this chapter, you will learn what those objects are; some of the more interesting properties, methods, and events they offer; and how best to put them to use in your own pages.

 This chapter does not present an exhaustive list of all the properties, methods, and events available for all the objects. I didn't want to bore you with all of that here. If you want a complete list, I have included one in Appendix C. In this chapter, I'll focus instead on interesting ways of putting some of these properties, methods, and events to use. I will, in the process, repeat the information from Appendix C that you need to know to understand the examples.

Browser Objects and the Object Hierarchy

Browser objects make accessing and using the capabilities of the Internet Explorer possible.

You will be working with these objects:

➠ **Window:** represents the window of the browser.

➡ **Frame:** a pane within a window. Corresponds directly to the frames you can create in HTML.

➡ **History:** the history of the user's browsing. Used to remember where the browser should go when you click the Back and Forward buttons.

➡ **Navigator:** contains properties that identify the current browser.

➡ **Location:** tracks the URL of the current page.

➡ **Scripts:** a list of all the scripts defined with the `<SCRIPT>` tag in the current window. These cannot be accessed or used in any way from VBScript.

➡ **Document:** represents the document currently loaded and displayed in the browser.

➡ **Links:** a list of all the links in the current document that the user can click on to go someplace else.

➡ **Anchors:** a list of all the anchors in the current page. Anchors include links, but they also include placeholders used to name certain parts of the document so that other links can jump directly to a paragraph in the middle of a long page, for instance.

➡ **Forms:** a list of all the forms on the current page. Forms are used to obtain information from the user and submit it to the web server for processing. For a complete discussion on creating and using forms, see Chapter 12.

➡ **Elements:** a list of the elements on the current page. Examples of elements include ActiveX controls and Java applets.

Wow. Those are a lot of objects to keep track of. It turns out that these objects aren't just a hodgepodge grab bag of stuff you can use. They are organized into an *object hierarchy.*

To explain what an object hierarchy is, allow me to return to the car example I used in the last chapter. I described a car as having properties like Color, Engine Type, and so on. It also had methods like Go and Stop, and I described an event like a head-on collision to which there was a response: an airbag popping out.

Now let's talk about other properties the car might have. In addition to things like Color, Engine Type, Purchase Price, and so on, it will also have properties like Transmission and Steering Wheel. A car wouldn't be much good if it didn't have these things, but if you look at the Steering Wheel more closely, you'll see that it, too, has properties. A steering wheel will have a Composition property that might hold the values *plastic* or *leather,* and it could have its own Color property. It might even have methods. Steer Right and Steer Left come to mind immediately. Therefore, the Steering Wheel, too, is an object, and at the same time it is a property of the car.

Thus, objects can have properties that are, themselves, complete objects, and if they are objects, they, too, could have properties that are objects. These objects within objects within objects can go to any level you like, and they end up forming an *object hierarchy*.

This note is only for those who've programmed in other object-oriented environments in the past.

This is not an inheritance hierarchy. It is a containment hierarchy. Inheritance is not supported in the COM/ActiveX model, at least not yet.

For example, look at Figure 6-1. This is a diagram of an object hierarchy containing all of the objects listed earlier. Look back at the description of the objects as you look at this diagram. The relationships should begin to make sense to you.

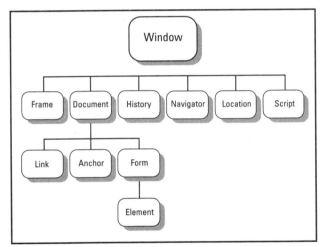

Figure 6-1: The browser object hierarchy.

The Window is the highest in the hierarchy. It makes sense that the Window object, which represents the window of the browser, would contain all the other objects. The Window contains the History object and the Location object, but the most important object it contains is the Document object, which represents the currently loaded page. Inside the Document are Links and Anchors, as you might expect.

I'll spend the rest of this chapter describing how to put the more interesting of these objects, properties, methods, and events to use in your own web pages. Again, for a complete, exhaustive reference of all the objects, properties, methods, and events, see Appendix D.

NOTE By the way, these same objects are available to JavaScript developers, and they work the same way there. These objects are also a part of the Netscape Navigator browser, so most any code you write using these objects should work in either browser.

The Window Object

I'll start at the top with the Window object. As you saw in the last section, the Window is the mother of all objects. It represents the browser window itself and provides a number of interesting properties and methods.

The Status Bar

The status bar is the gray bar at the very bottom of the browser window. It provides information on what the browser is doing. It indicates when the browser is trying to find a site or when it is loading a document or graphic.

Most of the time when the user is reading or working with a page that has already loaded, the status bar is blank. That makes it prime real estate for sending whatever information you like.

Putting the Status Bar to Work

Putting a message in the status bar is easy:

```
Window.Status = "Welcome to my terrific home page!"
```

Window refers to the Window object, and Status is a property of that object. This is exactly the same type of notation you used when you wanted to assign text that would appear in a label:

```
IeLabel1.Caption = "Welcome to my terrific home page!"
```

IeLabel1 is the ActiveX label control's name, and Caption is the property. You can access all of the browser object properties and methods this way.

You should know one additional thing about the Window object: it is considered the default object in the browser object hierarchy. This means that you don't even have to use the Window object's name when you refer to one of its properties or methods. You can simply refer to the method, and VBScript will figure out that you mean to refer to the Window object. For instance, this code would work just as well as the last code:

```
Status = "Welcome to my terrific home page!"
```

Window isn't specified, but VBScript figures it out. This is only true of the Window object. With all the other objects, you must specify both the object and the property or method you want to work with, separated by a period. Often I'll go ahead and specify the Window object, too, just to make it clear what I'm doing.

Because you can specify all the properties and methods of the Window object without referring to the Window object, all of those properties and methods are reserved words in VBScript. A reserved word is a word that the language itself uses: you can't use it to name your own variables or procedures. You can't name your own variable or subroutine MsgBox. Likewise, you can't name your own variable or subroutine Status.

For an example that describes how to create a scrolling marquee-style message across your status bar, see the section titled "Example: A Scrolling Status Bar Message" later in this chapter.

Alert, Confirm, and Prompt

Throughout this book, I've used MsgBox as a simple way to present information to the user and InputBox to obtain information from the user. Of course you learned about more sophisticated ways of doing this on the page using ActiveX controls, but these functions still work well for simple things.

The Window object has several more functions that provide functionality similar to the MsgBox and InputBox. They are Alert, Confirm, and Prompt.

Alert

The first is Alert:

```
Window.Alert "I'm glad you're here."
```

Alert is simpler than MsgBox. Although you can use MsgBox to display information simply (as shown in Figure 6-2), it also has optional parameters for changing the title bar text, the icon, and the kind of buttons that appear on the dialog box.

Figure 6-2: The MsgBox dialog box using the default arguments.

Alert doesn't have any of this. It simply displays a string in a dialog box with an OK button that looks like Figure 6-3.

Figure 6-3: The Alert dialog box.

Confirm

Confirm is another method of the window that displays a message. It has both an OK and a Cancel and can be used to allow the user to make a decision. If the user clicks OK, True is returned from the Confirm function; otherwise, False is returned. This makes it easy to drop a Confirm right into an If...Then statement:

```
If Confirm("Are you sure you want to do this?") Then
    ' Do it
End If
```

These lines produce a dialog box that looks like Figure 6-4.

Figure 6-4: Confirm dialog box.

Confirm is much simpler to use for simple decision-making like this than the corresponding MsgBox.

Prompt

Prompt displays a dialog box very similar to the InputBox dialog box. You send it a string to display in the dialog box to prompt the user, and you can also send a default value for the text box that appears on the dialog box.

```
Dim Name
Name = Prompt("What is your name?","Fred")
```

This code produces the dialog box in Figure 6-5.

Figure 6-5: The Prompt dialog box.

Prompt does not provide optional parameters that allow you to specify the dialog box's location on the screen, the title bar text, or an associated help file as InputBox does, but for most simple user prompts, it works great.

The second argument for Prompt specifies a default for the text box. Even though it is optional, you will probably want to include it anyway. If you don't, this will appear in your text box:

```
<undefined>
```

Strange huh? You'd think they'd go with something simple, like maybe putting nothing there at all.

Automated surfing: the Navigate method

The Window object allows you to control what document the user is looking at in the browser through the Navigate method. This is all it takes

```
Window.Navigate "http://www.edgequest.com"
```

and suddenly, you're there! This is handy if you want to create a command button (or almost any other ActiveX control) that works like a link. Just put a Microsoft Forms 2.0 CommandButton on your page and code something like the last code line for its Click event. Anytime you click the button, it will take you there.

Window events: OnLoad and OnUnload

Two events are associated with the Window object: OnLoad and OnUnload. OnLoad happens *immediately after* a page is loaded into the browser. OnUnload happens *immediately before* the page is unloaded (usually to load in a new page). These events are very handy places to write VBScript code. In fact, you are almost sure to use OnLoad in any reasonably sophisticated page to give you the chance to initialize variables and set things up the way you want them. You can use OnUnload to clean things up and do any housekeeping necessary before the page goes away.

Example: a Scrolling Status Bar Message

One common technique is to use the status bar as a scrolling marquee. The moving text attracts the user's attention, and the fact that it is scrolling means you can use it to display more information than the single line could normally present at one time.

The good news is that this is a really easy one to implement. It just takes a couple of global variables, a few extra lines in your Window OnLoad event, and a timer.

Here's what you do to add this functionality to an existing page. Add a Timer Object ActiveX control to the page. If you already have one or more timer objects on the page, make sure the names don't conflict.

Add these global variables:

```
CurLetter
Marquee
```

Add these lines to the end of your Window's OnLoad event:

```
CurLetter = 1
Marquee = "Hello and welcome to my very cool web page with
a scrolling " & _
   "marquee on the status bar!   "
IeTimer1.enabled = True
```

This assumes your timer's name is IeTimer1, of course. Now use this code in Listing 6-1 of your timer's event.

Listing 6-1: The timer's event to create a scrolling status bar.

```
Dim Show, NumOnEnd

CurLetter = CurLetter + 1
If CurLetter > Len(Marquee) Then CurLetter = 1

NumOnEnd = Len(Marquee) - CurLetter
Show = Right(Marquee, NumOnEnd)
Do Until Len(Show) > 125
    Show = Show & Marquee
Loop
Window.Status = Show
```

CurLetter keeps track of the first letter in the string that will appear in the status bar. Since the idea is to have the text march from right to left, that letter keeps advancing, so the first thing I do is increment CurLetter. By the same token, if CurLetter reaches the end of the Marquee string (that was initialized in the Window's OnLoad event), CurLetter starts over at 1. Then NumOnEnd finds out how many letters are left on the end of the string if you start at CurLetter. Show is assigned that string that starts with CurLetter.

Now, no matter how wide you make the Internet Explorer window, you can only ever display 125 letters on its status bar. If you try to display more than it can show, it just shows what it can. This makes it very easy to create the string that will be displayed. The only trick is that the string has to have at least 125 characters. If it isn't, the entire Marquee string is appended to the end. This is done again and again using the Do Until loop until the string is greater than 125 characters long. This ensures a continuously repeating message, no matter how short or long the message in Marquee is.

Finally, the completed string is assigned to the status bar. You can see the result in Figure 6-6.

Figure 6-6: The scrolling status bar.

The Document Object

The Document object is a property of the Window object, and so it appears below the Window in the object hierarchy. Document represents the web page inside the browser.

Colors, Colors, Colors

You might remember the properties for the <BODY> tag I discussed in Chapter 2 called BGCOLOR, TEXT, LINK, and VLINK. These allowed you to set the background color, the text color, the link color, and the visited link color for the page.

The Document object gives you access to these properties from VBScript. The properties here are called bgColor, fgColor, linkColor, and vLinkColor, which correspond exactly to their <BODY> tag property counterparts.

You can assign a value returned from the RGB function to these properties, or you can assign a string specifying the color name. Both of these lines are valid:

```
Document.bgColor = "Red"
```

```
Document.fgColor = RGB(0,0,130)
```

When an assignment is made to one of these properties, the entire page changes immediately.

Write method

One of the most useful methods in the entire browser object hierarchy is the Document's Write method. Document.Write lets you dynamically use VBScript to create a web page directly from your VBScript. This means that you can change what your page looks like depending on things that are happening at runtime.

For instance, suppose you wanted to create a simple page that provided multilingual support. Take a look at Listing 6-2.

Listing 6-2: The tri-lingual page.

```
<HTML>
<HEAD>
<TITLE>Language</TITLE>
</HEAD>
<BODY>
<SCRIPT LANGUAGE="VBScript">
<!—
Dim Lang

Lang = Prompt("What language do you prefer? Please enter
English, Spanish or French.","English")
If Lang = "Spanish" Then
    Document.Write "<h1>Hola</h1>"
```

```
    Document.Write "<h3>Encantado de conocerte</h3>"
    Document.Write "<h3>Que pasa?</h3>"
ElseIf Lang = "French" Then
    Document.Write "<h1>Bonjour</h1>"
    Document.Write "<h3>Enchante</h3>"
    Document.Write "<h3>Comment allez-vous?</h3>"
Else
    Document.Write "<h1>Hello</h1>"
    Document.Write "<h3>Nice to meet you</h3>"
    Document.Write "<h3>How are you?</h3>"
End If
-->
</SCRIPT>
</BODY>
</HTML>
```

Notice first that nothing is in the body of the HTML except the <SCRIPT> tag and the VBScript code. There is no text and no links.

In the VBScript code, I used Prompt to ask the user for a language preference (see Figure 6-7). Once the user types in a preference, the page is created dynamically using Document.Write. If the user enters **Spanish**, Spanish words greet the user (see Figure 6-8). If the user enters **French**, the corresponding French greeting appears (see Figure 6-9). Finally, any other response results in boring old English (see Figure 6-10).

Figure 6-7: What language do you prefer?

Look at the script again. I want to point out several things. Unlike most of the code in this book, the VBScript code in this example does not appear inside a subroutine, function, or event. This means that the code automatically executes as it loads. This is the *only* time you can do a Document.Write. If you ever see Document.Write in any procedure or event, it is an error because Document.Write can only write information to the page as it is being formed. Once all the HTML is loaded in, the page is fully formed and can't be added to or changed.

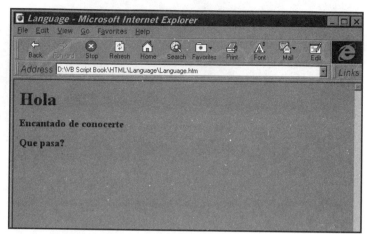

Figure 6-8: The Spanish page.

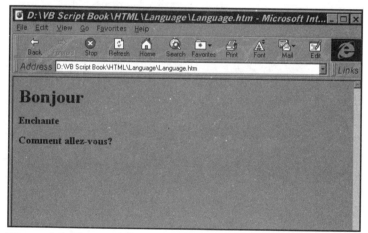

Figure 6-9: The French page.

Another interesting thing about the code is that I included not only text, but also tags. The fact is, you can put *anything* in a Document.Write statement that you could write by hand in your HTML page. All tags are fair game. You can even go so far as to create frames and forms dynamically on your page.

From time to time, you may see another Document method that works like Write. It is called WriteLn, and it takes the text you send and puts it on the web page, just like Write does. The only difference is that WriteLn adds a return at the end of the line. Remember that pressing return when you are entering HTML had no effect. If you want to add a return to the text you are entering, you can include a <br> or <p> tag in the Document.Write string.

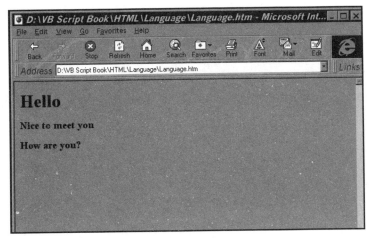

Figure 6-10: The English page.

You'll only see one instance where Write and WriteLn do something different. If you are already inside a <PRE> tag to indicate you are creating preformatted text, WriteLn will cause a real return to appear at the end of the line. <PRE> displays the text just as you enter it.

Example: Date- and Time-Based Greetings

The Date, Time, and Now functions are used to retrieve the current date and time from the user's system clock. Now returns the current date and time from the system clock, Date returns only the date, and Time returns only the time.

In this example I will use these functions in combination with Document.Write to create a friendly greeting for the top of your introductory page. Listing 6-3 shows the page.

Listing 6-3: A date- and time-based greeting introductory page.

```
<HTML>
<HEAD>
<TITLE>My Home Page</TITLE>
</HEAD>
<BODY>
<SCRIPT LANGUAGE="VBScript">
<!—
Option Explicit

Dim WD
```
(continued)

```
(continued)
If Time >= #12:00pm# And Time < #6:00pm# Then
    document.write "<h1>Good Afternoon! Welcome...</h1>"
ElseIf Time >= #6:00pm# And Time < #12:00am# Then
    document.write "<h2>Good Evening! Welcome...</h1>"
ElseIf Time >= #12:00am# And Time < #12:00pm# Then
    document.write "<h2>Good Morning! Welcome...</h1>"
End If

Select Case Weekday(Date)
Case 1
    WD = "Sunday"
Case 2
    WD = "Monday"
Case 3
    WD = "Tuesday"
Case 4
    WD = "Wednesday"
Case 5
    WD = "Thursday"
Case 6
    WD = "Friday"
Case 7
    WD = "Saturday"
End Select

document.write "<h4>Today is " & WD & ", the date is " &
Date & ". "
document.write "It is now approximately " & Time &
".</h4>"

Select Case Date
Case #1/1#
    document.write "<h4>Happy New Year!</h4>"
Case #1/11#
    document.write "<h4>Alexander Hamilton was born today,
1755</h4>"
Case #1/17#
    document.write "<h4>Benjamin Franklin was born today,
1706</h4>"
Case #2/3#
    document.write "<h4>Norman Rockwell was born today,
1894</h4>"
Case #2/14#
    document.write "<h4>Don't forget your
valentine...</h4>"
Case #2/22#
    document.write "<h4>George Washington was born today,
```

```
1732</h4>"
Case #3/3#
    document.write "<h4>Alexander Graham Bell was born
today, 1847</h4>"
Case #4/1#
    document.write "<h4>Beware the April fool...</h4>"
Case #4/18#
    document.write "<h4>Midnight ride of Paul Revere
happened today, 1775</h4>"
Case #5/10#
    document.write "<h4>Golden spike driven to connect
first transcontinental railroad today, 1869</h4>"
Case #6/6#
    document.write "<h4>Today was D-Day, 1944</h4>"
Case #7/4#
    document.write "<h4>Celebrate Independence Day.</h4>"
Case #7/8#
    document.write "<h4>The Liberty Bell was cracked today,
1835.</h4>"
Case #8/1#
    document.write "<h4>Francis Scott Key born today,
1779.</h4>"
Case #9/21#
    document.write "<h4>H.G. Wells was born today,
1866.</h4>"
Case #10/31#
    document.write "<h4>Watch for spooks and ghouls! It's
Halloween!</h4>"
Case #12/25#
    document.write "<h4>Merry Christmas!</h4>"
End Select

->
</SCRIPT>
</BODY>
</HTML>
```

Again, this code appears first in the body and outside of any procedure or
event. First, the Time function is checked to see what range it falls within.
Then, the user is offered a "Good Morning!," "Good Afternoon!," or "Good
Evening!," whichever is appropriate.

The Weekday function is then used in combination with a Select Case,
which fills in the WD variable with the correct day. That day is used in the
following two Document.Writes, which inform the user of the day, date,
and time.

Finally, the bulk of this routine is a giant `Select Case`, which looks at the current date and checks to see if it is significant in any way. I have included most of the major holidays, some birthdays of famous people, and days of important events. You could certainly pick up your own copy of *The Old Farmer's Almanac* and fill in as many days as you like. If this is for a corporate Intranet, you could include important company events and functions you want everyone to know about. The possibilities are endless!

The result looks something like Figure 6-11 (depending on what day it is).

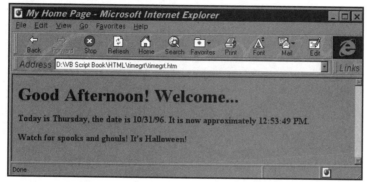

Figure 6-11: The date/time based greeting on Halloween.

If you are interested in seeing more examples putting `Document.Write` to work, see the section titled "Today's Random Picks" in Chapter 10.

The History Object

The Window object and the Document Object are the two most important objects in the browser object hierarchy, but the History object has a few interesting tricks up its sleeve as well.

This History object keeps track of where you've been in your web browser. It is what makes the Back and Forward buttons on Internet Explorer possible.

As you might expect, it offers those same features to you as a VBScript developer: `OHistory.Back` takes you back to the previous page. `History.Forward` takes you forward to the next page you looked at after the current one. Just like the buttons, you can't usually use Forward until you first use Back.

Summary

This chapter has provided you with a quick overview of some of the more interesting properties, methods, and events in the object hierarchy. It is by no means a list of all the cool stuff you can do with them, so feel free to check out Appendix D and start experimenting!

I began with the Window object and showed you its Status property; its `Alert`, `Confirm`, and `Prompt` methods; and then showed you how to change the page displayed in your browser with the Navigate method. Then I discussed the `OnLoad` and `OnUnLoad` events. Finally, I ended this section with an example showing how to create a scrolling message on the status bar.

I then launched into the Document object. I showed you the properties you needed to change the background, foreground, and link colors of your page dynamically and spent a lot of time with `Document.Write`. I ended the section with an example showing how to create date and time-based greetings. I finished up the chapter with the History object's Back and Forward methods.

Advanced Data Handling

Now you are ready to move on to some of VBScript's more advanced features. I assume that you feel completely comfortable with all the commands and concepts I covered in Chapter 4 and by putting them to use in the last couple of chapters, you have learned about all that you can do with the language. As you can see, using only the skills you've gained so far, you can go a long way in making your web site a more exiting place. With the advanced tools I show you in this chapter, you'll go even farther.

If you are in a hurry, you don't have to read every line of this chapter. It is a good idea, however, at least to skim over everything and take a little longer with these sections:

➡ Why You Need Conversion Functions

➡ Converting to a String

➡ Use Conversion Functions Liberally

➡ The Is... Functions

➡ Order of Evaluation

➡ Randomize and Rnd

➡ Working With Objects

The important thing is to know where you can come back if you find you need more detailed information on a specific topic like the conversion, string functions, and dates and times.

Interesting Stuff You Can Do with Variables

In Chapter 4, I introduced you to variables. You can use variables to store user input, you can do math with them, and you can display their contents in a message box or on a web page. In this section, I'll show you how to take total control over your variable data and provide more options in your web programming.

Subtypes and Conversion Functions

Unlike VBScript, most computer languages require that you identify the type of data a variable will hold when you first create the variable. For example, in Visual Basic, you might use this line to create a variable to hold a person's age:

```
Dim Age as integer
```

The variable's type is specified after the word *as*. In this case, it is an integer or a whole number. If later in your program you tried to execute this line:

```
Age = "Fred was here"
```

you would receive an error. Why? Because Visual Basic remembers that this variable was created to hold numbers and you tried to assign a string to it.

Data Types and Variants

In VBScript, all variables have the same data type. It's called a *variant*. A variant-type variable can hold anything: strings, numbers, or boolean values. You can create a variable, assign a string to it in one place, and then later assign a number to it. VBScript doesn't care. It allows you to use, reuse, and abuse variables in whatever way is convenient for you.

This might seem like a more flexible, easy-to-use way of doing things, and it is. Most of the time, you don't have to think about variable types at all. You simply create variables with Dim and use them however you like.

However, programmers generally consider it bad programming practice (or *unstructured programming*) to use variants unless they are absolutely necessary. This is because they can cause confusion, especially when a program becomes long and complicated. Because VBScript doesn't give you the option of declaring a variable's type, you have no choice but to use variants for everything.

Why You Need Conversion Functions

Is this a problem? It doesn't have to be. In the next couple of sections, I'll describe what kinds of problems you can run into when you use variants, and then I'll show you how to avoid those problems by using conversion functions.

Converting Decimal Numbers to Integers

What kind of trouble can you get into with variants? Well, all the way back in Chapter 4 you ran into a problem. You wanted to use the Rnd function to create a dice-rolling program. The problem came in when you found that Rnd returns a number between 0 and 1. Numbers like .423981 and .11384 don't fit on dice very well, so you multiplied the value by 6 and used the Int function to chop away any remaining numbers after the decimal point. Int is a *conversion* function. Conversion functions turn one kind of variable into another kind of variable. In this case, a decimal number into an integer.

Wait just a minute! Didn't I just finish saying that all variables have the *same* data type in VBScript? What are you converting if they are all the same? Well, it turns out that variables have two things: a type and a *subtype*.

A type is what the language enforces, just like when Visual Basic gave an error when "Fred was here" was assigned to a variable that had previously been declared an integer. VBScript doesn't really have any types, or you could say it has only one type: the variant. In any case, it doesn't ever give you an error just because you assigned a particular type of value to a variable.

A subtype, however, is determined by what data you put *into* the variable. The following code shows a different way of approaching the dice-rolling problem:

```
Dim Roll
Roll = Rnd * 6        ' A random number > 0 and < 6
Roll = Int(Roll) + 1
```

Roll, a variant variable (like all variables in VBScript), is created in the first line. In the second line, the value returned from Rnd is multiplied by 6 to create a random number that is greater than 0 and less than 6. At this point, the subtype of Roll is a decimal number. The next line converts the value in Roll into an integer using the Int function. The Int function chops off the numbers after the decimal point. After adding one, an integer is returned and assigned back to Roll. Now, the subtype in Roll is an integer. Its value has been converted.

Converting Strings for Comparison

One other example from Chapter 4 underscores the importance of conversion functions. The code in Listing 7-1 does not work as you might expect.

Listing 7-1: The faulty life calculator.

```
Option Explicit
Dim Life, Age, Left

Age = InputBox("How old are you?")

Life = 78      ' Average life expectancy

If Age > Life Then
    MsgBox("You should be dead!")
Else
    Left = Life - Age
    MsgBox("You have " & Left & " years left. Enjoy them!")
End If
```

As you probably remember from Chapter 4, this program tells you it thinks you should be dead, no matter what age you enter. Why does it do that? Follow it through. After the variables are created, Age is assigned whatever is returned from InputBox. Because InputBox always returns a string, you can be sure that Age now has a string subtype.

Next, Life is assigned a number (or an integer to be precise), so Life's subtype is now an integer.

Then comes the If...Then statement. This is where the problem occurs. Age, which has a subtype string, and Life, which has a subtype integer, are compared. When strings and integers are compared using the comparison operators like < and >, a string is *always* greater than a number. So the "You should be dead!" message box always appears.

To fix this problem, you must convert Age from a string into an integer so that it can be compared correctly, as in Listing 7-2.

Listing 7-2: The correct life calculator.

```
Option Explicit
Dim Life, Age, Left

Age = Int(InputBox("How old are you?"))
```

```
Life = 78      ' Average life expectancy

If Age > Life Then
   MsgBox("You should be dead!")
Else
   Left = Life - Age
   MsgBox("You have " & Left & " years left. Enjoy them!")
End If
```

The value returned from InputBox is immediately sent to the Int function and translated from a string into a number. Now, the comparison works correctly.

These two examples from Chapter 4 used the Int function to convert from a decimal number to an integer and from a string to an integer. You'll probably find that Int is one of the conversion functions you'll use the most, but there are many others. Another one that you'll probably use often is CStr to convert to a string.

Converting to a String

CStr converts variables with a subtype of integer, boolean, or date into a string. You will often use it to put variables in a format that can be shown to the user either through a message box or by assigning the string to an ActiveX label or edit control. This function is essential if you want to concatenate a number with one or more strings. The basic form looks like this:

```
stringvar = CStr(expression)
```

The *stringvar* is a variable that will hold the string returned from the function. The *expression* can be nearly anything. Usually it will be a variable holding a number, boolean, or date. It can also be an expression that evaluates to a number, boolean, or date.

If it is an expression, the expression is completely evaluated and the result is used.

If the result is a number, the number is just turned into a string version of that number.

If the result is a boolean, the string "True" or "False" will be returned.

If the result is a date, a string is created that presents the date in a readable format.

Some functions that expect a string will also accept a variable that holds a number and will automatically convert it. `MsgBox` is an example. Even when this is true, it is often a good idea to go ahead and use `CStr` to make it clear what you intend so that even though this works:

```
Dim x,y,z
x=5
y=19
z=x+y
MsgBox z
```

it is preferable to do this:

```
Dim x,y,z
x=5
y=19
z=x+y
MsgBox CStr(z)
```

 Another function in Visual Basic (not VBScript) that is commonly used to convert numbers to strings is called `Str`. If you ever look at a Visual Basic application, you are very liklely to see it. VBScript does not support `Str`. You wouldn't want to use it anyway because it doesn't do as good a job at conversions as `CStr`.

Converting to a Number

Unfortunately, VBScript does not provide a CNumber function that converts anything else to a number. Instead, it divides that functionality up into several different functions that can be divided into integer and decimal functions.

Integer Functions

What is an integer? A variable with an integer subtype holds a whole number, meaning that it doesn't have a fractional or decimal part. The numbers 3, 7, and 14 are integers. The numbers 3.14, 7.5, and 1.1 are not.

Four functions allow you to convert other subtypes to integers: `Int`, `Fix`, `CInt`, and `CLng`. Their basic forms look like this:

```
intvar = Int(expression)
```

```
intvar = Fix(expression)
```

```
intvar = CInt(expression)
```

```
intvar = CLng(expression)
```

The *intvar* is a variable that will hold the integer returned from the function. The *expression* is a string or a number that is to be converted to an integer subtype.

When converting a string to a number, they all work more or less the same. The differences come in when they are converting numbers with decimal parts into integers.

You might remember that in Chapter 4 I introduced you to Int. Like all of these functions, it takes a string or a noninteger number (a number with a decimal part) and returns an integer.

Int accomplishes this goal in the simplest possible way: it takes any fractional part and simply chops it off. This is the brute-force approach. Don't like numbers after the decimal point? Fine, lop them off. The number 8.9 becomes 8, and the number 2.1 becomes 2. Easy.

Fix also uses the meat-cleaver approach: referred to by more civilized folks as *truncation*. The difference is in how Int and Fix deal with negative numbers. Int returns the first negative number that is *less than* the value. Whereas Fix returns the first negative number that is *greater than* the value.

So for -3.7 Int would return -4 because it is the first integer less than -3.7. Fix would return -3 because it is the first integer greater than -3.7. Int and Fix only differ in how they deal with negative numbers. They both work exactly the same with positive numbers.

CInt is a more sophisticated function. Instead of simply lopping off the fractional numbers in one way or another, it rounds the number to the nearest whole number. So 8.9 is rounded to 9 and 2.1 is rounded to 2.

You might be wondering how CInt rounds numbers like 3.5 where the fractional part is exactly between the two whole numbers. The answer is a bit strange.

In math class, you were told that these numbers always round up. So 3.5 rounds to 4 and 14.5 rounds to 15. This is not the way CInt does it.

CInt rounds .5 numbers to the nearest even number. So 3.5 rounds to 4 and 14.5 rounds to 14. Why? I honestly don't know.

Table 7-1 provides many examples and then shows how each function would convert the fractional numbers to integers.

Table 7-1 Examples of How the Various Integer Functions Convert Fractional Numbers to Whole Numbers				
Original Number	Int	Fix	CInt	**Comment**
3.14	3	3	3	Int and Fix are always the same for positives
4.7	4	4	5	CInt rounds to the closest integer
-1	-1	-1	-1	
-3.7	-3	-4	-4	Int truncates up, and Fix truncates down
-4.2	-4	-5	-4	But CInt always rounds
4.5	4	4	4	For .5 numbers CInt rounds to the nearest even
1.5	1	1	2	

The last function to discuss is CLng, which converts the string or number into the subtype long. Long is another whole number subtype like integer. The difference is that a long variable can hold much larger numbers than integers can. In general, an integer can hold any value between about – 32,000 and 32,000. If you need something bigger than that, the long will probably handle it.

One other integer-conversion function is called CByte, which is like a smaller version of CInt. It converts the value to subtype byte, which is an integer between 0 and 255. A byte variable takes up less memory space than an integer, but it usually isn't enough to worry about. You probably won't need to use CByte for your web page applications.

Decimal Functions

A decimal number has a decimal point and numbers after the decimal point. They can also be called *fractional numbers*.

Two decimal functions allow you to convert strings or numbers into numbers that have a fractional part: CSng and CDbl. Their general forms look like this:

```
sngvar = CSng(expression)
```

```
dblvar = CDbl(expression)
```

In this case, *sngvar* represents a variable that will hold the single value returned from CSng, and *dblvar* represents a variable that will hold the double value returned from CDbl. The *expression* is, again, a string or number to be converted.

CSng converts a string or number into a variable with the subtype single. Single is short for *single-precision number*. (That certainly makes everything clear, doesn't it!) This just means that this number can hold normal size numbers that include fractional parts, like 3.1416, 2.79, and 9.5.

CDbl converts a string or number into a variable with the subtype double, which stands for (you guessed it!) *double-precision number*. The difference is similar to the difference between an integer and a long. A double can hold much bigger numbers than a single can. A double can also hold numbers that have a lot more digits after the decimal place. That's where the precision part comes in. If you have more numbers after the decimal place, it is more precise. Unless you are doing heavy-duty scientific measurements or something like that, a single will usually do everything you need.

 Another function in Visual Basic (not VBScript) that is commonly used to convert strings to numbers is called Val. Again, if you ever look at a Visual Basic application, you'd be very likely to see it, but VBScript does not support it.

It's All So Confusing! Just Tell Me Which Function to use!

You seem to have way too many functions to choose from when you are converting to a number. Which should you use?

If you are just working with whole numbers and you want to convert a string (say from an ActiveX edit control or InputBox), it doesn't matter whether you use Int, CInt, or Fix. You'll most commonly see developers use Int in these circumstances, though. That's why I went ahead and showed that one to you in Chapter 4.

If you are converting a decimal number into an integer, you have to decide if you care how it is done. Is it OK if the fractional part is just cut off? If so, Int or Fix work great. If not, you can use CInt to round the number to the closest integer. Use CLng only if you are working with very large numbers.

On the other hand, if you want to preserve the fractional part, you will probably want to use the CSng function to convert the string or number to a single-precision variable. Use CDbl only if you are working with numbers that have a lot of digits after the decimal point.

Converting to a Boolean

A boolean subtype holds the values True and False. You can convert a string or number into a boolean with the CBool function. Its general form looks like this:

```
boolvar = CBool(expression)
```

The *boolvar* is a variable that will hold the boolean value (True or False) that is returned from the function. The *expression* is a string or number to be converted.

This function is very simple. If the expression evaluates to 0, CBool will return False. If it evaluates to any other number, it returns True. If it cannot be evaluated as a number, it will generate a Type Mismatch error when the code executes in your web page. Here are some examples:

```
Dim x
x = CBool(7)
MsgBox(CStr(x))
```

Displays True.

```
Dim x
x = CBool("3.5")
MsgBox(CStr(x))
```

Displays True.

```
Dim x
x = CBool("0")
MsgBox(CStr(x))
```

Displays False.

```
Dim x
x = CBool("Fred")
MsgBox(CStr(x))
```

Causes a Type Mismatch error on the second line.

Converting to Dates and Times

One subtype is specifically designed to hold dates and time: the date subtype. You might expect that there would be a date subtype and a time subtype, but that isn't how it works. The date subtype holds both a date and a time. For a given variable, you may only use the date portion or you might only use the time portion, but you can use both.

Assigning and Comparing Date Subtype Variables

To assign a date to a variable so that it will be held as a `date` subtype, you must surround your date with *hash marks* (#), also called *pound signs*:

```
Dim Birthday
Birthday = #10/5/67#
```

The hash marks work just like quote marks surrounding a string: they tell VBScript to store the information as a date and/or time in a date subtype.

This is also the syntax you use if you want to compare a date in an `If...Then` statement:

```
If Birthday > #1/1/65# Then MsgBox("You are x-gen.")
```

The CDate Function

To convert a number or string into a date subtype, you use the CDate function. Its general form looks like this:

```
datevar = CDate(expression)
```

The *datevar* is a variable that will hold the date returned from `CDate`. The *expression* is a numeric or string variable or expression to be converted.

`CDate` is essential if you'll be obtaining dates from the user and then using the dates, especially if you want to compare dates using the =, ,, and > signs. If you try to compare two strings that hold dates, VBScript will compare them like it does any other strings: in alphabetical order. That doesn't always work for dates. For instance, if you are using strings:

```
"5/1/96" > "10/1/96"
```

However, if you are using variables with the date subtype:

```
#5/1/96# < #10/1/96#
```

So always be sure to convert a string holding a date into a variable with a date subtype using the `CDate` function as quickly as possible.

Converting Numbers to Dates

You might be curious how a number like 3.2 would be translated into a date. I know I was. To experiment, I created an HTML page with one button on it that had the ID `Test1Button`. The code in Listing 7-3 responds when the user clicks the button.

Listing 7-3: A test to see how CDate responds.

```
Sub Test1Button_Click()
Dim UserString, UserDate

UserString = InputBox("What would you like to convert to a
date?")
UserDate = CDate(UserString)
MsgBox CStr(UserDate)
End Sub
```

Sending "3.5" has exactly the same effect as sending the number 3.5, so this little application will allow you to test all the possibilities. Table 7-2 shows some of my results.

Table 7-2	Number Date Tests
Entered	**Result**
3.5	3:05:00 AM
13.25	1:23:00 PM
25.2	1/24/1900 4:48:00 AM
100.5	4/9/1900 12:00:00 PM
7	1/6/1900

If you enter a small number and a decimal portion, the number is interpreted as hours and minutes. If the number on the left of the decimal becomes greater than 12, it is assumed to be PM.

However, if the number on the left becomes greater than 24, the whole thing changes. The number on the left of the decimal is interpreted as the number of days after January 1, 1900. The number to the right of the decimal is the time, represented as a fraction of the day. If you enter a whole number, it is interpreted as the number of days after January 1, 1900.

I don't know why you'd ever use this capability, but it is interesting.

Converting Strings to Dates

What you are likely to do, though, is to convert a date from a string the user enters into a real date subtype. How does that work? Quite easily. Using the same program described in Listing 7-3, I tried some string-like dates. Table 7-3 presents the results.

Table 7-3	Date String Tests
Entered	**Result**
12/17/91	12/17/91
January 5	1/5/96
5-22	5/22/97
22 June	6/22/97
13/1	1/13/97

This time it is much more straightforward. You can enter the date in one of the many formats that `CDate` understands, and it converts that entry to the standard date format. If you don't specify the year, it assumes *this* year. This is a very handy capability. Often, you don't want to constrain your users or force them to enter a date in exactly the right way. Using `CDate`, your application can be very robust and forgiving and still end up working with one standard format.

Converting Strings to Times

What about times, though? Table 7-4 shows some more tests I tried.

Table 7-4	Time String Tests
Entered	**Result**
3:00	3:00:00 AM
10:52	10:52:00 AM
15:05	3:05:00 PM
3:05:55	3:05:55 AM
2 PM	2:00:00 PM
13pm	1:00:00 PM
17am	5:00:00 PM

You can specify AM or PM by including the letters in your string. If the hour given is greater than 12, it will be PM no matter what you specify. Again, this allows for a lot of flexibility in accepting user input of times.

 Be sure to do a Refresh in your browser after you see a Type Mismatch error. Once an error is displayed, the browser stops displaying any further errors on that page until you do another Refresh.

Stuff That Doesn't Work

I've shown you a variety of things that do work. Now, Table 7-5 shows you some entries that don't work.

Table 7-5	Stuff That Doesn't Work
Entered	**Result**
Today	Type Mismatch error
Yesterday	Type Mismatch error
Now	Type Mismatch error
30/30	Type Mismatch error
25:20	Type Mismatch error
32pm	Type Mismatch error
pm	Type Mismatch error

The DateValue and TimeValue Functions

The `DateValue` and `TimeValue` functions convert strings and numbers into dates or times. Their general form appears here:

```
datevar = DateValue(expression)
datevar = TimeValue(expression)
```

The *datevar* is a variable that will be assigned the value returned from either `DateValue` or `TimeValue` and will have the subtype date. The *expression* argument can be either a string or a number that represents a date.

These functions do the same thing as `CDate`, but each works with only one part of the date subtype: either the date or the time. `CDate` can work on either or both. Because of this, you probably won't need to use these functions very often.

Use Conversion Functions Liberally

I'd like to drive home one last point about conversion functions: use them liberally. Don't think that you should only use them when your code won't work without them. Use them throughout your code whenever you use a variable in a different way, even when VBScript would probably do the conversion for you automatically. Why? Because it keeps your code clear, and it helps you avoid some of the tricky problems that can occur when you thought VBScript would handle it but didn't. In short, making your code *self-documenting* helps. Programmers use the term *self-documenting* to refer to code that is used just to make things clearer, not necessarily to affect the way it works.

Here are some examples of places where you should use conversion functions:

➥ When you ask the user to enter a number into an ActiveX edit control, the Text property of the control is a string. Convert it to a number right away and then use it as a number. The same applies to information returned to you from an InputBox function.

➥ When you do math or compare two variables where one is a string and one is a number, always convert one of them to match the other, and always use + for addition only. When you want to concatenate strings, use &.

➥ When the user enters a date or a time, convert it from a string to a date subtype. This helps standardize its format and standardize the way you access it. Also, when you assign or compare a date, always use the hash marks (#) to set the date off, like you would use quotes around a string.

➥ When you have a number that has a decimal part but the user doesn't care to see that kind of detail, use Int or CInt to truncate or round the number to an integer.

Checking the Subtype

In the last section, I spent a lot of time describing what each subtype was and how you could convert other subtypes to it, but often, you need to find out more information about a variable before you attempt to convert it. Look at the example in Listing 7-4.

Listing 7-4: Are you X-Gen or Boomer?

```
Dim UserAge
UserAge = InputBox("Enter your birth date:")
If CDate(UserAge) > #1/1/65# Then
    MsgBox("You are definitely a member of the X-
Generation.")
Else
    MsgBox("Boomer Alert! Boomer Alert!")
End If
```

This code looks fine, and it works if the user enters a valid date for his or her birthday. If the user doesn't, the program will crash and display a Type Mismatch error. Because that isn't very user-friendly, you should try to find out if the date is valid before you use it. How do you do it? With an Is... function: IsDate, to be specific. Listing 7-5 shows the much more user-friendly Version 2.

Listing 7-5: Version 2 of X-Gen versus Boomer?

```
Dim UserAge
UserAge = InputBox("Enter your birth date:")
Do Until IsDate(UserAge)
  UserAge = InputBox("Please enter a valid date:")
Loop
If CDate(UserAge) > #1/1/65# Then
    MsgBox("You are definitely a member of the X-
Generation.")
Else
    MsgBox("Boomer Alert! Boomer Alert!")
End If
```

This program won't ever crash with a Type Mismatch because the value entered is checked at the top of the Do Until loop. IsDate returns a boolean value (True or False) indicating whether the string passed can be converted to a valid date. If it can't, the InputBox inside the loop executes. If another bad date is entered, the loop continues. When a valid date is finally entered, it is converted and compared, and the correct message box is displayed. If a valid date is entered the first time, the condition at the top of the loop fails, and the entire loop is skipped.

As you can see, the IsDate function can be pretty handy. In the next section, I'll describe all the Is... functions in more detail.

The Is... Functions

There are six Is... functions: IsNumeric, IsDate, IsArray, IsEmpty, IsNull, and IsObject. This is the general form for each of them:

```
boolvar = IsNumeric(expression)
boolvar = IsDate(expression)
boolvar = IsArray(expression)
boolvar = IsEmpty(expression)
boolvar = IsNull(expression)
boolvar = IsObject(expression)
```

The *boolvar* in each case represents a variable that will hold the boolean value returned from the function. The *expression* in each case represents a variable or expression that is to be evaluated by the Is... function.

These functions share many things in common. They all accept one expression as an argument, and they evaluate that expression. If the expression meets the requirements of the function, True is returned; otherwise, False is returned.

IsNumeric checks to see whether the argument sent is numeric or could be converted to a numeric value.

IsDate checks to see whether the argument is a date or time or if it could be converted to a date or time.

IsArray determines whether the expression is an array. For more on arrays, see Chapter 9.

IsEmpty checks to see whether the variable is empty. A variable is usually only empty after it has been created but before any value has been assigned to it. You can think of empty variables as not yet having a subtype.

IsNull checks for a specific value called Null. Null is not the same as 0. It is a special value that is often used in database programming. You probably won't use it much.

IsObject checks to see whether the expression refers to an object. For more on objects see the section titled "Working With Objects" later in this chapter.

VarType

VarType is a function you can use when you have no idea what a particular variable's subtype is and you want VBScript to tell you. Its general form looks like this:

```
intvar = VarType(varname)
```

The *intvar* is the variable that will hold a number indicating what subtype the variable is. The *varname* argument is the name of the variable to check. Notice that this argument expects a variable, not an expression.

Table 7-6 lists the values VarType returns and what they mean.

VarType can return one other kind of value. If the value returned is greater than 8,192, it indicates that the variable is an array. To find out what type of array, subtract 8,192 from the value returned and look up the result on the previous table. For instance, if 8,199 was returned, you know that the variable is an array of dates (8192 + 7). If it is an array of variants, 8,204 (8,192 + 12) will be returned. For more information on arrays see Chapter 9.

Table 7-6 The Values Returned by VarType and Their Meanings	
Value	Meaning
0	Empty: the variable has probably not been initialized
1	Null
2	Integer
3	Long integer
4	Single
5	Double
6	Currency (not used in VBScript)
7	Date
8	String
9	OLE Automation object
10	Error
11	Boolean
12	Variant (used only with variant arrays)
13	Other types of objects
17	Byte

String Functions

Strings are used for so many things that it is important to have a lot of tools to work on them, and VBScript won't fail you here. In this section, I'll describe the variety of functions available to manipulate strings, chop them up, and stick them back together again.

UCase and LCase

UCase and LCase force all the letters in a string to uppercase or lowercase. Their general forms look like this:

```
newstring = UCase(oldstring)
newstring = LCase(oldstring)
```

The *newstring* is a variable that will hold the string that has been changed to all uppercase or all lowercase (depending on the function called). The *oldstring* indicates the string passed as an argument. Notice that *oldstring* is *not* changed. The string that is in all upper- or all lowercase ends up in *newstring* leaving *oldstring* alone.

If you want to change a string without using another variable, though, you can do this:

```
Dim MyName
MyName = "Fred"
MyName = LCase(MyName)
```

Here, MyName is both the argument and the variable that receives the value back. The original value is what is sent ("Fred", in this case), and the new value is assigned to MyName when the function returns ("fred").

Why would you use UCase or LCase? One really common reason to use them is to make dealing with user input easier. Look at the code in Listing 7-6.

Listing 7-6: Checking user input, the hard way.

```
Dim Happy
Happy = InputBox("Are you happy with your life?")
If Happy = "yes" or Happy = "YES" or Happy = "Yes" Then
    MsgBox("Good for you!")
Else
    MsgBox("That's too bad. Keep your chin up!")
End If
```

Although your web pages don't usually pose philosophical questions, they do often need to interpret user input like this. If you only check for "yes", you will misinterpret the response if the user happens to have the Caps Lock key pressed, so you have to check all of the possibilities. You could do it another way. See Listing 7-7.

Listing 7-7: Checking user input, the easy way.

```
Dim Happy
Happy = InputBox("Are you happy with your life?")
If UCase(Happy) = "YES" Then
    MsgBox("Good for you!")
Else
    MsgBox("That's too bad. Keep your chin up!")
End If
```

Now it doesn't matter if the user typed **yes**, **YES**, **Yes**, or even **yEs**: your web page will interpret it correctly.

LTrim, RTrim, and Trim

When you are trying to understand what users typed, you can also be thrown when they add spaces to the beginning or the end of their input. They don't think anything about extra spaces, but if you compare *yes* with *_yes*, they won't match! That's where LTrim, RTrim, and Trim come into play. They trim any spaces from the beginning (LTrim), end (RTrim), or both (Trim). Their general forms look like this:

```
newstring = LTrim(oldstring)
newstring = RTrim(oldstring)
newstring = Trim(oldstring)
```

The *newstring* is a variable that will hold the string that has had its spaces removed. The *oldstring* indicates the string passed as an argument. Again, just as with UCase and LCase, *oldstring* is *not* changed. The string that is changed ends up in *newstring* leaving *oldstring* alone, but again, just like UCase and LCase, you can use the same variable in both places.

Listing 7-8 shows the same code used in Listing 7-7 with a Trim added to make the user input even more bulletproof.

Listing 7-8 Checking user input, even better.
```
Dim Happy
Happy = InputBox("Are you happy with your life?")
If Trim(UCase(Happy)) = "YES" Then
    MsgBox("Good for you!")
Else
    MsgBox("That's too bad. Keep your chin up!")
End If
```

You might be surprised to see a function call inside of another function call. Can you do that? Yep. The inner one is called first, and whatever is returned from it is used as the argument to the outer one. In this case, the Happy variable is converted to all uppercase, and the value returned is trimmed of spaces on both sides. The result of that is compared to "YES". Now users can type ___yeS, YEs___, or ____yes___, and it will still be interpreted correctly.

String and Space

String and Space produce long strings filled with characters. The general form for String looks like this:

```
strvar = String(num, char)
```

The *strvar* is a variable that is assigned a string filled with *num* number of *char* characters. An example will make this clearer:

```
Dim Stars
Stars = String(15,"*")
MsgBox(Stars)
```

The message box would display *×15. String generates a string with a character repeated the number of times specified.

Space is like a simplified version of String that allows you to create a string with a specified number of spaces in it. This is its general form:

```
strvar = Space(num)
```

The *strvar* is a variable that is assigned a string filled with *num* number of spaces.

StrComp

StrComp accepts two strings as arguments and returns a value indicating whether one string is less than, equal to, or greater than the other. The general form looks like this:

```
intresult = StrComp(string1, string2[, casesens])
```

If *string1* > *string2*, the value returned into *intresult* is 1.

If *string1* = *string2*, the value returned into *intresult* is 0.

If *string1* < *string2*, the value returned into *intresult* is -1.

If *casesens* is 1, the comparison will be *case-insensitive*: it will ignore whether the letters are upper- or lowercase. The default for *casesens* is 0, which means that the letter's case will be considered in the comparison.

Of course, most of the time when you want to compare strings, you'll simply use the comparison operators like this:

```
If string1 > string2 Then...
```

This works just fine. StrComp is only offered for convenience. Sometimes it is easier to use StrComp than to use the normal comparison operators when you are doing a lot of comparisons or if you are keeping track of the results from a lot of comparisons. For instance, you might use StrComp if you were writing a routine to sort numbers or strings or to search quickly through a large list of sorted numbers or strings.

Len

Len gives you the length (number of characters) in a string. Its general form looks like this:

```
intvar = Len(strvar)
```

The *intvar* is the variable that will receive the value returned indicating how many characters are in the string. The *strvar* is the string being evaluated.

Listing 7-9 shows an example of Len at work.

Listing 7-9: How long is your name?

```
Dim FullName
FullName = InputBox("Please enter your full name.")
If Len(FullName) > 14 Then
    MsgBox("My, what a long name you have...")
End If
```

After the user enters his or her name, its length is checked. If the name's length is longer than 14 letters, the message box informs the user of the obvious.

For a more real-world example, see the next section titled "Len, Left, Right, Mid, and InStr Examples" later in this chapter. Len is often used in conjunction with these functions.

Left, Right, and Mid

Left, Right, and Mid are key string handling functions. They allow you to do surgery on a string and tear it apart. Their general forms look like this:

```
newstr = Left(oldstr, num)
newstr = Right(oldstr, num)
newstr = Mid(oldstr, loc, num)
```

Left takes a number of characters from the left side of the string and uses them to create a new string. (See Listing 7-10.)

Listing 7-10: Left is used to extract the first name.

```
Dim FullName, FirstName
FullName = "William Allen Hatfield"
FirstName = Left(FullName, 7)
MsgBox(FirstName)
```

After the variables are declared and `FullName` is assigned, `Left` is called with the `FullName` and 7 as arguments. `Left` takes the first seven characters of `FullName`, creates a new string with them, and returns the new string. The new string is assigned to `FirstName` and displayed in a message box.

The message box would display `William`.

Right does the exact same thing for the right-hand side of the string. (See Listing 7-11.)

Listing 7-11: Left and Right extract the first and last names.

```
Dim FullName, FirstName, LastName
FullName = "William Allen Hatfield"
FirstName = Left(FullName, 7)
LastName = Right(FullName, 8)
MsgBox(LastName & ", " & FirstName)
```

This listing is the same as 7-10 except that now the last name is extracted using the `Right` function and both are displayed in the message box.

The message box would display `Hatfield, William`.

`Mid` allows you to create a string from anywhere inside another string. It takes three arguments: the string to start with, the location of the first character (counting from the left), and the number of characters to use. Listing 7-12 extracts the middle name.

Listing 7-12: Left, Right, and Mid extract the first, middle, and last names.

```
Dim FullName, FirstName, LastName, MiddleName
FullName = "William Allen Hatfield"
FirstName = Left(FullName, 7)
LastName = Right(FullName, 8)
MiddleName = Mid(FullName, 9, 5)
MsgBox(LastName & ", " & FirstName & " " & MiddleName)
```

MiddleName is assigned a string created by the Mid function. The string was created by taking starting with the ninth character and pulling off five characters total.

The message box displays Hatfield, William Allen.

InStr

InStr is probably the most handy string handling function you'll use. It makes it easy to find a bit of text within a string. Here's the general form:

```
pos = InStr([start, ]searchedstr, strtofind[, casesens])
```

This one will take a little more explaining. The *pos* is a variable that will hold the position where *strtofind* was found within *searchedstr*. The *start* argument is optional and specifies a character position within *searchedstr* to begin searching. If you don't specify start, it will start at the first character of *searchedstr*. The *casesens* argument is also optional. The default is 0, and with that it looks for an exact match. If you specify a 1 for *casesens*, it will do a *case-insensitive* search. In other words, it will ignore whether letters are in upper- or lowercase and just look for text that matches. If *strtofind* is not found within *searchedstr*, the value returned from InStr is 0.

One more thing to keep in mind: both *start* and *casesens* are optional. However, if you specify *casesens*, you *must* also specify *start*. You can, however specify *start* without *casesens*. I know this is confusing, and I don't know why it works this way, but the upshot is that these are the valid forms:

```
pos = InStr(start, searchedstr, strtofind, casesens)
pos = InStr(start, searchedstr, strtofind)
pos = InStr(searchedstr, strtofind)
```

If you want to make the search case-insensitive but you still want to start at the beginning, just use a 1 for *start* and then a 1 for *casesens*.

Let me show you some examples to make it clear. If you simply want to see if a bit of text can be found in a string, you can check to see if InStr is greater than 0. (See Listing 7-13.)

Listing 7-13: Sharing common interests?

```
Dim Leisure
Leisure = InputBox("What you enjoy doing in your leisure
time?")
If InStr(1, Leisure, "golf", 1) > 0 Then
```

```
    MsgBox("I like golf, too.")
Else
    MsgBox("Really. How nice. I had a cousin who did that
once.")
End If
```

If the user enters any of these strings, the first message box will be displayed:

```
I like golf.
Golf is my favorite thing to do after work.
Well, first of all, I really hate golf.
```

Of course the last one would make the conversation strange, but because the word was found, InStr will be greater than 0. Notice that I used the *casesens* optional argument. That made it possible to match on the second example as well as the other two. The capitalization is ignored, but, again, because I specified *casesens*, I had to specify *start*. Therefore, I just used 1 so that it would begin looking from the first letter.

Len, Left, Right, Mid, and InStr Examples

In this section, I'll show you some examples that use the most common string handling functions: Len, Left, Right, Mid, and InStr. After reading the last few sections, you should be familiar with their basic features, but I thought a few bigger examples might help you see how they can work together to accomplish a goal.

In the previous section titled "Left, Right, and Mid," I used an example that chopped up a full name into the first, middle, and last names. The problem is that I used hard-coded numbers to chop it up. The examples I'll show you in this section begin to create a more generalized solution that will find the first, middle, and last names for any full name that the user enters.

Listing 7-14 begins by finding the first name when a user types in a first and last name.

Listing 7-14: Find the first name.

```
Dim FirstLast, SpaceLoc, First
FirstLast = InputBox("Enter your first and last name.")
SpaceLoc = InStr(FirstLast," ")
If SpaceLoc > 0 Then
    First = Left(FirstLast, SpaceLoc - 1)
    MsgBox("Hello, " & First)
End If
```

After putting the full name into the `FirstLast` variable, `InStr` is executed to find the first space in the string. An `If...Then` checks to be sure there is a space in the string before executing the rest of the code. A `Left` function creates a new string from the first few characters of `FirstLast`. `SpaceLoc`, the result of the `InStr`, finds everything up to, but not including, the space (thus the - 1). This is the first name. Then, I can greet the user on a first-name basis.

Could you extend this to find the last name, too? Of course you could! Take a look at Listing 7-15.

Listing 7-15: Find the first and last name.

```
Dim FirstLast, SpaceLoc, First, Last, BeginLast, LastLen
FirstLast = InputBox("Enter your first and last name.")
SpaceLoc = InStr(FirstLast," ")
If SpaceLoc > 0 Then
    First = Left(FirstLast, SpaceLoc - 1)
    LastLen = Len(FirstLast) - SpaceLoc + 1
    Last = Right(FirstLast, LastLen)
    MsgBox("Hello, " & First)
    MsgBox(Last & " is a very nice last name.")
End If
```

This example just adds a few lines to the first example. It finds the location of the space and uses `Left` to extract the first name, just as the first one did. Then a couple of new variables are initialized. `LastLen` is the length of the last name, which is found by using `Len` to find the length of the entire string and then subtracting out the location of the space, plus one (so that the space, too, is subtracted out). Then `Last` is found by using the `Right` function to find the characters at the end that represent the last name. I use `LastLen` to give `Right` the number of letters in the last name.

Finally, the user is greeted and complemented on his or her last name.

As you can see, this all can get a little complicated, but I'm sure that these functions will never fail you. You can do surprisingly complex string manipulation with these tools.

But are they good enough to find the first, last, and middle name? Sure. Take a look at Listing 7-16.

Listing 7-16: Find the first, middle, and last name.

```
Dim FullName, Space1Loc, Space2Loc
Dim First, Last, Middle
```

```
Dim BeginMid, LenMid, BeginLast, LenLast

FullName = InputBox("Enter your first, middle and last
name.")
Space1Loc = InStr(FullName," ")
Space2Loc = InStr(Space1Loc+1,FullName," ")

If Space1Loc > 0 and Space2Loc > 0 Then
    First = Left(FullName, Space1Loc - 1)

    BeginLast = Space2Loc + 1
    LenLast = Len(FullName) - Space2Loc
    Last = Mid(FullName, BeginLast, LenLast)

    BeginMid = Space1Loc + 1
    LenMid = Len(FullName) - Space1Loc - LenLast - 1
    Middle = Mid(FullName, BeginMid, LenMid)

    MsgBox("First: " & First & "; Middle: " & Middle & ";
Last: " & Last)
End If
```

This time I find the first two spaces: the one between the first and middle name and the one between the middle and last name. Notice that I begin the search for the second space on the character after the first space. I then verify that both space locations are greater than zero.

The first name is easy. Its length is one less than the first space's location. I tackled the last name next. It begins on the character after the second space. Its length is the length of the string minus everything before the second space (including the space). After determining the location and the length, a simple Mid pulls it right out.

Finally, the middle name is the tricky one. It begins on the character after the first space. Its length is the length of the string minus everything before the first space (including the space), and also minus the length of the last name. The -1 subtracts out the space between the middle name and the last name. Whew! Now its just a simple Mid function to pull it out.

The message box gives up on the silly greetings and simply displays each variable labeled for what it is.

Date and Time Functions

VBScript has a rich variety of features for dealing with dates and times. In this section, you'll learn all about the date time functions and what they can do for you.

Date, Time, and Now

Date, Time, and Now all return the system clock's current information. Their general form looks like this:

```
datevar = Date
datevar = Time
datevar = Now
```

They don't take any arguments. Date returns the current date, Time returns the current time, and Now returns the current date and time. The *datevar* is a variable with a date subtype that will receive the result returned from the funtions. You'll recall from the discussion earlier in this chapter in the section titled "Converting to Dates and Times" that a date subtype holds both a date and a time, even though you may only use one or the other.

Remember that these functions pull their information from the machine they are running on, so if you use them in your web page, they will pull their information from the client machine where the user's browser is running. They will not pull their information from the web server. For an example, see the next section.

Day, Month, Year, Hour, Minute, and Second

Day, Month, Year, Hour, Minute, and Second allow you to access these six individual parts of a date variable individually. These are their general forms:

```
intvar = Day(datevar)
intvar = Month(datevar)
intvar = Year(datevar)
intvar = Hour(datevar)
intvar = Minute(datevar)
intvar = Second(datevar)
```

The *intvar* is a variable that will hold an integer returned from each function. This value will be the component of the date or time that the function is intended to extract. The *datevar* argument is a variable with a subtype of date. Listing 7-17 shows an example using Now along with these functions.

Listing 7-17 Greeting with a fancy date notice.

```
Dim CurDate, ThisDay, ThisMonth, ThisYear
CurDate = Date
ThisDay = Day(CurDate)
ThisMonth = Month(CurDate)
ThisYear = Year(CurDate)
MsgBox("Greetings on this " & CStr(ThisDay) & "th day of
the " & _
    CStr(ThisMonth) & "th month in the year of our Lord " &
CStr(ThisYear))
```

This is the kind of thing you'll see in the message box:

```
Greetings on this 9th day of the 9th month in the year of
our Lord 1997.
Greetings on this 20th day of the 12th month in the year
of our Lord 1998
```

Of course, if you catch it on a bad day, it could stumble:

```
Greetings on this 1th day of the 1th month in the year of
our Lord 1999
```

But nothing's perfect, I suppose.

Weekday

Weekday is an easy way to find out what day of the week a particular date falls on. Its general form looks like this:

```
intvar = Weekday(datevar)
```

When passed *datevar*, a variable with a date subtype, Weekday returns into *intvar*, a number indicating what day of the week it is. The number it returns corresponds to the days of the week as described in Table 7-7.

Table 7-7 Values Returned from Weekday **and the Day of the Week They Correspond to**

Returned	Day of Week
1	Sunday
2	Monday
3	Tuesday
4	Wednesday
5	Thursday
6	Friday
7	Saturday

Listing 7-18 shows an example.

Listing 7-18: What day is it?

```
Dim ThisWeekday, ThisDate
ThisDate = Date
ThisWeekday = Weekday(ThisDate)
Select Case ThisWeekday
Case 1
    MsgBox("Today is Sunday")
Case 2
    MsgBox("Today is Monday")
Case 3
    MsgBox("Today is Tuesday")
Case 4
    MsgBox("Today is Wednesday")
Case 5
    MsgBox("Today is Thursday")
Case 6
    MsgBox("Today is Friday")
Case 7
    MsgBox("Today is Saturday")
End Select
```

Most of the time if you need to use Weekday, you can use it just as I described, but I didn't mention one other optional argument. The actual form of Weekday looks like this:

```
intvar = Weekday(datevar[, startday])
```

The startday argument allows you to specify a different starting day of the week. That is, instead of the week starting on Sunday, as it does on most calendars, you could create a workweek calendar that started on Monday and make Saturday and Sunday the last two days of the week. To do this, you'd just call the function this way:

```
ThisWeekday = Weekday(ThisDate, 2)
```

The value 2 for the second argument indicates that you want Monday (normally the second day) to be considered the first day. Then, when you interpret the day coming back from the Weekday function, you have to take this into account. If it is Tuesday, the Weekday function will return 2 because Tuesday is the second day of our workweek calendar. If today were Sunday, Weekday would return 7. Listing 7-18 would have to be modified to look like Listing 7-19 to work with this new calendar.

Listing 7-19: What day is it on the new workweek calendar that begins on Monday?

```
Dim ThisWeekday, ThisDate
ThisDate = Date
ThisWeekday = Weekday(ThisDate, 2)
Select Case ThisWeekday
Case 1
    MsgBox("Today is Monday")
Case 2
    MsgBox("Today is Tuesday")
Case 3
    MsgBox("Today is Wednesday")
Case 4
    MsgBox("Today is Thursday")
Case 5
    MsgBox("Today is Friday")
Case 6
    MsgBox("Today is Saturday")
Case 7
    MsgBox("Today is Sunday")
End Select
```

Although I wanted to describe this extra argument so that you'd know about it, I don't think it's something you'll find yourself using very often.

DateSerial and TimeSerial

DateSerial and TimeSerial let you add and subtract time easily. Their general forms look like this:

```
datevar = DateSerial(yearint, monthint, dayint)
datevar = TimeSerial(hourint, minuteint, secondint)
```

The *datevar* is a variable that will receive the value returned from the function and will have the subtype date. The *yearint*, *monthint*, and *dayint* arguments can either be actual numbers, variables, or expressions. The same holds true for *hourint*, *minuteint*, and *secondint*.

Listing 7-20 shows an example using `DateSerial`.

Listing 7-20: Figuring the date the project will be done.

```
Dim ThisDay, ThisMonth, ThisYear, MoreDays, Done
ThisDate = Day(Now)
ThisMonth = Month(Now)
ThisYear = Year(Now)
MoreDays = CInt(InputBox("How many more days until your
project is done?"))
Done = DateSerial(ThisYear, ThisMonth, ThisDay + MoreDays)
MsgBox("You'll be done on " & CStr(Done))
```

After the variables are created and `ThisDate`, `ThisMonth`, and `ThisYear` are initialized with their values for the current date, the user is asked to enter the number of days until the project is completed, which is immediately converted to an integer before it is placed in `MoreDays`.

Then `DateSerial` is used by passing these individual parts of today's date and adding `MoreDays` to `ThisDay`. This works, even if the total for the *dayint* argument is greater than the number of days that could be in a month. For instance, if today was January 1, 1997 and I entered 45 for days to completion, `DateSerial` would know to kick the `Month` forward by one to February and calculate the days from there.

The same holds true for the other arguments. Just add the number of days, months, years, hours, minutes, or seconds to the appropriate function's argument, and you'll get a valid date that is that far ahead of the date sent. You can also subtract values:

```
Done = DateSerial(ThisYear, ThisMonth, ThisDay - MoreDays)
```

This line would subtract the number of days entered and give you a date in the past.

More on VBScript Math

VBScript comes with a fairly complete set of basic math functions. You are already familiar with using +, -, *, and / for standard calculations. In this section, I'll introduce some of the more advanced math capabilities.

Order of Evaluation

When you have a long equation, you need to understand how VBScript evaluates it in order to know what the right answer will be. Here's an example:

```
Result = 3 + 5 * 2
```

What will `Result` hold after this line executes? Well if VBScript simply reads left to right, the answer would be 3 + 5 = 8 * 2 = 16, but if you try it out, you'll find that the value in Result is actually 13. Why? Because VBScript always performs multiplication and division (* and /) before addition and subtraction (+ and -), so it actually does it this way: 5 * 2 = 10 + 3 = 13.

What if you wanted to do the addition first? Can you force VBScript to do it in the order you want? Yes. You use parentheses:

```
Result = (3 + 5) * 2
```

Operations in parentheses are performed first, and then everything else. You can even have parentheses inside of parentheses. In that case, the deepest buried operations are performed first, and then it works its way out.

The order in which the different parts of an expression are evaluated is called the *order of precedence* or *order of evaluation*.

Whenever you are unsure about how VBScript will evalutate a long expression, place parentheses to indicate the exact order you want the calculation done. That way, you'll always be sure to have the correct answer.

Integer Division and Mod

When you do division with the / operator, you usually end up with a decimal number, even if you were dividing two integers. That's becuase most division doesn't come out nice and neat.

Do you remember when you were back in grade school and you were first learning to do long division? Since the teacher didn't want to get into the whole complexity of decimal numbers and fractions, you were probably taught to divide it out and provide the answer with a *remainder*. The remainder is what was left over that didn't go into the number equally. You can do that kind of division in VBScript, too. (See Listing 7-21.)

Listing 7-21: Integer division with a remainder.

```
Dim DividedBy, DividedInto, Answer, Remainder
DividedInto = InputBox("What number do you want to divide
into?")
DividedBy = InputBox("What number do you want to divide
by?")
Answer = DividedInto \ DividedBy
Remainder = DividedInto Mod DividedBy
MsgBox("The answer is " & CStr(Answer) & ", Remainder " &
CStr(Remainder))
```

Notice that the operator I used here was not / (slash). It is \ (back slash). Back slash does *integer division,* and the result of integer division is always an integer. Then, if you want the remainder, you can do a Mod with the same two numbers. Notice that Mod is not a function. It is an operator just like +, -, *, /, and \. You put the two numbers on either side of it just as you would with any other operator.

Of course you don't have to use \ and Mod together. Sometimes you just want the number of times a given number goes into another, without regard to any remainder. Sometimes you might also be interested in just the remainder or *modulo* of the number.

Sgn and Abs

Sgn determines whether a number is positive, negative, or zero. Here's the general form:

```
sign = Sgn(expression)
```

The *expression* argument can be any numeric expression. The value returned into *sign* will be -1 if the expression evaluates to a negative number, 0 if it's 0, and 1 if it's positive.

Abs returns the absolute of a number: that is, the number without a sign. Its general form is

```
num = Abs(expression)
```

The *expression* argument is any valid numeric expression. Returned to *num* is the evaluated expression's value without any sign. So -34 would return 34 and 12 would return 12.

Exponents and Square Roots

Exponents are numbers that are *raised to the power* of another number. 5, raised to the power of 3 is a shorthand way of saying 5 times itself 3 times, or 5 * 5 * 5 equaling 125. You indicate powers in VBScript using the ^ (caret) operator. Listing 7-22 squares (raises to the power of 2) any number entered.

Listing 7-22: Squaring numbers.

```
Dim Value
Value = CInt(InputBox("Enter a value"))
MsgBox(CStr(Value) & " squared is " & CStr(Value^2))
```

If 5 is entered, the message box reads

```
5 squared is 25
```

If 10 is entered, it reads

```
10 squared is 100
```

So, if 5 squared is 25 and 10 squared is 100, the square root is just the opposite. 25's square root is 5, and 100's square root is 10. To find the square root of a number in VBScript, use the Sqr function. (See Listing 7-23.)

Listing 7-23: Finding the square root of numbers.

```
Dim Value
Value = CInt(InputBox("Enter a value"))
MsgBox(CStr(Value) & "'s square root is " &
CStr(Sqr(Value)))
```

Trigonometry Functions: Sin, Cos, Tan, and Atn

The functions in this section are mathematical functions to help you solve trigonometry-type problems in your programs. These are the basic building blocks, and you can build more complex functions using these if you need to. You can find a whole table full of the formulas to build more complex functions in the VBScript documentation.

I'm not going to spend a lot of time detailing each of these functions for two reasons. First, if you need them, chances are you already know what they do, and if not, you might want to go rummaging though the attic for your old trig book from high school. Second, you are just not all that likely to need them when developing cool web pages.

Sin returns the sine of an angle. Its general form is this:

```
sine = Sin(angle)
```

Sin accepts the argument *angle*, which is a number representing an angle in radians, and returns the sine of the angle passed. The value returned will be a decimal number between -1 and 1.

Cos returns the cosine of an angle. Its general form is this:

```
cosine = Cos(angle)
```

Cos accepts the argument *angle*, which is a number representing an angle in radians, and returns the cosine of the angle passed. The value returned will be a decimal number between -1 and 1.

To convert degrees to radians, use this expression:

```
radians = degrees * pi/180
```

To convert the other way, use this expression:

```
degrees = radians * 180/pi
```

There is no constant in VBScript for pi, so just use 3.1415926535897932.

Tan returns the tangent of an angle. Here's its general form:

```
tangent = Tan(angle)
```

Tan accepts the argument *angle*, which is a number representing an angle in radians, and returns the tangent of the angle passed.

Atn returns the arctangent of a number. This is the general form:

```
arctangent = Atn(num)
```

The *num* argument is the ratio of two sides of a right triangle. Returned is the corresponding angle in radians. The range of the result is -pi / 2 to pi / 2.

Log and Exp

Log returns the natural logarithm of the number. Its general form looks like this:

```
log = Log(num)
```

The *num* argument is the number you want to find the natural logarithm for. The natural logarithm is the log to base *e*. The *e* here is approximately 2.718282.

You can calculate different base logarithms with this function. Just use the following equation:

```
logn(x) = log(x) / log(n)
```

For example, to find the base-10 for x, you'd write

```
log10 = log(x) / log(10)
```

Exp returns e (approximately 2.718282) raised to a given power. The general form is this:

```
exp = Exp(power)
```

The *power* argument determines what power you want to raise e to. If the result is higher than 709.782712893, you'll receive an error.

Randomize and Rnd

In creating cool web pages, you are probably most likely to use the two math functions Randomize and Rnd.

You've already met Rnd. That is the function you used in Chapter 4 to generate random numbers, but I wanted to introduce you to it more formally here. This is its general form:

```
num = Rnd([gen])
```

The *gen* argument is a number that tells Rnd how to generate its random number. Rnd returns into *num* a random number between 0 and 1.

When you used Rnd, you didn't pass an argument. That's generally the best way to use it. It just keeps generating new random numbers that way.

Do you really want to know what that gen argument does in the Rnd function? The reason I side-stepped that discussion is because I doubt you'll need it, but for those of you who really must know, here's the scoop.

If you provide a negative number for Rnd, it will use that number as the seed and will produce the same "random" number each time.

If you pass a zero as an argument, Rnd will use the last seed used to generate a random number and produce the same number it did last time.

If you pass a postive number as an argument, it does exactly the same thing it does when you provide no argument at all.

Randomize Solves the Problem of Repeating Sequences

If you've used Rnd a lot, you might have discovered that every time you reload or refresh the page, the same series of numbers is provided. For instance, imagine you have a dice rolling page that rolls the dice three times and shows you the results. You load the page and it generates a 5, a 3, and a 1. Then you refresh the page. You'll note that the values again are 5, 3, and 1. The numbers are random, but it gives you the same sequence each time.

To fix this problem, you need Randomize. Here's its general form:

```
Randomize [seed]
```

The *seed* argument is a number used to seed or generate a random number.

You see, computers can't create a number out of thin air like we can. They can only generate numbers based on other numbers. So to simulate creating a random number, the computer has to have a number to start with. That number is the seed.

You can provide a seed here, but every time this line executes, it will seed the generator with the same number and produce the same sequence again. What you really want to do is leave the argument off. When you do this, VBScript uses the system's clock as the seed for the random number.

Because the clock is very likely to be different every time the program is run, you'll see a different sequence of numbers.

You only need to use `Randomize` once before you do any `Rnd` functions. That will seed the generator correctly, and you'll get a different sequence every time.

Try out the dice rolling program in Listing 7-24.

Listing 7-24: A dice rolling program to test `Randomize`.

```
Dim Roll1, Roll2, Roll3
rem Randomize
Roll1 = Int(Rnd * 6) + 1
Roll2 = Int(Rnd * 6) + 1
Roll3 = Int(Rnd * 6) + 1
MsgBox("The rolls were " & CStr(Roll1) & ", " & _
    CStr(Roll2) & ", " & CStr(Roll3))
```

First try running it a few times as it is with the `Randomize` commented out. You should see the same sequence of numbers each time your refresh the page. Then take the comment in front of the `Randomize` out and try it again. The sequence should be different each time.

Generating Exactly the Random Number You Need

Back in Chapter 4, I showed you a trick to get VBScript to give you a random number between 1 and 6 to simulate rolling dice. I used that same trick again in Listing 7-24. You multiply the result from `Rnd` by the maximum number you want, use `Int` to chop off any decimal part of the number, and add 1:

```
num = Int(Rnd * topnum) + 1
```

You can use that formula to generate random numbers between 1 and any other number, but suppose you want to generate random numbers between 100 and 200. Is there a way to do that? Sure.

```
Num = (200 - 100 + 1) * Rnd + 100
```

Or, more generally,

```
num = (topnum - bottomnum + 1) * Rnd + bottomnum
```

where *bottomnum* and *topnum* are the lowest and highest numbers you want to be in the range.

Working with Objects

You have already been introduced to the concept of an object. An object is an entity that contains properties, methods (built-in functions), and events. You also learned about two common types of objects that you work with in VBScript: ActiveX controls and objects that are built-in to the browser. Now you'll learn how you can use variables to refer to objects.

As an example for this section, I'll use the web page called lblcolor.htm that was included on your CD-ROM in the folder titled Chap07. Open this page in Control Pad and follow along as I describe it. It has three Label Objects with the IDs IeLabel1, IeLabel2, and IeLabel3. They each have Captions that read like this:

```
This is Label 1
```

```
This is Label 2
```

```
This is Label 3
```

Below the labels is some text which says:

```
Click on the label above that you wish to change and then
click on the button below to indicate which color you want
to change it to.
```

Below the text are four command buttons. The buttons don't have any caption, but their background colors are set to red, yellow, green, and blue.

Finally, below the four buttons is one long button that has the Caption "What Is The Current Label?"

To use the page, just click on a label and then click on a button. The label changes to the color of the button. Click on the bottom long button to find out which label is the current one (the one you last clicked on). See Figure 7-1.

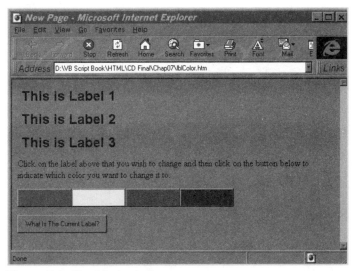

Figure 7-1: The label coloring page.

Object Variables and Assignment

Variables that are designed to hold objects are declared just like any other variable: with the Dim statement:

```
Dim CurLabel
```

If you get into the Script Wizard for this page and look under Global Variables, you'll see that CurLabel is declared as a normal global variable.

Now look at the Window object's OnLoad event script. There is only one line. It looks like this:

```
Set CurLabel = IeLabel1
```

This line assigns the CurLabel variable to hold IeLabel1, which is an ActiveX Label Object control on the page. Notice, though, that I didn't just use the normal "*variable* = *value*" syntax. Instead I had to use the Set statement. Set allows you to assign an *object* to a variable. Because working with objects is different than working with normal values, I must use the Set statement.

Now that CurLabel holds IeLabel1, I can use CurLabel to access all the properties and methods of IeLabel1 *through* CurLabel. All I have to do is write

```
CurLabel.property = value
```

or

```
CurLabel.method
```

and it works the same as if I were using IeLabel1.

Interesting, but how is that helpful? Well, it turns out that it is very helpful on this page. Whenever the user clicks on a label, IeLabel3 for instance, a line of code like this executes:

```
Set CurLabel = IeLabel3
```

Then, in the color buttons, it only takes one line of code. Here's the code for RedButton:

```
CurLabel.ForeColor = RedButton.BackColor
```

At this point in your code, you don't care which label is current. You just use CurLabel to change its foreground color, the color of the text. You change it to the background color of the RedButton, which is, of course, red. Simple.

Just think how you would have to write the code for this page if you didn't use a variable to hold the current object. You'd have to keep track of the current object by using a current object integer variable. Then you'd have to write several lines of code in each color button to make it work. The red button would look something like this:

```
If CurrentLabelNum = 1 Then
    IeLabel1.ForeColor = RedButton.BackColor
ElseIf CurrentLabelNum = 2 Then
    IeLabel2.ForeColor = RedButton.BackColor
ElseIf CurrentLabelNum = 3 Then
    IeLabel3.ForeColor = RedButton.BackColor
End If
```

And if you had more labels, it would become even more complicated!

Instead, all you need is one line.

Comparing Object Variables

What does the code look like that goes in the clicked event of the "What Is The Current Label?" button? It looks like this:

```
If CurLabel Is IeLabel1 Then
    MsgBox("Label 1 is the current label.")
ElseIf CurLabel Is IeLabel2 Then
    MsgBox("Label 2 is the current label.")
ElseIf CurLabel Is IeLabel3 Then
    MsgBox("Label 3 is the current label.")
End If
```

Here, you do need an If...Then structure because you don't want to access a property or method. You want to tell the user which one of the three labels is the current one, but it isn't so bad because you only have this code in one place.

You'll notice something interesting here. The comparison doesn't use the = sign as you might guess. Instead it uses Is. What's Is?

Is is an operator that allows you to compare two *objects* to see if they refer to the same thing. In this case, we want to see if CurLabel is IeLabel1, 2, or 3. You can't use = when comparing two objects. You must always use Is, and that's the only time you'll use Is, too, by the way. Use it only when comparing two objects.

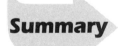

Summary

This chapter has covered a lot of ground. I began by discussing the concept of a variant and the meaning of a variant's subtype. That naturally led to conversion functions that are used to change a variable from one subtype to another.

Then came the string functions for slicing and dicing strings. The corresponding date and time functions came next, followed by more than everything you ever wanted to know about VBScript math.

Finally, I ended this chapter by discussing objects in more detail and showing you how to put objects into variables.

Arrays

An array is a special kind of variable. Actually, an array is a whole group of variables. The difference is that the whole group shares the same name.

What is an Array?

Here's an example.

Let's say I have a wife and two children. Now suppose that we, as a family, have made the decision that everyone in our household from now on will be called by the name Fred. My wife is Fred, I am Fred, and both the children are named Fred.

This is nice and cozy, but it does pose some problems. For instance, how do we refer to each other? and how do others refer to us individually? Well, to solve this problem, we each decided to take a number. My wife is 1 (ladies always go first), I am 2, and the children are 3 and 4.

Now imagine that someone calls on the phone. I pick it up and say "Hello."

"Hi. Could I speak to Fred please?"

"Ah, could you be more specific?"

"Oh, yes, I'm sorry. Could I speak to Fred 1?"

"Of course," I say as I hand the phone to my wife.

This little example describes exactly how array variables work. In an array, you might have any number of variables with the same name, and you can access each individual variable by referring to its number.

Why Would I Want to Do That?

Although the concept is simple, understanding why you'd want to do such a thing is a different matter.

Suppose you were writing a game where there could be three players. The game logic might look like Listing 8-1.

Listing 8-1: A three player game without loops or arrays.

```
Dim FirstPlayer, SecondPlayer, ThirdPlayer
FirstPlayer = InputBox("Enter the first player's name.")
SecondPlayer = InputBox("Enter the second player's name.")
ThirdPlayer = InputBox("Enter the third player's name.")
...
MsgBox("Your turn, " + FirstPlayer)
...
' Code for player 1's turn
...
MsgBox("Your turn, " + SecondPlayer)
...
' Code for player 2's turn
...
MsgBox("Your turn, " + ThirdPlayer)
...
' Code for player 3's turn
...
```

 You'll notice in this chapter that I've reverted to my Chapter 4 habit of using `InputBox` and `MsgBox` for input and output. In Chapter 4, I did it because you didn't yet know about other ways of doing input and output from VBScript. Now you know that the web page itself and the ActiveX controls on the web page will provide the best ways of communicating with the user. In this chapter, however, I use `InputBox` and `MsgBox` to keep it simple and focus on the techniques I'm teaching. Otherwise, I'd continually have to be saying things like, "OK now imagine you're on a page with three radio buttons and a text box with the names...."

The problem with this method is that the code for each player's turn is exactly the same. You would just be repeating the same code three times over. Whenever you find yourself repeating code one after another like this,

you should think about putting it into a loop. Maybe a `For...Next` loop
(see Listing 8-2).

Listing 8-2: A three player game with a loop.

```
Dim FirstPlayer, SecondPlayer, ThirdPlayer, PlayerNum
FirstPlayer = InputBox("Enter the first player's name.")
SecondPlayer = InputBox("Enter the second player's name.")
ThirdPlayer = InputBox("Enter the third player's name.")
...
For PlayerNum = 1 To 3

    If PlayerNum = 1 Then
        MsgBox("Your turn, " + FirstPlayer)
    ElseIf PlayerNum = 2 Then
        MsgBox("Your turn, " + SecondPlayer)
    Else
        MsgBox("Your turn, " + ThirdPlayer)
    End If
...
    ' Code for each player's turn
    ...
Next
...
```

This solution works. Now you only have one copy of the code for the
player's turn, and you didn't have to duplicate it again and again. But this
introduces another problem. When you wanted to use the player's name,
you had to create a big `If...Then` structure to do it. In fact, any time you
want to refer to the name of a player, you'll have to do that. How annoying.
Isn't there an easier way?

Of course there is. With arrays. Take a look at Listing 8-3.

Listing 8-3: A three player game with loops and an array.

```
Dim PlayerNum, PlayerName(3)

For PlayerNum = 1 To 3
    PlayerName(PlayerNum) = _
        InputBox("Enter player " + CStr(PlayerNum) + "'s
name.")
Next
...
For PlayerNum = 1 To 3
    MsgBox("Your turn, " + PlayerName(PlayerNum))
```

(continued)

```
(continued)

    . . .
    ' Code for each player's turn
    . . .
Next
. . .
```

This solution is *much* better. Why? Because now any time you need to refer to a player's name, you can do it with the PlayerName array. The Dim statement created the array when you put PlayerName and the 3 in parentheses after it. That caused VBScript to create an array of three variables, all with the name PlayerName. Then, whenever you want to refer to one of the player's names, you just give it the appropriate number, again in parentheses after the variable name. It simplifies the code to display the message box (by eliminating the big If...Then), and it also cleaned up the InputBox code at the beginning of the listing. Instead of asking to fill in each variable one at a time, you just loop through, executing the same line three times.

 For more information on CStr see the section titled "Converting to a String" in Chapter 7.

Do I Really Need Arrays?

Now you might be thinking, "Yea, it cleaned up the code a little bit, but I don't think it's a big deal. Why do I need to use arrays?" The answer is simple. In the previous example, I used a three player game. Imagine instead that you are tracking a list of employees and you want to calculate the amount of money to give them in pay this week. You have to do this by multiplying their hours worked by their hourly wage. No problem. By the way, there are a hundred employees! Now you *need* loops and arrays (see Listing 8-4).

Listing 8-4: Figuring the weekly pay for 100 employees.

```
Dim EmpRate(100), EmpHours(100), WeeklyPay(100), EmpNum
. . .
For EmpNum = 1 To 100
    WeeklyPay(EmpNum) = EmpRate(EmpNum) * EmpHours(EmpNum)
Next
. . .
```

Three arrays are created: one for the rate of pay per hour, one for the hours worked this week, and the third to hold the amount to pay that this program will calculate. Finally, a regular variable is created to use in the For...Next loop to keep track of which employee you are working on each time.

Assume that the EmpRate array and the EmpHours array are filled in with the right values after they are declared. That code isn't shown but would happen some time after the Dim and before the For...Next loop.

Finally, the weekly pay is calculated in the loop, so the first time through, the EmpNum is 1. The first element of the WeeklyPay array is set equal to the EmpRate array's first element times the EmpHours array's first element. The key thing to remember about these arrays is that array element 1 for each array refers to the information for employee 1. Another way to say it is that the first employee's rate is multiplied by the first employee's hours to find the first employee's weekly pay. The same happens for the second employee, the third employee, and so on.

Now you've done in three lines what it would have taken you a hundred lines and a multitude of variables to do without a loop and arrays. You should begin to see how arrays can simplify things, especially when you are working with a lot of information that you want to process in a loop.

 Throughout these examples I've been making an assumption that isn't quite true. Imagine you declare an array like this.

Dim Name(20)

You might think that this would create 20 Name variables numbered 1 to 20. Although using that assumption won't ever get you into trouble, it isn't quite the truth. You are actually creating an array of 21 names numbered 0 through 20. Every time you create an array in VBScript, the first element is always 0. That doesn't mean you have to use the 0th element. You can ignore it and start with 1 if it is more convenient, but it is there.

You'll notice throughout this book that I usually ignore this 0th element just to keep it simple. You'll probably want to do the same.

Doing the Wave

Often in sporting events, the crowd will show its spirit by doing *the wave*. It starts on one end when people slowly stand up and raise their arms, then lower their arms, and sit down. They do this in sequence. You do it just a second or two after the fan on your left, and the fan on your right does it a second or two after you. If it's done right, it looks like a giant wave is traveling across the stadium.

What if you took inspiration from this sporting ritual and decided to make the letters on your web page do something similar. You could use it for a headline or for the lead-in to something on your page for which you wanted to attract attention.

In a section titled "Simple Property Changes and Cool Effects" in Chapter 5, I showed you how to create many interesting, attention-getting effects by changing the properties of a label. The wave will require a little more work, though. You want to change the properties of each letter individually, not the entire word or phrase. So to do that, you'll have to make each letter a separate label.

Building the Foundation

Read through all the steps in this section before starting:

1. Create a new HTML page by choosing New HTML from the File menu in Control Pad. Put 13 ActiveX "Label Object" controls on it.

2. Set each label's ID to IeLabel1 through IeLabel13.

3. Set each label's Height and Width properties to 20. When you set and apply these values, they might automatically change to something like 20.25. If that happens, don't worry about it. Control Pad is coming as close to what you asked for as it can.

4. Set the Caption on each label so that each has one letter and together they will spell *COOL VBSCRIPT* (all capital letters). Note that Label5 will have a space as its caption. Leave all the rest of the properties at their default values.

When you have many similar ActiveX controls on a web page, it may be easier to go through the normal process of creating and setting the properties for the first one and then copying and pasting everything between the <OBJECT> and </OBJECT> tags (including the tags themselves) as many times as required. Then you can go through and modify things like the Caption and the ID right in the HTML <PARM> tag.

5. Finally, add an ActiveX Timer Object control. Set its ID to IeTimer1, and set Interval to 100. Set its Enabled property to False.

Now that you have all the labels for the headline finished, it is time to do some scripting:

1. Get into the Script Wizard. (You can choose it from the Tools menu.)

2. Create a new global variable. (Right-click in the Insert Actions pane and choose New Global Variable.)

3. Type this for the new global variable's name:

    Letters(20)

4. Create two more global variables. Their names should be

   ```
   NumLetters
   CurLetter
   ```

5. Now create a script for the Window object's OnLoad event. (Double-click Window in the Select an Event pane and then click to select OnLoad.) Be sure to click the Code View radio button at the bottom of the screen so that you can type in your code.

6. Enter the code in Listing 8-5.

Listing 8-5: The code for the Window OnLoad event.

```
NumLetters = 13
Set Letters(1)=IeLabel1
Set Letters(2)=IeLabel2
Set Letters(3)=IeLabel3
Set Letters(4)=IeLabel4
Set Letters(5)=IeLabel5
Set Letters(6)=IeLabel6
Set Letters(7)=IeLabel7



Set Letters(8)=IeLabel8
Set Letters(9)=IeLabel9
Set Letters(10)=IeLabel10
Set Letters(11)=IeLabel11
Set Letters(12)=IeLabel12
Set Letters(13)=IeLabel13
CurLetter = 1
IeTimer1.Enabled = True
```

Letters is an array that will hold ActiveX Label Object controls. They are all set up here in the OnLoad event of the window so that they are available throughout the rest of the page. NumLetters identifies the number of the last letter. The Letters array is filled, and the CurLetter is initialized to 1. You'll remember that Letters was created as a 20 element array. That is just so that you can change the phrase at the top to be up to 20 characters long without changing the Dim statement where it is created. All you have to do is add the labels, increase NumLetters here, and add the Set lines to initialize the array elements.

For more information on object variables and the Set command see the section titled "Working With Objects" in Chapter 7.

Finally, IeTimer1's Enabled property is set to True. I could have just set the IeTimer1's Enabled property to True when I created it, but if I did that, there's a chance it might fire off while the OnLoad event is executing, before I've had a chance to do all my initialization. Instead I set the control to False when it was created and then set it to True at the end of the OnLoad event.

After this event executes, you can access and manipulate all the labels of the phrase individually through the Letters array. This makes it quick and easy to do all sorts of things.

Now, before you finish, there's one more thing you should do.

1. Get out of the Script Wizard.

2. Go to the top of the listing and find the first <SCRIPT> tag.

3. Hit return a few times after the HTML comment to make space to add a VBScript line of code.

4. Add this line:

```
Option Explicit
```

This is a line of code you should add to the top of every project you work on. It tells VBScript to force you to declare a variable with a Dim statement before you use it. If you use Option Explicit and forget to declare a variable, VBScript will let you know right away. This makes debugging much easier.

That's all there is to it. Now save your work:

1. Save this page under the name letters.htm. You can use this as a starting point for lots of projects and experiments.

2. Save it again under the name wave1.htm. This is the name of the project that you'll work on now. By saving it twice, you'll ensure that letters.htm stays the way it is and you can come back and start new projects from this same foundation later.

3. When you are ready to start a new project using this foundation, open letters.htm in Control Pad and immediately save it out to a new name: the name of your new project.

A Simple Wave

I'll start with a simple wave.

1. Get into the Script Wizard and enter Listing 8-6 into the IeTimer1's Timer event script.

Listing 8-6: The Timer's code.

```
Dim LetNum
If CurLetter = NumLetters Then CurLetter = 1 Else
CurLetter = CurLetter + 1
For LetNum = 1 to NumLetters
    If LetNum = CurLetter Then
        Letters(LetNum).FontSize = 18
        Letters(LetNum).FontBold = True
    Else
        Letters(LetNum).FontSize = 12
        Letters(LetNum).FontBold = False
    End If
Next
```

2. Save the page and try it out.

You should see something that looks like Figure 8-1. Except that the big bold letter moves across from left to right, one letter at a time and then starts over.

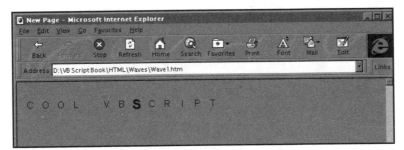

Figure 8-1: The simple wave.

Not bad. Now take a look back at Listing 8-6. What is happening there? Well, first off, keep in mind that this is the `Timer` event of a `Timer` control. It is triggered every 100 milliseconds, or 10 times a second. Each time, `CurLetter` is incremented until it equals `NumLetters`, and then it is goes back to 1. This tracks which letter is the current one: that is, which one will be enlarged.

Then, a loop runs through each of the letters and checks to see if it is the current letter. If it is the current letter, the `FontSize` is set to 18, and `FontBold` is set to `True`. For all the other letters, the `FontSize` is set to 12, and `FontBold` to `False`.

That's simple enough, but it isn't as visually interesting as it could be. Let's try another way.

Wave 2.0

The first version of the wave simply made one letter bigger and then moved that bigger letter across the phrase from left to right. To make it more like an actual wave, it would be nice if the letters grew increasingly bigger until they were the biggest size and then became smaller again until they were back down to the smallest size. Then this wave could really travel across the letters.

That's the ideas behind version 2.0:

1. Open letters.htm and Save As, naming the new page wave2.htm.

2. Get into the Script Wizard and enter the code in Listing 8-7 into the `IeTimer1's Timer` event script.

3. Save the page and try it out.

Listing 8-7: The Timer's code.

```
Dim LetNum

If CurLetter = NumLetters Then CurLetter = 1 Else
CurLetter = CurLetter + 1

For LetNum = 1 to NumLetters
    If LetNum = CurLetter -2 Then
        Letters(LetNum).FontSize = 14
        Letters(LetNum).FontBold = False
    ElseIf LetNum = CurLetter -1 Then
        Letters(LetNum).FontSize = 16
        Letters(LetNum).FontBold = False
    ElseIf LetNum = CurLetter Then
        Letters(LetNum).FontSize = 20
        Letters(LetNum).FontBold = True
    ElseIf LetNum = CurLetter +1 Then
        Letters(LetNum).FontSize = 16
        Letters(LetNum).FontBold = False
    ElseIf LetNum = CurLetter +2 Then
        Letters(LetNum).FontSize = 14
        Letters(LetNum).FontBold = False
    Else
        Letters(LetNum).FontSize = 12
        Letters(LetNum).FontBold = False
    End If
Next
```

The result should look something like Figure 8-2, except of course that it's moving.

The code in Listing 8-7 is really just an extension of the code in Listing 8-6. CurLetter is incremented as before. In the loop this time, though, I not only look to see if I am on the CurLetter, I also check to see if I am on CurLetter -2, -1, +1, and +2. If I am on any of these, I set the font to the appropriate size to create the wave effect. CurLabel is the biggest, those on either side of it are second biggest, and those further out still are third biggest. Finally, all other letters are set to font size 12. FontBold is set to False except for the one that matches CurLetter where it is True.

Figure 8-2: The Wave 2.0 in action.

Wave 3.0: A Different Twist

After creating Wave 2.0, I wondered whether I should make CurLetter the first big one and have the letters become smaller afterward (on the left side) but not on the right.

1. With wave2.htm in Control Pad, do a Save As and name the new page wave3.htm.

2. Go into the Script Wizard and delete the last two ElseIf clauses (being careful not to delete the final Else clause). When you are done, it should look like Listing 8-8.

3. Save the page and try it out.

Listing 8-8: Wave 3 Timer code.

```
Dim LetNum

If CurLetter = NumLetters Then CurLetter = 1 Else
CurLetter = CurLetter + 1

For LetNum = 1 to NumLetters
    If LetNum = CurLetter -2 Then
        Letters(LetNum).FontSize = 14
```

(continued)

```
(continued)
          Letters(LetNum).FontBold = False
     ElseIf LetNum = CurLetter -1 Then
          Letters(LetNum).FontSize = 16
          Letters(LetNum).FontBold = False
     ElseIf LetNum = CurLetter Then
          Letters(LetNum).FontSize = 20
          Letters(LetNum).FontBold = True
     Else
          Letters(LetNum).FontSize = 12
          Letters(LetNum).FontBold = False
     End If
Next
```

The result should look a lot like Figure 8-3.

This probably shouldn't be Wave 3.0 because it is really a different effect altogether, but as you can see, the code is identical except for the missing lines.

Wave 4.0: Adding Color

Color can be an effective tool in adding attention-getting text to your web page. In this final version of the Wave, I'll include the lines I took out to create Wave 3.0, but I'll also add some color.

Figure 8-3: Wave 3.0 in action.

1. Start over with letters.htm and Save As to call the new page wave4.htm.

2. Add the code in Listing 8-9 to the IeTimer1's Timer event.

3. Save the page and try it out.

Listing 8-9: Wave 4's Timer event.

```
Dim LetNum

If CurLetter = NumLetters Then CurLetter = 1 Else
CurLetter = CurLetter + 1


For LetNum = 1 to NumLetters
    If LetNum = CurLetter -2 Then
        Letters(LetNum).FontSize = 14
        Letters(LetNum).FontBold = False
        Letters(LetNum).ForeColor = 120
    ElseIf LetNum = CurLetter -1 Then
        Letters(LetNum).FontSize = 16
        Letters(LetNum).FontBold = False
        Letters(LetNum).ForeColor = 200
    ElseIf LetNum = CurLetter Then
        Letters(LetNum).FontSize = 20
        Letters(LetNum).FontBold = True
        Letters(LetNum).ForeColor = 250
    ElseIf LetNum = CurLetter +1 Then
        Letters(LetNum).FontSize = 16
        Letters(LetNum).FontBold = False
        Letters(LetNum).ForeColor = 200
    ElseIf LetNum = CurLetter +2 Then
        Letters(LetNum).FontSize = 14
        Letters(LetNum).FontBold = False
        Letters(LetNum).ForeColor = 120
    Else
        Letters(LetNum).FontSize = 12
        Letters(LetNum).FontBold = False
        Letters(LetNum).ForeColor = 0
    End If
Next
```

The result should look a lot like Figure 8-4.

You can't really tell the color change from the figure very well, of course, but it should produce a pretty impressive effect on your screen. The color, even though it is just several shades of red, adds to the feeling of depth and makes it work better.

You could take the last two ElseIf clauses out to make an effect like Wave 2 with color, also, if you like. That's easy enough, but I hope this exercise has your mind working on new ideas for manipulating text and headlines on your pages. The possibilities are nearly endless. When you watch television or look at other web pages or software packages, look for different ways they've manipulated or animated the text to make it more interesting. Then see if you can do the same thing in VBScript. One software package that has lots of neat text stuff is the trivia game "You Don't Know Jack." I'm sure you'll find many others.

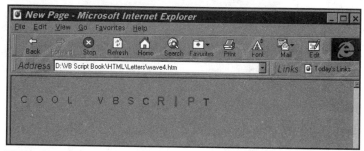

Figure 8-4: Wave 4.0 in action.

Two-Dimensional Arrays

The arrays that you've looked at so far are *one-dimensional* arrays: that is, you could picture them as a row of numbers like Table 8-1.

Table 8-1	The EmpHours **Array**
Element	Value
1	40
2	42
3	38
4	41
...	...
98	42
99	51
100	47

VBScript also allows you to create *two-dimensional* arrays. A two-dimensional array looks more like the data in Table 8-2, which shows the number of points scored by several students in several basketball games.

Table 8-2
Number of Points Scored by Students in Several Basketball Games

Student	Game 1	Game 2	Game 3	Game 4
1	4	2	6	2
2	0	2	4	4
3	8	12	10	14
4	4	4	8	6
5	3	4	6	4
6	8	6	10	8

Instead of one row of numbers whose value you can access with an index number, you have both rows and columns, and you access a particular bit of information by specifying its row and column. Listing 8-10 shows what the code would look like to create and fill in one column of an array like the one pictured in Table 8-2.

Listing 8-10: Creating and filling in the points-scored array.

```
Dim PointsScored(6,4), Game, Student
Game = InputBox("What game did you just play")
For Student = 1 to 6
    PointsScored(Student, Game) = InputBox("How many points
did Student " + _
        CStr(Student) + " score?")
Next
```

You create a two-dimensional array using the Dim statement with a variable followed by parentheses, just like the single-dimensional array was. This time, however, you have two numbers inside the parentheses, separated by a comma. This indicates the maximum number of rows and columns. In this case, there are 6 students (rows) and 4 games (columns).

The code then finds out which game was just played and then fills in that particular column of the array with the number of points scored by each student. If you did this several times for several different games, you could fill in the entire array, or if you wanted the user to enter all the information at once, you could use code like that in Listing 8-11.

Listing 8-11: Filling in the entire points-scored array at once.

```
Dim PointsScored(6,4), Game, Student
For Game = 1 To 4
    For Student = 1 to 6
        PointsScored(Student, Game) = _
           InputBox("How many points did student " +
CStr(Student) + _
           " score in game " + CStr(Game) + "?")
    Next
Next
```

The input box would go through all the possibilities asking for points starting with

```
How many points did student 1 score in game 1?
```

continuing with

```
How many points did student 2 score in game 1?
```

and finally ending up with

```
How many points did student 6 score in game 4?
```

If you run this example on your machine, be aware that it will force you to go through all 24 input boxes. You can't get out of it by pressing Cancel on the dialog box or even by trying to close down Explorer. Just keep pressing Enter until it stops!

Just as one-dimensional arrays work well with For...Next loops, so two-dimensional arrays work well with *nested* For...Next loops. If you want to brush up on nested loops, you might want to take a look back at the section titled "Loops Inside of Loops" in Chapter 4.

Listing 8-12 shows some code you might use to display information from the array.

Listing 8-12: Creating and filling in the points-scored array.

```
...
Game = InputBox("What game do you want to check on?")
Student = InputBox("What student do you want to see points
for?")
MsgBox("Student " + Student + " in game " + Game + _
```

```
      " scored " + PointsScored(Student, Game) + " points.")
...
```

After asking what game and student the user wants to see, this listing displays a message box with a message that would end up looking something like this:

```
Student 1 in game 3 scored 6 points.
```

Two-dimensional arrays can do lots more than store basketball points. In fact, they have many uses, including:

➡ A chart indicating the number of miles to travel from one city (the row) to another city (the column)

➡ Sales figures for several salesmen (rows) over the last several months (columns)

➡ The blood pressure of all the people in a hospital (rows) over the last three weeks (columns)

 In this list, I indicated what information might be represented by rows and what other information would be represented by columns. Is there any reason why one should be a row and another the column? Couldn't you have sales figures for several months be the rows and the salesmen be the columns?

Of course. You can set it up however you like, but however you set it up, make sure it is intuitive and makes sense to you (and anybody else who might work with your code). Although you can set up your array however you want, you must be consistent in the way you access it once you set it up. In other words, if you use this line to fill in the second salesman's sales for the fourth month:

```
Sales(2,4) = 2575
```

you can't access that same value later this way:

```
MySales = Sales(4,2)
```

Row 2, column 4 is completely different from row 4, column 2, no matter what the rows and columns represent!

Multidimensional Arrays

Naturally the next question is, can you have a three-dimensional array?

Sure. Instead of picturing the array as a table with rows and columns now, though, you will want to imagine it as an array of tables, or perhaps as a three-dimensional cube with height, width, *and* depth.

In fact, you can have a four-dimensional array. This one is a lot tougher to picture in your mind. Five dimensions, six dimensions...is there any end? Yes, in fact, there is. VBScript supports up to 60-dimensional arrays.

Just because it's possible doesn't mean it's a good idea. I highly recommend sticking with one- or two-dimensional arrays and using several of them if required. You can very easily lose track of what's going on if you go much higher than that.

Multidimensional arrays are a bad idea for several reasons. Not only are they hard to keep track of, but you can quickly use up a lot of the computer's memory if you aren't careful. For example:

```
Dim MyArray(10,10)
```

This statement creates an array with 10 rows and 10 columns. That means that it sets aside room for 10x10 or 100 variables.

Now think about this:

```
Dim MyArray(10,10,10)
```

This three-dimensional array takes up 10x10x10 or 1,000 variables. Adding a fourth dimension of the same size increases the number of variables to 10,000. That's a lot of memory!

String Arrays

So far, all the arrays I've shown you have been used to hold numbers, but you can store strings in arrays just as easily. Listing 8-13 allows the user to look up the phone number for a friend from the list.

Listing 8-13: Phone number lookup.

```
Dim Name(10), Phone(10), LookupName, NameIndex
Name(1)="Melanie Hatfield"
Phone(1)="555-3422"
Name(2)="Paul Logston"
Phone(2)="555-6622"
Name(3)="Mike LaFavers"
Phone(3)="555-3444"
Name(4)="Brad Jones"
```

```
Phone(4)="555-2411"
...
LookupName = _
    InputBox("Enter name of the person's phone number you
need.")
For NameIndex = 1 To 10
    If Name(NameIndex) = LookupName Then
        MsgBox(Name(NameIndex) + _
            "'s phone number is " + Phone(NameIndex))
    End If
Next
```

The first thing I do is create two single-dimensional arrays to hold 10
names and 10 associate phone numbers. Then I fill in each element one by
one with the information I want it to hold.

After asking the user which name to look for, `NameIndex` loops from 1 up
to 10. Each `Name` array element is compared to the `LookupName` and if
there is a match, the associated phone number (the one with the same
index) is displayed. The result would look something like this:

```
Paul Logston's phone number is 555-6622.
```

I can hear someone out there asking, "Yes, you could have implemented
this with one two-dimensional array instead of two one-dimensional
arrays." The code would look like Listing 8-14.

Listing 8-14: The phone number lookup implemented with a two-dimensional array.

```
Dim NamePhone(10,2), LookupName, NameIndex
NamePhone(1,1)="Melanie Hatfield"
NamePhone(1,2)="555-3422"


NamePhone(2,1)="Paul Logston"
NamePhone(2,2)="555-6622"
NamePhone(3,1)="Mike LaFavers"
NamePhone(3,2)="555-3444"
NamePhone(4,1)="Brad Jones"
NamePhone(4,2)="555-2411"
...
LookupName = _
    InputBox("Enter name of the person's phone number you
```
(continued)

```
(continued)
need.")
For NameIndex = 1 To 10
    If NamePhone(NameIndex,1) = LookupName Then
        MsgBox(NamePhone(NameIndex,1) + _
            "'s phone number is " + NamePhone(NameIndex,2))



    End If
Next
```

In this solution, a row exists for each name and phone number. Column 1 holds the name, and column 2 holds the phone number.

For my part, I think the two one-dimensional array solution is more straightforward.

Dynamic Arrays

So far, all the arrays you've seen have been set to a fixed size when they were created. The problem is, you don't always know how big you need for the array to be when you begin. That's when *dynamic arrays* come in handy.

Dynamic arrays are declared with a Dim statement and parentheses, just like normal arrays, but a dynamic array doesn't include a number inside the parentheses. Instead, once you know the number, you can use the ReDim statement to set it.

Listing 8-15 picks up on the example of a multiplayer game I used earlier in this chapter. Suppose that between 1 and 4 players can play your game, but each game could be different. How do you set up an array to handle it? Well, you could always set the array to hold 4 and simply not use those you don't need, but that would be wasteful. Instead, you can use dynamic arrays.

Listing 8-15: Revisiting the multiplayer game.

```
Dim PlayerName(), NumPlayers, PlayerIndex

NumPlayers = CInt(InputBox("How many players are there?"))
ReDim PlayerName(NumPlayers)

For PlayerIndex = 1 To NumPlayers
```

```
    PlayerName(PlayerIndex) = _
        InputBox("Enter player " + CStr(PlayerIndex) + "'s
  name.")
  Next
```

The `PlayerName` array is declared dynamically without specifying the number of elements it will have.

The user enters the number of players, and `ReDim` sets the size of `PlayerName`. A loop then goes through each player to get their name.

You can use `ReDim` anywhere in your VBScript code, but it must execute before the dynamic array is used. You can even use it more than once. If you decide later that an array needs to be bigger than what you originally `ReDim`med it for, you can write a line like this:

```
ReDim Preserve PlayerName(4)
```

The `Preserve` tells VBScript to preserve any data in the array already and just change its size. If you don't use `Preserve`, the array is re-initialized, and all your data will be lost.

Remember, too, that you can still lose data even if you use `ReDim Preserve`. If you originally `ReDim`med the array to hold three elements and then you do a `ReDim Preserve` to make it two elements, you will lose any data that was in the third element. Be careful!

Again, this may seem like a small convenience until you start thinking about bigger numbers. Perhaps it is a page that tracks employees for a company. You may have 5 employees in the company, or you may have 500. That's a big difference, and it doesn't make a lot of sense to use 500 elements when you only need 5.

On the other hand, don't use dynamic arrays all the time just because they are more flexible. They aren't nearly as efficient with memory, and they execute more slowly than static arrays. If you do know ahead of time how big your array needs to be or you can get pretty close, use a static array and identify its size when you create it. If you don't know what size it needs to be, dynamic arrays can be handy.

UBound

There is a function in VBScript that is designed to help you when you work with dynamic arrays. Its name is `UBound` and its general form looks like this:

```
Num = UBound(ArrayName[, Dimension])
```

An example will help you understand what it can do for you:

```
Dim Employees()
...
ReDim Employees(50,3)
...
MsgBox CStr(UBound(Employees))
```

This code declares a dynamic array and later sets it to be a two-dimensional array that is 50 by 3. Later still, the UBound of the array is displayed in a message box. What will appear? 50. That is the upper bound (the highest possible array element) for the first dimension of the array.

 The VBScript documentation provided from Microsoft says that UBound will give you 49 in the case above. They say it will always give you one less than the number the array was declared for. That would be very confusing and fortunately, it's not true. VBScript works as I describe here.

How do you get the upper bound for the second dimension?

```
MsgBox CStr(UBound(Employees,2))
```

The result displayed in the message box is 3, the highest possible array element for the second dimension.

 There is also an LBound function in VBScript that gives you the lower bound or the lowest possible element for an array. This isn't a big deal in VBScript, though, since all arrays begin with 0. The reason LBound exists is because the full-blown Visual Basic development environment gives you the ability to start arrays at other numbers. Since VBScript doesn't, you won't probably ever have a need for LBound.

Erase

You should know about one more command in VBScript that works with arrays: Erase. This is its general form:

```
Erase array
```

The *array* argument is the name of any array (without parentheses).

Erase does different things depending on the type of array you send as an argument. If you send a static array (one that you specified the size when it was created), it simply re-initializes the array. In other words, if it is a string array, it sets all the elements to the empty string (""). If it is a numeric array, it sets all the elements to 0.

If it is a dynamic array, though, Erase actually frees all the memory allocated for the array. This is a nice feature to use if you need a big array for just a short time, but you don't want to take up all that memory for the whole application. Just remember that you can't use a dynamic array after you Erase it until you do another ReDim.

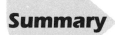

Summary

I began this chapter by describing what arrays are and why you might need such a thing. Then I described simple, static arrays and showed you how an array holding ActiveX Label Object controls could do some pretty neat tricks. Next, I described the other kinds of arrays you can create in VBScript: multidimensional arrays, string arrays, and dynamic arrays. Finally, I described the Erase command. You now have more than enough information to tackle any tough data-crunching page that comes along.

Debugging and Error Handling

I'll attack the related topics of debugging and error handling. In order to create robust web pages that do more than display text and pretty pictures, you have to write computer programs — even if the programs are as simple as those you create with VBScript. But with any sort of programming comes bugs. I'll show you how to use VBScript itself to hunt them down and kill them.

The two topics identified in the title of this chapter are related, but different. *Debugging* is the process of finding and removing errors in your VBScript page. These errors can range from simply misspelling the name of a VBScript command to complex logic errors.

Error handling, on the other hand, refers to the code that you write to make sure your page doesn't stop working when the user uses your page — no matter what they do. Even after your page works perfectly and has no bugs, users can still often create errors. How? By typing in their name when you were expecting them to type in their age or by doing one of a hundred other odd and unexpected things. Don't think they won't! Users have a way of coming up with ways of manipulating your page that you wouldn't believe they'd do in a million years, so you have to be ready for them. Some programmers like to refer to error handling as *bulletproofing* their code. A cynical person might prefer *idiotproofing*. Either way, you must do it.

I'll discuss each topic separately. I'll start with debugging.

Debugging

The term *bug* was coined when a moth was caught in a relay of one of the very earliest computers causing it to give incorrect results. Since that time, a bug has come to mean any error in a program that causes it to work incorrectly.

Debugging, then, is the process of removing bugs from your programs, and it is the thing programmers spend as much of their time doing as anything else.

Most of the VBScript programs you'll write to activate your web pages won't be as complex as an accounting program or a computer game, but that doesn't mean you won't spend time debugging. You'll probably end up spending a lot of time. So the question is, how do you do it?

What is the Process?

What is the process you go through to kill a bug? Well, it is exactly like tracking down a rattling noise that your car makes when you accelerate or a problem in your telephone line that results in no dial-tone. In fact, it is just like the process of fixing problems in any reasonably complex system.

The first step is to analyze what you know. What is the problem? How does it show itself? When does the problem occur? What else is going on at that time? Does it happen at any other times? Once you've answer some of these fundamental questions, you'll begin to have a place to start. Go in and look at the code that is running when the problem happens.

One of the most powerful techniques you can use is called *desk-checking* or *pretending you're the computer*. You do just that. Pretend like you are the computer and walk through the code line by line and keep track of what happens. If a line of code uses a variable, think about what value that variable has before it reaches this line, and what it is afterward. Are you making an assumption that isn't true? This sort of walking-through helps you see things much more as the computer sees them.

The Tools of the Trade

In order to make the process of debugging simpler, most languages and development environments have a complete set of debugging tools. The most common tool, simply called the *debugger*, allows you to desk-check the code right on the screen. It executes your code in slow motion right in front of you, one line at a time. At any point, it allows you to stop, check variable values, and see where things stand.

The bad news is that VBScript doesn't have a debugger. In fact, it has no built-in debugging tools at all. That's right! You're on your own.

Fortunately, you can do some things to make up for this problem. I'll spend the rest of this section discussing those techniques.

Setting up Your Environment

If you were using a modern, professional development tool like Visual Basic or Visual C++ you'd not only have a host of cool debugging facilities, but also a convenient, consistent, straightforward environment in which to work. Again, VBScript has no such beast yet.

 Notice that I said *yet*. That's important. As VBScript becomes more common and more people develop in it, you can bet that it will only be a matter of time before development environments and debugging tools are offered by other companies — and maybe even offered by Microsoft. Microsoft has yet to announce how much support its planned Internet Studio will provide for VBScripters.

The Basic Drill

As I've used VBScript, I've set up my environment for development so that it is pretty convenient. I'll describe how I set things up here, and you can use my technique or adapt it to suit yourself.

First, I always have two applications running when I'm creating a new page or modifying an old one:

➡ Microsoft Control Pad

➡ Microsoft Internet Explorer 3.0

I load up the page I want to work with in Control Pad, and then I load up the same page in Internet Explorer. I then follow these steps:

1. Make modifications in Control Pad.
2. Save the page.
3. Switch over to Internet Explorer.
4. Click the Refresh button.
5. Check the page to see if it is correct.

This routine allows you to see the results of your changes quickly and easily as soon as you make them. They also speed the process of making a change, seeing how it worked, changing it again, and checking the result.

 Always, always, always click the Refresh button, even after you just loaded up a new page in Internet Explorer. If you have loaded up that same page earlier, Internet Explorer is likely to load up that earlier version from its cache rather than the new copy on your hard drive. If you click the Refresh button, you force the browser to go back to the original file on the hard drive and load a fresh copy.

You may find yourself in a situation where you are making changes, but the changes don't seem to be reflected in the page when you try it out. If you do, you need to check a couple of things:

➡ Make certain that you are both saving the page *and* clicking Refresh in the browser — in that order.

➡ Make sure that you still have the same document in both Control Pad and Internet Explorer. If you change the name using Save As in Control Pad, don't forget to load up the new page in Internet Explorer.

A Couple of Hitches

This process works well, but you need to supplement it in a couple of cases. First, if you ever need to do a search or search and replace, you'll quickly find that there are no menu items available for this in Control Pad. Second, if you receive an error message in Internet Explorer, it will usually give you a line number within the HTML page of the line of code that caused the problem, but Control Pad doesn't show you what line of the HTML file you are on. In fact, you have no way to find a line by its line number except to start at the top of your file and count as you press the down-arrow key. That may work with an error on line 34 but not for an error on line 519, as you may see when you use lots of ActiveX controls on your page.

So you need another tool that can provide these capabilities.

Windows Notepad won't work. Although it does provide the search and replace capabilities, it doesn't tell you what line you are on and doesn't have any built-in way of jumping to a line, given its line number.

There is another editor that comes with Windows 95. It is called Edit. The downside is that Edit is a DOS program. To run it, all you have to do is choose Run from the Start menu and type Edit. The editor launches. (If it goes to full-screen text mode, just press Alt-Enter to turn it into a window.) Although Edit isn't a Windows program, it does have a menu bar across the top that you can use, just like a Windows application. Choose File ➪ Open and then locate your HTML file on your hard drive. Windows 95 Edit even works with long file and directory names, which is pretty unusual for a DOS application.

Don't use copy and paste to paste code into the editor. It takes a long time to paste a large number of lines and, for some reason, the code's indentation gets screwed up. It is much easier just to load the page from the hard drive after you've saved it in Control Pad.

Once you have loaded your HTML page, you will notice that the current cursor's row and column appear at the bottom right of the screen. You can simply scroll down with the cursor keys or page down until you find the line number you are searching, and, of course, it has complete Search and Replace capabilities built-in, too.

If you loath using DOS, text-mode applications, you could look for a shareware or freeware editor on the Internet that works in Windows. Even the simplest of them will probably have the capabilities you need.

There is just one problem with introducing another editor, either Windows or DOS. When you have the code in two different editors (Control Pad and whatever other editor you decide to use), you run the risk of becoming confused. Which editor has the most up to date code in it? Which did you change last? If you save out the wrong one, you could lose your changes. Be careful where you are making changes.

When I do this, I use Control Pad as my primary editor and only use the second editor when I need one of the features Control Pad doesn't have. I use it to find lines based on their line number and to search for things, but when I need to make changes to the actual page, I try to always do that in Control Pad. That way, I always know the latest version of my page is there. Some situations occur where I need to Search and Replace a lot. In these cases, I have to do it in the other editor. As soon as I'm done, I save the changes and load the new document up in Control Pad, and I'm back to where I was.

 You may be asking yourself, why go through all this trouble? Why not just get a really good editor — maybe even one optimized for creating HTML — and forget about Control Pad. If it doesn't even have line numbers and search/replace, it doesn't deserve serious consideration.

Normally I would agree, but the problem is that Control Pad is the only tool out there that gives you such an easy-to-use interface for adding and modifying ActiveX controls on your page. If you are going to be using ActiveX controls a lot — and I bet you are — it is tough to throw away Control Pad.

If you prefer, you could use another editor as your primary editor, though. Then you'd use Control Pad just as a supplement whenever you need to add a new ActiveX control or modify one already on the page. Do what works best for you.

Common Errors and Their Causes

Now that you've got your tools selected and a process down for moving around among them and developing with them, all you have to do is create your page and start debugging.

A debugging session usually begins by trying out your newly created page and getting an error message.

Loadtime Errors

There are two kinds of errors you'll get in VBScript. The first is a loadtime error, which happens when you first load your page into Internet Explorer. The second is a runtime error, which happens after the page is loaded and in the course of using the page.

Listing 9-1 would cause a loadtime error.

Listing 9-1: This page would cause a loadtime error.

```
<SCRIPT LANGUAGE="VBScript">
<!—
Dim a, b, c

a = "dog"
b = 7
c = a * b
—>
</SCRIPT>
```

You can't multiply a variable holding a string together with a variable holding a number. When you load this page in Internet Explorer, Figure 9-1 shows what you see.

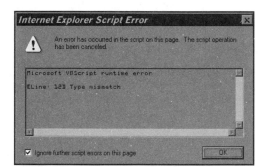

Figure 9-1: The loadtime error message.

You might notice that the error messge dialog box says, "Microsoft VBScript runtime error." It will always say that regardless of when the error occurred, but this error clearly happened at loadtime when it was bringing up the page.

What does *Type Mismatch* mean? A Type Mismatch error occurs when you try to use one type of variable in a situation where you should be using another type. I tried to multiply a number and a string, but the types did not match. VBScript would have preferred two numbers.

Often a Type Mismatch error like this can be an indicator that you should have used a conversion function (like `Int` or `CStr`) to convert information from one type to another before you do math or other things with it.

Be aware, however, that you will see the Type Mismatch error pretty often. Many times when you see it, the error won't have anything to do with the type of data you store in a variable. Take Listing 9-2, for instance.

Listing 9-2: Another loadtime, Type Mismatch error.

```
<HTML>
<HEAD>
<SCRIPT LANGUAGE="VBScript">
<!-
MssgBox "Hello everybody!"
->
</SCRIPT>
<TITLE>Test Page</TITLE>
</HEAD>
<BODY>
<h1>Test Page</h1>
</BODY>
</HTML>
```

This time, I have simply misspelled a command (two s's in `MsgBox`). This also causes a Type Mismatch error. Most languages would flag something like this as *a syntax error*, but VBScript seems to throw type mismatch errors and syntax errors all into the same bucket and calls them *Type Mismatch*. Don't let this throw you off.

You can also receive a Type Mismatch error when you have Option Explicit specified. Option Explicit means you don't want VBScript to allow you to create variables on the fly without first creating them with a `Dim` statement. If you use Option Explicit and then you refer to a variable that has not been declared with `Dim`, the error you will receive is a Type Mismatch on the line where the variable is used.

So whenever you receive a Type Mismatch error, first look for stupid mistakes like misspelling command names, misspelling your own variable names, or forgetting to declare a variable.

Runtime Errors

As I mentioned, runtime errors happen after the page is loaded. Usually they occur in the process of using a page like after you clicked a button or did something else that caused code to execute.

The Example Page

Let me describe a little more complicated example now. Imagine a page with three Label Object controls: named `Label1`, `Label2`, and `Label3`. Each is on a different line with a different word or set of words in their Captions. Then below all three is a Microsoft Forms 2.0 CommandButton. In Internet Explorer it might look like Figure 9-2.

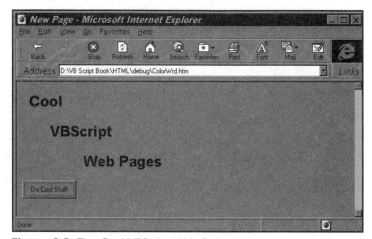

Figure 9-2: The Cool VBScript Web Page page.

By the way, this page is on your hard drive if you've installed the CD-ROM from the back of this book.

A global variable is declared that looks like this:

```
Words(3)
```

The Window's `OnLoad` event code looks like Listing 9-3.

Listing 9-3: The Cool VBScript Web Page Window `OnLoad` event.

```
Set Words(1) = Label1
Set Words(2) = Label2
Set Words(3) = Label3
```

This associates the array elements with the three labels on the page. Sometimes it's easier to refer to controls with an array rather than by their original name.

Object Doesn't Support Property or Method

The only other event that has any code is the button's `Click` event (see Listing 9-4).

Listing 9-4: The CoolButton's `Click` event.

```
Dim CurWord, RandRed, RandGreen, RandBlue

RandRed = Int(Rnd * 255)+1
RandGreen = Int(Rnd * 255)+1
RandBlue = Int(Rnd * 255)+1

For CurWord = 1 To 3
    Labels(CurWord).Color = RGB(RandRed, RandGreen,
RandBlue)
Next
```

This code generates three random numbers between 1 and 255 and then plugs those numbers into the RGB function to create a random color. The loop goes from 1 to 3 so that all the labels' colors are set.

This page doesn't give you an error when you load it up, but when you push the button you receive an error that looks like Figure 9-3.

The message says "Object doesn't support this property or method," and, if you edit one of the label objects, you'll find that, sure enough, `Color` isn't in the `Properties` window. The property you want to change is `ForeColor`. Once you change `Color` to `ForeColor`, it works.

Whenever you receive the "Object doesn't support this property or method" error, check these things:

➡ Am I using the right object?

➡ Have I spelled the object name correctly?

➡ Am I using the right property/method?

➡ Is the property/method spelled correctly?

Bear in mind that different ActiveX controls are often created by different companies and one may use one name for a property or method and another might use a completely different name. Be sure you know the property with which you are working. You can always edit the object to find its properties or go into the Script Wizard to find its properties and methods.

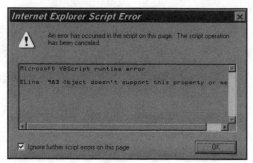

Figure 9-3: The error.

Another Cause for "Object doesn't support" Errors

Like Type Mismatch, this error (and most of the errors in VBScript, it seems) do not always describe the situation exactly right. For instance, imagine you had `ForeColor` correct in the previous application, but you forgot to put the `Set` commands in the Window's `OnLoad` event, as in Listing 9-5.

Listing 9-5: The `OnLoad` event minus the `Set` commands.

```
Words(1) = Label1
Words(2) = Label2
Words(3) = Label3
```

This would cause the same error: "Object doesn't support this property or method" on the first line. It is confusing because no properties or methods are there! Always remember to use `Set` whenever you are working with objects.

You'll notice, if you try it out, that when you leave off the `Set` commands in the `OnLoad` event that the error seems to occur when the page is loaded. That does not make it a loadtime error. It is a runtime error. The code just happens to be in the `OnLoad` event that happens immediately after the page is loaded.

Object Required

Now, walk through one more scenario with me using this application. Go back to the button's `Click` event, but this time, imagine that it was coded like Listing 9-6.

Listing 9-6: The CoolButton's bad `Click` event.

```
Dim CurWord, RandRed, RandGreen, RandBlue

RandRed = Int(Rnd * 255)+1
RandGreen = Int(Rnd * 255)+1
RandBlue = Int(Rnd * 255)+1

For CurWord = 1 To 3
    Labels.ForeColor = RGB(RandRed, RandGreen, RandBlue)
Next
```

The difference is the second to last line. Instead of this:

```
Labels(CurWord).ForeColor = RGB(RandRed, RandGreen,
RandBlue)
```

The line looks like this:

```
Labels.ForeColor = RGB(RandRed, RandGreen, RandBlue)
```

The (CurWord) was left off. What error does this generate? Figure 9-4 has the answer.

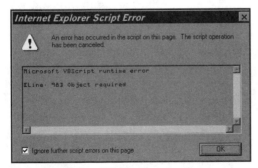

Figure 9-4: The "Object Required" error.

The error is "Object Required." This happens when you refer to a property or method, but the object itself isn't right. Again, look for misspellings and also situations like this where you left off the array index.

Tracking Insects

Now you are familiar with some of the common errors you'll run into as you debug your applications — and also where to start looking for the problem.

The most insidious bugs are those that don't produce an error, or, if they do, the error makes no sense whatsoever. In these cases, it is time to break out the debugging techniques in this section and settle down to some serious bug hunting.

Tracing Code With MsgBox

The word tracing often refers to the kind of online desk checking I described that you can do with a debugger in other development environments. Because you don't have a debugger in VBScript, you have to find other ways of tracing your code.

Tracing includes two primary activities:

➡ Identifying the flow of the program

➡ Finding out what value different variables have at different times

What does VBScript offer to accomplish this? Only its own built-in input/output commands. The simplest and most convenient, I think, is the `MsgBox` command.

Identifying a Program's Flow

I can't count the number of times when I've just stared at a routine and said, "I just don't see how this could be happening. It looks *right*!"

These are often the times to start tracing the program's flow. Where is it going? You may assume that certain lines are executing, but are they?

I'll create an example to serve as a basis for our discussion. It has an obvious bug in it that you will probably see right away but pretend that you don't so that I can demonstrate this process.

Imagine you have a window with a text box, button, and label on it. It looks something like Figure 9-5.

When you click the button, the code in Listing 9-7 executes.

Listing 9-7: The EvaluateButton's `Click` event.

```
Dim Returned
Returned = EvaluateStatus(Int(StatusTextBox.Text))
StatusLabel.Caption = Returned
```

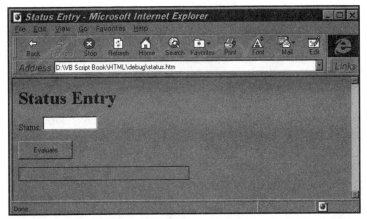

Figure 9-5: The Status Entry page.

It calls a function passing the information entered in the text box as an integer. (Let's assume, for now, that the user will always enter a valid number.) Then a value is received back from the function and that value is placed in the Caption of the label.

So far so good. Listing 9-8 shows you the code for the function.

Listing 9-8: The EvaluateStatus **function.**

```
If Stat > 200 Then
    EvaluateStatus = "Abnormally High"
End If

If Stat < 200 Then
    EvaluateStatus = "Normal"
End If
```

The value the function receives is named Stat, which is checked to see if it is over 200. That indicates an abnormally high status. If it is, EvaluateStatus (the return value for the function) is set to the string "Abnormally High". If the Stat is less than 200, the returned value is "Normal".

When testing it, the developer types in a value and clicks the button, but nothing appears in the label. What could be wrong?

If you didn't see the problem right away, the first thing you might want to do is to insert a new line, first thing in the function:

```
MsgBox "In the EvaluateStatus function"
```

Then try the page again. That will allow you to check the flow of the program to make sure that it actually made it into the function. If the function never actually is called for one reason or another, that would explain very well why the label isn't being filled in with text.

When you try the page, the message box does appear. Now, at least, you know for sure that the function is being called.

What's the next step? Look at the function. Is the code inside the If...Then statements being called? Add this line inside the first If...Then, above the assignment:

```
MsgBox "Inside first If...Then. Stat > 200."
```

Add this one inside the second If...Then, above the assignment:

```
MsgBox "Inside second If...Then. Stat < 200"
```

Now when the page is loaded up, the value entered, and the button pressed, two message boxes should appear. The first indicates that the function is called, and then a second indicates which If...Then has executed.

Here is the first unexpected result! Only the one message box appears, so, although the function is being called, neither of the If...Then's is being triggered. Now the question is very pointed. Is it possible that a value could be entered that would not trigger *either* If...Then? At this point, it would become obvious to you as you look at the function (if it wasn't already before) that a value of exactly 200 would, in fact, slip through.

To fix the problem, the second If...Then should probably be changed to look like this:

```
If Stat <= 200 Then
```

The process I've demonstrated is a very simple example of the kind of tracing you are likely to do a lot of in VBScript. You obviously don't want to put a MsgBox command on every other line just to be sure everything is executing. Assume everything will work until you see evidence to the contrary, and you will! It will be either in the form of a page that doesn't work as planned (as in this example) or in the form of an error message. Either way, begin to use your logical deduction skills as well as your intuition to figure out what has gone wrong. If you have a strong inclination to try something even though it doesn't make any sense logically, try it. Often it can uncover additional clues that will lead to the answer. This process can be every bit as rich and complex as a good detective novel.

Finding Variable Values

Another way to approach the problem would have been to focus on the value of variables. If you worked on the problem this way, you might add this line first in the function:

```
MsgBox "Stat = " & CStr(Stat)
```

That would not only tell you if the function was getting called but also that it was receiving the value you were expecting.

Then, if you wanted to check to see what value was being returned, you could change the function so that it looked like Listing 9-9.

Listing 9-9: The new `EvaluateStatus` function.

```
Dim ReturnValue
MsgBox "Stat = " & CStr(Stat)
If Stat > 200 Then
    ReturnValue = "Abnormally High"
End If

If Stat < 200 Then
    ReturnValue = "Normal"
End If
MsgBox "ReturnValue = " & ReturnValue
EvaluateStatus = ReturnValue
```

You'll notice that I added the variable `ReturnValue` and assigned the results of the `If...Then` statements to it instead of to `EvaluateStatus` directly. I had to do this if I wanted to display the value. I could have, instead, tried to do this:

```
MsgBox "ReturnValue = " & EvaluateStatus
```

This would confuse VBScript. When VBScript sees the name of a function inside an expression like this, it *calls the function* — even when it is already in the function.

Yes, it is legal to call a function inside that same function. The technique is called recursion, and I wouldn't recommend you mess with it unless you have a very specific reason to do so. It can become very confusing.

To avoid this potential mess, I had to introduce another variable and use it in the `MsgBox` and then assign it to `EvaluateStatus` last thing.

If I were now to load this page in Internet Explorer, I'd see that the first `MsgBox` would inform me that the value 200 was in fact received in the function, but that `ReturnValue` was empty by the time it was finished. This might lead me to suspect that the `If...Then` statement code wasn't executing, and if that didn't cause me to see the problem, I could put the additional `MsgBox` commands inside the `If...Then`s to verify that they weren't executing.

As you can see, the processes of using `MsgBox` to trace the flow and to check the value of variables at different points are complementary tactics. You'll use them together all the time. These are probably your biggest and most commonly used allies in the fight against bugs.

Tracing Code With the Status Bar or Label

The problem with `MsgBox` is that you have to click the OK button every time one comes up. If you are tracing the flow of a complex page, you may end up clicking through a dozen or more of them. Isn't there an easier way?

Yes, there is. You could use the status bar to indicate what's going on. You display text in the status bar by coding a line like this:

```
Window.Status = "Hello out there!"
```

This will display the text in the string on the status bar at the bottom of the Internet Explorer window.

This is an easy way to indicate that you have in fact arrived at a particular point in the program. You can even display the value of variables this way.

The problem with this technique is that it doesn't stop the flow of the program like the message box does, and if you overwrite a message too quickly with a new message, you may not have time to read the first one. Even worse, Internet Explorer itself uses the status bar to give the user feedback about what it is doing, so it could easily overwrite something you've put there.

Another option is to create ActiveX labels on your page to use just for debugging. Then you can have as many labels as you like, and you can fill different ones in at different parts of your application. This helps avoid the overwriting problem you have with the status bar but introduces the new problem of adding extra ActiveX controls to your page.

Each of these techniques has advantages and disadvantages. I usually prefer the simplicity of the message box over the other methods, even if it is tedious at times to click through each one of them. Again, use what you like best.

A More Comprehensive Solution

There is one other option, but it requires a little more setup initially. You add one ActiveX list box to your page and one subroutine. The new subroutine looks like Listing 9-10.

Listing 9-10: The `AddMsg` **subroutine.**

```
MessageListBox.AddItem Msg
```

`AddMsg` receives one argument: `Msg`. All it does is call the `AddItem` method of the list box and insert the string passed into the list box. This assumes, of course, that the name of the list box is `MessageListBox`.

Now you can change the button's `Click` event to look like Listing 9-11.

Listing 9-11: The new button's `Click` **event.**

```
Dim Returned
AddMsg "Before EvaluateStatus call"
Returned = EvaluateStatus(Int(StatusTextBox.Text))
AddMsg "After EvaluateStatus call"
StatusLabel.Caption = Returned
```

Change the `EvaluateStatus` function to look like Listing 9-12.

Listing 9-12: The new `EvaluateStatus` **function.**

```
Dim ReturnValue

AddMsg "In EvaluateStatus function. Stat = " & CStr(Stat)

If Stat > 200 Then
    ReturnValue = "Abnormally High"
    AddMsg "Inside first If...Then. Stat > 200"
End If

If Stat < 200 Then
    ReturnValue = "Normal"
    AddMsg "Inside second If...Then. Stat < 200"
End If

AddMsg "End of EvaluateStatus function. ReturnValue = " &
ReturnValue

EvaluateStatus = ReturnValue
```

I've added calls to the `AddMsg` subroutine throughout the program. Then when I load the page, enter a value, and click the Evaluate button, Figure 9-6 is what you see.

The benefit of this approach is obvious. There's no clicking, clicking, clicking though message boxes, and you see a complete list of the messages all in one spot.

The downside is that you have to create an extra ActiveX control on your page — at least while you're debugging — and you have to create the subroutine, but if the logic is complex, this can be a really nice approach.

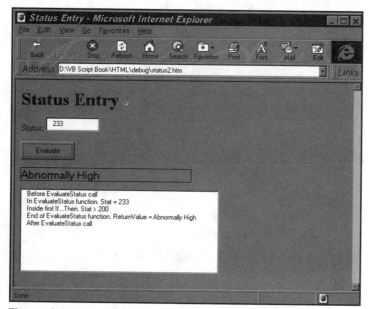

Figure 9-6: After the button is clicked.

If you want, you could expand this method so that you don't have to put the list box and subroutine in and take them out again every time you want to update and retest the page.

Here's what you do. Create a new global variable and call it `Debug`. In the Window's `OnLoad` event, code a line that sets the `Debug` variable to either True or False. Then code a statement that sets the `Visible` attribute to whatever `Debug` is (making it visible if `Debug` is True and invisible if it is False).

Finally, in the `AddMsg` subroutine, add an `If...Then` statement that only executes the `AddItem` line if `Debug` is True.

Once you've done all this, you can turn debug mode on or off just by changing how Debug is initialized in the OnLoad event. If it is True, the list box is made visible and the AddMsg routine will work. If not, the list box disappears, and calling AddMsg has no effect at all.

This way, you can put calls to the AddMsg subroutine throughout your code and just leave them there when you are done. They won't have any effect when Debug equals False and if you ever need to work on the page again, the whole structure will still be there!

Error Handling

Error handling is a part of development, not debugging. It is the process of writing code that will handle all the possible things that might happen to your program and handling them appropriately.

Most error handling revolves around the user. That's because, no matter what the program does or what other hardware or software it interfaces with, the most unpredictable element is always the user. That's even more true with VBScript where the interaction with the rest of the system or other applications is severely limited.

So in this section I'll focus my attention there: dealing with user input gracefully, no matter what they throw at you.

On Error Resume Next

Most modern computer languages offer some sort of error handling mechanism. VBScript, in an effort to keep it small and simple, does not. Well, it almost doesn't. In this section, I'll introduce you to the On Error Resume Next statement and show you how you can use it for rudimentary error handling.

Again, the best way to show you is through an example, so imagine a page that has a set of controls similar to the one in the last section: a text box, a command button, and a label.

This time, though, you enter your age, and the program calculates how old you are in dog years (see Figure 9-7).

The only code for this page is in the CalculateButton's Click event. That code is in Listing 9-13.

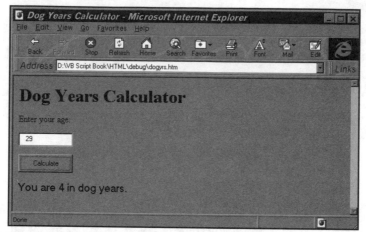

Figure 9-7: Dog-years calculator.

Listing 9-13: The `CalculateButton's` `Click` **event.**

```
Dim DogAge

' Integer division, ignoring any remainder
DogAge = Int(AgeTextBox.Text) \ 7

OutLabel.Caption = "You are " & CStr(DogAge) & " in dog
years."
```

This code converts the `Text` property of the text box into an integer and uses integer division (note the backslash instead of the slash for normal division) to divide it by 7. Then the result is converted to a string and concatenated with descriptive output.

This is very straightforward, and it works, too. As long as the user doesn't enter anything we're not expecting.

Suppose, however, that the user accidentally enters this:

```
1 2
```

This is a 1 and 2 separated by a space. `Int` won't like it. What if the user enters something like this:

```
Get lost
```

The Int function really won't like that. In fact, it will cause a Type Mismatch error on the line where Int tries to convert it.

This is where On Error Resume Next can come in handy. Listing 9-14 shows an updated Click event.

Listing 9-14: The CalculateButton's **updated** Click **event.**

```
Dim DogAge

On Error Resume Next

' Integer division, ignoring any remainder
DogAge = Int(AgeTextBox.Text) \ 7

If Err.Number <> 0 Then
    If Err.Number = 13 Then
        OutLabel.Caption = "Invalid age. Please enter a
number."
    Else
        MsgBox CStr(Err.Number) & ": " & Err.Description
    End If
Else
    OutLabel.Caption = "You are " & CStr(DogAge) & " in dog
years."
End If
```

On Error Resume Next tells VBScript, "Look if there are any errors, don't go nuts and tell the user about it. Just keep going like nothing happened, and everything will be OK."

Because VBScript doesn't just give up anymore when you use this command, you can check for errors after the fact to see if you can do anything about them. How? By using the Err object.

Err is a simple object that is built into VBScript. It has several properties and a couple of methods. The most important properties are Number and Description. These, as you might expect, give you the current error's number and description. If the user enters a string that can't be converted to a number by Int, it will always generate a Type Mismatch error. Type Mismatch's error number is 13.

 How do you figure out what error number a particular error is? Well, just set up your code so that the error will happen, put an On Error Resume Next in and then a line like this right after the line where the error will occur:

```
MsgBox CStr(Err.Number) & ": " & Err.Description
```

Then you'll know the error number, and you'll be able to see the description to make sure it was the error you expected.

So what does this routine do? The `On Error Resume Next` line appears first thing after the `Dim` statement. Then `Int` attempts the conversion. If the conversion caused an error, I check to see if it was an error 13. If it was, I let the user know that he or she needs to enter a valid age. If it happened to be some other error that I didn't anticipate, I simply display the error number and message.

If no error occurs, I display the results of the calculation.

`On Error Resume Next` only works for the procedure or event you are currently in. If you want to use it throughout your page, you'll have to specify it in each routine.

TIP If you plan to use `On Error Resume Next` in your VBScript applications, be sure you wait to add it in until the page is completely debugged. If you're not careful, it can cause VBScript simply to ignore an error that you need to discover.

Preventive Error Handling

The approach I just showed you works well, but I think another approach to error handling is very important. I call it *preventative* error handling.

I think the technique I just outlined is a bit reminiscent of closing the barn door after the cow has already escaped, if you'll allow me the Midwestern cliché. In other words, it waits until an error has happened before it tries to clean things up.

A better approach is to anticipate errors and try to avoid them before they happen. For instance, the `Click` event for the example used in the last section could be written like Listing 9-15.

Listing 9-15: Preventive error handling.

```
Dim DogAge

If IsNumeric(AgeTextBox.Text) Then
    ' Integer division, ignoring any remainder
    DogAge = Int(AgeTextBox.Text) \ 7
    OutLabel.Caption = "You are " & CStr(DogAge) & " in dog
years."
Else
   OutLabel.Caption = "Invalid age. Please enter a number."
End If
```

The `IsNumeric` function looks at a string and determines whether it can be converted to a number, and it returns a True or False so it can be used right inside the `If...Then` statement as I've done here. Only once I'm sure it can be converted successfully, do I call the `Int` function. If it cannot, I tell the user about the problem.

I can also use an `IsDate` function to see if a string can successfully be converted to a date and/or time.

This approach ends up being more concise and a better solution since the problem is handled before it becomes an error, not after.

Does this mean you should never use `On Error Resume Next`? No. Sometimes you cannot do preventive error handling, and there are undoubtedly times when it just makes more sense to use `On Error Resume Next`. Use your own judgment.

For more information on preventive error handling, see Chapter 12. My discussion there on validation and formatting goes into more detail about the ways you can make sure your data is good before using it. Although the discussion there is focused on making sure data is correct before sending it to the server, the same techniques apply to making sure it is correct before you use it for anything.

Summary

After describing the way to set up your environment and the process you should go through when writing and debugging your applications, I described a number of common errors and how to go about fixing them. After that, I gave you some tools for tracing your program's execution: the message box, the status bar, and label controls. Then I described a more comprehensive strategy that works well for large or complex pages.

After I finished talking about debugging, I launched into the topic of error handling. I showed you what `On Error Resume Next` does and how you can use the `Err` object to handle errors after they happen. Finally, I addressed the topic of preventive error handling that attempts to handle potential problems before they turn into errors.

Cool VBScript Web Page Examples

In this chapter I'm going to show you how to put all these new skills to work in creating some real full-blown web page projects. The first project is pure entertainment: a puzzle game that's very addictive. The second is practical: a series of recipes that automatically adjust their ingredients based on the serving size you enter. The last one is educational: a math practice page that generates an endless number of problems and another that provides a timed test. Either way, the computer tracks which ones you get right and wrong. Finally, at the end of this chapter, I've included a section called "Techniques for Your Own Pages," which provides a few smaller examples that you could integrate into any page you create to make it come alive.

Creating Cool VBScript Pages

By now you have a pretty solid understanding of how VBScript works and what mechanics are involved in using it in a web page. What you don't yet have is an example of a full-blown web page blending the best of HTML and VBScript. The examples in this chapter will provide that. That said, there's lots of room for improvement in these examples and I'll end each section by discussing some of my ideas for making them better. I'm sure you'll be able to think of lots of your own. So take these examples, use them as a starting point for your own pages (similar or different), and make them your own.

Light-It-Up!

Light-It-Up! is a puzzle game with a 5-by-5 grid of buttons that you can press to toggle their color from white to black or from black to white. The catch is that when you press one button, not only that button, but all the ones around it are also toggled: white to black and black to white. The goal of the game is to turn all the lights on: to make all the buttons white. Figure 10-1 shows what a game in progress looks like.

It is similar to a popular hand-held game from Tiger Electronics, Inc. called Lights Out. You may have seen ads on TV or seen the game in the store.

For being such a simple idea, Light-It-Up! is incredibly addicting. You immediately begin to see patterns and ways of manipulating the colors to change them. Like Tetris and Solitaire attest — the best games are always the simple ones.

Creating the HTML and ActiveX Controls

It is always easiest to think through what you are going to need and then implement that using HTML and ActiveX controls before you ever start writing your VBScript code. I know it's tempting to go in and just start writing VBScript, but if you do you'll end up having to jump in and out of the Script Wizard every time you think of a new control you need.

For this project, the main thing you are going to need is a playing field. The playing field for this game is simple: 25 buttons in five rows of five. The easiest way to do it is to use the Insert ActiveX Control menu option to create a single Microsoft Forms 2.0 CommandButton and be very careful to get it just as you want. Table 10-1 lists the properties to change and the values to set them to. Leave the rest at their default values.

Table 10-1 The Properties to Change for the First Game-Board Button	
Property	**Value**
ID	Button1
Height	24
Width	37
BackColor	00000000 - Unknown (Go to the color dialog box and find black.)

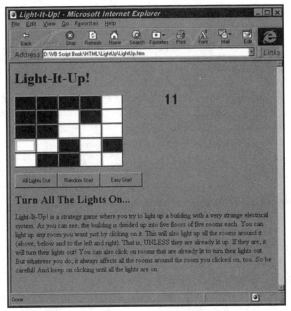

Figure 10-1: A Light-It-Up! game in progress.

The problem is, you need 25 of these guys. It wouldn't be much fun to do what you just did 25 times! It isn't necessary either. Just select the HTML object tag (everything between <OBJECT ...> and </OBJECT>) and press Ctrl-C. That copies it to the clipboard. Now move the cursor to the line just after </OBJECT> and press Ctrl-V. The HTML is pasted in. Keep pressing Ctrl-V until you have five button objects. Now type this on a line by itself:

```
<br>
```

Now paste five more in! Keep pasting five, adding a line break and pasting five until you have five sets of five.

You have just created 25 identical ActiveX controls on your page in five rows of five each. You only have one thing left to do. Rename them. Right now they all have the same name: Button1. It's a little tedious, but you'll have to go to each control and name it incrementally: Button1, Button2, Button3, up to Button25. Don't edit each one. Just change the ID property in the HTML object tag. For instance, for the second one change this:

```
<OBJECT ID="Button1" WIDTH=49 HEIGHT=32
```

To this:

```
<OBJECT ID="Button2" WIDTH=49 HEIGHT=32
```

TIP You can often change a property right in the HTML <OBJECT> tag rather than having to edit the object. As you can see in this example, it can potentially save you a lot of time. Be careful, though. Not all properties are available, and some properties are specified differently in the HTML than they are when you edit the object. The Width and Height, for instance, will not be the same value in the HTML as you set them when you created or modified the object. That's because they are measuring with two different units.

Now save your page under the name LightUp.HTM and look at it in the browser. If you add an <h1> header above your HTML controls that says Light-It-Up!, it should look like Figure 10-2.

Now you need to add just a few more controls. You can start by adding three more Microsoft Forms 2.0 CommandButtons below the grid you just created, but don't use the copying method to create these. These will be normal buttons the user clicks to initiate actions. You'll probably want a <p> between the grid and these buttons to give them some space. Table 10-2 summarizes the buttons and their properties. Leave the Height and Width and everything else at the default value.

Table 10-2	The Buttons below the Grid.
Property	**Value**
ID	AllOutButton
Caption	All Lights Out
ID	RandomStartButton
Caption	Random Start
ID	EasyStartButton
Caption	Easy Start

I added one more ActiveX control on the page just to keep things interesting. It is a counter for the number of times the user has clicked on the grid. This adds an additional element of challenge not only to solve it but to do it in the fewest clicks possible. I wanted this timer to appear beside the board near the top, but I didn't want it immediately beside it.

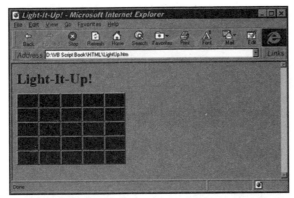

Figure 10-2: The header and the game board are ready to go!

Go up to the first set of five buttons on the grid. Make a couple of free lines right before the `<br>`, insert a Microsoft Forms 2.0 Label control, and set the properties using Table 10-3.

Table 10-3 The Properties for the Label that Keeps Track of the Number of Clicks.

Property	Value
ID	ClickLabel
Font	24pt MS Sans Serif, Bold (Go into the font dialog box to set these values.)
Height	29
Width	95
Caption	0 (That's zero, not O.)
TextAlign	3 - Right

The font is large, but the width is much longer than it needs to be to hold the two or three digits it will need to hold. The extra length, along with the alignment of the text to the right, will put the desired space between the grid and the counter.

Finally, I added the lines in Listing 10-1 after the row of buttons at the bottom of the grid and before the `</BODY>`. By the way, if you haven't been saving this page as you've been creating it, now would probably be a good time to do so.

Listing 10-1: The description text.

```
<p>
<h2>Turn All The Lights On...</h2>
Light-It-Up! is a strategy game where you try to light up
a building
with a very strange electrical system. As you can see, the
building is divided up into five floors of five rooms
each. You can
light up any room you want just by clicking on it. This
will also light
up all the rooms around it (above, below and to the left
and right). That
is, UNLESS they are already lit up. If they are, it will
turn their lights
out! You can also click on rooms that are already lit to
turn their lights
out. But whatever you do, it always affects all the rooms
around the
room you clicked on, too. So be careful! And keep on
clicking until
all the lights are on.<p>
```

A building with a strange electrical system? OK, it's a little lame, but it is customary to come up with back-stories that justify a game's existence even when it is obviously a very abstract logic puzzle. This is the best one I could concoct. I also thought about describing it as splashing paint on a wall but....

The page should look very much like its final form (see Figure 10-3).

Now it's time for the fun part.

Writing the Game

We will do most of this section from within the Script Wizard. I highly recommend that you get out of the Script Wizard every now and then to save the page. It isn't any fun to work on scripting for a half an hour and lose it all just because you accidentally press the Esc key and the dialog box closes, disposing of all your changes.

You'll also want to get out to check out your handiwork in Internet Explorer, of course.

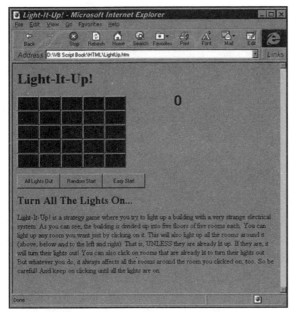

Figure 10-3: All the controls and text are there.

Creating the Global Variables

The first thing you'll need is a way of referring to the button controls in the grid. Something easier than Button7, Button15, and so on. Therefore, create a global variable that looks like this:

```
Grid(5,5)
```

Grid is a two-dimensional array. In a moment, I'll fill it in with the appropriate buttons. That provides a nice, easy way to tell what buttons are above and below the current button. Determining which button is above Button7 is difficult without doing a little math, but the button above Grid(2,2) is Grid(1,2), and the one below is Grid(3,2). Remember that the custom is to use the first number to specify the rows and the second one to specify the columns.

While you're at it, create two more global variables:

```
Black
White
```

These will hold the values for these colors. They just provide a shorthand to make the code easier to write and easier to read.

Initializing the Global Variables

Now you need to initialize these variables. As usual, the best place for that is the OnLoad event of the Window object. Listing 10-2 shows you what it should look like.

Listing 10-2: The Window's OnLoad event initializes the global variables.

```
Set Grid(1,1) = Button1
Set Grid(1,2) = Button2
Set Grid(1,3) = Button3
Set Grid(1,4) = Button4
Set Grid(1,5) = Button5
Set Grid(2,1) = Button6
Set Grid(2,2) = Button7
Set Grid(2,3) = Button8
Set Grid(2,4) = Button9
Set Grid(2,5) = Button10
Set Grid(3,1) = Button11
Set Grid(3,2) = Button12
Set Grid(3,3) = Button13
Set Grid(3,4) = Button14
Set Grid(3,5) = Button15
Set Grid(4,1) = Button16
Set Grid(4,2) = Button17
Set Grid(4,3) = Button18
Set Grid(4,4) = Button19
Set Grid(4,5) = Button20
Set Grid(5,1) = Button21
Set Grid(5,2) = Button22
Set Grid(5,3) = Button23
Set Grid(5,4) = Button24
Set Grid(5,5) = Button25

White = RGB(255,255,255)
Black = RGB(0,0,0)
```

To make entering all those set lines easier, type in the first five and then copy and paste them five times. Then, just go back and change the grid numbers and button numbers. White and Black are initialized using the RGB function.

Create the Flip Subroutine

Now you have a grid that you can refer to using row and column coordinates and an easy way to refer to colors. The next thing to do is create a routine that changes a button's color. Create a new procedure. The header for the procedure should be this:

```
Sub Flip(GridX, GridY)
```

The procedure's body is in Listing 10-3.

Listing 10-3: The Flip subroutine.

```
If GridX >= 1 And GridX <= 5 And _
    GridY >= 1 And GridY <= 5 Then
        If Grid(GridX, GridY).BackColor = White Then
            Grid(GridX, GridY).BackColor = Black
        Else
            Grid(GridX, GridY).BackColor = White
        End If
End If
```

Flip receives two coordinates into the grid and toggles the color for the button at that coordinate, but it first checks to be sure that coordinate is within range. If the coordinates are out of range, this routine does nothing.

Create the Splash Subroutine

Now create another procedure. Its header should look like this:

```
Sub Splash(GridX,GridY)
```

and its body is in Listing 10-4.

Listing 10-4: The Splash subroutine.

```
Flip GridX,GridY
Flip GridX+1,GridY
Flip GridX-1,GridY
Flip GridX,GridY+1
Flip GridX,GridY-1
ClickLabel.Caption = CStr(Int(ClickLabel.Caption)+1)
```

Splash is what will be called from an individual button on the grid when it is pressed. The button will send its coordinates into the Splash subroutine. Splash will then call Flip with the coordinates sent, for the grid coordinates just to the left and right, and for the coordinates below and above. I don't have to bother checking to see if these grid coordinates are within range because Flip has that built in. If I ask Flip to flip the button at coordinates (3,6), it will just ignore it and do nothing.

Finally, I increment the number of clicks label. I have to do some gymnastics with the conversion functions here. Here's what's happening: I convert the original value from a string to an integer so that I can add one to it. The result is converted back into a string so that it can be assigned back to the Caption property of the ClickLabel and displayed.

Call Splash from All the Grid Buttons

This is going to be the most tedious part of the VBScript code. You need to go to the click event for each button in the grid, starting with Button1 and add the following line of code to their Click event:

```
Splash 1,1
```

Actually, you'll need to change that for each button. That one will work for Button1. Button2's Click event should look like this:

```
Splash 1,2
```

And Button5's Click event should look like this:

```
Splash 1,5
```

You have the idea. Button6's Click event should look like this:

```
Splash 2,1
```

Remember that the first number should increase after every five buttons. You should never be sending a coordinate greater than 5. Button25's Click event should look like this:

```
Splash 5,5
```

Once you have all those done, you have the basic framework for the game in place! In fact, you can start playing the game right now.

Trying it Out

Save the page and load it up in Internet Explorer. Try clicking on a button. That button and all the ones around it should turn white. Now click on the button beside the first one (which is now white). That button and the first button you clicked should turn black again but all the rest of the buttons around it should turn white.

Play with it a while. See if you can light them all up, or at least all but one or two. If you've never played a game like this before, you'll probably begin to see the attraction.

What if You Win?

If you are lucky enough to turn on all the lights, you'll notice one thing: the game doesn't even seem to notice. No fireworks, no flashing lights — nothing. This is somewhat anticlimactic after all that hard work.

Go back to Control Pad and see if you can remedy that situation.

Create a new procedure with this header:

```
Sub CheckForWin()
```

Use the code in Listing 10-5.

Listing 10-5: The CheckForWin subroutine.

```
Dim Rows,Cols, Win
Win = True
For Rows = 1 To 5
    For Cols = 1 To 5

        If Grid(Rows,Cols).BackColor = Black Then Win =
False
    Next
Next

If Win = True Then
    MsgBox "You Win! And it only took you " &
ClickLabel.Caption & " clicks!"
End If
```

This subroutine starts off with the optimistic assumption that the user has won. Then, using a nested For...Next loop (a loop within a loop), it goes through each and every button and checks to see if it is Black. If it is, it sets Win to False. When the loops are done, an If...Then checks to see if Win is still True. If it is, a message box is displayed congratulating the user.

All right, so it's not fireworks and flashing lights. I'll leave that for you to implement. A very cool addition here would make use of the grid for a cool graphical effect. You could make the grid buttons flash on and off randomly, or you could create an exploding design that starts in the middle of the grid and grows outward. Using the grid, you could do lots of things with a little creativity.

Calling CheckForWin

Hold on a second! When is this subroutine called? Right now it isn't? Where should it be called? Well, whenever the board could become all White. Every click, once the Splash is done, it could happen. That's where the call should be: at the end of the Splash subroutine. Listing 10-6 shows the Splash subroutine with the call added.

Listing 10-6: The Splash **subroutine with the call to** CheckForWin.

```
Flip GridX,GridY
Flip GridX+1,GridY
Flip GridX-1,GridY
Flip GridX,GridY+1
Flip GridX,GridY-1
ClickLabel.Caption = CStr(Int(ClickLabel.Caption)+1)
CheckForWin
```

Now, every time the user clicks a button to change the board, your page will check to see if he or she has won.

Get out of the Script Wizard and save the page.

If you won when you played the game the first time, you might want to try to load the page up in Internet Explorer and see if you can win again to be sure the CheckForWin message box is displayed. Lighting the entire building up from an all black building isn't easy, so you might want to wait to test this feature until we implement the code for the Easy Start button.

All Lights Out

After I reached this point in creating the page, I decided that I needed some different ways of starting the game or restarting it when you're stuck. That's when I added the buttons along the bottom of the grid.

The first one is called All Lights Out, and it does just as it says: it returns the board to the way it was when the page was loaded, all black.

Before you write the code for the Click event of this button, though, create a new procedure. Its header should look like this:

```
Sub ColorGrid(Color)
```

and its body is in Listing 10-7.

Listing 10-7: The ColorGrid subroutine.

```
Dim Rows,Cols

For Rows = 1 To 5
    For Cols = 1 To 5
        Grid(Rows,Cols).BackColor = Color
    Next
Next
```

This routine accepts a color and then sets the entire grid to that color. Technically it could be any value returned from the RGB function, but for this page, you'll only ever send it the global variables Black or White.

Now that AllOutButton's Click event should be easy. It's in Listing 10-8.

Listing 10-8: The AllOutButton's very simple Click event.

```
ColorGrid(Black)
ClickLabel.Caption = "0"
```

The first line calls the new subroutine with Black. The second line resets the ClickLabel counter to 0 because the user wants to start over.

We have one button down and two more to go.

Random Start

To provide the user with nearly endless gaming possibilities, I decided to add this button to provide a random starting board from which to work. It was also a bit selfish in that it also meant that I didn't have to create dozens of predesigned boards. If users don't like a board, they can just keep clicking this button until they find one they do like and work from there. If they are very, very lucky, the random program will actually start them with all the buttons White and they'll win automatically! Of course, this will only happen 1 out of every 33,000,000 times (according to my calculations), but it is possible.

Listing 10-9 shows the code for the RandomStartButton's OnClick event.

Listing 10-9: The `RandomStartButton`'s `OnClick` **event.**

```
Dim Rows,Cols

Randomize
For Rows = 1 To 5
    For Cols = 1 To 5
        If Rnd > .5 Then
            Grid(Rows,Cols).BackColor = Black
        Else
            Grid(Rows,Cols).BackColor = White
        End If
    Next
Next

ClickLabel.Caption = "0"
```

I used another nested loop here to be sure it visits every single button. I use the Rnd function here which, you remember, returns a decimal number between 0 and 1. In this case, if it is greater than .5 (which it should be about half the time), I set the current button to Black; otherwise, it is set to White. This should result in roughly half black and half white squares each time, although for any given time, you could have a lot more black or a lot more white. It's all random!

Easy Start

If you've tried to play this little game from an all-black start or even one of the random boards, you know that it can be tough. In order to avoid scaring away new players, I've included five predesigned boards that users can solve relatively quickly. That's not to say you can't get lost on a bunny trail and get stuck with these boards, too. You can, but these are much easier to solve than a random distribution.

What does the code look like? See Listing 10-10.

Listing 10-10: The `EasyStartButton's Click` **event.**

```
Dim Rows, Cols, Choice

Randomize



Choice = Int(Rnd * 5)+1
Select Case Choice
Case 1
    ColorGrid(Black)
    For Rows = 1 To 5
        Grid(Rows, 3).BackColor = White
    Next
    For Cols = 1 To 5
        Grid(2, Cols).BackColor = White
        Grid(4, Cols).BackColor = White
    Next
Case 2
    ColorGrid(White)
    Grid(1,3).BackColor = Black
    Grid(3,3).BackColor = Black
    Grid(5,3).BackColor = Black
Case 3
    ColorGrid(White)
    For Rows = 1 To 5

        If Rows <> 3 Then
            Grid(Rows, 2).BackColor = Black
            Grid(Rows, 5).BackColor = Black
        End If
    Next
    Grid(1,4).BackColor = Black
    Grid(5,4).BackColor = Black
Case 4
    ColorGrid(White)
    For Rows = 2 To 4
        Grid(Rows, 1).BackColor = Black
```

(continued)

```
(continued)
          Grid(Rows, 5).BackColor = Black

    Next
      For Cols = 2 To 4
          Grid(1, Cols).BackColor = Black
          Grid(5, Cols).BackColor = Black
      Next
      Grid(3,3).BackColor = Black
Case 5
      ColorGrid(Black)
      For Rows = 1 To 3
          Grid(Rows,2).BackColor = White
          Grid(Rows,4).BackColor = White
      Next
      For Rows = 3 To 5
          Grid(Rows,1).BackColor = White
          Grid(Rows,5).BackColor = White
      Next
      For Cols = 2 To 4
          Grid(1,Cols).BackColor = White
          Grid(5,Cols).BackColor = White
      Next
End Select

ClickLabel.Caption = "0"
```

This is a long bit of code, but it is all pretty simple. A random number between 1 and 5 is generated and then the `Select Case` statement branches off based on the random value. Case 1 sets the grid to all black and then draws three white lines using two `For...Next` loops. The resulting board looks like Figure 10-4.

Case 2 sets the grid to all white and then flips three individual buttons. The result looks like Figure 10-5.

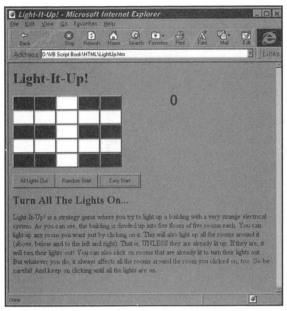

Figure 10-4: The first Easy Start board.

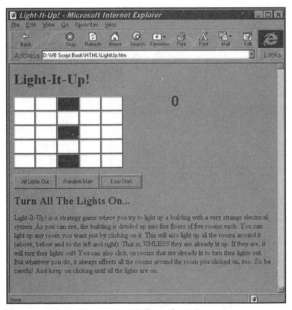

Figure 10-5: The second Easy Start board.

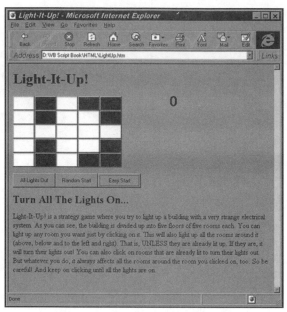

Figure 10-6: The third Easy Start board.

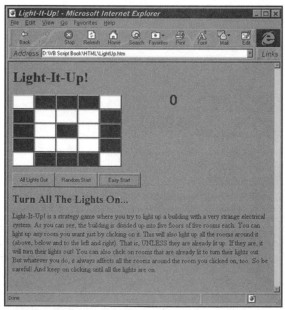

Figure 10-7: The fourth Easy Start board.

Case 3 also sets the grid to all white and then draws two lines across the board skipping over row 3. Finally it sets two buttons individually. The result is Figure 10-6.

Case 4 turns the grid white, draws four black lines within two For...Next loops, and sets one button individually. The result is Figure 10-7.

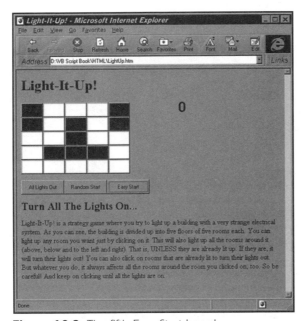

Figure 10-8: The fifth Easy Start board.

Finally, Case 5 sets the grid to black and then uses three For...Next loops to create six lines. Figure 10-8 is the result.

There's no magic about the way I set these boards up. After I determined what I wanted the board to look like, I just tried to write the code that would create a board like that in the fewest lines of code.

The last line resets the click counter to 0 because the user is starting a new game.

Ideas for Making it Better

A nice addition to this game would be a more easy start, predesigned levels. How do you come up with easy levels? Just start with an all white board, click between five and ten times, and try to make an interesting pattern. By working backwards from a completed board and not using too many clicks to create it, you'll be assured of creating a starting point that can, potentially, be solved in the same number of moves you used to create it.

It would also be nice if users could choose a specific easy start board and start it over whenever they wanted. You could even provide a start-over feature for the randomly created boards, too. To do it, you'd have to create another 5 by 5 grid, this time of boolean variables where `True` is `White` and `False` is `Black`. You'd have to fill in this new grid whenever the user started over (any time the click counter is set back to 0). Then in the Start Over button, just clear the game grid and use the boolean to set the board up as it was.

Here's another idea: provide hints. Give users a button that they can press to receive a hint for their first move only on each Easy Start game board. Usually a hint on the first move is all they'll need to set them off and running in the right direction.

A Dynamic Recipe Book

Recipes are valuable information in some circles, but not so valuable that you don't want to give them away! In fact, the World Wide Web is an ideal place for sharing old family recipes with the world.

Because it's the web and because dynamic pages are so easy with VBScript, why not go beyond a simple recipe? You can make the recipe dynamic by automatically adjusting the ingredients to match whatever serving size the user enters. That way, a dinner for 2 can become a dinner for 20 with just the click of a button.

Figure 10-9 shows the index for this recipe book.

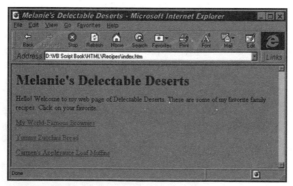

Figure 10-9: Recipe book index.

All right, perhaps *book* is too strong a word to use because we only have three recipes, but I've provided you with a framework for easily using what I've done to create your own recipe pages and include as many as you want!

When you click on the first link in the index page, you'll see the page in Figure 10-10.

I've listed the ingredients at the top, and I've put the directions in the text box in the middle. At the bottom, I've provided the number of servings that this recipe creates. If you want to change the number of servings, simply type a different number into the Serves text box and click the Change button. The ingredients at the top of the page are immediately adjusted for the new number of servings. Nifty.

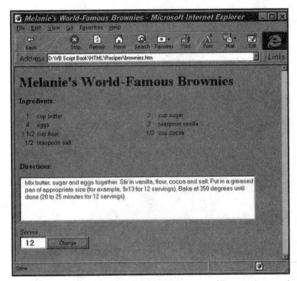

Figure 10-10: Melanie's World-Famous Brownies recipe page.

Figures 10-11 and 10-12 show the other two recipe pages I've created.

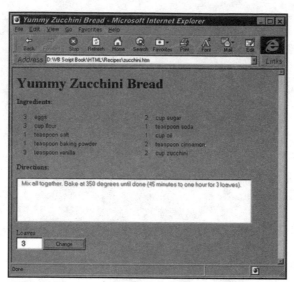

Figure 10-11: Yummy Zucchini Bread recipe page.

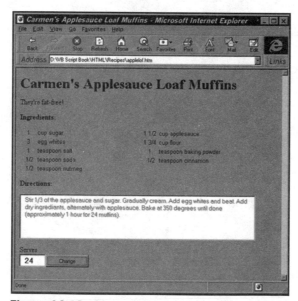

Figure 10-12: Carmen's Applesauce Loaf Muffins recipe page.

Creating the Index Page

The index page is a no-brainer. Just some simple HTML (see Listing 10-11).

Listing 10-11: The index page.

```
<HTML>
<HEAD>
<TITLE>Melanie's Delectable Deserts</TITLE>
</HEAD>
<BODY>
<H1>Melanie's Delectable Deserts</H1>
Hello! Welcome to my web page of Delectable Deserts. These
are
some of my favorite family recipes. Click on your
favorite.<p>
<A HREF="brownies.htm">My World-Famous Brownies</A><p>
<A HREF="zucchini.htm">Yummy Zucchini Bread</A><p>
<A HREF="applelof.htm">Carmen's Applesauce Loaf
Muffins</A><p>
</BODY>
</HTML>
```

Just a simple page with three links, this page assumes the other pages will be in the same directory as the index.

Melanie's World Famous Brownies

My wife Melanie loves to bake, and she makes few things better than brownies. So when I decided to do this project, this was my first choice for recipes. The card she gave me looked something like this:

---

1 cup butter

2 cups sugar

4 eggs

2 teaspoons vanilla

1 1/2 cups of flour

1/2 cup of cocoa

1/2 teaspoon of salt

Mix butter × sugar × eggs. Stir in vanilla, flour, cocoa and salt. Put in a greased 9×13 pan. Bake at 350 degrees 20 to 25 minutes. Serves 12.

We should be able to make a web page out of this. In fact, if you didn't want the web page to figure the ingredients dynamically based on the servings entered, it would be a piece of cake (no pun intended). You could do it all in HTML.

But that wouldn't be any fun, would it? Besides, adjusting the servings shouldn't be too tough. It's just a little math, right?

Creating the HTML and ActiveX controls

Now it's the time to create a brand new HTML page to hold the recipe. This new page will be the one that you see if you click on "My World Famous Brownies" on the Index page you created earlier.

I struggled a little bit on this page about what should be an ActiveX control and what should be simple HTML text. At first, I made the ingredient amounts ActiveX controls and the ingredient descriptions simple HTML text, but I had a tough time aligning them so that they looked right. I ended up making both the amount and the description separate ActiveX Labels.

This means, though, that you end up with 20 labels on the page for a simple ten ingredient recipe. I have limited this page to ten, but you could easily extend it if you like.

So after giving the page a title and an <h1> header identifying the recipe, I added an <h4> level header to identify the list as Ingredients.

Then come the labels. I used two Label Object ActiveX controls for each ingredient. Table 10-4 summarizes the properties I set for each.

Table 10-4 The Properties for the Ingredient Amount and Description.

Property	Value
ID	AmountLabel1
Alignment	4 - Centered
Height	15
Width	30
Caption	(empty)
FontName	Arial
FontSize	10

ID	DescLabel1
Alignment	3 - Left Centered
Height	15
Width	175
Caption	(empty)
FontName	Arial
FontSize	10

In order to make a total of 10 sets of controls, you'll want to use the same copy and paste method I described in the last example. Select the <OBJECT> tags that create these two controls, press Ctrl-C to copy them to the clipboard, move the cursor down below, and press Ctrl-V to paste them. After you have two amount/description pairs, add a <br> so that only two ingredients are listed per line. Now select both sets of controls (4 controls total) and the <br> tag and copy it to the clipboard. Paste in 4 more times to give a total of 10 amount/description pairs on lines.

Now you must go back and rename them. The first two should be named AmountLabel1 and DescLabel1 as in Table 10-4. You'll have to change the second to AmountLabel2 and DescLabel2, the third to AmountLabel3 and DescLabel3, and so on up to AmountLabel10 and DescLabel10. You don't have to edit the object to do each of these, though. Just change this line:

```
<OBJECT ID="AmountLabel1" WIDTH=40 HEIGHT=20
```

to this:

```
<OBJECT ID="AmountLabel2" WIDTH=40 HEIGHT=20
```

and so on through all the <OBJECT> tags.

Now the hard part is over. Listing 10-12 shows what the rest of the page looks like.

Listing 10-12: The bottom part of the Brownies page.

```
<OBJECT ID="AmountLabel10" WIDTH=40 HEIGHT=20
    CLASSID="CLSID:99B42120-6EC7-11CF-A6C7-00AA00A47DD2">
        <PARAM NAME="_ExtentX" VALUE="1058">
        . . .
        <PARAM NAME="BotPoints" VALUE="0">
    </OBJECT>
```

(continued)

```
(continued)
     <OBJECT ID="DescLabel10" WIDTH=233 HEIGHT=20
      CLASSID="CLSID:99B42120-6EC7-11CF-A6C7-00AA00A47DD2">
         <PARAM NAME="_ExtentX" VALUE="6165">
         ...
         <PARAM NAME="BotPoints" VALUE="0">
     </OBJECT>
<br>
<h4>Directions:</h4><p>
     <OBJECT ID="DirectionsTextBox" WIDTH=533 HEIGHT=100


     CLASSID="CLSID:8BD21D10-EC42-11CE-9E0D-00AA006002F3">
         <PARAM NAME="VariousPropertyBits"
VALUE="2894088217">
         <PARAM NAME="ScrollBars" VALUE="2">
         <PARAM NAME="Size" VALUE="14111;2646">
         <PARAM NAME="FontEffects" VALUE="1073750016">
         <PARAM NAME="FontHeight" VALUE="200">
         <PARAM NAME="FontCharSet" VALUE="0">
         <PARAM NAME="FontPitchAndFamily" VALUE="2">
         <PARAM NAME="FontWeight" VALUE="0">
     </OBJECT>
<p>
Serves<br>
     <OBJECT ID="ServesTextBox" WIDTH=60 HEIGHT=28
      CLASSID="CLSID:8BD21D10-EC42-11CE-9E0D-00AA006002F3">
         <PARAM NAME="VariousPropertyBits"
VALUE="746604571">
         <PARAM NAME="Size" VALUE="1582;741">
         <PARAM NAME="FontEffects" VALUE="1073741825">
         <PARAM NAME="FontHeight" VALUE="240">
         <PARAM NAME="FontCharSet" VALUE="0">
         <PARAM NAME="FontPitchAndFamily" VALUE="2">
         <PARAM NAME="FontWeight" VALUE="700">
     </OBJECT>
<OBJECT ID="ChangeButton" WIDTH=96 HEIGHT=27
 CLASSID="CLSID:D7053240-CE69-11CD-A777-00DD01143C57">
     <PARAM NAME="Caption" VALUE="Change">
     <PARAM NAME="Size" VALUE="2540;709">
     <PARAM NAME="FontCharSet" VALUE="0">
     <PARAM NAME="FontPitchAndFamily" VALUE="2">
     <PARAM NAME="ParagraphAlign" VALUE="3">
     <PARAM NAME="FontWeight" VALUE="0">
</OBJECT>
</BODY>
</HTML>
```

Of course you don't want to type in the `<OBJECT>` tags by hand. Use Table 10-5 along with the Insert ActiveX Control menu option in Control Pad to add the three controls at the bottom of the page.

Table 10-5 The Three ActiveX Controls at the Bottom of the Brownies Page.

Property	Value
Microsoft Forms 2.0 Text Box	
ID	DirectionsTextBox
Enabled	False
Font	10pt MS Sans Serif
Height	75
Width	400
Multiline	-1 - True
Text	(empty)
WordWrap	-1 - True
Microsoft Forms 2.0 TextBox	
ID	ServesTextBox
Font	12pt MS Sans Serif, Bold
Height	21
Width	45
Microsoft Forms 2.0 CommandButton	
ID	ChangeButton
CaptionChange	
Height	20
Width	72

That's all you need for the page itself. Save the page. When you load it up in Internet Explorer, it should look like Figure 10-13.

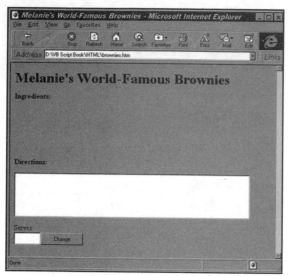

Figure 10-13: The HTML and ActiveX controls are done.

Activating Your Page with VBScript

Now you are ready to make the page come alive with VBScript, and you really don't have all that much code to write.

Creating the Global Variables

This page uses three global variables. The first two are arrays:

```
Amount(10)
AmountForStandard(10)
```

Amount holds the labels where the amounts are displayed. As in the last example, it is easier to refer to a series of controls through an array rather than by names like AmountLabel7 and AmountLabel9. The description labels are only filled in once, so they don't need an array for accessing them.

AmountForStandard holds on to the values that are displayed for the standard servings when the page is first displayed:

```
StandardServings
```

StandardServings holds the number of servings displayed when the page is first displayed.

I'll talk more about each of these in the next couple of sections. Once you see how they are used, they will make more sense to you.

Initializing the Global Variables

After the global variables are created, you need to give them values. As usual, the Window's `OnLoad` is the place to do that (see Listing 10-13).

Listing 10-13: The Window's OnLoad event initializes the global variables.

```
StandardServings = 12
AmountForStandard(1) = 1
AmountForStandard(2) = 2
AmountForStandard(3) = 4
AmountForStandard(4) = 2
AmountForStandard(5) = 1.5
AmountForStandard(6) = .5
AmountForStandard(7) = .5
AmountForStandard(8) = 0
AmountForStandard(9) = 0
AmountForStandard(10) = 0

DescLabel1.Caption = "cup butter"
DescLabel2.Caption = "cup sugar"
DescLabel3.Caption = "eggs"
DescLabel4.Caption = "teaspoon vanilla"
DescLabel5.Caption = "cup flour"
DescLabel6.Caption = "cup cocoa"
DescLabel7.Caption = "teaspoon salt"
DescLabel8.Caption = ""
DescLabel9.Caption = ""
DescLabel10.Caption = ""

Set Amount(1) = AmountLabel1
Set Amount(2) = AmountLabel2
Set Amount(3) = AmountLabel3
Set Amount(4) = AmountLabel4
Set Amount(5) = AmountLabel5
Set Amount(6) = AmountLabel6
Set Amount(7) = AmountLabel7
Set Amount(8) = AmountLabel8
Set Amount(9) = AmountLabel9
Set Amount(10) = AmountLabel10

DirectionsTextBox.Text = "Mix butter, sugar and eggs
together. Stir in vanilla, flour, " & _
```

(continued)

```
(continued)
    "cocoa and salt. Put in a greased pan of appropriate
size (for example, 9x13 for " & _
    "12 servings). Bake at 350 degrees until done (20 to 25
minutes for 12 servings)."

ServesTextBox.Text = CStr(StandardServings)

ChangeButton_Click
```

When a page is first displayed, it shows a standard, common number of servings for the recipe and the associated ingredient amounts. This information is saved in the StandardServings variable and AmountForStandard array. That way, when you need to calculate new ingredient amounts because the user has entered a new number of servings, you'll have something to work from (more on this later).

The first thing done is that the StandardServings variable and AmountForStandard array are filled in with the appropriate values. Notice that if the recipe calls for "1 1/2 cups flour" (as this does in the fifth ingredient) you must put 1.5 in the associated spot in the AmountForStandard array. Convert any fractions to their associated decimal numbers when you fill in the array.

Next, the DescLabels are filled in directly. Those won't change after they are initially set.

Next, the Amount array is associated with the AmountLabel controls so that they can be quickly and easily referenced later.

The DirectionsTextBox is filled in with the directions for this recipe. The value in this control won't change either. The ServesTextBox is then filled in with the value in StandardServings.

Notice that nowhere in this routine were the actual ingredient amounts filled in on the page. I filled in the AmountForStandard array but not the actual controls on the page. That's because I let the standard update routine do it for me. The last line calls the subroutine that executes when the user clicks the ChangeButton.

The ChangeButton

The only other VBScript code on this page is in the Click event of the ChangeButton. Listing 10-14 shows what it looks like.

Listing 10-14: The ChangeButton's Click **event.**

```
Dim Ingred, NewAmount, AmountForOne
Dim WholeString, Fractional, AmountString

For Ingred = 1 To 10
    If AmountForStandard(Ingred) <> 0 Then
        AmountForOne =
AmountForStandard(Ingred)/StandardServings
        NewAmount = Int(ServesTextBox.Text) * AmountForOne

        ' The code below is intended to make use of
        ' common fractions when appropriate.
        ' Additional fractions could be added and the ranges
        ' adjusted so that the fractions shown are more
        ' accurate.
        Fractional = NewAmount - Int(NewAmount)
        If Int(NewAmount) = 0 Then
            WholeString = ""
        Else
            WholeString = CStr(Int(NewAmount))
        End If
        If Fractional >= .9 Then
            AmountString = CStr(Int(NewAmount) + 1)
        ElseIf Fractional < .1 and Int(NewAmount) > 0 Then


            AmountString = WholeString
        ElseIf Fractional >= .1 And Fractional < .3 Then
            AmountString = WholeString + " 1/4"
        ElseIf Fractional >= .3 And Fractional < .4 Then
            AmountString = WholeString + " 1/3"
        ElseIf Fractional >= .4 And Fractional <= .55 Then
            AmountString = WholeString + " 1/2"
        ElseIf Fractional >= .55 And Fractional < .7 Then
            AmountString = WholeString + " 2/3"
        ElseIf Fractional >= .7 And Fractional < .9 Then
            AmountString = WholeString + " 3/4"
        End If
        Amount(Ingred).Caption = AmountString
    End If
Next
```

The entire routine is one big loop that goes from the first to the tenth ingredient in the recipe to update each one based on the new number of servings entered by the user. The first thing inside the loop, the `AmountForStandard`'s current array element is checked. If it is 0, that indicates that this ingredient isn't used. For instance, the Brownies recipe has only seven ingredients, so the last three elements in the `AmountForStandard`'s array are 0. If the value for the current ingredient is 0, the whole thing is skipped.

Assuming it isn't, `AmountForOne` is calculated. This takes the ingredient amount for the standard number of servings and divides it by the number of servings. This results in the amount of the ingredient to make one serving. The next line then multiplies this by the number of servings requested by the user to find out how much of this ingredient is needed. That's all the math that's necessary to make the calculation.

When I first created this page, that's all the work I did, but I ended up with a page that asked for things like this:

```
2.79 cups button
.99 eggs
4.12 teaspoons sugar
```

Obviously the average cook wouldn't be too happy about these measurements. When you cook, you usually see fractions, not decimal numbers. So I added the big `If...Then...ElseIf` structure you see in this routine now. It first separates the fractional part of the number from the whole part of the number. Then it looks at the fractional part and decides what would be the closest fraction.

You might not like the divisions I've made. They are very rough and not terribly even. They are simply intended to associate decimal numbers with approximate fractions. If you wanted to add more fractions (like 1/8, 3/8, 5/8, and 7/8) and make a little better divisions than I did, you could make it much more accurate.

At any rate, the result I end up with is a string that looks something like this: "2 3/4," and that is what I assign to the amount label's `Caption`.

Try it out!

Save the page and try it out in Internet Explorer. Try half the number of servings. Does it cut the ingredient amounts in half? Try twice the number of servings. Does it double the ingredient numbers? Now try weird numbers of servings. You'll probably notice if you try a serving size of 1 or 2, you can see some of the ingredient amounts to end up blank. That's because the number is too small to register as 1/4 based on my `If...Then...ElseIf` statement.

Making a Generic Recipe Page

This page was designed to be used and reused to create a variety of recipes. To make this task easier, you might want to save this page under a different name (like, say, Recipe.HTM) and then massage it so that you can use it as a template to copy from when you are ready to make new recipes.

After you save the page under a new name, go to the title and main header and change them to something generic like "Recipe."

Next, go into the Window's OnLoad event and change the code so it looks like Listing 10-15.

Listing 10-15: The generic recipe page's Window OnLoad event.

```
StandardServings = 1
AmountForStandard(1) = 0
AmountForStandard(2) = 0
AmountForStandard(3) = 0
AmountForStandard(4) = 0
AmountForStandard(5) = 0
AmountForStandard(6) = 0
AmountForStandard(7) = 0
AmountForStandard(8) = 0
AmountForStandard(9) = 0
AmountForStandard(10) = 0

DescLabel1.Caption = ""
DescLabel2.Caption = ""
DescLabel3.Caption = ""
DescLabel4.Caption = ""
DescLabel5.Caption = ""
DescLabel6.Caption = ""
DescLabel7.Caption = ""
DescLabel8.Caption = ""
DescLabel9.Caption = ""
DescLabel10.Caption = ""

Set Amount(1) = AmountLabel1
Set Amount(2) = AmountLabel2
Set Amount(3) = AmountLabel3
Set Amount(4) = AmountLabel4
Set Amount(5) = AmountLabel5
Set Amount(6) = AmountLabel6
Set Amount(7) = AmountLabel7
Set Amount(8) = AmountLabel8
Set Amount(9) = AmountLabel9
Set Amount(10) = AmountLabel10
```

(continued)

```
(continued)
DirectionsTextBox.Text = "Directions. Directions.
Directions."

ServesTextBox.Text = CStr(StandardServings)

ChangeButton_Click
```

Basically, you are just setting the `StandardServings` to 1, all the `AmountForStandard` elements to 0, and all the description labels to an empty string.

Creating New Recipes

Now Recipe.HTM is your template. Whenever you want to create a new recipe page, just follow these steps:

1. Load up Recipe.HTM in Control Pad.

2. Immediately save it under a new name.

3. Change the HTML title and the `<h1>` header at the top to the name of the recipe.

4. Go into the Script Wizard and edit the `Window`'s `OnLoad` event.

5. Set the numbers in the `AmountForStandard` assignments to the amounts for each ingredient.

6. Type in the measure (cup, teaspoon, tablespoon, and so on) and the ingredient in the string assigned to the description labels.

7. In the `DirectionsTextBox` assignment, type in the directions for the recipe.

8. Save the changes you made.

That's it! After that you'll have a new recipe page ready to add to your Internet cookbook. Don't forget to add a link to it from your index page!

On the CD-ROM I also have recipes for Yummy Zucchini Bread and Carmen's Applesauce Loaf Muffins. Take a look at them for additional examples (or good deserts for your next dinner).

Math Practice and Drills

Nothing could be more dull and frustrating than math drills, so why include it as an example? Well, I think that computers have a vast, mostly untapped, capability to make even the dullest subject fascinating. Educational software is becoming better and better, but I don't think we've even begun to scratch the surface of what's possible.

The World Wide Web makes it all the more compelling, so how can you create interesting, educational web pages using VBScript?

Well, this certainly isn't the final answer, but I thought I would show you an example of an educational page that helps students learn multiplication tables by providing plenty of problems, infinite patience, and immediate feedback.

By the way, in the last two examples I walked you through the process of creating the pages step-by-step. For this example, I'll take a higher level approach and show you the highlights of the process of developing these pages. If you want to see more detail, all the code for both pages is available on the CD-ROM.

Multiplication Practice

The first page I created was designed for use by a student to practice multiplication problems at his or her own pace. It isn't timed, and it grades the problems when the student presses a button to indicate he or she is ready. The score is tallied, and the student is informed. The student then has the ability to go back and work on those questions that were incorrect again and again until he or she gets them right.

Figure 10-14 shows what the completed page looks like in Internet Explorer.

Creating the HTML and ActiveX Controls

The HTML in this page is pretty straightforward, so I won't spend much time there. The ActiveX controls are a little more interesting.

Just as in the last couple of examples, this page includes a number of identical controls one after another. The best way to do it is to create one and copy and paste the HTML <OBJECT> tag as you did before.

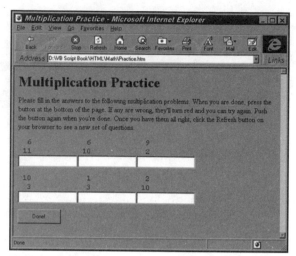

Figure 10-14: The math practice page.

This time, though, there are two rows of three labels each and then one row of text boxes. For the labels I used the ActiveX Label Object, and for the text boxes I used Microsoft Forms 2.0 TextBox. You only have a couple of key properties to set for these controls. All of them must use the Courier New font. Courier New is a *monospaced* font. Monospace means that every character takes up the same width. Normally a *W* takes up more space than an *I*. With a monospace font, that isn't true. The reason you want a monospace font here is so that the numbers will line up correctly.

The second property to be concerned about is the width. Make sure that both the labels and the text boxes are all the same width. I used 100, but you could use whatever you like.

Finally, users can click on one simple Microsoft Forms 2.0 CommandButton at the bottom when they are finished. This grades the test and tells them the results.

Adding VBScript

This is a pretty simple page. Only two events have VBScript code: the `Window`'s `OnLoad` event and the `DoneButton`'s `Click` event. Before I could write that code, though, I needed to create some global variables. These are the ones I created:

```
Num1(10)
Num2(10)
Answer(10)
NumProbs
Tries
```

As you can see, I created three separate arrays for this page to track the label holding the first number in each problem (Num1), the second number (Num2), and the text box that will hold the user's answer (Answer). Although I declared the arrays for holding 10 elements, I didn't use all of them, so NumProbs indicates the number of actual problems on the page. Tries counts the number of attempts the user makes before getting all the problems correct.

Listing 10-16 shows the code for the Window's OnLoad event.

Listing 10-16: The Window's OnLoad event.

```
Dim Prob, First, Second

Randomize
NumProbs = 6
Set Num1(1) = Prob1Num1
Set Num1(2) = Prob2Num1
Set Num1(3) = Prob3Num1
Set Num1(4) = Prob4Num1
Set Num1(5) = Prob5Num1
Set Num1(6) = Prob6Num1

Set Num2(1) = Prob1Num2
Set Num2(2) = Prob2Num2
Set Num2(3) = Prob3Num2
Set Num2(4) = Prob4Num2
Set Num2(5) = Prob5Num2
Set Num2(6) = Prob6Num2

Set Answer(1) = Prob1Answer
Set Answer(2) = Prob2Answer
Set Answer(3) = Prob3Answer
Set Answer(4) = Prob4Answer
Set Answer(5) = Prob5Answer
Set Answer(6) = Prob6Answer

For Prob=1 to NumProbs

    First = CStr(Int(Rnd * 12)+1)
    Second = CStr(Int(Rnd * 12)+1)

    If Len(First) < 2 Then
        Num1(Prob).Caption = "  " & First
    Else
        Num1(Prob).Caption = " " & First
    End If
```

(continued)

```
(continued)
    If Len(Second) < 2 Then
        Num2(Prob).Caption = "  " & Second
    Else
        Num2(Prob).Caption = " " & Second
    End If

Next
```

After assigning the labels and text boxes to their appropriate array elements, I go through each problem and generate random numbers between 1 and 12 to multiply together. The two If...Then...Else structures add one space to the left of the number if it is a two-digit number and only one space if it is a one-digit number. This lines up the numbers correctly with each other and with the text edit below.

Finally, Listing 10-17 shows the DoneButton's Click event.

Listing 10-17: The DoneButton's Click event.

```
Dim Prob, NumRight

NumRight = 0
For Prob = 1 To NumProbs
    ' If they didn't answer or typed in garbage, it's wrong
    If Not IsNumeric(Answer(Prob).Text) Then
        Num1(Prob).ForeColor = RGB(255,0,0)
        Num2(Prob).ForeColor = RGB(255,0,0)
        Answer(Prob).ForeColor = RGB(255,0,0)
    Else
        ' If they typed in a number, check to see if it's
right
        If  (Int(Num1(Prob).Caption) *
Int(Num2(Prob).Caption) = _
            Int(Answer(Prob).Text)) Then
                NumRight = NumRight + 1
                Num1(Prob).ForeColor = RGB(0,0,0)
                Num2(Prob).ForeColor = RGB(0,0,0)
                Answer(Prob).ForeColor = RGB(0,0,0)
        Else
            Num1(Prob).ForeColor = RGB(255,0,0)
            Num2(Prob).ForeColor = RGB(255,0,0)
            Answer(Prob).ForeColor = RGB(255,0,0)
        End If
```

```
   End If
Next


Tries = Tries + 1

If NumRight = 0 Then
   MsgBox("You didn't get any of them right. Try again.")
ElseIf NumRight = 6 Then
   MsgBox("You got them all right! Good Job! And it only
took you " & _
      CStr(Tries) & " tries.")
Else
   MsgBox("You got " & CStr(NumRight) & " right out of " &
_
      CStr(NumProbs) & " problems.")
End If

DoneButton.Caption = "Try Again!"
```

The loop goes through each problem on the page. If the user didn't enter anything or entered something other than numbers, the question is counted wrong. This means that the NumRight counter isn't incremented and that the problem labels and text box have their text color turned red (so the user knows which ones were wrong).

If the user did enter a number, the routine goes on to do the math itself and compares the user's results to its results. If they match, NumRight is incremented, and the text color of the problem is turned black. It is turned black because users can try several times on the same problems and if they got it wrong last time, the text might be red. I set it back to black here to let them know that the problem is correct now.

If the number they entered does not match, NumRight is not incremented, and the label and text box text are turned red.

Next, the Tries variable is incremented. Each time you press the DoneButton, it counts as one try. Tries is never really initialized, but when it was created, it had the value 0. When the user wants a new set of problems, he or she will Refresh the page and that will automatically reset Tries back to 0.

The If...Then...Else statement checks to see how many the user got right and informs him or her. The DoneButton caption is changed after the first time to "Try Again!".

Trying it Out!

Try the page out. Each time you load up the page, either initially or by pressing the Refresh button, you will see a new set of problems. You can then continue working on the problems until you get them all right. It's simple, but effective.

Multiplication Test

I decided to create a timed version of the multiplication page. This would be used for a test or for timed drills. It is very similar to the last page I created. In fact, I used that page as a foundation for creating this one, so as I go over this one, I'll only describe the things that are different.

Creating the HTML and ActiveX Controls

Again, the HTML here is simple, and the ActiveX controls are almost identical to the first page. With three exceptions. First, and most simply, I added a Start button to the bottom of the page. When the user uses this page, the questions don't appear until they click the Start button.

Second, I added another `Label Object` called `TimerLabel` after the first row of problem labels (just after `Prob3Num1`). Its `Alignment` is `Centered`, `FontSize` is `20`, and its `Height` and `Width` are about 29 by 53. The `Caption` is empty at the start. It will be filled in later when we know how many seconds the user wants on the clock before beginning.

Finally, there is the timer itself. I used a `Timer Object` and placed it at the bottom of my page, although you could place it anywhere you like because it isn't actually visible to the user. The `ID` is `Timer`, the `Interval` is `1000` (which evaluates to about a second), and `Enabled` is `False`. The timer will be enabled when the user clicks the Start button.

Adding VBScript

Much of the code for this page is the same as the last page, but several things have been added and shifted around, so I'll show you each routine in roughly the order that it would execute.

The Global Variables

The global variables are the same as for the last page with these exceptions:

➡️ There is no `Tries` variable

➡️ A `TimeLeft` variable has been added to keep track of the seconds as they count down.

The Window's OnLoad Event

The `Window`'s `OnLoad` event for this page appears in Listing 10-18.

Listing 10-18: The Window's OnLoad event.

```
Dim Prob

Randomize
NumProbs = 6
Set Num1(1) = Prob1Num1
Set Num1(2) = Prob2Num1
Set Num1(3) = Prob3Num1
Set Num1(4) = Prob4Num1
Set Num1(5) = Prob5Num1
Set Num1(6) = Prob6Num1

Set Num2(1) = Prob1Num2
Set Num2(2) = Prob2Num2
Set Num2(3) = Prob3Num2
Set Num2(4) = Prob4Num2
Set Num2(5) = Prob5Num2
Set Num2(6) = Prob6Num2

Set Answer(1) = Prob1Answer
Set Answer(2) = Prob2Answer
Set Answer(3) = Prob3Answer
Set Answer(4) = Prob4Answer
Set Answer(5) = Prob5Answer
Set Answer(6) = Prob6Answer

TimeLeft = InputBox("How many seconds do you need on the
timer?")

Do Until IsNumeric(TimeLeft)
   TimeLeft = InputBox("Please enter a valid number of
seconds for the timer.")
Loop
TimeLeft = Int(TimeLeft)

TimerLabel.Caption = CStr(TimeLeft)
```

The arrays are initialized, just as they were in the last page.

Then the user is asked, using an input box, how many seconds he or she wants on the clock to answer the questions. A Do Until loop ensures that the time entered is numeric and then the variable TimeLeft is converted to hold the numeric equivalent of the value entered. This is done so that the timer can easily subtract one each time it clicks.

Finally, the timer label is filled in with the appropriate value.

The Start Button

The next logical place to look is the Start button. Its Click event is in Listing 10-19.

Listing 10-19: The Start button's Click event.

```
Dim First, Second

' Stop user from clicking Start multiple times
StartButton.Enabled = False

For Prob=1 to NumProbs

    First = CStr(Int(Rnd * 12)+1)
    Second = CStr(Int(Rnd * 12)+1)

    If Len(First) < 2 Then
        Num1(Prob).Caption = "   " & First
    Else
        Num1(Prob).Caption = "  " & First
    End If
    If Len(Second) < 2 Then
        Num2(Prob).Caption = "   " & Second
    Else
        Num2(Prob).Caption = "  " & Second
    End If

Next

Timer.Enabled = True
```

The first thing I do is disable the Start button so that the user doesn't press it multiple times. Then, the loop goes through all the problems and fills them in. This code is identical to the code that was at the bottom of the Window's OnLoad event in the last page.

Lastly, the Timer is enabled to start the clock.

The Timer

Once every second, the Timer event executes. Listing 10-20 shows you what it does.

Listing 10-20: The Timer **event.**

```
TimeLeft = TimeLeft -1
TimerLabel.Caption = CStr(TimeLeft)

If TimeLeft = 0 Then
    'Stop timer right away so it doesn't click again
    Timer.Enabled = False
    MsgBox("Times Up!")
    DoneButton_Click
End If
```

First thing, one second is ticked off the timer, and the timer label is updated.

Then it checks to see if they are out of time. If they are, the timer disables itself and informs the user. The last line calls the routine that would normally be called if the user clicked the DoneButton. What happens there? Glad you asked.

The DoneButton

If the user finishes before the counter reaches 0, he or she can click the DoneButton. Listing 10-21 shows what happens in that case.

Listing 10-21: The DoneButton's Click **event.**

```
Dim Prob, NumRight

' Stop the timer
Timer.Enabled = False

' Disable Done! button so they can't try again
DoneButton.Enabled = False
```

(continued)

(continued)

```
NumRight = 0
For Prob = 1 To NumProbs
    ' If they didn't answer or typed in garbage, it's wrong
    If Not IsNumeric(Answer(Prob).Text) Then
        Num1(Prob).ForeColor = RGB(255,0,0)
        Num2(Prob).ForeColor = RGB(255,0,0)
        Answer(Prob).ForeColor = RGB(255,0,0)



    Else
        ' If they typed in a number, check to see if it's
right
        If  (Int(Num1(Prob).Caption) *
Int(Num2(Prob).Caption) = _
            Int(Answer(Prob).Text)) Then
                NumRight = NumRight + 1
                Num1(Prob).ForeColor = RGB(0,0,0)
                Num2(Prob).ForeColor = RGB(0,0,0)
                Answer(Prob).ForeColor = RGB(0,0,0)
        Else
            Num1(Prob).ForeColor = RGB(255,0,0)
            Num2(Prob).ForeColor = RGB(255,0,0)
            Answer(Prob).ForeColor = RGB(255,0,0)
        End If
    End If
Next

If NumRight = 0 Then
    MsgBox("You didn't get any of them right. You need more
practice!")
ElseIf NumRight = NumProbs Then
    MsgBox("You got them all right! Good Job!")
Else
    MsgBox("You got " & CStr(NumRight) & " right out of " &
_
        CStr(NumProbs) & " problems.")
End If
```

First, the timer is disabled so that it stops the countdown, and then the Done button is disabled so the user doesn't click on it multiple times. Then comes the big loop that checks each problem to see if it's right. This code is nearly identical to the code in the Done button of the first page. It counts up the number right and highlights in red the ones that were missed.

Again, as in the last page, users are informed of their score. This time, they can't keep trying, though.

Try it Out!

This will put your skills to the test. How long will it take you to answer six multiplication questions? Now we'll find out for sure if you memorized those tables in school!

Once you click the Start button, the counter starts clicking off second by second. There's no bonus for finishing early, so make sure you have them all right.

 If you didn't notice it on the last page, you probably will now that time is of the essence on this page. You can't simply press the Tab key to move from one text box to the next. I couldn't find any way to make this possible. Controls on a form automatically do it, but ActiveX controls on a page don't. There are `TabIndex` properties, but they only work when the controls are on a Layout control.

Making it Better

You could easily extend these pages to do a whole lot more. First off, you could make them do addition, subtraction, and division problems, and you could add more problems per page.

To make it more educational, you could add hints and tips to help the user understand what he or she did wrong and how to do it right.

You could even add several pages before this one that actually teach the concepts practiced and tested with these pages. Then you'd have a complete self-study course.

Techniques for Your Own Pages

The last three examples have shown you what a complete page integrating VBScript can look like and what kinds of things it can do.

In this section, I'd like to change the focus a little and show you some smaller tidbits that you can take and use in your own pages to dress them up and make them come alive.

Still More Attention-Getting Text

I have to admit, finding clever ways of manipulating text through a single label control or multiple controls has become a bit of an obsession with me. It is so much fun to come up with new and clever ideas for simple tools like a timer and Label Object. Once the user has these two ActiveX controls, a surprising variety of effects are possible. I've already shown you some of them in Chapter 5. Among them...

- Making text look like it is coming closer and then going away by incrementally changing the font size
- A sign hanging by a nail that slowly swings back and forth
- Switching quickly back and forth between two font sizes
- Switching quickly back and forth between two colors, like dull red and bright red
- Fading slowly to brighter, then duller and back to brighter colored text

Then in Chapter 8, after showing you what an array was, I gave you some more ideas. These were all based on the idea of creating a header where each letter was a separate label control and could be controlled separately. Among those...

- One letter after another is enlarged and then shrunk to its original size giving the impression of movement from left to right.
- In addition to the one letter each letter beside the big letter was a little smaller and the letters beside those smaller still until they reached the text's normal size. This wave traveled across the text from left to right, as well.
- A colorful version of the previous wave where the biggest letter is also the brightest in color and the color dulls as the letters get smaller. Normal sized letters are black. Again this pattern moves across the phrase from left to right.

Now I have a few more ideas I'd like to share with you.

The Letters.HTM Foundation

In a section titled "Building the Foundation" in Chapter 8, I provided detailed step-by-step directions for creating a page called Letters.HTM. This page provided the foundation for the rest of the Wave pages in that chapter. I also mentioned that you could use it as a platform for your own experimentation with attention-getting text.

All the examples in this section will use Letters.HTM as their foundation, so go back and pick up the one you created in Chapter 8 or use the one I created and included on the CD-ROM that came in the back of this book.

Just to refresh your memory, Letters.HTM was composed primarily of 13 Label Objects that were assigned to an array in the Window's OnLoad event. There was also a Timer Object on the page that was used to manipulate the labels. The timer object was enabled at the end of the Window's OnLoad event.

Color Kaleidoscope

One really easy attention-getter is to change the colors of the letters in the title quickly and randomly.

For this page, I changed the label's FontSize property to 20 and the timer Interval to 200.

Then I put the code in Listing 10-22 in the Timer event.

Listing 10-22: The Timer event.

```
Dim ThisLet, ForeRed, ForeGreen, ForeBlue

Randomize

For ThisLet = 1 To NumLetters
    ForeRed = Int(Rnd * 255) + 1
    ForeGreen = Int(Rnd * 255) + 1
    ForeBlue = Int(Rnd * 255) + 1
    Letters(ThisLet).ForeColor = RGB(ForeRed, ForeGreen,
ForeBlue)
Next
```

With the Interval set at 200 miliseconds, this code will execute five times a second. It just goes through all the letters and changes their ForeColor to a random RGB value. The result is quite colorful, as you can imagine (see Figure 10-15).

Figure 10-15: A less-than-colorful rendition of a very colorful headline.

If you put this on a white or light-colored page, you might want to replace the first three lines inside the loop with these lines.

```
ForeRed = Int(Rnd * 128) + 1
ForeGreen = Int(Rnd * 128) + 1
ForeBlue = Int(Rnd * 128) + 1
```

This will keep all the colors generated on the darker end of the spectrum so it doesn't look like certain letters disappear when they turn white or yellow.

You can combine this technique with other text techniques to provide an instantly festive atmosphere on any page.

FontFrenzy

A popular technique used in television takes a word or phrase and quickly cycles through different fonts either for the entire phrase or for each letter individually. You can do the same thing on your pages easily enough. This time, instead of starting with Letters.HTM, go ahead and start with the page from the last section (Color Kaleidoscope).

Add this to the body tag:

```
BGCOLOR=WHITE
```

Change the timer's Interval to 150.

After you get in the Script Wizard, create these two new global variables.

```
FontsAvail(20)
LastFont
```

Change the Window's OnLoad event so that it looks like Listing 10-23.

Listing 10-23: FontFrenzy's Window OnLoad event.

```
NumLetters = 13
Set Letters(1)=IeLabel1
Set Letters(2)=IeLabel2
Set Letters(3)=IeLabel3
Set Letters(4)=IeLabel4
Set Letters(5)=IeLabel5
Set Letters(6)=IeLabel6
Set Letters(7)=IeLabel7
Set Letters(8)=IeLabel8
```

```
Set Letters(9)=IeLabel9
Set Letters(10)=IeLabel10
Set Letters(11)=IeLabel11
Set Letters(12)=IeLabel12
Set Letters(13)=IeLabel13
CurLetter = 1

FontsAvail(1) = "Arial"
FontsAvail(2) = "Arial Black"
FontsAvail(3) = "Arial Narrow"
FontsAvail(4) = "Book Antiqua"
FontsAvail(5) = "Bookman Old"
FontsAvail(6) = "Century Gothic"
FontsAvail(7) = "Comic Sans MS"
FontsAvail(8) = "Copperplate Gothic Bold"
FontsAvail(9) = "Copperplate Gothic Light"
FontsAvail(10) = "Courier New"
FontsAvail(11) = "Garamond"
FontsAvail(12) = "Impact"
FontsAvail(13) = "Lucida Handwriting"
FontsAvail(14) = "Lucida Sans"
FontsAvail(15) = "Mistral"
FontsAvail(16) = "MS LineDraw"
FontsAvail(17) = "News Gothic MT"
LastFont = 17

IeTimer1.Enabled = True
```

The lines that were added are the initialization of the new global variables. The `FontsAvail` array holds the name of up to 20 fonts that you think are likely to be available on the user's machine. `LastFont` identifies the last valid array element. The fonts I've used here are likely to be on most Windows 95 machines.

The timer's event should look like Listing 10-24.

Listing 10-24: FontFrenzy's Timer event.

```
Dim ThisLet, ForeRed, ForeGreen, ForeBlue, ThisFontName,
ThisBold, ThisItalic

Randomize

For ThisLet = 1 To NumLetters
    ForeRed = Int(Rnd * 130) + 1
    ForeGreen = Int(Rnd * 130) + 1
```

(continued)

```
(continued)
    ForeBlue = Int(Rnd * 130) + 1
    ThisFontName = FontsAvail(Int(Rnd * LastFont)+1)
    If (Int(Rnd * 2)+1) = 1 Then ThisBold = True Else
ThisBold = False
    If (Int(Rnd * 2)+1) = 1 Then ThisItalic = True Else
ThisItalic = False

    Letters(ThisLet).ForeColor = RGB(ForeRed, ForeGreen,
ForeBlue)
    Letters(ThisLet).FontName = ThisFontName
    Letters(ThisLet).FontBold = ThisBold
    Letters(ThisLet).FontItalic = ThisItalic
Next
```

I've used the same technique as I did in Color Kaleidescope to change the colors randomly. You'll notice this time, though, that I've limited the colors to the darker end of the spectrum so that they look nice on the white background. In addition, I randomly pick a font from the array and also randomly decide to set bold or italic.

This produces a nice effect (see Figure 10-16).

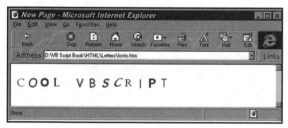

Figure 10-16: The FontFrenzy in action.

You might also want to try this effect without the color changes to see if that works better on your page.

Bouncers

This is another fun variation on the Color Kaleidoscope. Start with that page and change the Timer event so that it looks like Listing 10-25.

Listing 10-25: Bouncers Timer event.

```
Dim ThisLet, ForeRed, ForeGreen, ForeBlue
```

```
Randomize

For ThisLet = 1 To NumLetters
    ForeRed = Int(Rnd * 255) + 1
    ForeGreen = Int(Rnd * 255) + 1
    ForeBlue = Int(Rnd * 255) + 1
    Letters(ThisLet).ForeColor = RGB(ForeRed, ForeGreen,
ForeBlue)
    Letters(ThisLet).Alignment = (Int(Rnd * 9))
    Letters(ThisLet).Angle = (Int(Rnd * 20)-10)
Next
```

This time, in addition to setting the color to a random value, the `Alignment` and `Angle` are also modified.

The `Alignment` property determines where, in the control, the text appears. It can have one of nine values: left top, centered top, right top, left centered, centered, right centered, left bottom, centered bottom, and right bottom. The numbers associated with these values are 0 through 8.

You'll notice that the +1 that is usually on the lines where random numbers are generated isn't there. When you take it off, it generates a number between 0 and one less than the number you multiplied by. So (`Int(Rnd * 9)`) produces a random number between 0 and 8. This has the effect of making the letters bounce around within the area the size of their control.

`Angle` is a property you've already seen. It determines the angle at which the text appears. The default 0 puts the text on a straight horizontal line reading from left to right. The value 90 sets the text on edge so that the letters are sideways and the text reads down. In this routine, I'm assigning a random value generated by (`Int(Rnd * 20)-10`). This will produce a random number between -10 and 10. Just enough to put them off kilter and add to the jumble effect.

The results can be seen in Figure 10-17.

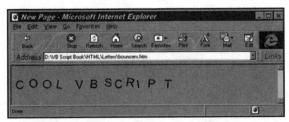

Figure 10-17: Bouncing letters.

I've commented out the color lines in the page I've included with the CD-ROM in the back of this book. I like it better without them. It makes the other effects more visible. Again, do whatever works best for your page!

Playing the Slots

And now for something completely different....

This effect is intended to simulate the look of a slot machine. Start again with Letters.HTM and increase the FontSize of all the labels to 20. In the Script Wizard, add this global variable:

```
LettersPhrase
```

Be sure to note that it is LettersPhrase, not LetterPhrase.

Change the Window's OnLoad event so that it looks like Listing 10-26.

Listing 10-26: Slots Window OnLoad event.

```
NumLetters = 13
Set Letters(1)=IeLabel1
Set Letters(2)=IeLabel2
Set Letters(3)=IeLabel3
Set Letters(4)=IeLabel4
Set Letters(5)=IeLabel5
Set Letters(6)=IeLabel6
Set Letters(7)=IeLabel7
Set Letters(8)=IeLabel8
Set Letters(9)=IeLabel9
Set Letters(10)=IeLabel10
Set Letters(11)=IeLabel11
Set Letters(12)=IeLabel12
Set Letters(13)=IeLabel13

For CurLetter = 1 To NumLetters
    LettersPhrase = LettersPhrase &
Letters(CurLetter).Caption
Next

For CurLetter = 1 To NumLetters
    Letters(CurLetter).Caption = Chr(Int(Rnd * 26) + 65)
Next

CurLetter = 1
IeTimer1.Enabled = True
```

The code that is different here are the two `For...Next` loops at the bottom. The first goes through all the labels and concatenates their `Captions` so that the `LettersPhrase` global will hold a string that represents the original value of the phrase on the page. The next loop goes through each of the letters and puts a random letter in it.

The Timer event code is in Listing 10-27.

Listing 10-27: Slots `Timer` **event.**

```
Dim ThisLet, CurCorrect, RandLet

Randomize

For ThisLet = 1 To NumLetters
    CurCorrect = Mid(LettersPhrase, ThisLet, 1)
    If Letters(ThisLet).Caption <> CurCorrect Then
        RandLet = Int(Rnd * 27) + 65 'Generate one more
than needed
        If RandLet = 91 Then RandLet = 32 'Use the one more
for a space
        Letters(ThisLet).Caption = Chr(RandLet)
    End If
Next

CurLetter = CurLetter + 1
If CurLetter > NumLetters then CurLetter = 1
```

Each time the timer clicks, this loop goes through each letter and sees if it happens to have the right letter in it. If it doesn't, a random number is generated between 65 through 91.

The computer uses numbers to represent everything, so every letter and symbol on your keyboard has an associated number. This number is often referred to as its ASCII value (*American Standard Code for International Interchange*, if you must know). You can convert numbers into their associated letters by using the `Chr` function. `Chr(65)`, for instance returns *A*. You can turn letters into their associated numbers by using the `Asc` function. `Asc("A")` returns 65. This is handy because, although you can't generate random letters, you can generate random numbers within a certain range and then convert them to letters.

So in this case, I convert the random number into a letter and put that letter in the current label control. The `If...Then` checks to see if the number is 91. If it is, it uses this special case to insert a space (which has the ASCII value 32) into the control. I had to do it this way because there's no way to tell the computer to generate a random number between 65 and 90, and, by the way, throw an occasional 32 in there sometimes.

Notice, though, that once a character is the correct one in the right place for the original phrase, it is no longer changed. Each letter takes different amounts of time to get it right, and sometimes one or two take longer than the rest. The odds say it will all work out, given enough random chances. You can see the results in Figure 10-18.

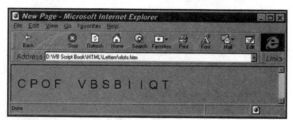

Figure 10-18: Slots in action.

Spinners

This effect makes use of the angle property to spin each individual letter as though it were a wheel on a giant vehicle. Each letter, in turn, stops when it finally is turned right side up and jumps to a larger font size. This has the effect of making it look like the letter has clicked into place.

To create this one, begin again with Letters.HTM. Change the labels' FontSize to 20.

The Window's OnLoad event should look like Listing 10-28.

Listing 10-28: Spinners Window OnLoad event.

```
NumLetters = 13
Set Letters(1)=IeLabel1
Set Letters(2)=IeLabel2
Set Letters(3)=IeLabel3
Set Letters(4)=IeLabel4
Set Letters(5)=IeLabel5
Set Letters(6)=IeLabel6
Set Letters(7)=IeLabel7
Set Letters(8)=IeLabel8
Set Letters(9)=IeLabel9
Set Letters(10)=IeLabel10
Set Letters(11)=IeLabel11
Set Letters(12)=IeLabel12
```

```
Set Letters(13)=IeLabel13
CurLetter = 0
IeTimer1.Enabled = True
```

There's not much here except setting the `CurLetter` to 0. Listing 10-29 shows you the Timer event.

Listing 10-29: The Spinners `Timer` event.

```
Dim ThisLet

If Letters(NumLetters).Angle = 0 Then
    CurLetter = CurLetter + 1
    If CurLetter > 1 Then Letters(CurLetter-1).FontSize =
24
End If

If CurLetter <= NumLetters Then
    For ThisLet = CurLetter To NumLetters
        Letters(ThisLet).Angle = Letters(ThisLet).Angle - 20
    Next
Else
    IeTimer1.Enabled = False
End If
```

For this routine, you'll probably find it easier to look at the second `If...Then` first. The second `If...Then` checks to see if the `CurLetter` is at the end of the phrase. If not, all the letters between `CurLetter` and the last letter have their angle property decreased by 20. This has the effect of tilting them to the left, or, stated better, moving them counterclockwise.

Once the `CurLetter` does reach the end, this timer is disabled. So the upshot is, all the letters are spinning.

Now look back up at the top `If...Then`. It checks to see if the angle of the last letter is 0. Because all the letters are changed together, this actually is checking to see where all the letters are. In other words, if all the letters are sitting upright, the code inside the `If...Then` executes. What happens? The `CurLetter` is incremented and the previous letter's font size is increased. Now, because the loop at the bottom part of the routine goes from the `CurLetter` forward, that previous letter won't be disturbed any more.

The upshot looks like Figure 10-19.

Figure 10-19: The Spinners spinning.

It seems that one letter each revolution is clicked into place and stops spinning. It starts with the first letter and goes from left to right, but it seems that the V in VBScript rotates twice before it clicks into place. Why?

Because the space before it is a separate label control and it has to have a turn to rotate and click into place, too, even if you don't see it happening.

A Marquee Using Only Labels and VBScript

Marquees are a very popular way of presenting information on web pages. You'll find all kinds of marquees implemented using Java or an ActiveX control, but you don't need any of that fancy stuff to create a marquee. You can do it with nothing more than a label, a timer, and a little VBScript ingenuity.

Start off again with the Letters.HTM page. Change all the label `Caption`s to a single space and set their `FontSize` to 24.

Get into the Script Wizard and create a global variable.

```
Marquee
```

You only need to add one line to the `Window`'s `OnLoad` event. Add it just before the last line (`IeTimer1.Enabled = True`):

```
Marquee = "WELCOME TO MY VBSCRIPT-ENHANCED WEB PAGE..."
```

This initializes the string that will scroll across your marquee. You can put any string here you want to display.

Now use the code in Listing 10-30 for the Timer event.

Listing 10-30: The Marquee Timer event.

```
Dim Show, NumOnEnd, NumToWrap, DisplayLetter
```

```
CurLetter = CurLetter + 1
If CurLetter > Len(Marquee) Then CurLetter = 1

NumOnEnd = Len(Marquee) - CurLetter
If NumOnEnd < NumLetters Then


    NumToWrap = NumLetters - NumOnEnd
    Show = Right(Marquee, NumOnEnd) + Left(Marquee,
NumToWrap)
Else
    Show = Mid(Marquee, CurLetter, NumLetters)
End If

For DisplayLetter = 1 To NumLetters
    Letters(DisplayLetter).Caption =
Mid(Show,DisplayLetter,1)
Next
```

This is the same technique I used in Chapter 6 when I described how to create a scrolling status bar message.

The `CurLetter` in this routine indicates which letter appears in the first marquee position. It is incremented each time this Timer event is triggered. When it reaches the end, it starts over at 1.

`NumOnEnd` counts the number of characters left from the `CurLetter` to the end of the string. If that isn't greater than the number of letters in the marquee, an additional number of characters from the *beginning* of the string are added onto the end. This is how the message wraps around. Then `Show` is filled with a string containing those end characters concatenated with enough beginning characters to fill out the marquee.

On the other hand, if the `NumOnEnd` is long enough to fill the marquee, the portion of that string needed is simply placed into the `Show` variable.

Finally, the last loop chops apart the `Show` string one character at a time and displays the characters in the marquee. You can see the result in Figure 10-20.

Dropped Letter

I saved my favorite for last. This is a very simple effect. All of the letters are perfectly still and standing at attention, except for one. It seems to have broken off and fallen down. It only hangs by a single nail and swings back and forth.

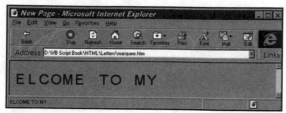

Figure 10-20: The VBScript marquee.

Start, once again, with Letters.HTM. Change the `Alignment` property for `IeLabel8` to `2 - Right Top`. For some odd reason, this puts the letter in the lower right-hand corner of the control. Either the control doesn't work correctly or I'm missing something. But anyway, you want the letter to appear in the lower right corner of the control. Use whatever setting makes that happen. For me it's `2 - Right Top`.

Get into the Script Wizard and add a global variable:

```
Direction
```

Initialize the global by adding this line near the bottom of the `Window`'s `OnLoad` event, just before `IeTimer1.Enabled = True`:

```
Direction = -1
```

Then, of course, the key event is the Timer event (see Listing 10-31).

Listing 10-31: The Dropped Letter's `Timer` event.

```
Letters(8).Angle = Letters(8).Angle + 10 * Direction
If Letters(8).Angle = -30 or Letters(8).Angle = 0 Then
Direction = Direction * -1
```

That's right! It's only two lines. Because you only have one letter to deal with, the 8 is hard-coded. The first line adds 10 to the `Angle` property. Actually, it adds `10 * Direction`. `Direction` is initialized to -1, so it actually subtracts 10 the first time this executes.

The second line checks to see if the angle is -30 or 0. If it is either one, DirSection is multiplied by -1. Because -1 times -1 = 1, the `Direction` keeps switching back and forth between 1 and -1.

The result is that the `Angle` starts at 0, goes to -10, -20, and finally to -30. That's when the second line kicks in changing Direction to 1. That causes the first line to start adding 10 and so it goes from -30 to -20 to -10 and back to 0 where the process starts over again. See Figure 10-21.

I played around with lots of different tilts and Alignments until I found this one that looks pretty authentic. Do your own experimenting to see if you can come up with other effects.

The Quote for Today is a simple, interesting quote from a noted statesmen, scientist, or entertainer. It will often be at the top or bottom of a page just to entertain or make you think.

Today's Cool Web Site is an interesting web site that you want to relay to others. It may or may not have anything to do with the content on your web page.

Quote for Today

The Quote for Today is easy to implement. Listing 10-32 shows you how.

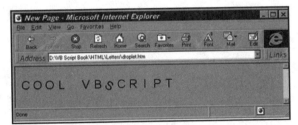

Figure 10-21: The letter has dropped.

Listing 10-32: Quote for Today.

```
<HTML>
<HEAD>
<TITLE>My Web Page</TITLE>
</HEAD>
<BODY>
<h1>Welcome To My Web Page</h1>
<SCRIPT LANGUAGE="VBScript">
<!-
Option Explicit

Randomize

document.write "<p><h2>Quote for Today:</h2>"
```

(continued)

(continued)

```
Select Case Int(Rnd * 13) + 1
Case 1
    document.write "You may not realize it when it happens,
but a kick in " & _
        "the teeth may be the best thing in the world for
you. - Walt Disney<p>"
Case 2
    document.write "If there's nothing wrong with me, maybe
there's something " & _
        "wrong with the universe. - Beverly Crusher in Star
Trek, The Next " & _
        "Generation's episode Remember Me<p>"
Case 3
    document.write "A great many people think they are
thinking when they are " & _
        "merely rearranging their prejudices. - William
James<p>"
Case 4
    document.write "One striking difference between a cat
and a lie is that a cat " & _
        "has only nine lives. - Mark Twain<p>"
Case 5
    document.write "People are like tea bags. They don't
know their own strength " & _
        "until they get into hot water. - Dan McKinnon<p>"
Case 6
    document.write "You've got to be very careful if you
don't know where you are " & _
        "going, because you might not get there. - Yogi
Berra<p>"
Case 7
    document.write "Everyone needs deadlines. Even the
beavers. They loaf around " & _
        "all summer, but when they are faced with the
winter deadline, they work like " & _
        "fury. If we didn't have deadlines, we'd stagnate. -
Walt Disney<p>"
Case 8
    document.write "The first time I walked into a trophy
shop, I looked around and " & _
        "thought to myself, Man this guy is good. - Fred
Wolf<p>"
Case 9
    document.write "Computers are useless. They can only
give you answers. - Pablo " & _
        "Picasso<p>"
```

```
Case 10
    document.write "A foolish consistency is the hobgoblin
of little minds... - Ralph " & _
        "Waldo Emerson<p>"
Case 11
    document.write "It's easy to think that as a result of
the extinction of the dodo, we " & _
        "are now sadder and wiser, but there's a lot of
evidence to suggest that we are " & _
        "merely sadder and better informed. - Douglas
Adams, Last Chance to See<p>"
Case 12
    document.write "Imagination is more important than
knowledge. For knowledge is " & _
        "limited, whereas imagination embraces the entire
world, stimulating progress, giving " & _
        "birth to evolution. - Albert Einstein<p>"
Case 13
    document.write "Violence is the last refuge of the
incompetent. - Salvor Hardin, in " & _
        "Foundation by Isaac Asimov<p>"
End Select
->
</SCRIPT>
</BODY>
</HTML>
```

You must type the VBScript tag and code into the page by hand. You can't use the Script Wizard to write code that isn't associated with a procedure or an event, as you need to do here. You can put this code anywhere in your document where you want the quote to appear. After using document.write to display the header, a random number between 1 and 13 is generated. The big Select Case then uses document.write to print a quote based on the number generated.

Why is this a "Quote for Today"? Aren't users going to see a different quote every time they go back to this page? Probably not. Once a page is downloaded to the browser, it is held in the browser's *cache*. A cache is just a place on the hard drive for storing web pages that have been visited recently. If the user goes back to this page the same day they've been there before, the browser will just pull the page from the cache, instead of downloading it again, so the user will see the same quote again. The only way it will change is if the user presses the Refresh button, which forces the browser to go out and download the page again. If the user does this, a new quote will likely appear.

If you have a site you want people to visit often (and who doesn't!), you'll probably want to add a lot more quotes than I've included here. Otherwise, the user will start seeing the same quotes again and again. You should probably start with at least 30 to 50 quotes or more if possible. You can buy anthologies of famous quotes in book form or on CD-ROM. You might even be able to find interesting web pages full of quotes you can borrow.

Today's Cool Web Site

Another interesting feature you often see on cool pages is a Cool Web Site to visit. You can implement this just like you did the Quote for Today. Add the lines in Listing 10-33 to the page created in the last section, just before the end of the script.

Listing 10-33: Today's Cool Web Site.

```
document.write "<h2>Today's Cool Site:</h2>"
Select Case Int(Rnd * 10)+1
Case 1
    document.write "<a
href='http://www.edgequest.com'>EdgeQuest</a>"
Case 2
    document.write "<a
href='http://www.gamesdomain.com'>Games Domain</a>"
Case 3
    document.write "<a
href='http://www.discovery.com'>Discovery Channel
Online</a>"
Case 4
    document.write "<a href='http://www.cnet.com'>C|Net
Online</a>"
Case 5
    document.write "<a href='http://www.idg.com'>IDG
Productions</a>"
Case 6
    document.write "<a href='http://www.scifi.com'>The Sci-
Fi Channel: The Dominion</a>"
Case 7
    document.write "<a href='http://www.usatoday.com'>USA
TODAY</a>"
Case 8
    document.write "<a
href='http://www.gigaplex.com'>Gigaplex: Books, music, " &
_
        "TV, theatre and more</a>"
Case 9
    document.write "<a
href='http://www.sunnyside.com/lib/htdocs/diningout.html'>D
```

```
ining " & _
      "Out On the Web</a>"
Case 10
   document.write "<a
href='http://www.disney.com'>Disney</a>"
End Select
```

Again, the idea is simple. Print a header, choose a random number, and
Select Case off the number to choose which site to display. Notice this time
that I use the `<a>` tag inside quotes with `document.write` to make an
anchor. Remember, anything you can do in a web page, you can do
dynamically with `document.write`.

You'll also want to add a lot more sites so that this doesn't begin repeating
itself quickly, too. Like the quotes, 30 to 50 would be a good start. The best
place to begin is probably your own Favorites list.

The finished page looks like Figure 10-22.

Figure 10-22: Quote for Today and Today's Cool Web Site page.

Summary

I began with three fully developed examples of putting VBScript
to work in the real world: A cool game, a dynamic recipe book,
and an educational page for teaching math skills. I finished up
by showing VBScript techniques you can implement in your own
pages to create attention-getting text, a Quote for Today, and
Today's Cool Web Site.

Serverless Databases

I'll begin by describing what client/server and intranet development is and how it has affected business today. Then I'll describe what a serverless database is and how it is implemented in VBScript, and I'll provide a real-world example.

Client/Server and Intranets

One of the biggest buzzwords in the computer industry and business in general — after the Internet and all its associated buzzwords — is *client/server*. What does the term *client/server* mean?

Client/server usually refers to a way of organizing a computer system so that it has a central repository of information and several other computers that sit on people's desks and access the repository. The central repository is often called the *database server*, and the other computers are called the *clients*.

This organization is often designed to replace old, expensive mainframe systems. A mainframe system is one giant machine accessed by everyone through dumb terminals. They are called *dumb terminals* because they aren't computers themselves. They just provide access to the one big computer.

The problem with mainframes is that they cost a lot of money to buy and maintain, and they begin to run too slow when a lot of people access them at the same time. A client/server system works better because the server doesn't do all the processing. The clients do most of the work and only ask the server to help out as needed.

For instance, a user might ask to see all the employees in Human Resources. The client would ask the server to provide the information, and once the client received the information, it would show it to the user. Then, if the user wanted to sort the employees by last name or narrow it down so to see the managers, for instance, the client can do that all by itself without going back to the server. This distributes the processing so that the server does some of it, but the client does lots of it. That's where the term *distributed processing* originates.

This should sound familiar to you. My description of distributed processing applies as much to the Internet as it does to traditional client/server systems. In fact, many people think that the ultimate fulfillment of the client/server dream is the Internet and that the Internet is the best client/server platform in existence. Thus, many companies have shifted their efforts. Instead of developing standalone client/server systems, they are creating *intranets*. An intranet is nothing more than an *internal* Internet. Using the same technologies that make the Internet successful, companies are creating client/server solutions for their business problems and implementing them as complex web pages.

How Does VBScript Fit in?

VBScript is not the final answer for everything you need to create an intranet for client/server applications. In an intranet, you will usually have a web server that also acts as the database server providing information to clients through their web browsers, so a lot of technology is involved in getting an intranet up and going. The good news is that there are ways you can implement database pages using VBScript alone. That's what serverless databases do.

A *serverless* or *client-side* database, as its name implies, does away with the idea of a server altogether. Instead, it does all its processing and data-retrieval on the client side. Serverless databases are limited, and you can't use them for all the things that you can use a normal database for, but they are a great alternative for some problems and offer distinct advantages. What's better: you can implement them completely in VBScript!

If you have more extensive needs, believe me, the companies that make Internet and intranet servers are building in so many features that each new release makes it easier to do more and more powerful stuff. Both Microsoft and Netscape are competing hard for this market. This is where you will want to use HTML forms on the client side to submit data to a server for processing, but even here VBScript has many uses. See Chapter 12 for more information on this topic.

Serverless Databases

Serverless databases provide an interesting way to supply information to your users. It is a simple idea and an easy concept to implement, but it offers a lot of power and flexibility to your users. I'll show you what a serverless database is and what kind of VBScript code is necessary to put one together, and then I'll demonstrate by showing you a real-world example.

What's a Serverless Database?

Instead of requesting data from a server and then receiving that data back, a serverless database brings everything with it. The web page includes not only the user interface and the VBScript code to accept input and display the output, but it also contains the data itself.

Advantages

When the user asks for information in a serverless database, the page simply searches through its information and displays it. This method carries several obvious benefits:

➡ It is extremely fast because there is no delay in requesting or retrieving data across the Internet or intranet network.

➡ It completely eliminates any burden on the server by doing everything in the browser on the client machine.

➡ It is easy to implement and can be done completely with VBScript. No other server software or complicated setup is necessary.

Disadvantages

Great! So if serverless databases are so cool why don't we use them for everything? Well, there are some significant disadvantages, too:

➡ You can't give the user the ability to update the data. The data is hard-coded in the web page and the VBScript in the page itself must be changed to update the data, add new records, or delete old records.

➡ If the database is large, it can extend the time it takes to bring up the page initially. All the data is built into the page and must be downloaded from the server before the page is displayed in the browser.

Good Serverless Databases

Given these advantages and disadvantages, what types of databases are best suited for implementation as serverless databases? I'd say databases with these characteristics:

➡ Small- to medium-sized databases.

➡ Contains data that seldom changes.

Examples? I think any of these would make good serverless databases:

➡ An employee roster or phone list

➡ An area code lookup

➡ A zip-code lookup

➡ Ratings and reviews of local restaurants, hotels, or malls

➡ Common dog breeds and their defining characteristics (with pictures!)

➡ Books and magazines currently available on a particular topic

➡ Conference rooms available and the equipment in each

I'm sure you can think of many more and can begin to discover ways you can put them to use in your own pages.

How Do I Do it in VBScript?

Let's say you've decided to create an area code lookup page as a serverless database. What information do you need to store? Well, this is a simple one. You just need the area code and its associated location (usually a state and any major cities), so you use two string arrays: one holds the area code and the other holds the state/city information.

Yes, it's true, you could use a numeric array to store the area codes because they are always a three-digit number, but the rule of thumb that I use is this: if you need to do math on it, make it a numeric variable; otherwise, make it a string. This helps minimize the number of times that you have to convert it from a string into a number and back again.

If you were going to store more data for each individual item (as you might do for an employee roster), you simply use as many arrays as you need. You might have one for the employee's name (or one for the first name and a second for the last name); another array for the address; another for the city, state, and zip; and perhaps another array (this one numeric) to hold the employee's salary.

The key to this arrangement is that each array is the same size, and a given index cuts across all the arrays and gives you all the information for one element. For example, you can retrieve employee 21's name from Name(21), employee 21's address is in Address(21), and the same employee's phone number is in Phone(21).

You should create these as global, fixed arrays. Global because you will need to access them in a number of places throughout the page, and fixed because you should know the exact number of elements once you enter them. Because this number won't change as the user works with the web page, you do not need to use dynamic arrays.

Once you create these arrays, you must fill them in with data. The Window's OnLoad event is probably the best place to do this. Just use normal VBScript assignment statements. It will look something like Listing 11-1.

Listing 11-1: An example of filling in arrays to create a serverless database.

```
Name(1) = "Fred Smith"
Address(1) = "101 Main Street"
CityState(1) = "Upland, IN 42003"
Phone(1) = "(317)998-7886"
Name(2) = "George Johnson"
Address(2) = "1650 W. 9th St."
CityState(2) = "Marion, IN 43222"
Phone(2) = "(317)443-2233"
Name(3) = "Mary Hinkley"
...
```

Whew! That looks like a lot of work, and yes, it is. Typing in these assignment statements will be the most tedious part of creating your serverless database application. You must enter all the data this way, but once you're done, you have all the data you need, neatly contained right inside the web page.

Finally, you must add ActiveX controls to your page so that the user can enter information to search for, and then you have to write the code that takes the user's input, locates it, and displays the information. You can use a variety of methods to do this, and I'll show you some of them in the examples to come.

The State/Area Code Serverless Database

In this example, I'll show you how to create a state/area code database and a lookup page. This idea works well as a serverless database because area codes are relatively stable and don't change that often from one year to the next. The United States also has a limited number of area codes, so the size of the database won't be too large.

Creating a Simple Page

The simple search will allow the user to type in an area code and then see the corresponding city/state, if it is found. You can add controls and VBScript code later to do other kinds of searches, but for the moment, I'll focus on creating a page to do the simple search first.

 As with the other examples in the book, the completed State/Area Code Database page is included on the CD-ROM that comes in the back of this book. You can either walk through this chapter and use my instructions to create your own page or you can bring up the one I created and follow along as I describe its various parts.

What do you need to get started? Begin by creating a simple HTML page like the one in Listing 11-2.

Listing 11-2: The basic HTML page.

```
<HTML>
<HEAD>
<TITLE>State/Area Code Database</TITLE>
</HEAD>
<BODY>
<h1>State/Area Code Database</h1>
Ever get a phone number for a person or a company and
wonder where,
exactly, you were calling? Now you don't need to wonder a
minute
longer. Just type the area code into the edit below and
I'll look it up and
give you the state and maybe even a major city that the
area code
covers. It couldn't be easier. You can also type the name
of a state
or city and I'll find the area code that goes with it.<p>
This page is still under construction and currently only
supports states
```

```
which are either partially or fully in the Eastern Time
Zone.<p>
<p>
Area Code: <br>
    <OBJECT ID="AreaCodeTextBox" WIDTH=60 HEIGHT=24
 CLASSID="CLSID:8BD21D10-EC42-11CE-9E0D-00AA006002F3">
    <PARAM NAME="VariousPropertyBits" VALUE="746604571">
    <PARAM NAME="Size" VALUE="1588;635">
    <PARAM NAME="FontCharSet" VALUE="0">
    <PARAM NAME="FontPitchAndFamily" VALUE="2">
    <PARAM NAME="FontWeight" VALUE="0">
</OBJECT>
<p>
<OBJECT ID="FindStateButton" WIDTH=96 HEIGHT=32
    CLASSID="CLSID:D7053240-CE69-11CD-A777-00DD01143C57">
        <PARAM NAME="Caption" VALUE="Find State">
        <PARAM NAME="Size" VALUE="2540;847">
        <PARAM NAME="FontCharSet" VALUE="0">
        <PARAM NAME="FontPitchAndFamily" VALUE="2">
        <PARAM NAME="ParagraphAlign" VALUE="3">
        <PARAM NAME="FontWeight" VALUE="0">
    </OBJECT>
<p>
    <OBJECT ID="FindStateLabel" WIDTH=391 HEIGHT=49
 CLASSID="CLSID:978C9E23-D4B0-11CE-BF2D-00AA003F40D0">
    <PARAM NAME="Size" VALUE="10336;1305">
    <PARAM NAME="FontHeight" VALUE="200">
    <PARAM NAME="FontCharSet" VALUE="0">
    <PARAM NAME="FontPitchAndFamily" VALUE="2">
    <PARAM NAME="FontWeight" VALUE="0">
</OBJECT>
<p>
```

Listing 11-2 contains three ActiveX controls. I recommend you use
Microsoft Control Pad to add them to your web page. Table 11-1 identifies
what type of ActiveX controls to use and what to set their properties to.

The Height and Width values in Table 11-1 are the values you should enter
into the Property window as the values for those properties. When you are
finished creating the ActiveX control, you might notice that the Height and
Width specified in the <OBJECT> tag in the HTML has different values.
That's because VBScript uses a different unit of measurement in the
Property window than the <OBJECT> tag does in the HTML. Don't worry
about it. Just be aware that they will be different.

Table 11-1 The Three ActiveX Controls and Their Properties on the Simple Web Page

Microsoft Forms 2.0 TextBox

Property	Value
ID	AreaCodeTextBox
Height	18
Width	45

Microsoft Forms 2.0 CommandButton

ID	FindStateButton
Caption	Find State

Microsoft Forms 2.0 Label

ID	FindStateLabel
Caption	(empty)
Height	37
Width	293
Font	10pt MS Sans Serif

I just used the Microsoft Forms 2.0 controls that come with Internet Explorer to keep it simple. I don't need to do anything fancy with the controls, so these will work just fine.

Most of this page should be self-explanatory. The TextBox is used to enter the area code, and the button is pressed when the user wants to search. You might, however, be curious about why you would put a big label on the page with nothing in it. That label will present the information found when the user clicks the button. I could have flashed a message box on the screen, but this way the user doesn't have to click the message box OK button, and the information stays on the page until he or she does another search.

Save the page under the name ACLookup.HTM. If you load the page in Internet Explorer, it should look something like Figure 11-1.

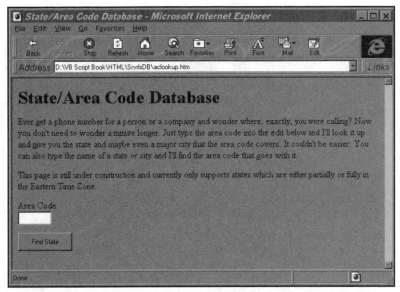

Figure 11-1: The State/Area Code Database page.

Creating Variables and Filling Them in

Now that you have a basic page the next step is to create the variables that will hold the information. Create these three global variables:

```
AC(100)
State(100)
NumACs
```

The AC array will hold the area codes, the State array will hold the corresponding state/city information for each area code, and NumACs is a variable that will hold the number of the last element in the arrays.

I have declared these arrays to hold 100 elements. On the page I included on disk, I did not use all 100 elements. I only entered the area codes for the states in the Eastern time zone. If you were going to enter the rest of the area codes, you would probably have to make the arrays bigger.

Now that you have a place to put the information, it's time to fill it in. Listing 11-3 shows what your Window's event code should look like.

Listing 11-3: The Window's event script.

```
NumACs = 69

AC(1) = "207"
State(1) = "Maine (Entire State)"
AC(2) = "603"
State(2) = "New Hampshire (Entire State)"
AC(3) = "802"
State(3) = "Vermont (Entire State)"
AC(4) = "413"
State(4) = "Massachusetts (Western)"
AC(5) = "508"
State(5) = "Massachusetts (Eastern, Except Boston)"
AC(6) = "617"
State(6) = "Massachusetts (Boston)"
AC(7) = "860"
State(7) = "Connecticut (Entire State, Except Bridgeport)"
AC(8) = "203"
State(8) = "Connecticut (Bridgeport)"
...
AC(97) = ""
State(97) = ""
AC(98) = ""
State(98) = ""
AC(99) = ""
State(99) = ""
AC(100) = ""
State(100) = ""
```

I've omitted a large chunk of the assignments in the middle, but you can check out the page included on the CD-ROM if you want to see the whole thing. The idea here is to give you an impression of how it works.

As I mentioned, I've only entered the area codes for states in the Eastern time zone. That turned out to be a total of 69 area codes, so that's what I initialized NumACs to. Once I went beyond 69, I went ahead and assigned empty strings to the rest of the elements in the array even though it wasn't necessary. If you do decide to continue this and fill in the rest of the area codes, this will give you a place to start.

Writing the Search Code

Now that the page is created and the data is all filled in, all that's left to do is the search. This code, as you might expect, will be written in the Click event of the FindState button. Listing 11-4 shows the code.

Listing 11-4: The FindState **button's** Click **event.**

```
Dim AreaCode, Index, Found

AreaCode = Trim(AreaCodeTextBox.Text)
If Not (IsNumeric(AreaCode) And Len(AreaCode) = 3) Then
    MsgBox("Invalid area code. Try again.")
    Exit Sub
End If

Index = 0
Do Until Found or Index = NumACs
    Index = Index + 1
    If AC(Index) = AreaCode Then
        Found = True
    End If
Loop

If Found = True Then
    FindStateLabel.Caption = "Area Code " & AreaCode & _
        " found. The location is " & State(Index) & "."
Else
    FindStateLabel.Caption = "Area Code " & AreaCode & "
was not found."
End If
```

The first thing I have to do is figure out if the value the user entered is valid. By *valid* I don't mean that it is one of the items in my list. I just mean does it look, roughly, like an area code. So I first trim any spaces from the input and the check to see if it is numeric and its length is 3. If so, it is good. If not, I display a message box and exit this subroutine.

Once that part of the code is done, you can assume that the input is valid. Therefore, the next step is to do the search. Instead of using a For...Next loop here, I decided to use a Do Until...Loop. That's because if I find the element I'm looking for, I don't want to continue looping though all the rest of them, I just want to break out. The Do Until...Loop gives me that flexibility. The downside is that I have to initialize and increment the index variable myself, which is no big deal.

Inside the loop, I use an If...Then statement to check to see if the current AC variable is equal to what the user entered. If it is, the Found variable is set to true, which will stop the loop; otherwise, it just keeps going.

Because the loop could end in two ways (either by finding the value or running through all the elements and not finding it), I check Found to see whether it is True. If it is, I use the label to give the user the information about the area code's state. If not, I tell the user that the area code wasn't found.

That's all there is to it! Save the page and try it out with Internet Explorer.

Extending the Page with Another Search

This page works well if you have an area code and are curious about its location, but it doesn't give you the area code for a specific city or state. It could, however.

Change the page so that the lines in Listing 11-5 are added after the FindStateLabel and before the </BODY> tag.

Listing 11-5: Lines to add to the basic HTML page after the
FindStateLabel.

```
<p>
State/City:<br>
    <OBJECT ID="StateTextBox" WIDTH=137 HEIGHT=24
     CLASSID="CLSID:8BD21D10-EC42-11CE-9E0D-00AA006002F3">
        <PARAM NAME="VariousPropertyBits"
VALUE="746604571">
        <PARAM NAME="Size" VALUE="3634;635">
        <PARAM NAME="FontCharSet" VALUE="0">
        <PARAM NAME="FontPitchAndFamily" VALUE="2">
        <PARAM NAME="FontWeight" VALUE="0">
    </OBJECT>
<p>
<OBJECT ID="FindACButton" WIDTH=96 HEIGHT=32
    CLASSID="CLSID:D7053240-CE69-11CD-A777-00DD01143C57">
        <PARAM NAME="Caption" VALUE="Find Area Code">
        <PARAM NAME="Size" VALUE="2540;846">
        <PARAM NAME="FontCharSet" VALUE="0">
        <PARAM NAME="FontPitchAndFamily" VALUE="2">
        <PARAM NAME="ParagraphAlign" VALUE="3">
        <PARAM NAME="FontWeight" VALUE="0">
    </OBJECT>
<p>
    <OBJECT ID="FindACLabel" WIDTH=391 HEIGHT=49
     CLASSID="CLSID:978C9E23-D4B0-11CE-BF2D-00AA003F40D0">
        <PARAM NAME="Size" VALUE="10336;1305">
        <PARAM NAME="FontHeight" VALUE="200">
        <PARAM NAME="FontCharSet" VALUE="0">
```

```
        <PARAM NAME="FontPitchAndFamily" VALUE="2">
        <PARAM NAME="FontWeight" VALUE="0">
</OBJECT>
```

Again, you'll want to use the Control Pad to add the ActiveX controls rather than typing the OBJECT tag stuff in by hand. Use Table 11-2 to find the control types and properties.

Table 11-2 The ActiveX Control Types and Properties for the Extended Page

Microsoft Forms 2.0 TextBox

Property	Value
ID	StateTextBox
Height	18
Width	103

Microsoft Forms 2.0 CommandButton

ID	FindACButton
Caption	Find Area Code

Microsoft Forms 2.0 Label

ID	FindACLabel
Height	37
Width	293
Font	10pt MS Sans Serif

These controls are very similar to the first set of ActiveX controls on the page. They are designed to accept a city or state name (or even part of a name) and then return the associated area code.

Save the page. If you load the page in Explorer, it will look like Figure 11-2.

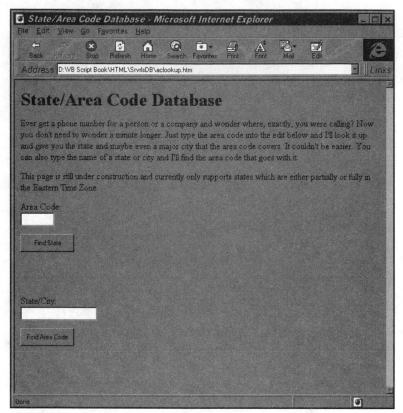

Figure 11-2: The State/Area Code Database page extended with new search controls.

Of course to make them work, you'll have to write some code. As you might suspect the key event is the FindACButton's Click event. The code for it is in Listing 11-6.

Listing 11-6: The FindACButton's Click **event script.**

```
Dim StateRequested, Index

StateRequested = Trim(StateTextBox.Text)

If Len(StateRequested)= 0 Then
    MsgBox("Invalid State/City. Please try again.")
    Exit Sub
End If

Index = 0
Do Until Found or Index = NumACs
```

```
    Index = Index + 1
    If InStr(UCase(State(Index)), UCase(StateRequested)) >
0 Then
        Found = True
    End If
Loop

If Found = True Then
    FindACLabel.Caption = State(Index) & " has the area
code " & AC(Index) & "."
Else
    FindACLabel.Caption = StateRequested & " was not
found."
End If
```

Again, just as in the last search, you first need to ensure that the input is valid. The test here is much less stringent. All I do is trim any spaces and make sure that the user did, in fact, type something in (the length of the string is greater than 0). If not, I display the error message and jump out of this routine.

You could require the user to enter at least three characters, if you wanted. He or she isn't going to see a very meaningful result otherwise. It's up to you.

The loop then searches the array. I use a `Do Until...Loop` and increment an `Index` variable myself just as I did in the last search button.

The primary difference in this search, though, is that I do more than a straight comparison. I use `InStr` to find out if what the user entered is *anywhere within* the `State` array element. This way the user can type just the state or just the city, and it will still be found.

Another thing you'll notice is that I use the `UCase` function to convert both the `State` array element and the text that was entered to uppercase. That makes the search *case-insensitive*. In other words, if the user types **boston**, it will still match on "Massachusetts (Boston)".

Finally, I fill in the `FindACLabel` with the information if it was found, and if it wasn't, I let the user know.

Creating Other Serverless Databases

You can use the area code database as a foundation for creating other serverless database pages. The first step is to evaluate the information and figure out how many pieces of data you want to keep for each record.

Then, create that many arrays, and start filling them in.

The part of your page that will be the most different for other serverless databases is the user interface. You will have to decide which elements users will most likely to want to search. You'll also have to determine if you want multiple records returned as a result. In the area code database, I quit searching after I find a match, but I could have implemented it so that if the user enters Indiana, it would return all four area codes for that state. Instead, it just returns the first one it finds.

How do you show multiple records on the screen? You could use multiple labels, or you could use a list box and simply add a row to the list box for each record that matches.

Another approach is to use frames. Divide the screen across the middle and use the top half for searching and then use the Document.Write method to create a web page for the bottom frame showing the results.

Updating Serverless Databases

I mentioned at the beginning that one of the downsides to serverless databases is that the user can't directly update the data from a web page. While that's true, there is no reason you couldn't use a form to allow the user to send you information so that you can update the page yourself. You could create an application on the server that takes user input and sends it to you in the form of an e-mail. If you think the change makes sense, you can go in and modify the VBScript in the page to make the update.

For details on how forms work and how you can use VBScript with forms, see Chapter 12.

Summary

I began by describing what a serverless database is, what its advantages and disadvantages are, and what kinds of databases are best implemented that way. Then, I gave you an overview of what is involved in creating a serverless database in VBScript. Finally, I demonstrated those techniques by creating the State/Area Code Database page that let a user search for an area code by state or for a state by area code.

Data-Entry Forms, Validation, and Formatting

12

This chapter discusses entry-edit forms designed to send information to a web server. I'll focus on the client side of the effort and demonstrate how you can make use of VBScript to perform validation, formatting, and context-sensitive help. In the process, I'll show you how to create a web survey page to collect information from people who visit your site.

Web Server Databases and Forms

If you decide that your database needs are more complex or too sophisticated for a serverless database, you'll need to set up a database on your web server. Once you do this, you can let users edit, update, and delete information right from a web page. This is a powerful capability. It also becomes a potentially dangerous situation.

You want to make sure that only those people you want updating your database have the security access to do it. Perhaps you have a situation where anyone can add a record, but you only want those who understand the database to update or delete records. However you decide to set it up, most of these security concerns will be handled at the server.

Once you have security taken care of, though, you still have to watch for other things. You want to make sure, at a minimum, that the data added to your database is valid and in the correct format. Even when a user mistypes, that's where VBScript can help. In this section, I'll demonstrate the creation of a web survey page that will allow people who visit your web site to tell you about themselves.

I won't spend time discussing how to set up your server with a database or how to implement the communications between your web server and the database. That would occupy an entire book in itself, especially because there are so many ways to go about doing it. In this section, I will concentrate on the client side of the equation and show you how to implement validation and formatting there.

HTML Forms

Throughout this book, I have used ActiveX controls any time I needed to obtain information from the user, but there is another way to do it. It is a method that has been available to web page developers for a lot longer than ActiveX controls have: HTML Forms.

An HTML form is a portion of your HTML page that you set aside specifically to receive input from the user. `<FORM>` is just a tag like other HTML tags that surround the portion of the page that will serve as the form.

Within the form, you can use several tags to identify the kinds of controls you want to place on the form. These controls are very simple and are only used for the most basic input and output.

The best way to describe how forms work is to present a simple example. Take a look at Listing 12-1.

Listing 12-1: A simple form.

```
<HTML>
<HEAD>
<TITLE>Sign Up</TITLE>
</HEAD>
<BODY>
<H1>Sign Up</H1>
Please enter your name and e-mail address below to sign up
for our exciting new electronic newsletter which will be
delivered to your e-mail box every month for the next year.
<FORM Action="/nwsltr/signup.exe" Method="POST"
Name="SignUpForm">
Enter your name: <br>
    <INPUT Type=text Size=40 Name="Name" MaxLength=50>
```

```
<p>
Enter your e-mail address: <br>
    <INPUT Type=text SIZE=40 Name="Email" MaxLength=70>
<p>
    <INPUT Type=Submit Value="Send Comments">
</FORM>
</BODY>
</HTML>
```

First, the page has a title, a header, and some text. Then, the form begins. The <FORM> and </FORM> surround the area that will contain the form. Inside the form, you can use any of the normal HTML tags you'd use anywhere else with several additional tags only allowed within forms. Figure 12-1 shows you how this page would look in Internet Explorer.

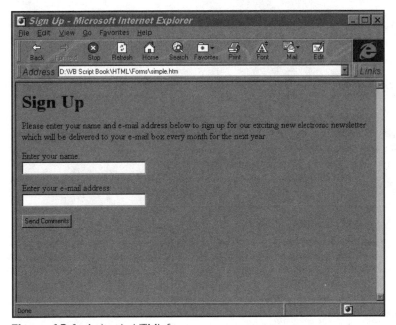

Figure 12-1: A simple HTML form.

The <FORM> Tag Pair

Take a look at the properties specified for the <FORM> tag. Action identifies what should happen when this form is completely filled out and submitted to the server. Often this is the name of a file that will be executed on the server to receive the information and process it. This might be a CGI (Common Gateway Interface) application, an ISAPI (Internet Server Application Programming Interface, used with Microsoft Internet Information Server), or even an OLE server running on the web server. You'll have to check out your server documentation to see how best to implement the application to receive and process the data.

The second property is Method. The two options here are POST and GET. These describe how the information is sent back to the server. GET only works well with small amounts of data, and POST is more commonly used. Again, the way you've implemented your server application will determine what this property's value should be.

The last property is Name. Although you can get by without naming the form, you need to name it if you plan to work with it from VBScript.

The <INPUT> tags

Inside the form are a series of <INPUT> tags, which are used to create a variety of controls inside a form. In this case, I've used it to create two text boxes and a button.

The first two <INPUT> tags have the same value for their Type property: Text. This means that they are simple text boxes that receive text the user types. In this case, it gives the user the opportunity to type in a name and e-mail address.

Size determines how long the text box is. The number indicates the number of characters that could be visible at once. MaxLength sets the maximum number of characters the user can type into the text box. When MaxLength is not specified, the user can enter any number of characters in the text box. When MaxLength is larger than Size (or MaxLength isn't specified at all), the text box will scroll horizontally once it is filled with characters to let the user enter more text than can be seen at once. This allows you to save screen space and, at the same time, provide all the room the user needs.

Finally, Name allows you to give the control a name. This works exactly like ID for ActiveX controls. Again, it isn't required, but it is a very good idea to specify a unique name for each one if you want to work with them in VBScript.

Now look at that last `<INPUT>` tag. It creates a Submit button. `Value` simply describes what text should appear on the button. When this submit button is clicked, the information in the other controls on the form are bundled together and sent off to the server automatically.

A Web Survey

All of the features of forms, including the controls and the automatic capability to submit the information to the server, are built into HTML itself and supported by almost any browser that supports HTML these days. You don't need ActiveX controls or VBScript to do forms.

If you have VBScript, though, you can do a lot of things to make forms better. Here are some examples:

➡ Validating information before it is sent to the server to be sure it is correct

➡ Formatting data so that it looks the way the server expects

➡ Providing context-sensitive help describing what input is expected for each control

I'll demonstrate how to implement each of these in the course of creating a web survey page that allows you to gather some basic information about those who surf your site.

Getting the HTML Right

The first part of the work in creating a form has nothing to do with VBScript. It is purely an HTML process. Take a look at Listing 12-2.

Listing 12-2: The HTML page, including the form for filling out the survey.

```
<HTML>
<HEAD>
<TITLE>Survey</TITLE>
</HEAD>
<BODY>
<H1>Survey</H1>
```

(continued)

(continued)

```
This is a survey of questions to find out more about the
folks who
visit my site and the internet population in general. I'll
be posting the
results of this survey soon, so take a few minutes and
make your
voice heard!
<FORM Action="/survey/ques.exe" Method="POST"
Name="SurveyForm">
What is your first and last name? <br>
    <INPUT Type=Text Size=40 Name="Name" MaxLength=50>
<p>
What is your e-mail address? <br>
    <INPUT Type=Text Size=40 Name="Email" MaxLength=70>
<p>
What is your phone number? <br>
    <INPUT Type=Text SIZE=40 Name="Phone">
<p>
How old are you? <br>
    <INPUT Type=Text SIZE=10 Name="Age">
<p>
What is your gender? <br>
    <INPUT Type=Radio Name="Gender" Value="Male"
CHECKED>Male
    <INPUT Type=Radio Name="Gender" Value="Female">Female
<p>
How often do you use the internet? <br>
    <SELECT Name="UseInternet">
    <OPTION>Just every once in a while
    <OPTION>Once a week
    <OPTION>A couple of times a week
    <OPTION>Almost every day
    <OPTION>When DON'T I use the internet?
    </SELECT>
<p>
Any additional comments you'd like to make?<br>
    <TEXTAREA Name="Comments" Rows=5 Cols=50>Cool!
    </TEXTAREA>
<p>
    <INPUT TYPE=Submit VALUE="Send Survey">
    <INPUT TYPE=Reset VALUE="Reset">
</FORM>
</BODY>
</HTML>
```

This HTML produces a page that looks like Figure 12-2.

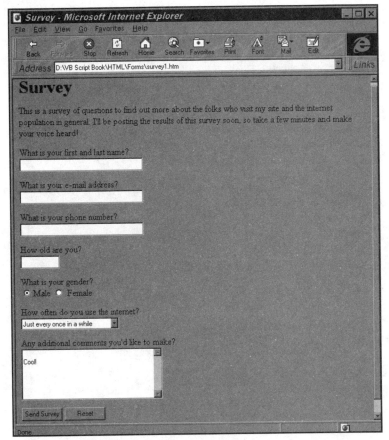

Figure 12-2: The Survey page in Internet Explorer.

Although the form controls are not nearly as flexible as ActiveX controls, you can see that you have a good variety to choose from when creating a page for user input.

HTML Form Radio Buttons

The four edits are simple text edits like those I described in the last section. The fifth one, though, produces radio buttons. Radio buttons (sometimes also called *option buttons*) provide a series of mutually exclusive options from which the user can choose. In other words, the user can only choose one from the list. Because that's how gender normally works, radio buttons are a good choice for this bit of data.

How do you make radio buttons? Just use Radio as the value associated with the Type property of the <INPUT> tag. Create a separate <INPUT> tag for each radio button and set the Name of all the buttons that go in the same group to the same value. This is different than it is for most other controls. Usually you'll want to be careful to give each control a different name, but radio buttons work together. Although they appear in the HTML as separate `<INPUT>` tags, they really represent different options for the same question. The two radio buttons in the survey have the name `Gender` indicating that they work together. If you had another set of radio buttons on the page, you would want to give them a different name.

Set `Value` to the information you want returned if the user chooses this option. Notice that you still have to put the text to label the radio button after the `<INPUT>` tag, even though it is probably the same as the information you put in the `Value` property. The `Value` property is not used to label the radio button. It just determines what is sent back to the server if the user chooses that option.

The last thing to notice is the word *CHECKED* inside the `<INPUT>` tag for the first radio button. This determines which will be the default value for the group when the page is first displayed. It's always a good idea to make one of your radio buttons (usually the first one) the default.

HTML Form Dropdown List Boxes

Next comes the `<SELECT>` and `<OPTION>` tags. These tags, inside a form, allow you to create a dropdown list box or combo box. It works the same as a set of radio buttons in that it lets the user choose one option from a list, but it takes up less space on your page. Radio buttons are usually only used for very short simple lists like gender. Whenever you have a longer list, a dropdown list box is usually better.

How is it done? Well, the `<SELECT>` tag is the important one. Here is where you give the control a name. Then the `<OPTION>` tags within the `<SELECT>` allow you to specify lines that appear in the list. The first `<OPTION>` tag is also used as the default value in the dropdown list box. Notice that the text for each option appears *outside* the `<OPTION>` tag.

HTML Form Memo Fields

Finally the last control is indicated by the `<TEXTAREA>` tag, which allows you to create a big, multi-line memo field where the user can enter larger bits of text, like a paragraph of comments. In addition to providing a name, you specify the height and width in characters using the `Rows` and `Cols` properties. Any text that appears within the `<TEXTAREA>` tag pair (in this case, the word *Cool!*) acts as a default value in the memo field.

HTML Form Submit and Reset Buttons

You've already seen the submit button in the last example. It automatically sends all the information in the form off to the server for processing. The reset button looks exactly the same except that its Type property is set to Reset. This button clears all the input so that the user can start over, if he or she wants.

Adding Validation

The page, as it sits now, would work, assuming you have the server set up appropriately.

Users could type in as little or as much as they wanted. They could even type in totally nonsensical information, and it would be happily transmitted across the Internet back to the server and processed. What you need is *validation*, which simply means making sure the data is correct, or at least as correct as it can be.

Of course, the server itself could validate on the data. That is, in fact, the way it was done before scripting languages like VBScript became available, but that is a wasteful process. It takes time for the information to reach the server. The server must take time away from other tasks to process the bad data, and then the user must wait even longer for a message to transmit back just to say that the data is invalid.

But if you do your validation in VBScript, it is executed on the client — right in the browser on the user's machine — before it is ever sent to the server. The big benefit for the user is immediate feedback. Without any waiting at all, the user is informed of problems, and he or she can fix them and try sending again. This significantly increases the chances that by the time the server receives it, it's correct.

Where Do You Put the Validation?

The first question to answer is where the validation code should be placed. What object and what event? Well, when do you want the validation to occur? You probably want it just before the information is submitted.

You could do it in the Click event of the Submit button, but there is a better place. An event is associated with the form itself called OnSubmit. You should write a function in response to this event and do your validation there.

Be careful, though. Your first inclination will be to go into the Script Wizard, choose the `SurveyForm` object, click the `OnSubmit` event, and begin writing code. This will *not* work. If you do this, you'll notice a line of text above the text box where you normally type in your code. The line of text looks like this:

```
<FORM NAME=SurveyForm OnSubmit=...>
```

Any code you write here will be placed after the `OnSubmit` property of the `<FORM>` tag. This is not the place to write your validation code. If you do (or you call a function here to do your validation) you won't be able to tell VBScript to *cancel* the submit if the validation finds errors. If you can't cancel the submit, there's not much point in doing the validation in the first place, so your best bet is not even to include the `OnSubmit` property for the `<FORM>` tag.

So where do you write your validation code? Just create a separate function and name it this way:

```
FormName_OnSubmit
```

where *FormName* is the name of your form. When you do, VBScript will understand from the name that you want to execute this function when the form is submitted and will do that for you automatically.

To create a function for the form on this Survey page, you can either use the Script Wizard or simply write the function yourself in the HTML. Either way, you'll want to name the function `SurveyForm_OnSubmit`. The name alone will be enough to connect it to the form's `OnSubmit` event. The actual steps you should take to create this function follow.

I'll extend the survey so that it has minimal validation just to give you a feel for how it should work. Here are the steps to adding validation to the HTML page back in Listing 12-2.

1. Get into the Script Wizard.

2. Right-click on the Insert Actions pane on the right and choose New Procedure from the menu.

3. The code pane (at the bottom of the Script Wizard window) had the following line at the top:

   ```
   Sub Procedure1()
   ```

4. Change that line to read like this:

```
Function SurveyForm_OnSubmit()
```

5. Type the code in Listing 12-3 into the lower part of the code pane.

6. Now get out of the Script Wizard by clicking OK.

7. Make sure that the <FORM> tag line in your HTML still reads like this:

```
<FORM ACTION="/survey/ques.exe" METHOD="POST"
        NAME="SurveyForm">
```

Listing 12-3: The simple validation code.

```
If Trim(SurveyForm.Name.value) = "" Then
    MsgBox("You must enter your name.")
    SurveyForm_OnSubmit = False
Else
    SurveyForm_OnSubmit = True
End If
```

I specifically asked you to check the <FORM> tag at the end there to make sure that OnSubmit property wasn't specified.

To edit this procedure again in the Script Wizard, follow these steps:

1. Get into the Script Wizard.

2. Double-click on the Procedures object in the Insert Actions pane on the right.

3. A list of all the procedures on this page will appear. Right-click on SurveyForm_OnSubmit.

4. From the popup menu, choose Edit.

5. The procedure will appear below for you to edit.

Now look at Listing 12-3. You'll notice a couple of interesting things about it. First, when you refer to a control on a form, you have to add a prefix to it with the form name like this: *SurveyForm.Name.* That's because you could have more than one form on a page and VBScript has to know which one you want to use.

Next, notice the property of the Name text box I am checking is Value. If this were an ActiveX control, I'd be checking the Text property, but all the form controls use the property Value to indicate what's in them.

If you haven't worked with functions much, you might also be thrown off by the use of SurveyForm_OnSubmit. This is the name of the function, but I assign values to the name within the function. Back in Chapter 4, I told you that this is how you specify the value that is *returned* when the function ends.

So, all this function does is check to be sure that the users entered something into the name text box. If they did, it returns True; otherwise, it returns False. This returned value tells VBScript whether it should go ahead with the submit. If False is returned, the submit is canceled. True indicates that the submit should continue.

 There is another way of validating and submitting forms. Instead of using a Submit button, you can use a standard HTML form button and then place your validation in the onClick event of the button. If you do it this way, you then have to call the Submit method manually if all the validation passes.

To do this, replace your Submit button with a line of HTML like this:

```
<INPUT Type="Button" Name="SendButton" Value="Send Survey">
```

Then, put all the validation code in the SendButton_OnClick subroutine. If all the validation passes, be sure to put this line in the subroutine:

```
SurveyForm.Submit
```

This calls the form's built-in Submit subroutine that does the same thing that a standard Submit button would do if it were clicked: send the form information off to the server.

Feel free to use whichever method you like best.

Writing the Validation for the Page

Now that you understand where to put the validation code and how to cancel the submit if the validation fails, it should be a simple matter to add validation for the rest of the page. Take a look at Listing 12-4. Replace the code in your SurveyForm_OnSubmit function with this. It does all the validation for the entire page.

Listing 12-4: The complete validation code in the
SurveyForm_OnSubmit **function.**

```
Dim ErrMsg
```

```
ErrMsg = ""

If Trim(SurveyForm.Name.value) = "" Then
    ErrMsg = ErrMsg & "You must enter your name. "
End If

If Trim(SurveyForm.Email.Value) = "" Then
    ErrMsg = ErrMsg & "You must enter your e-mail address.
"
Else
    If InStr(SurveyForm.Email.Value, "@")=0 Then
        ErrMsg = ErrMsg & "E-mail address is invalid. "
    End If
End If

If Trim(SurveyForm.Phone.Value) <> "" Then
    If Len(SurveyForm.Phone.Value) < 10 Then
        ErrMsg = ErrMsg & "Enter complete area code and
phone number.  "
    End If
End If

If SurveyForm.Age.Value <> "" Then
    If Not IsNumeric(SurveyForm.Age.Value) Then
        ErrMsg = ErrMsg & "Age is invalid. "
    Else
        If Int(SurveyForm.Age.Value) < 5 Or
Int(SurveyForm.Age.Value) > 150 Then
            ErrMsg = ErrMsg & "Age is out of range. "
        End If
    End If
End If

If ErrMsg = "" Then
    SurveyForm_OnSubmit = True
Else
    MsgBox ErrMsg
    SurveyForm_OnSubmit = False
End If
```

This is a long function, but nothing is too complex about it. A local variable called ErrMsg is created and initialized first. Then I check to see if the user entered his or her name. If not, I assign a string to ErrMsg indicating that the name is required. Notice that I did not do a direct assignment as you might expect:

```
ErrMsg =   "You must enter your name. "
```

Instead, I assigned `ErrMsg` to equal the value *currently in* `ErrMsg` concatenated with the error message:

```
ErrMsg =   ErrMsg & "You must enter your name. "
```

Because the `ErrMsg` variable started out with the value of an empty string ("") , whether I assign it directly or concatenate it doesn't really matter much. The result is the same.

You'll notice that I don't just do this concatenation thing with only the first error message. I do it throughout the entire function. That way, if the user neglects to enter his or her name and phone number, both error messages are displayed. How? Look at the last few lines of the function. An `If...Then` statement checks to see if `ErrMsg` still contains an empty string by the time it goes through all the validation tests. If it does, the data must be perfect, so `SurveyForm_OnSubmit` is assigned a value of True. If not, a message box is displayed showing the `ErrMsg` string. If, as I mentioned earlier, both the name and e-mail address were missing, the error message would look like this:

```
You must enter your name. You must enter your e-mail
address.
```

This is nice for the user. If you just display the first error message you came to and gave up, the user only knows that one thing is wrong. The user could fix that and try to submit again only to find another problem. This way, he or she receives a list of all the problems at once and can go fix them all before trying to submit again.

Validating the Name and E-Mail Address

Now that you understand the basic structure of the error messages on this page, look back up at the top at the actual validation code again. You've already seen the validation for the name, so look at the e-mail validation. An e-mail address is also required, so if it isn't there, an error message is generated. If, on the other hand, an e-mail address is present, I check to be sure that an @ sign is somewhere in it. Because I know that the e-mail address must have one, I can be sure that the information entered is invalid without it.

Validating the Phone Number

The phone number, on the other hand, is not required. So first I check to see if the user entered one. If not, I go on. If the user did, however, I want it to be valid. Because you can't enter a valid phone number (with area code) in fewer than ten digits, I make sure the user at least did that.

Validating the User's Age

The next question asks the user's age. Again, the user doesn't have to enter it, but if he or she does, I want to be sure first that they entered a numeric value. I use the function `IsNumeric()` to check this out. If the entry is not numeric, an error message is generated. If it is, I go on to a further check. An age of less than 5 or greater than 150 is probably not valid so I flag that, too.

Validating Gender

The next question on the survey asks the user's gender. Because this is implemented with radio buttons and a default radio button is chosen from the beginning, there is no way that it could be invalid. I'm not saying it couldn't be incorrect, but it will always be valid. This is the benefit of using radio buttons and dropdown list boxes. Because the user is given a fixed number of options and can only choose among them, the user cannot possibly enter invalid data. Use both radio buttons and dropdown list boxes everywhere they are appropriate to minimize your validation work.

Validating Use of the Internet and Comments

Because the question on using the Internet is a dropdown list box, I don't need to do any validation on it, and because comments are very freeform, I don't need any validation there either. Therefore, I'm done!

A Final Word on Validation

As you can see from this example, validation does not ensure that the data is correct. There's no way it could. It just helps users see where they forgot to answer an important question or where they accidentally typed something wrong. It won't keep someone from deliberately typing in false information.

Nevertheless, validation can be an important tool in keeping your data as clean and correct as possible, and with VBScript, it becomes as simple and convenient to implement as it is to use.

Adding Formatting

Formatting is another area where VBScript can help you on the client side of your data-entry applications. Sometimes the user types data in using a particular format. The format isn't wrong, but it also isn't what the server expects.

This happens all the time. For instance, a user might enter times and dates in any of these ways:

3/5/68

22-4-96

January 3rd, 1807

3pm

5:15am

5 o'clock

None of these are *wrong*, per se. They are all valid ways that different people might choose to represent dates and times. Other people would easily understand any of them, but computers are more picky about their data. They generally tend to want it in one form.

Therefore, you have two choices. You can tell users what format to put it in and keep displaying error messages (through your validation code) until they get it right, or you can look at what they've entered and see if you can't put it in the right format yourself before you send it off. The second option is certainly more user friendly, but it isn't always possible. You will spend a long time trying to think up every possible way the user might try to enter some data. The best option is usually a hybrid of the two options.

Rethinking the Phone Number

Let me step back from the formatting discussion for a moment to talk about the survey's phone number. You probably noticed that the validation code I wrote for the phone number was pretty weak. (See Listing 12-5.)

Listing 12-5: The validation code for the phone number.

```
If Trim(SurveyForm.Phone.Value) <> "" Then
    If Len(SurveyForm.Phone.Value) < 10 Then
        ErrMsg = ErrMsg & "Enter complete area code and
phone number.  "
    End If
End If
```

Nearly anything could get through this validation if it was long enough, but how could you tighten up the validation?

Well, the first step is to think of the different ways a user might enter the phone number. For simplicity's sake, let's assume that the phone number is a standard, American phone number and doesn't need to include any international codes. A brainstorming session to think of all the possible ways a user might enter a phone number might result in Table 12-1. I'll use this as my basis for my new, tighter validation.

Table 12-1   Common Ways of Entering a Phone Number

Phone number	Comment
111-222-3333	These first two are probably the most common
(111)222-3333	
(111) 222-3333	Notice the extra space between the parentheses and the 2
111 222 3333	Using spaces as separators
1112223333	Using no separators at all

The smallest of the group is ten characters long, so the original test was right on target. You could also add a validation test to reject anything longer than 14 characters because that is the longest of the bunch.

Suppose the server is expecting it in a specific format. You might even be able to choose the format that the server accepts, but generally it will only accept one. How do you make all these valid options fit?

Formatting the Phone Number

Probably the easiest one for the server to digest would be a phone number with no formatting at all. That is the best way to store it, and if you wanted to show formatting later, you could add it then. Therefore, you want to strip out all the formatting characters and leave only a ten digit number that looks very much like the last entry in Table 12-1.

Now remove the portion of the validation code that does the validation for the phone number and replace it with the code in Listing 12-6.

Listing 12-6: The new phone number validation and formatting.

```
Phone = Trim(SurveyForm.Phone.Value)
If Phone <> "" Then
    If Len(Phone) < 10 or Len(Phone) > 14 Then
        ErrMsg = ErrMsg & "Invalid phone number.  "
    Else
        Index = 1
        Do Until Index = Len(Phone)
            If Mid(Phone, Index, 1) = " " Or Mid(Phone,
Index, 1) = "(" Or _
                Mid(Phone, Index, 1) = ")" Or Mid(Phone,
Index, 1) = "-" Then
                    Phone = Left(Phone, Index-1) &
Right(Phone, Len(Phone)-Index)
            Else
                Index = Index + 1
            End If
        Loop
        If Not IsNumeric(Phone) Or Len(Phone) <> 10 Then
            ErrMsg = ErrMsg & "Invalid phone number. "
        Else
            SurveyForm.Phone.Value = Phone
        End If
    End If
End If
```

The first thing I do is put the phone number into a local variable. This is done primarily so that I don't have to type **SurveyForm.Phone.Value** every time I want to use it. I trim any spaces off the ends while I'm at it.

Then I check to see if it is empty. If it is, I simply go on; otherwise, I check to see if it is between 10 and 14 characters long. If it is in one of the formats I identified in Table 12-1, it should be within that range.

Next comes the actual formatting. In this case, I'm removing formatting so that only the numbers are left. I go through each character, one-by-one to see if it is a formatting character. The four that showed up in Table 12-1 were the space, right and left parentheses, and a dash. If the current character is any of these, I use the `Left` and `Right` functions to concatenate everything on the left of the character with everything to the right of the character, conveniently leaving out the current character. This has the effect of pulling it right out of the middle of the string.

You'll notice that I use a `Do...Until` loop here instead of a `For...Next` loop. I did that because I wanted to control when the loop variable (in this case a local variable named Index) was incremented. I didn't want to increment it each time. Why? Well, take a look at Figure 12-3. If you are at position four in the string and you decide that it is a formatting character and remove it, the string is now different. The new character at position four is the one *after* the one you just examined (and removed), so it is the next one you want to examine. Therefore, when you remove a character, you don't want to increment the counter or else you'll skip right over a character you want to examine. You only increment the counter when the character is not removed.

```
Before removal:
111-555-9999
   ↑

After removal:
111555-9999
   ↑
```

Figure 12-3: After removing the current character, the next one you want to look at is in the same position.

The `If...Then` statement checks to see if it should be removed. If so, it removes it; otherwise, the `Index` is incremented and the loop continues.

Assuming the user entered his or her phone number using one of the formats in Table 12-1 (or something very similar), you should be left with a stream of exactly ten numbers at the end of this loop. So after the loop, I check to make sure that only numbers are left (using the `IsNumeric` function) and that the length is exactly 10. If not, an error message is generated; otherwise, the local variable's new formatted value is plopped in to the edit to replace what the user typed before it is sent off.

A Final Word on Formatting

Formatting can involve changing the input from the user in any way you see fit so that the server will be better able to digest it. It is more user-friendly than simple validation because instead of just kicking it out, it tries to be flexible and work with what the user has provided. Like validation, it is limited. It can't turn bad data into good data, but it is a nice tool to have in your toolbox for creating easy-to-use, flexible entry-edit pages.

Adding Context-Sensitive Help

Context-sensitive help is help that is associated with what you are doing now. Instead of just providing page after page of documentation, context-sensitive help seeks to provide you with little bits of information just at the point where you need them.

For instance, on an entry-edit window you might run across a text box that isn't labeled very well, and you aren't quite sure what to enter there. If context-sensitive help were available, you could pop up a little window or look down at the status bar to find more information.

You could use several ways to provide context-sensitive help to your users. The simplest and most straightforward is to use the status bar.

On the survey page, create a new subroutine called `ContextHelp`. If you are doing it in the Script Wizard, change the line at the top that says

```
Sub Procedure1()
```

to, instead, say

```
Sub ContextHelp(Item)
```

This subroutine will be called whenever the cursor (sometimes called the *focus*) is on one of the controls on the form. It will pass the name of the control where it has just landed. Listing 12-7 shows you the code that should make up the `ContextHelp` subroutine.

Listing 12-7: The `ContextHelp` subroutine.

```
Select Case Item
Case "Name"
```

```
         Window.Status = "Please enter your full name."
Case "Email"
         Window.Status = "Please enter your internet e-mail
address."
Case "Phone"
         Window.Status = "Please enter your day-time phone
number."
Case "Age"
         Window.Status = "Please enter your age."
Case "Gender"
         Window.Status = "Please choose Male or Female to
indicate your gender."
Case "Student"
         Window.Status = "Please choose Yes or No to indicate
whether or not you are " & _
              "currently a full-time college student."




Case "University"
         Window.Status = "Please enter the name of the
university you attend."
Case "Graduate"
         Window.Status = "Please enter the year you expect to
graduate from college."
Case "UseInternet"
         Window.Status = "Please click the button and choose the
statement which best " & _
              "describes how often you use the internet."
Case "Comments"
         Window.Status = "Please enter any additional
comments you'd like to make " & _
              "about this site or this survey."
End Select
```

The routine is nothing more than a giant Select Case statement that looks
at the string sent in and then sets the status bar to a string that provides
additional information about the control. Some of these don't end up giving
much more information than the control labels did, but I'm sure you'll do a
much better job than I of creating your own context-sensitive help.

The only thing left to do is call it. Begin by choosing the onFocus event of
the Name control of SurveyForm in the Select Event pane on the left of the
Script Wizard. The line above the code box at the bottom is this:

```
<INPUT NAME=Name OnFocus=...>
```

This indicates that whatever you type here will be assigned to the `OnFocus` property in the `<INPUT>` tag. This is fine because you only want to write one line of code: the subroutine call. Type this:

```
ContextHelp("Name")
```

and for `Email`'s `OnFocus` event code type this:

```
ContextHelp("Email")
```

You'll just keep doing this for all the controls. You'll notice that the radio buttons actually count as two controls even though they have the same name. You'll also notice that they only have one event you can code for: `onClick`. Go ahead and put this line in the `onClick` event of both `Gender` radio buttons:

```
ContextHelp("Gender")
```

All the rest should be easy. Don't bother putting anything in the `onClick` event of the submit and reset buttons.

Now try it out. You should be able to tab to or click on any control and see its associated line of help in the status bar. The only exceptions are the radio buttons. If you click on them, you'll see the help but not if you tab to them. There's no way around this because they don't have an `onFocus` event.

Summary

I began this chapter by introducing you to HTML forms and their associated controls. From there, I showed you how to validate data before it is sent to the server and how to reformat the data so that it is in a more digestible form. Finally, I described a simple method for adding context-sensitive help to any data-entry page.

Glossary

Appendix A

This appendix contains a pretty complete glossary of the terms and buzzwords used throughout this book. I've included it because I know how frustrating it can be to keep all the terminology straight as you are first learning.

If you ever stumble upon a word or phrase that looks unfamiliar to you, check the text where you're reading to see if it is defined there. I've tried to define any unfamiliar words the first time I use them in the text. If you don't find a definition there, check here.

+ — Addition operator. Used to add two numbers or variables together.

- — Subtraction operator. Used to subtract one number or variable from another.

* — Multiplication operator. Used to multiply two numbers or variables together.

/ — Division operator. Used to divide one number or variable by another.

action pane — the right pane of the Script Wizard, which is used to copy into the editor a call to an object's method or a reference to an object's property. See *Script Wizard*.

ActiveX — a generic name that refers to the technologies Microsoft is using to *activate* the Internet. Instead of just viewing web pages that present text and graphics, ActiveX technologies seek to liven up the experience. To add things like animation, sound, and video to pages to make them more engaging and more interactive. The ultimate goal is to make web pages indistinguishable from the interactive multimedia CD-ROM applications you run today on your computer.

ActiveX control — a bit of code that provides a useful tool or user interface element to your web pages. Think of a button, a text box, a slider bar, or an animation viewer. You can create all of these things as ActiveX controls and dropped onto your web page to make it more entertaining and interactive.

ActiveX scripting — a standard for writing scripting languages for the Internet that Microsoft developed. Both VBScript and JScript (Microsoft's JavaScript language) are ActiveX scripting languages. This standard makes it easy for others to develop their own scripting languages for a specific purpose or audience. See *scripting*.

Anchors object — a browser object that represents a list of all the anchors in the current page. Anchors include links, but also include placeholders used to name certain parts of the document so that other links can jump directly to a paragraph in the middle of a long page, for instance. See *browser objects* and *object hierarchy*.

argument — a variable or value that is passed to a function or subroutine so that it can use it. You send the value to a subroutine by listing it after the subroutine's name in the order expected. You send the value to a function by placing it inside parentheses after the function name. See *procedure*, *subroutine*, and *function*.

array — a series of variables that all have the same name. The individual variables in an array are referenced by using their index or associated number. See *one-dimensional arrays*, *two-dimensional arrays*, *multidimensional arrays*, *static array*, and *dynamic array*.

assignment — the process of putting a value into a variable. Variables can be assigned new values as often as you like in your VBScript program. See *variable*.

attribute — See *property*.

boolean — a type of variable that can contain only two possible values: True and False.

bottom-tested loop — a loop that checks to see if its condition is satisfied at the bottom of the loop. In this case, because the check is at the bottom, the code inside the loop will always be executed at least once. See *top-tested loop*.

browser objects — objects that are built into the browser and allow you to control and manipulate both the browser and the page it contains. See *object hierarchy*, *Window object*, and *Document object*.

bug — an error in the syntax or logic of a program that causes it to work incorrectly. See *debugging*.

bullet-proofing — making an application so that it anticipates every possible action a user might take and responds appropriately. See *error handling*.

case-insensitive — an adjective describing a computer language or operating system. It indicates that the system does not distinguish between upper- and lowercase letters, so *Fred*, *FRED*, and *fred* are all the same.

case-sensitive — an adjective describing a computer language or operating system. It indicates that the system distinguishes the difference between upper- and lowercase letters, so *Fred* is different from *FRED* or *fred*.

characteristics — See *property*.

client — a computer on a network that accesses a server to update and share information and resources. See *server* and *client/server*.

client/server — describes a way of organizing computers on a network that has a primary computer (the server) containing shared information, like files and database data, and a bunch of other computers (the clients) that access the server to update and share information. This has become a very popular alternative in many companies to large, expensive mainframes. See *intranet*.

client-side database — See *serverless databases*.

code — a program listing or a portion of one.

COM — a high-level specification created by Microsoft that identifies the way that objects interact with each other. ActiveX controls and OLE controls are implementations of this specification.

command — a function or subroutine built into VBScript that allows you to do something.

comments — a portion of a computer program that is set apart to describe what is going on. Comments help those who will maintain or update the program in the future. Comments have no effect on the program or how it runs. Comments in HTML begin with <!- and end with ->. Comments in VBScript are always only one line long, and the line begins with the command REM or the apostrophe (').

concatenation — the act of sticking two strings together to form one long string.

conversion functions — VBScript functions that are designed to change a variable from one subtype to another. Int, for instance, converts a decimal number or a string into a whole number. CStr converts a decimal number or a whole number into a string. See *Int* and *CStr.*

converting variables — the process of changing a variable from one subtype to another. For instance, you might convert a string entered by the user into a number so that you can perform arithmetic on it. See *conversion functions* and *subtype.*

CStr — a VBScript conversion function that converts decimal numbers and integers into strings. Often used to prepare data to be displayed on a web page or in a message box. See *conversion functions.*

database — a structured store of information which allows easy update and retrieval.

Date — a VBScript function that returns the current date from the system clock on the user's machine. See *Time* and *Now.*

debugger — a piece of software included with most computer languages that allows the programmer to watch as a program executes in slow-motion, line-by-line and allows the programmer to stop at any time and check the value held in variables. VBScript, unfortunately, does not have a debugger. See *debugging.*

debugging — the process of removing syntactical and logical errors from code so that it performs as desired. See *bug.*

decimal numbers — numbers that contain a decimal point and numbers to the right of the decimal point. Also called fractional numbers. See *integer, truncation,* and *rounding.*

declare — to create a variable before it is used. In VBScript you use the Dim statement to declare variables.

declaring a variable — the process of creating a new named storage place for data. Variables are declared or created using the Dim statement in VBScript. See *variable*, *declare*, and *initialization*.

desk-checking — a technique used in debugging that involves walking through the code step-by-step as the computer would to locate a problem.

distributed processing — a way of organizing computers on a network so that an application can execute some of its code on one machine and other code on another machine. This flexibility allows developers to balance applications and optimize them so that they run best. See *client/server*.

Document object — a browser object that represents the document currently loaded and displayed in the browser. See *browser objects* and *object hierarchy*.

document.write — See *write method*.

Do...Loop — a VBScript looping statement that allows you to execute a piece of code until a condition is True or until it is False. See *loop*, *nested loop*, and *For...Next*.

dynamic array — an array that is not set to any size at all when it is created. After it is created, its size is later set and possibly reset as it is used. See *array* and *static array*.

editor — a computer program designed to allow people to enter text. Often, programmers use special editors to write computer programs or HTML documents.

Elements object — a browser object that represents a list of the elements on the current page. Examples of elements include ActiveX controls and Java applets. See *browser objects* and *object hierarchy*.

error handling — refers to code that is designed to anticipate and intercept problems which could cause the program to crash or behave unexpectedly.

event — something that can happen to an object. For instance, a button can be clicked. You can write code that executes in response to an event.

event pane — the left pane of the Script Wizard that is used to specify what object and event you want to write a script for. See *Script Wizard*.

execute — to cause a computer to process a program and to do what it says.

expression — a series of variables and values strung together with operators. Expressions can always be evaluated down to one final value. See *order of precedence*.

form — a tag in HTML that gives you a place to put built-in HTML controls. Then in VBScript you reference them through the Form object. After data has been entered, the form can be used to submit data to the server. See *validation* and *formatting*.

formatting — the process of changing the way the data looks so that the server can more easily digest it. See *form*.

Forms object — a browser object that represents a list of all the forms on the current page. Forms are used to obtain information from the user and submit it to the web server for processing. See *browser objects* and *object hierarchy*.

For...Next — a VBScript looping statement that counts the number of times you execute a piece of code. You can count from any number up to any other number. See *loop, nested loop*, and *Do...Loop*.

Frame object — a browser object that represents a pane within a window. Corresponds directly to the frames you can create in HTML. See *browser objects* and *object hierarchy*.

FrontPage — a WYSIWYG (What-You-See-Is-What-You-Get) HTML editor that allows you to type text and format it much as you would do in a word processor, and it generates the associated HTML tags. See *WYSIWYG*.

function — a piece of code that is separated off from the rest of the program and given a name of its own. The subroutine's code executes when its name is called from another piece of code. Information can be passed to the subroutine when it is called in the form of arguments. The arguments that a subroutine receives are defined when the subroutine is first created. A function is distinguished from a subroutine in that it also returns a single value back to the code which originally called it. This is called the return value. See *procedure* and *subroutine*.

global variable — See *script-level variable*.

History object — a browser object that represents the history of the user's browsing. You use a History object to remember where the browser should go when you click the Back and Forward buttons. See *browser objects* and *object hierarchy*.

HTML — stands for *Hypertext Markup Language*. The standard way of formatting text on the Worldwide Web. Its capabilities continue to expand with each new browser release, but it is not a full-fledged computer language.

HTML Assistant Pro — an HTML editor designed to ease the process of creating HTML pages by making common tags easily available from menus and button bars. See *editor*.

HTML document — See *HTML page*.

HTML page — a file that contains HTML forming a document to be displayed through a web browser.

idiot-proofing — See *bullet-proofing*.

IeTimer1 — the default name of the Internet Explorer Timer ActiveX control from Microsoft. See *timer*.

If...Then...Else — a VBScript statement that allows you to test and compare variables with other variables and values and then make a decision about what to do. The condition comes after the If. The portion of code after the Then executes if the condition is True, and the portion after the Else executes if the condition is False.

initialization — describes the process of assigning the first value to a variable. Often the first value a variable has will have a big impact on how the program works with that variable. See *variable* and *assignment*.

InputBox — a VBScript command that allows you to display a dialog box with a prompting message and an edit box to allow the user to enter a number or a string of text.

InStr — a VBScript function that searches for a small string inside of a larger string. If InStr finds the smaller string, the command returns the character number in the larger string where it was found. See *Len, Left, Right,* and *Mid*.

Int — a VBScript function that accepts a string or a decimal number and converts it to a whole number. This funciton is often used to convert input from the user that is accepted as text (either through the InputBox or an ActiveX text box).

integer — a whole number; a number without a decimal part. See *Int*.

Internet Assistant — a series of products from Microsoft that allow you to use their Microsoft Office suite of products to create web pages of different types. For instance, the Word Internet Assistant allows you to create web pages in much the same way as you create Word documents, and it generates the HTML tags for you. See *WYSIWYG*.

Internet Explorer — the web browser designed by Microsoft. It supports all the latest HTML tags and all the newest Internet standards including plug-ins, Java applets, ActiveX controls, JavaScript, and VBScript.

intranet — a derivation of the word *Internet* that describes a company's internal use of Internet technology to make it easy to share information with other parts of the company. This technology provides a standard platform on which client/server applications can be built. See *client/server*.

Is — a VBScript operator that is used to compare two variables to see if they hold the same object. Use `Is` instead of equals when comparing objects. See *Set*.

Is... functions — a series of VBScript functions that allow you to check the subtype of the variable to find out what kind of information it holds. Each returns True or False to indicate whether it holds that particular type of data or data which can be converted into that type of data. For instance, `IsNumeric` returns a True if the variable it was passed holds a number or a string that can be safely converted to a number. See *conversion functions*.

Java — an extremely popular programming language developed by Sun Microsystems. Based on C++, Java was designed to be a truly multiplatform language for both the source code and the compiled code. This made it a natural fit for developing small web applications called applets. Java applets are different from JavaScript and VBScript in that they are written and compiled once and then associated with a web page using the `<OBJECT>` tag, much as ActiveX controls are. Whereas the scripting languages are coded right in the web page, alongside the HTML, and the source code is downloaded with the page and executed by the browser. In practice, scripting languages are used to tie together and orchestrate multiple Java applets and ActiveX controls to make them all work together as a cohesive page.

JavaScript — a scripting language with a syntax loosely based on Java, which itself was based on C++. JavaScript is used to do all the same kinds of things that VBScript does, but it isn't as easy to learn for a non-programmer. See *Java*.

LCase — a VBScript function that converts a string into all lowercase letters. Numbers and symbols are not changed. See *UCase*.

Left — a VBScript function that takes a number of characters from the left side of the string and uses them to create a new string. You specify the number of characters. See *Len*, *Right*, *Mid*, and *InStr*.

Len — a VBScript function that will tell you how many characters are in a string. See *Left*, *Right*, *Mid*, and *InStr*.

Links object — a browser object that represents a list of all the links in the current document that the user can click on to go someplace else. See *browser objects* and *object hierarchy*.

load-time error — an error that happens in your VBScript code as its page is being loaded into the browser initially. These errors are usually syntactical problems. See *run-time error*.

local variable — a variable declared inside a subroutine or function. A local variable is created when it is declared and doesn't exist anymore when the procedure ends. It can only be accessed, assigned, and used inside the procedure where it was declared. See *script-level variable*.

Location object — a browser object that tracks the URL of the current page. See *browser objects* and *object hierarchy*.

loop — a type of VBScript statement that causes certain bits of code to execute multiple times. How many times they execute can be determined by a predefined number (as is often the case with a `For...Next` loop) or by a condition becoming True or False (as is often the case with a `Do...Loop`). See *nested loop*, *For...Next*, and *Do...Loop*.

message box — a dialog box that presents information and usually several buttons that allow the user to make a decision.

method — a subroutine or function that is bundled into an object. Methods are called by first typing the object name, then a period, then the subroutine/function name, followed by the arguments as you normally would. Methods are not commands that are built into VBScript, but rather subroutines or functions that are built into specific objects you can use, like ActiveX controls.

Mid — a VBScript function that takes a number of characters from the middle of the string and uses them to create a new string. You specify the starting character and number of characters to take. See *Len*, *Left*, *Right*, and *InStr*.

MsgBox — a VBScript command that allows you to display a flexible message dialog box that presents some text and buttons to the user.

multidimensional arrays — an array of more than one dimension. See *array*.

Navigator — the web browser designed by Netscape. It supports most of the latest HTML tags and newest Internet standards. It does not support ActiveX controls (unless you have a third-party plug-in) and although it supports JavaScript, it does not support VBScript.

Navigator object — a browser object that contains properties that identify the current browser. See *browser objects* and *object hierarchy*.

nested If...Then — an If...Then statement within another If...Then statement. You can continue to nest If...Then statements as many times as you need to.

nested loop — a loop inside a loop. You can have a For...Next loop inside another For...Next loop, a Do...Loop inside a For...Next loop, or any other combination. The innermost loop continues until it is completely done before the outer loop goes to a second loop.

Now — a VBScript function that returns the current date and time from the system clock on the user's machine. See *Date* and *Time*.

object — bundles together variables and functions/subroutines to create a useful entity. Variables bundled into an object are called *properties*. Functions/subroutines bundled into an object are called *methods*. An object can also have associated events and defined responses to those events. ActiveX controls are the most common type of object you'll use in VBScript.

object hierarchy — an organization of objects where some objects are contained within other objects. The browser objects, for instance, are organized into an object hierarchy where the Window object, representing the browser window, contains the Document object which represents the document within the window. See *browser objects*, *Window object*, and *Document object*.

<OBJECT> tag — an HTML tag used to indicate that an object should be embedded into the HTML page. The <OBJECT> tag provides all the information about what the object is and where it can be found. It is often associated with <PARM> tags that specify properties of the object. Common <OBJECT> tags are Java appletes and ActiveX controls. See *<PARM> tag*, *ActiveX control*, and *Java*.

OLE — a standard for dividing large applications down into smaller pieces and then allowing those pieces to communicate and be put together in different ways to solve problems. OLE originally stood for *Object Linking and Embedding,* but it is now known only by the initials.

OLE Control — ActiveX controls are actually a *superset* of OLE controls. That is, OLE Controls are a particular type of ActiveX control. There are other types of ActiveX controls that don't require so much in the way of interface specifications and therefore are looser and smaller. These ActiveX controls are the ones specifically designed for the Internet. Thus, it is accurate to say that all OLE Controls are ActiveX controls. It is also accurate to say that the new kind of ActiveX controls designed for the Internet are slimmed down versions of their OLE Control counterparts.

one-dimensional arrays — an array that represents one series of numbers individually indexed by one number. See *array.*

On Error Resume Next — a VBScript statement that causes the procedure to continue executing even if it runs into an error. This allows your script to check for the error after it has occurred and do something about it. See *run-time error.*

OnLoad event — an event of the Window browser object that happens when a page is first loaded into a window. This is a good place to write VBScript code to initialize variables and set up the page the way you want it. See *Window object.*

OnUnload event — an event of the Window browser object that happens when a page is being unloaded from the window in order to load a different page. You can code any clean up or housekeeping code you need to here before the page ends. See *Window object.*

Option Explicit — a VBScript command that should be placed at the top of every VBScript page you write. It tells VBScript not to allow variables to be created automatically. That is, it tells VBScript to force you to declare all your variables with a Dim statement before you use them. This helps you avoid bugs that appear simply because you mistyped a variable name.

order of evaluation — See *order of precedence.*

order of precedence — refers to the way a computer language figures out the value represented by an expression. For instance, all the multiplication and division is done before the adding and subtracting. Different languages have slightly different ways of evaluating expressions, so it is important to know how VBScript does it. See *expression.*

page — a single file displayed in a web browser that can be scrolled up and down to view it all.

parameter — See *argument*.

<PARM> tag — an HTML tag used in association with the <OBJECT> tag to specify an object's properties when it is created. See *<OBJECT> tag*.

preventive error handling — a way of approaching error handling that involves trying to stop errors before the occur. Instead of waiting for the error to occur and handling it then, the preventive approach attempts to head off problems before they turn into errors. See *error handling*.

procedure — a generic name that refers to both subroutines and functions in VBScript.

program — a set of detailed instructions that tell the computer what to do. This term is often used synonymously with software and application.

property — a variable which is bundled into an object. A property can be changed to define what the object will look and act like.

Randomize — a VBScript command that seeds the random number generator with the current value in the system clock. If you don't use Randomize in your pages where you use the Rnd command, each time you load the page, you'll receive the same sequence of numbers. Randomize makes sure they are different each time. You need to call Randomize only once at the beginning of your page. See *random number* and *Rnd*.

random number — a number that is, effectively, drawn from a hat. Random numbers come in no particular order and over time end up more or less equally distributed over the entire range. See *Rnd* and *Randomize*.

remarks — See *comments*.

reserved word — a word used by VBScript as a command or constant. Examples include *Dim*, *For*, *Loop*, and *True*. You cannot use reserved words as names for your variables or procedures.

return value — the value returned from a function back to the code which called it.

RGB — a VBScript function that allows you to pass three numbers between 0 and 255 to represent the red, green, and blue intensities of a single color. The long integer that is returned holds the number that represents the color you described.

Right — a VBScript function that takes a number of characters from the right side of the string and uses them to create a new string. You specify the number of characters. See *Len*, *Left*, *Mid*, and *InStr*.

Rnd — a VBScript command that returns a random decimal number that is greater than zero and less than one. Rnd can be multiplied to produce random decimal numbers or random integers for any range. See *random number* and *Randomize*.

rounding — one method of converting a decimal number into a whole number. Rounding involves examining the decimal portion of the number and choosing a whole number to represent it that is closest to the decimal number. See *Int*, *truncation*, and *conversion functions*.

run — See *execute*.

run-time error — an error that happens as a page is being manipulated and used by a user. Often these are logic errors. See *load-time error*.

scope — describes when and where a variable can be accessed. If a variable is declared in a procedure, the scope is said to be *local*. This means that the variable only exists as long as the procedure is running and that it can only be accessed from within the procedure. Contrast local scope to global scope. A *script-level* or *global* variable exists for as long as the page is loaded and can be accessed from anywhere within the page. See *script-level variable* and *local variable*.

scripting — the process of writing code that appears right in the web page, alongside the HTML. The source code is downloaded with the page and executed by the browser. See *ActiveX scripting*.

script-level variable — a variable that is declared in VBScript outside of any procedure. Script-level variables are global in scope, meaning they can be accessed from anywhere throughout the page. See *local variable*.

Scripts object — a browser object that represents a list of all the scripts defined with the <SCRIPT> tag in the current window. These cannot be accessed or used in any way from VBScript. See *browser objects* and *object hierarchy*.

<SCRIPT> tag — a tag in an HTML document that specifies that the information to follow will be a scripting language program. The end tag </SCRIPT> indicates when the program is over and the HTML document begins again.

Script Wizard — a part of Microsoft Control Pad that lets you quickly and easily write code for specific objects and events. See *action pane* and *event pane.*

Select...Case — a VBScript statement that allows you to look at one variable and do many different things based on the value of that variable.

server — a centralized computer that holds shared files, database data, and even access to computing resources like printers and Fax modems. See *client* and *client/server.*

serverless database — a type of database that brings all its data down to the client and provides access to it there. It is extremely fast and efficient for small to medium-sized databases, but it doesn't easily allow for updates. See *database* and *client/server.*

Set — a VBScript statement that assigns an object to a variable. Set is only used when working with object. When assigning a normal value (like a number or a string) to a variable you do not use Set. See **Is**.

statement — See *command.*

static array — an array which is set to a specific size (number of elements) when it is created. See *array* and *dynamic array.*

Status bar — the gray bar at the bottom of the browser window that is used to provide information on the status of the browser. You can use the status bar used from VBScript to provide other types of feedback to the user including help on the use of specific controls.

string — a series of letters, numbers, and symbols all strung together to be used for some purpose. Strings are usually surrounded by double quotes inside a program and can be held in variables.

string arrays — an array that holds string values. See *array.*

structured programming — a way of approaching programming that brings structure, discipline, and consistency to the code. Structured code is much easier to maintain and change later than unstructured code. See *unstructured programming.*

subroutine — a piece of code that is separated off from the rest of the program and given a name of its own. The subroutine's code executes when its name is called from another piece of code. Information can be passed to the subroutine when it is called in the form of arguments. The arguments that a subroutine receives are defined when the subroutine is first created. See *procedure* and *function*.

subtype — a description of the kind of data that is actually, currently being held in a variable, be it a number, string, or boolean value. Although all variables in VBScript are of type variant, they also have a subtype which describes what kind of data they are actually holding now. This subtype can be changed with conversion functions. See *type, converting variables*, and *conversion functions*.

tag — a word in an HTML document surrounded by greater-than and less-than signs to indicate that it is used to format or describe the document, as in: <TAG>. Tags often are used to surround a bit of text to indicate that the text should be formatted in a particular way. Surrounding text is done by placing the tag at the beginning and an end tag at the end. End tags are indicated with a / before the tag name, as in: </TAG>.

three-dimensional arrays — an array that represents several series of numbers that could be pictured in the form of a cube. Each element is addressed by the combination of three indexes. See *array*.

Time — a VBScript function that returns the current time from the system clock on the user's machine. See *Date* and *Now*.

timer — a type of ActiveX control that has an `Interval` property and a `Timer` event. The `Interval` specifies how often the `Timer` event is triggered. For instance, if the `Interval` contains the value 500, the `Timer` event will be triggered twice a second because the value in interval represents a number of milliseconds.

top-tested loop — a loop that checks to see if its condition is satisfied at the top of the loop. If the condition is satisfied the first time the code executes, the loop is skipped altogether and never even executes once. See *bottom-tested loop*.

tracing — the process of stepping through code line-by-line to find a problem. See *debugger*.

truncation — one method of converting a decimal number into a whole number. Truncations involve simply chopping off the decimal part of the number. See *Int, rounding*, and *conversion functions*.

two-dimensional arrays — an array that represents several series of numbers that could be pictured in the form of a grid. Each element is addressed by the combination of two indexes. See *array*.

type — a description of the kind of data that can be held by a variable, be it numbers, strings, or boolean values. In most languages, you must specify the type of the variable when it is declared. VBScript doesn't support different variable types. The only variable type in VBScript is the variant. A variant can hold information of any type. However, when a value is assigned to a variant in VBScript, it automatically sets the variable's subtype to be whatever type of data was assigned to it. Therefore, if you create a variable called Name, it is a variant. If you assign the string "Fred" to the variable Name, it is still a variant, but its subtype is *string*. See *converting variables*, *subtype*, and *conversion functions*.

type conversion — See *converting variables*.

UCase — a VBScript function that converts a string into all uppercase letters. Numbers and symbols are not changed. See *LCase*.

unstructured programming — the opposite of structured programming. An approach to programming that is haphazard and careless. Code that is unstructured is very difficult to maintain and change later. This type of code is often referred to as *spaghetti code*. See *structured programming*.

URL — Universal Resource Location. The web address found at the top of most web browsers indicating the name of the web site accessed.

user — the person who will ultimately browse to your web page and use it. The experience this person has is what all this work concerns.

validation — the process of ensuring, as far as possible, that the data entered is correct. See *form*.

variable — a named place in memory where information can be stored. Variables are created or *declared* by using the Dim statement in VBScript. They can then have values assigned to them and can have their values checked using If...Then statements. Variables generally hold one of three different kinds of information: strings, boolean values, and numbers. A string is a series of letters, numbers, and symbols, usually surrounded by quotes. Boolean values are either True or False. Numbers can be either integers (whole numbers) or decimal numbers (ones that have a decimal point and numbers after it). See *assignment* and *initialization*.

VBA — stands for *Visual Basic, Applications Edition*. VBA is a computer language based on Visual Basic that is integrated with applications, like word processors and spreadsheets, allowing advanced users of these products to extend and customize their capabilities. VBScript is a subset of VBA and Visual Basic.

VBScript — stands for *Visual Basic, Scripting Edition*. VBScript is an Internet scripting language. It is a complete, yet simple programming language that allows you to extend the capabilities of your web page. Although it is not as full-featured as Visual Basic or C++, VBScript provides all the features you need to do almost anything in a web page that you could do in any other application running on your computer.

Visual Basic — a development environment designed to help software developers quickly and easily create intricate Windows applications that solve problems. When it was introduced, it was revolutionary. It did for computer programming what What-You-See-Is-What-You-Get (WYSIWYG) word processors did for the task of typing in documents. It made the whole process more visual and much easier to understand. Because of this, Visual Basic is easier to learn and allows programmers to write applications much faster than traditional programming languages like C or C++. VBScript is a subset of VBA and Visual Basic.

Window object — a browser object that represents the window of the browser. See *browser objects* and *object hierarchy*.

write method — a method of the Document object that allows you to send HTML to the page from your VBScript code as it is being created. This allows the pages to be more dynamic and change how they look based on the time of day or other variables. See *Document object*.

WYSIWYG — *What-You-See-Is-What-You-Get*. An acronym originally created to describe Word processors that showed different fonts and styles right on the screen as they would appear when they were printed. Today, the term is applied to HTML editors that allow you to work in an environment similar to a word processor and have the HTML tags generated for you automatically. See *FrontPage* and *Internet Assistant*.

VBScript and Visual Basic

If you are already a Visual Basic developer, you are well on your way to developing very cool web pages with VBScript. Because VBScript is a strict subset of Visual Basic, all you really have to learn is what you *can't* do in VBScript. That, along with a little information on the browser objects and the way the user interface works in VBScript, and you'll be creating web pages that are every bit as cool as your Visual Basic applications.

I'll start off by discussing the biggest differences between VBScript and Visual Basic and after that I'll get into some specifics on the language: what's included and what's not.

The Big Differences

First, VBScript is not a standalone product. You can't go to the store and buy a copy. It is, instead, a part of Microsoft Internet Explorer, and whenever you want to run and test your applications, you will do it through Internet Explorer. The corollary to this is that your final product, when writing VBScript, will not be an .EXE file. It will be a web page with your source code in it. The code is compiled and executed when the page is loaded in the browser, and, as you might expect, your source code is visible to users if they select View Source for your page in their browser.

Second, VBScript has no development environment. There is no editor, no debugger, and no programming tools to make your life simpler. You simply use the same tool you currently use to create web pages. That said, you can use some small applications and utilities to ease the pain of adding

ActiveX controls to your page and scripting. The ActiveX Control Pad that I've shown you how to use in this book is free and makes it much easier to add controls and script. It doesn't quite qualify for a complete development environment, but it's much better than Notepad! Another environment that promises to be even better is Microsoft Front Page 97. It has all the Control Pad capabilities built-in, plus it includes a very easy-to-use WYSIWYG HTML editor. When Microsoft's Internet Studio is released, it will provide even more flexibility.

Third, input and output work very differently in VBScript. You don't use forms like you do in Visual Basic. You use web pages. There is a lot of similarity, however. You can drop ActiveX controls on your web pages and interact with them much like you do with a form, and you still have access to `MsgBox` and `InputBox` if you need them.

Fourth, with VBScript you have a set of built-in browser objects that allow you to access and manipulate the browser window and the currently loaded document. This is a powerful feature and will allow you to supplement for your loss of forms.

Finally, the languages themselves are different: VBScript only supports a subset of what Visual Basic can do. I'll spend the rest of this chapter discussing those language differences.

Changes to the Language

In order to understand the differences between VBScript language and Visual Basic language, it is best to take a look at the design goals of VBScript.

Microsoft created VBScript to serve three purposes:

- To be a client-side scripting language that could be used alongside HTML
- To be server-side script language for creating dynamic web pages on the fly
- To be a free scripting language that can be incorporated into any application to allow user scripting and customization capabilities

In this book, I've focused my attention on the first use of VBScript, but you'll want to keep your eyes open for the other two. Both are interesting, and you'll be ready to make use of them because it's the same VBScript language used in them all.

Clearly these purposes called for a very different language from the full-blown Visual Basic development environment. By the same token, it didn't make sense to create a totally new language that everyone would have to learn. Therefore, the decision was made to use a strict subset of Visual Basic. This not only makes it easy to learn, but it also aids in porting applications from one environment to another.

So it will be a strict subset, but what should be left out? Microsoft had three goals that it wanted VBScript to attain:

➡ Simplicity

➡ Safety

➡ Portability

These goals were used to drive the decision about what was left in and what was taken out. I'll discuss each of these goals and the implications they had on the language.

Simplicity

I use the word *simplicity* here to mean several things.

Microsoft wanted VBScript to be easy to learn for those who didn't already know Visual Basic. Therefore, the language needed to be clean, straightforward, and simple. At the same time, it had to be strong enough to be a usable tool for creating dynamic web pages.

In addition, the final size of the DLL that would contain VBScript (and be included in Internet Explorer) needed to be small. That way, if it was updated, the user could easily, maybe even automatically, download the newest version.

Finally, the full-blown version of Visual Basic has a lot of old functions and syntaxes that are supported purely for backward compatibility to the many earlier versions of Microsoft Basic, including QuickBasic. These simply bloat the language and confuse the newcomer about how things should be done. These needed to be dropped in the new slimmed-down, Internet-savvy VBScript.

What does all this mean? Plenty.

Data Types? What Data Types?

The first and most breathtaking change for a Visual Basic programmer is the complete absence of data types. That's right! Everything in VBScript is a variant. You might call it a structured programmer's nightmare!

Consequently, while you still need to declare all your variables with `Dim` (assuming you are faithfully using `Option Explicit`), you will not use an `As` clause after the variable name to declare its type.

You might think that this also means that all type-conversion functions go away, too. This is not the case. A few like `CCur`, `CVar`, and `CVDate` are gone, but most of them are still available. In fact, they become more important than ever because, although variants have no type, they do have a subtype that is set based on the values assigned to them. You should keep track of this and convert the value whenever necessary. For this reason, it is a very good idea to pretend that the variables have a data type even when they don't. In other words, don't take advantage of the fact that your variable is a variant by putting a string in it in one place and a number in it in a different place. You will only confuse yourself and end up with strange errors.

Thus, the loss of variable types ends up making your job tougher, not easier. Fortunately, you'll find that most VBScript applications aren't nearly as complex and data-rich as the average Visual Basic application. At least that's true today.

Trailing Data Type Characters

In Visual Basic, you can declare a string by using a $ after the variable name, like this:

```
Dim Address$
```

This is not usually considered good programming practice, and the `As` clause after the variable name is preferred.

In VBScript it is not an option. All the trailing data type characters are gone as are all the functions and system variables with a trailing data type character like `Hex$`, `Environ$`, `Chr$`, and `Format$`. Fortunately most of these have a corresponding function or variable without the trailing data type character, and all those are available in VBScript.

Strings

Strings may be held in variants, but some of the string capabilities are not a part of VBScript. You cannot create fixed length strings, for instance. They are all dynamic length strings. In addition functions like LSet, RSet, Format, Str, Val, and StrConv are not available.

Most of the string functions are available, however. CStr, Left, Right, Mid, and InStr are all available, but only the Mid function is available, not the Mid statement. That means that you can't use Mid to change characters in the middle of a string. You can only use it to obtain characters from within the string.

Un-Constant

Constants are also gone: not just the Const keyword for creating your own constants, but also all the Visual Basic-defined constants like vbOK and vbCancel. You may choose to use variables, with some sort of naming standard as constants, but there is no enforcement by the language to keep their value from changing.

Arrays and User-Defined Types

Arrays are supported but in a limited form. They can be multidimensional and either static or dynamic, depending on your needs, but they cannot have indexes numbered as you please. Each dimension's index must start with 0. The declaration

```
Dim Names(100)
```

creates 101 elements numbered 0 to 100. This declaration

```
Dim Names(10 to 50)
```

would be invalid. Likewise, Option Base is unavailable.

User-defined types (Type...End Type) are not supported at all.

Optional Arguments

Optional arguments are not available in VBScript, so the IsMissing function goes away, as does the Optional keyword and the ParamArray.

Select Case

Select Case is still available, but in a much trimmer form. You can't do all the fancy stuff you can in Visual Basic. In fact, it is very simple. You can only compare the test value versus one or more values after the Case, separated by commas. No greater-than or less-than or ranges.

Clearing Out the Chaff: Goto and Gosub

Finally Microsoft has axed the old, outdated holdovers in Visual Basic that were left to provide backward compatibility to QuickBasic and previous versions of Microsoft Basic: most notably Goto and Gosub.

Before Microsoft Basic was as robust as it is today, it was difficult to do some things without Goto and Gosub, but that was a long time ago, and I don't think anyone will miss these old-timers. They go along with their cousins On/Goto, On/Gosub, On Error Goto, line numbers, and even line labels.

Other Sacrifices to Simplicity

Here is a list of other functions, operators, and keywords that were chopped away to keep VBScript simple, straightforward, and small:

- DoEvents
- Timer
- The Like operator
- All the financial functions
- TypeName
- Conditional compilation
- Collections
- With...End With
- Debug.Print, End, and Stop
- Property Get/Let/Set
- Public and Private
- New (for creating a new object)
- Erl and Error (although the Err object and its properties are available)
- Resume and Resume Next

Safety

Safety is a broad term that is often bantered about in the Internet arena along with *security* and *privacy*. These concerns will grow into the inevitable law-enforcement arm of the new Internet world. Just as the Wild West had to submit to the law of the Sheriff and ultimately government and police, so the taming of the Internet will come about when the concerns of the many outweigh the unlimited freedom of the few.

How does safety affect a scripting language? Well mostly it is a matter of protecting against viruses. You might be surprised to think that a virus could be written in something like a scripting language, but if you think about it, it makes a lot of sense. A web page is distributed far and wide very quickly, and the code automatically executes when the page is downloaded, without any intervention from the user. Anyone who was bitten by the Microsoft Word Macro virus knows just how annoying a scripting language virus can be.

How do you keep viruses from being written in VBScript? Well, you can't, really, but you can try to make them a little less harmful by removing any too-powerful capabilities from the language. That's just what Microsoft did.

File Input and Output and Database Access

All file input and output commands have been removed from VBScript. You cannot create, modify, copy, or delete files on the client's hard drive. You can't even save information to be used later. This lack of any persistent storage is probably one of the most frustrating things about VBScript.

 Cookies are one exception to this rule. A cookie is a simple text file that is stored on the client machine and referenced by your web site. You can use cookies to store persistent information, but your use of it is limited. You simply identify what you want to store and Internet Explorer handles the text file creation and maintenance.

Likewise, VBScript does not provide any database access.

Dynamic Data Exchange (DDE)

All Dynamic Data Exchange commands have been removed, so you cannot take control of DDE-aware applications with `LinkExecute` or use `LinkPoke`, `LinkRequest`, or `LinkSend` to share information.

Other Sacrifices to Safety

There are several other changes made to keep VBScript safe. Declare is gone, so you won't be making DLL calls. In addition, object manipulation capabilities offered by `GetObject` and `TypeOf` are gone.

Portability

The last important goal VBScript was to attain was portability. In fact, Microsoft is so dedicated to portability that the company has offered the VBScript source code for free to anyone who wants to port it to a platform where it isn't already implemented. This is more than a philanthropic desire on Microsoft's part to see all platforms enriched. It is a blatant attempt to make VBScript the universal scripting language everywhere and set a de facto standard, and as a Visual Basic and VBScript developer, that's OK by me!

This goal did mean that certain Windows-specific stuff had to go, though: like the `Clipboard` object. Also gone is all the graphics routines (like `Circle`, `Line`, `Point`, `Print`, and so on), although the `RGB` color function is still available.

Also gone are the commands for manipulating user interface objects like `Arrange`, `ZOrder`, `SetFocus`, `Hide`, `Show`, `Load`, `Unload`, `Move`, `AddItem`, `RemoveItem`, `Refresh`, and `PrintForm`.

Printing commands like `EndDoc`, `NewPage`, and `PrintForm` are also gone.

Finally, environmental commands and variables like `Environ`, `SendKeys`, `Command`, `AppActivate`, `Shell`, and `Beep` are also gone.

ActiveX Controls Versus OLE Controls

One last topic that I wanted to throw in here is the relationship between OLE Controls (OCXs) and ActiveX controls. This is a topic that has caused a lot of confusion, and I wanted to help clear some of it up.

One reason this topic can be so confusing is that different authors, depending on their knowledge of the subject and the audience they are trying to address, will say very different things. You may have heard that

ActiveX controls is just the new name for OLE Controls, or you may have heard (as I said earlier in this book) that they are slimmed down, Internet-savvy versions of OLE Controls.

The fact is that the COM specification identifies the way that objects interact with each other. It is a high level specification. OLE Controls are one implementation of this specification. ActiveX controls are actually a *superset* of OLE controls: OLE Controls are a particular type of ActiveX control. There are other types of ActiveX controls that don't require so much in the way of interface specifications and therefore are looser and smaller. These ActiveX controls are the ones specifically designed for the Internet. Thus, it is accurate to say that all OLE Controls are ActiveX controls. It is also accurate to say that the new kind of ActiveX controls designed for the Internet are slimmed down versions of their OLE Control counterparts.

Therefore, you may expect people to continue referring to OLE controls as OLE controls to distinguish them from this other kind of Internet-optimized ActiveX control, but that hasn't happened. Microsoft is eager for everyone to believe that there are already hundreds of ActiveX controls out there. Although that is technically true (because ActiveX controls include the large base of OLE controls designed for Visual Basic), it is a bit misleading because most of these aren't optimized for use on the Internet.

In any event, the upshot is that Microsoft has consistently used the term ActiveX control for everything and the industry has followed, and although most of the ActiveX controls out there weren't designed with the Internet in mind, they can be imbedded in a web page and automatically downloaded like any other ActiveX control.

Summary

I began this appendix by identifying several major differences between VBScript and Visual Basic. I then went on to describe the three major design goals of VBScript and what the implications were to the language. Finally, a section describing the real difference between OLE Controls and ActiveX controls ended this chapter.

Browser Object Hierarchy Reference

This appendix is a reference to the browser object hierarchy. This object hierarchy is built into Internet Explorer and Netscape Navigator and can be accessed from either VBScript or JavaScript to manipulate and control the browser. For examples of how to put the more interesting of these tools to work in your own web pages, see Chapter 6.

A Word on Typography and Naming Standards

In this chapter, I will often use a template to describe how to call the methods of these objects. The templates will look something like this.

```
document.write string
```

or

```
[variable =]prompt [string][,default]
```

Text written normally is used exactly as it is written. Text in italics indicates that you will replace that text with something the italics describes (like a variable or a string). The square brackets indicate that the portion within is optional.

You'll probably notice an interesting naming standard that Microsoft has adopted as you look through the properties, methods, and events associated with these objects. The first letter is always lowercase, but if the property/method/event consists of more than one word, the words after the first are capitalized. Here are some example:

```
name
defaultStatus
setTimeout
```

I have followed their standard in this appendix, but you can write your code however you like because VBScript ignores capitalization altogether.

The Basic Hierarchy

Figure D-1 is a diagram of the browser object hierarchy. Descriptions of the objects appear below.

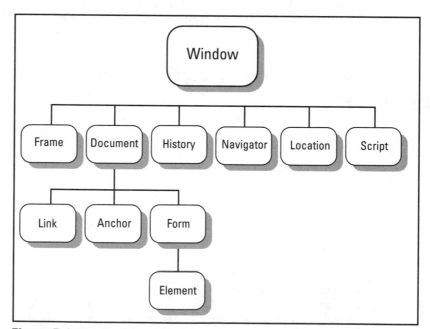

Figure D-1: The browser object hierarchy.

Here is a basic description of each object:

- **Window:** represents the window of the browser.

- **Frame:** a pane within a window. Corresponds directly to the frames you can create in HTML.

- **Document:** represents the document currently loaded and displayed in the browser.

- **History:** the history of the user's browsing. Used to remember where the browser should go when you click the Back and Forward buttons.

- **Navigator:** contains properties that identify the current browser.

- **Location:** tracks the URL of the current page.

- **Script:** a list of all the scripts defined with the `<SCRIPT>` tag in the current window. These cannot be accessed or used in any way from VBScript.

- **Link:** a list of all the links in the current document that the user can click on to go someplace else.

- **Anchor:** a list of all the anchors in the current page. Anchors include links, but also include placeholders used to name certain parts of the document so that other links can jump directly to a paragraph in the middle of a long page, for instance.

- **Form:** a list of all the forms on the current page. Forms are used to obtain information from the user and submit it to the web server for processing. I'll discuss these later.

- **Element:** a list of the elements on the current page. Examples of elements include ActiveX controls and Java applets.

This appendix describes each object, its properties, methods, and events.

The Window Object

The Window is at the top of the browser object hierarchy. If you want to find out more information on the objects that are properties of the Window object, see their associated section in this appendix.

Normally when you refer to properties and methods in VBScript, you are required to prefix them with their associated object using dot-notation:

```
window.status = "Almost finished..."
```

You can do this with the window object if you like, but it isn't required. Every script you write takes the window object for granted and doesn't require you to specify it. Although the previous line of code will work, this one will, too:

```
status = "Almost finished..."
```

Because this is so, all properties and methods of the window object are considered keywords in VBScript and may not be used as variable or subroutine/function names.

Window Properties

The Window object has 11 properties, which may all be accessed and changed unless otherwise noted:

➡ name: the name of the window.

➡ defaultStatus: holds the default message that is displayed in the status bar (the gray bar at the bottom of the Internet Explorer window). The default message is the one that is displayed when nothing else is displayed there.

➡ status: holds the text that is currently in the status bar. You can use this to change that text.

➡ parent: the parent window. This comes into play when you have frames within a window. Each frame is considered its own separate window and the container of that frame is the parent window. Parent cannot be changed.

➡ self: an object that refers to the current window. The window object and its property self always refer to the same thing. This one also comes into play in multiframe windows, but it isn't something you'll use everyday. Self cannot be changed.

➡ top: an object that refers to the highest level parent window. When you have frames inside of frames, this always refers to the highest level window. Top cannot be changed.

➡ frames: the list of Frames. Cannot be changed. See the section titled "The Frames" later in this appendix.

➡ location: the Location object for the current window. See the section titled "The Location Object" later in this appendix.

➡ history: the History object for the current window. See the section titled "The History Object" later in this appendix.

➡ navigator: the Navigator object for the current window. See the section titled "The Navigator Object" later in this appendix.

➡ document: the Document object loaded into this window. See the section titled "The Document Object" later in this appendix.

Window Methods

The Window object has six methods: Alert, Confirm, Prompt, SetTimeout, ClearTimeout, and Navigate. There are two additional methods, Open and Close, that have been documented but not yet implemented.

alert

```
alert string
```

This method displays a message box with an exclamation point icon, an OK button, and the text you provide. It works essentially like a simplified message box statement.

Example

```
alert "The page is not available"
```

confirm

```
[variable = ]confirm string
```

This method displays a message box with a question mark icon and both an OK and a Cancel button. This is another simplified version of the message box function. confirm returns True if the user clicked OK; otherwise, it returns False.

Example

```
Dim Answer
Answer = confirm "Do you want to go on?"
If Answer = True Then
...
```

prompt

```
[variable =]prompt [string][,default]
```

Very much like the VBScript's InputBox funtion, prompt displays *string* and provides a text box for the user to type a response. prompt returns whatever the user typed. Unlike InputBox, prompt allows you to specify a default value for the text box.

Example

```
Dim UserName
UserName = prompt "Please Enter Your Name","Fred"
If UserName <> "Fred" Then Alert "You're not Fred!"
```

The methods alert, confirm, and prompt all create a separate modal window and display it to the user. A modal window is one that forces you to respond to it before you can do anything else on the page. If you try to click on other elements of the page, you will only receive a beep from the system. Because of this, you should use them sparingly. Users find them annoying if they are used too often. The same is true for VBScript's MsgBox command.

What are the alternatives? Use the Window object's status property to give users feedback on the status bar instead of flashing up an alert and use ActiveX controls on the page to receive user feedback instead of flashing up a prompt.

setTimeout and clearTimeout

```
[IDVariable =]setTimeout StringExpression, milliseconds
clearTimeout IDVariable
```

setTimeout allows you to set a timer that will go off in the amount of time specified in *milliseconds*. When that time is passed and the timer goes off, *StringExpression* is evaluated and the subroutine/function or method it refers to is called. To cancel the timer before it goes off, call *clearTimeout* with the *IDVariable* containing the value returned from setTimeout.

Be aware that the first argument to setTimeout is a string. Although you are specifying the name of a subroutine, function, or method, it will be in quotes or in a string variable holding the name. I point this out because it is very unusual to see a subroutine, function, or method used as a string in VBScript.

In addition, even if you do not want to specify any arguments for a subroutine or function in setTimeout, you must still place the empty parentheses after the subroutine or function name.

By the way, when you call a method, you put the object's name inside the quotes, too. As in:

```
IDNum = setTimeout "adder.increment()",1000
```

Example

A page contains a button. A global variable named idnum is declared. The following code appears in the Window's onLoad event script (see "Window Events" later in this appendix):

```
idnum = setTimeout("TimesUp()",3000)
```

This code appears in the subroutine TimesUp():

```
MsgBox "Time's Up!"
```

This code appears in the button's Click event script subroutine:

```
clearTimeout idnum
```

Once the page is loaded, if the user doesn't click the button within three seconds, a message box appears that says

```
"Times Up!"
```

If the user does click the button, a message box appears that says

```
"You're just too quick for me..."
```

The "Times Up!" message box does not appear after the user clicks the button.

navigate

```
navigate URLString
```

This method changes the current page to the one specified by the URL in *URLString*.

TIP The URL specified in URL string can be either relative or absolute, but don't get lazy and use something like `www.microsoft.com`. It won't work. You must include the `http://` at the beginning.

Example

```
navigate "http://www.microsoft.com"
```

open and close

Microsoft has documented two more functions for the Window object called `open`, which opens a new browser window with a specified URL to be loaded into it and displayed, and `close`, which closes a specified window.

Neither of these two functions are implemented in Internet Explorer 3.0, but I strongly suspect that you will see them in Internet Explorer 4.0. That's because version 4 will be fully integrated into the user interface of Windows 95 and Windows NT operating systems and will need this type of functionality.

Window Events

There are two window events: `onLoad` and `onUnload`. `onLoad` occurs immediately after a document has completely finished loading into the browser. `onUnload` occurs just before a document in the window is cleared from view so another document can be loaded. These events are perfect spots for placing initialization code and final cleanup and housekeeping. Name your subroutines:

```
Sub window_onLoad()
```

and

```
Sub window_onUnload()
```

Remember, you don't have to worry about capitalization. It will work no matter how you capitalize it.

If you want to write code for these events using the Script Wizard, simply double-click the window object in the event pane (on the left), and you will see the onLoad and onUnload events appear under it. Simply click on one and begin entering your VBScript code in the editor below as you would for any event.

 Don't do things in the onLoad or onUnload that will take a long time. Users will be frustrated if they have to wait a long time before they can interact with your page or go to another page. Also, avoid using any modal dialog boxes like alert, confirm, prompt, InputBox, or MsgBox in either of these events. In addition to annoying the user, these will kill an automated web page downloading application.

The Frame Object

Frames have all the same properties, methods, and events that the Window object does. They are in almost every respect a window. The only difference is that a frame is loaded as part of a parent window frameset. For more information on Frames and how they work, see the Chapter 2 section titled "Frames" and the Chapter 6 section titled "Frames."

The Document Object

The Document object is the biggest and probably the most important of the browser objects. It has no events, but it has 13 properties and 5 methods.

Document Properties

The document object includes a number of properties that allow you to maintain the colors that are used to display the page: linkColor, vLinkColor, aLinkColor, bgColor, and fgColor. The color you assign to these properties may be either an RGB value or a string indicating the color's name. An RGB value is a value returned by the RGB function discussed in a section in Chapter 5 titled "Writing Your VBScript in Code View." The string values that VBScript accepts indicating a color's name are the same ones you used to set these colors from HTML. They are listed in Table D-1.

Table D-1	**The Standard Color Strings that can be Specified for** `linkColor`, `vLinkColor`, `aLinkColor`, `bgColor`, **and** `fgColor`.		
Aqua	Black	Blue	Fuchsia
Gray	Green	Lime	Maroon
Navy	Olive	Purple	Red
Silver	Teal	White	Yellow

➡ `linkColor` and `vLinkColor`: allow you to find out the color of links and visited links (respectively). They also allow you to change those colors, but only if you put the statements to do so *outside* of any subroutine or function so that they execute at the time the page loads. If you attempt to change these properties on the Click event script for a button, for instance, no change will be made. Microsoft says they had to implement it this way because the performance hit would be too great to go back and change the link colors after the page is loaded.

➡ `aLinkColor`: supported for Netscape Navigator compatibility, but has no effect in Internet Explorer. In Navigator, when you click and hold the mouse button down over a link, that link will change to the active link color specified by this property.

➡ `bgColor` and `fgColor`: holds the background and foreground (text) colors for the web page (respectively). You can change these at any time.

➡ `location`: the URL of the document. This is not the same as the location property for the Window object. The Window's location was an *object* with a number of properties, all of which could be changed. This location is just a *string* (not a complete object), and it contains the complete URL. This one may not be changed because a document can have only one address. Changing a document's address doesn't make any sense. If you want to change which document is displayed in the browser, you want to change the Window's location object.

➡ `lastModified`: provides the date that the page was last changed. This cannot be changed.

➡ `title`: provides the document's title: the text between `<TITLE>` and `</TITLE>` in the HTML. This cannot be changed.

➡ `cookie`: a string that is stored on the *client* machine and is associated with your server and subdirectory. A different cookie is stored for each web server that uses this facility, but Internet Explorer takes the responsibility for naming and tracking the cookies on the client. This is the only method provided for permanent storage in standard VBScript. The string can be any length you like and is often used to store many pieces of information in the form `DataName1=DataValue1;DataName2=DataValue2`, and so on. This works in a way similar to Window's INI files, but there are no built-in functions that allow you to specify a `DataName` and return the associated `DataValue` or to let you add or change a `DataName/DataValue`. You will have to search through the string by hand or write those functions yourself. VBScript string manipulation commands are found in a section titled "Strings" in Chapter 8.

➥ `referrer`: the URL of the page where you clicked on a link to get to this page. In other words, if you are on a page that has a link to another page that you click on, you are taken to the new page and the old page's URL (the one with the link) is placed into referrer. This allows you to customize a page depending on where the user came from. For instance, often a Back link is provided in the page. If the referrer is used as the URL for this Back link, you can be assured that no matter where the user came from to reach this page, your Back link will work. This property is only filled in if this page was arrived at by clicking on a link. If the user arrived here by typing the URL by hand or choosing a Favorite, this property will be NULL.

➥ `anchors`: a list of anchor objects, one for each anchor in the document.

➥ `links`: a list of the link objects, one for each link in the document.

➥ `forms`: a list of form objects, one for each form in the document.

Document Methods

The document methods all revolve around writing data to the document.

write and writeln

```
document.write string
```

The `write` method takes *string* and places it at the current location in the document. If you want to use `document.write` to customize your page, you should use it outside of any subroutine or function and at exactly the location in the HTML document where you want your customized text written. You cannot use `document.write` to modify the current page after it is completely loaded.

If you want to accept input from a user and then dynamically create output to show to a user on the same page, there is a way to do it. Create two or more frames, collect input in one frame, and use the `document.open`, `document.write`, and `document.close` to create a new document dynamically for another frame. Remember that each frame is effectively its own Window object and each has a separate document object.

Whatever is in *string* is sent to the HTML document as if it had been typed into the document exactly that way. In other words, you can include more than just text that you want printed. Any valid HTML can be written to the document using document.write including <OBJECT> tags. (You could even do <SCRIPT> tags. Hmm...)

```
document.writeLn string
```

This command is exactly the same as document.write except that it puts a new line character at the end. Remember, though, that a new line character doesn't usually do anything in an HTML document unless it is within a <PRE> (preformatted text) tag pair. If you want text with a new line character at the end, you are better off using document.write with a
 (line break) or <p> (end of paragraph break) tag at the end.

Example

```
document.write "This is a bit of text.<p>This is a second
line of text.<p>"
```

open and close

```
document.open
document.close
```

open and close allow you to create a new document dynamically. Usually you will issue an open, followed by a series of document.write method calls to fill the page and then a document.close. The text created is not displayed until the document.close executes.

Do not attempt to do this with the current document that houses the script you are executing right now. Calling document.open clears the current document with the intent of creating a new one, but that also clears the script as it's running — not a good idea. Because of this, usually you will see these commands used in a multiframe window where one frame's script opens, writes to, and then closes another frame's script.

clear

```
document.clear
```

`clear` cleans out the current page and leaves a blank one. Again, don't do this for the document where the script resides, and always be sure and do a close before you clear. Clearing an open document can cause unexpected results.

It is not necessary to do a clear on a document before you do an `open`. `open` automatically does a clear before it starts.

The History Object

The History object tracks where you've been, just in case you might want to go there again.

History Properties

There is only one property for the History object: `length`. It provides you with the length of the history list (that is, the number of URLs it currently holds).

History Methods

back

```
history.back
```

This method moves backward in the history one step. It is exactly the same as if the user clicked the Back button in the browser.

forward

```
history.forward
```

This method moves forward in the history one step. It is exactly the same as if the user clicked the Forward button in the browser.

Microsoft documents that the `back` and `forward` methods take one argument. That argument is a number indicating how many back or forward it should go in the history list. Although you won't receive an error if you pass an argument, it will still only go forward or back one, no matter what number you pass. This is either an error in the documentation (as I suspect) or a bug in Internet Explorer.

go

```
history.go num
```

Goes to the *num* element in the history list.

Example

```
history.go 1 ' Go to the first item in the history list
history.go history.length  ' Go to the last item in the
history list
```

This is the way Microsoft documents the `go` method. JavaScript in Netscape works differently. It accepts a relative number so that `history.go -3` would take you three back in the history from where you are now and `history.go 2` would take you two forward in the history. However, as implemented in Internet Explorer, `go` doesn't seem to work either way. I hope this is something that is fixed in the near future.

The Navigator Object

The Navigator object is included in the object hierarchy to maintain compatibility with Netscape Navigator's JavaScript object model. It doesn't contain many useful properties or methods.

If you use Navigator properties, you must prefix them with the object name navigator as in:

```
codename = navigator.appCodeName
```

This is true for all objects properties and methods in the browser object hierarchy *except* for the Window object.

Navigator Properties

These properties exist mostly to allow the scripter to find out what browser they are working in:

➡ appCodeName: holds the code name for the application. The code name for Netscape Navigator as it was being developed was *Mozilla*. The name arose from the fact that it was attempting to compete with Mosaic and it had a lizard as a mascot. This property is sometimes checked by JavaScript applications to see if the browser is Netscape and has all the capabilities that, at one time, only Netscape had. Because Internet Explorer now has all those capabilities, it also returns Mozilla so that older JavaScript code will work correctly with it.

➡ appName: holds the name of the browser application. Internet Explorer returns *Microsoft Internet Explorer*.

➡ appVersion: holds the version of the browser. Internet Explorer returns 2.0. This is, of course, wrong because Internet Explorer is in version 3.0. The reason it returns 2.0 is because that is the current production version of Netscape Navigator. Again, as with appCodeName, it is important to maintain backward compatibility with older JavaScript. Actually the full text returned is this: *2.0 (compatible; MSIE 3.0A; Windows 95),* or something similar depending on your release and operating system.

➡ userAgent: used when sending information from the browser to a web server to identify what type of client is sending it. Currently it is just a combination of the appCodeName and appVersion. Internet Explorer returns *Mozilla/2.0 (compatible; MSIE 3.0A; Windows 95).*

There are no Navigator methods or events.

The Location Object

The Location object holds properties associated with the URL of the currently loaded page. Changing any of these properties causes the browser to navigate to the newly specified page.

Location Properties

Here are the Location properties:

➡ href: the string containing the URL for the current page. Example: http://www.microsoft.com/devonly/index.htm

➡ protocol: the protocol portion of the URL. Does not include the // that appear between the protocol and the hostname. Those only appear in the href. Example: http:

➡ host: the name of the host web server machine. Example: www.microsoft.com

➡ port: the port number of the server. This is seldom used.

➡ hostname: this is a combination of the host and the port. If no port is specified (which is usually the case), it is identical to the host.

➡ pathname: the path and file name of the document you are viewing. Example: /devonly/index.htm

➡ search: the query request portion of the URL. The next time you search for something using one of the web search engines, look at the URL after you click Search. You'll notice that in addition to the normal parts of a URL, you'll find a bunch of gibberish at the end that spells out exactly your search criteria. Each search engine uses a different "language" here, but whatever it is, it is stored in this property of the location object.

➡ hash: the anchor within the page that indicates exactly where, in a long page, you want the browser to be looking. You'll remember from Chapter 2 that when you want to go to a particular anchor, you append the name of that anchor to the web page address using the pound or hash symbol (#). That's how this property gets its name. You can set the hash property to force the browser to jump to a particular anchor, but when you do, the page will reload before jumping to the anchor. When you assign a value to hash, you may include the # symbol as the first character. If you don't, Internet Explorer will add it for you.

You might wonder, as you look at these properties, why there is an href, which includes the entire URL and then separate properties for each of the individual parts of the URL. This is really just a convenience for you. If you want to stay on the same document on the same server but you want to jump to a different anchor, you can simply change the hash property. You don't have to go through and parse and reassemble a string containing the entire URL.

The Location object has no methods or events.

The Anchor and Link Objects

Anchors, you will recall, are used primarily for two different things. Most often, they create a link to another document on this site or another web site. Anchors can also identify a place in a document with a name so that other anchors can create links that go right to a specified location in the middle of a long document, for instance.

Anchor Object

```
document.anchors(index).name = string
```

anchors is an array of all the occurrences of the <A> tag in the document. The *index* identifies which one you want to work with, and *string* is a name you want to assign to the tag.

Link object

```
document.links(index).name = string
```

links is an array of all the anchors that have an HREF property defined and therefore provide a way to link to another location.

The link properties are identical to the Location object properties. See "Location Object" earlier this chapter for details.

There are three events for the Link object:

- **mouseMove:** happens again and again as the user moves the mouse over the link. The event script handler for this event receives four arguments:
- **x** and **y:** the current location of the mouse pointer relative to the link.
- **shift** and **button:** the current state of the shift keys and mouse button, respectively.
- **onMouseOver:** triggered every time the user moves the mouse over a link.
- **onClick:** happens immediately after the user clicks on a link but before the new page is loaded.

The Form Object

Form provides a method of presenting a group of intrinsic (built-in) controls to users so that they can enter information that will then be sent back to the web server for processing, usually with a CGI application.

Forms are HTML-based and were the most common method for creating interactivity on web pages before the advent of scripting languages like VBScript. They were also the only way of presenting controls to the user to accept input before the advent of ActiveX controls.

Many of the things that used to require you to use forms can now be done with ActiveX controls and VBScript right on the client without any server interaction at all. While this means that forms aren't as important as they used to be, it doesn't mean you won't ever use them. When you do want to send data to the database server so that the user can update a database or sign a guest book, forms are still a good option.

The forms array is a property of the document. You can have as many forms as you like on one web page. Then, inside each form, there are any number of elements — intrinsic controls that collect the data.

Form Properties

➡ `elements`: a list of element objects, one for each intrinsic control in the form. This cannot be changed.

➡ `action`: a string containing the URL indicating where the form's data should be sent when it is submitted for processing.

➡ `target`: specifies where the page returned from the web server as a result of a submission should be placed. Often in a multiframe window, the form will remain on the screen while the results returned from the server will appear in another frame.

➡ `method`: holds the value `"GET"` or `"POST"` indicating the format used for sending the information to the server. `"GET"` indicates that the arguments should be appended onto the URL indicated in the action property and opened as though it were a link. You often see this used with search engines. `"POST"` indicates that the data should be sent as a separate HTTP post transaction.

➡ `encoding`: indicates if the data being submitted is encoded. This must be a valid MIME type.

Form Methods

```
document.forms[index].submit
```

Sends a form's information to the web server. This is exactly the same as the user clicking a Submit button.

Form Events

`onSubmit` happens immediately before data is sent to the server. If a function is used as the event handler for this event rather than a subroutine, the function can return `True` or `False` indicating whether the submit should take place or not. This allows you to write a validation routine that is executed `onSubmit` and verify that all the data entered looks good before sending it off.